Certificate Paper C04

2011 Syllabus

FUNDAMENTALS OF BUSINESS ECONOMICS

For assessments in 2013 and 2014

CIMA

Study Text

In this October 2012 edition

- A **user-friendly format** for easy navigation
- Regular **fast forward** summaries emphasising the key points in each chapter
- **Assessment focus points** showing you what the assessor will want you to do
- **Questions** and **quick quizzes** to test your understanding
- **Question bank** containing objective test questions with answers
- A full index

BPP Learning Media's **i-Pass** product also supports this paper.

FOR ASSESSMENTS IN 2013 AND 2014

First edition July 2011
Second edition October 2012

ISBN 9781 4453 6473 5
Previous ISBN 9781 4453 7779 7
eISBN 9781 4453 9114 4

British Library Cataloguing-in-Publication Data
A catalogue record for this book is available from the British Library

Published by

BPP Learning Media Ltd
BPP House, Aldine Place
142-144 Uxbridge Road
London W12 8AA

www.bpp.com/learningmedia

Printed in the United Kingdom by Polestar Wheatons

Hennock Road
Marsh Barton
Exeter
EX2 8RP

Your learning materials, published by BPP Learning Media Ltd, are printed on paper sourced from sustainable, managed forests.

Contents

The BPP Learning Media Study Text

Aims of this Study Text

To provide you with the knowledge and understanding, skills and application techniques that you need if you are to be successful in your exams

This Study Text has been written to cover the **Fundamentals of Business Economics** syllabus.

- It is **comprehensive**. It covers the syllabus content. No more, no less.
- It is written at the **right level**. Each chapter is written with CIMA's precise learning outcomes in mind.
- It is targeted to the **assessment**. We have taken account of guidance CIMA has given and the assessment methodology.

To allow you to study in the way that best suits your learning style and the time you have available, by following your personal Study Plan (see page (vii))

You may be studying at home on your own until the date of the exam, or you may be attending a full-time course. You may like to (and have time to) read every word, or you may prefer to (or only have time to) skim-read and devote the remainder of your time to question practice. Wherever you fall in the spectrum, you will find the BPP Learning Media Study Text meets your needs in designing and following your personal Study Plan.

To tie in with the other components of the BPP Learning Media Effective Study Package to ensure you have the best possible chance of passing the exam (see page (v))

Learning to Learn Accountancy

BPP Learning Media's ground-breaking **Learning to Learn Accountancy** book is designed to be used both at the outset of your CIMA studies and throughout the process of learning accountancy. It challenges you to consider how you study and gives you helpful hints about how to approach the various types of paper which you will encounter. It can help you **focus your studies on the subject and exam**, enabling you to **acquire knowledge**, **practise and revise efficiently and effectively**.

The BPP Learning Media Effective Study Package

Recommended period of use	The BPP Learning Media Effective Study Package
From the outset and throughout	**Learning to Learn Accountancy** Read this invaluable book as you begin your studies and refer to it as you work through the various elements of the BPP Learning Media Effective Study Package. It will help you to acquire knowledge, practise and revise, efficiently and effectively.
Three to twelve months before the assessment	**Study Text and Interactive Passcards** Use the Study Text and Interactive Passcards to acquire knowledge, understanding, skills and the ability to apply techniques.
Throughout	**i-Pass** **i-Pass**, our computer-based testing package, provides objective test questions in a variety of formats and is ideal for self-assessment.
One to six months before the assessment	**Practice & Revision Kit** Try the numerous assessment-format questions, for which there are full worked solutions where relevant prepared by BPP Learning Media's own authors. Then attempt the two mock assessments.
From three months before the assessment until the last minute	**Passcards** Work through these short, memorable notes which are focused on what is most likely to come up in the assessment you will be sitting.

Help yourself study for your CIMA assessment

Assessments for professional bodies such as CIMA are very different from those you have taken at college or university. You will be under **greater time pressure before** the assessment – as you may be combining your study with work. There are many different ways of learning and so the BPP Study Text offers you a number of different tools to help you through. Here are some hints and tips: they are not plucked out of the air, but **based on research and experience**. (You don't need to know that long-term memory is in the same part of the brain as emotions and feelings - but it's a fact anyway.)

The right approach

1 **The right attitude**

Believe in yourself	Yes, there is a lot to learn. Yes, it is a challenge. But thousands have succeeded before and you can too.
Remember why you're doing it	Studying might seem a grind at times, but you are doing it for a reason: to advance your career.

2 **The right focus**

Read through the Syllabus and learning outcomes	These tell you what you are expected to know and are supplemented by Assessment focus points in the text.

3 **The right method**

The whole picture	You need to grasp the detail - but keeping in mind how everything fits into the whole picture will help you understand better. • The **Introduction** of each chapter puts the material in context. • The **Syllabus content, Learning outcomes** and **Assessment focus points** show you what you need to **grasp**.
In your own words	To absorb the information (and to practise your written communication skills), it helps to **put it into your own words**. • **Take notes.** • Answer the **questions** in each chapter. You will practise your written communication skills, which become increasingly important as you progress through your CIMA assessments. • Draw **mindmaps**. • Try **'teaching' a subject** to a colleague or friend.
Give yourself cues to jog your memory	The BPP Learning Media Study Text uses **bold** to **highlight key points**. • Try **colour coding** with a highlighter pen. • Write **key points** on cards.

4 **The right review**

Review, review, review	It is a **fact** that regularly reviewing a topic in summary form can **fix it in your memory**. Because **review** is so important, the BPP Learning Media Study Text helps you to do so in many ways. • **Chapter roundups** summarise the 'fast forward' key points in each chapter. Use them to recap each study session. • The **Quick quiz** is another review technique you can use to ensure that you have grasped the essentials. • Go through the **Examples** in each chapter a second or third time.

Developing your personal Study Plan

BPP Learning Media's **Learning to Learn Accountancy** book emphasises the need to prepare (and use) a study plan. Planning and sticking to the plan are key elements of learning success.
There are four steps you should work through.

Step 1 **How do you learn?**

First you need to be aware of your style of learning. The BPP Learning Media **Learning to Learn Accountancy** book commits a chapter to this **self-discovery**. What types of intelligence do you display when learning? You might be advised to brush up on certain study skills before launching into this Study Text.

BPP Learning Media's **Learning to Learn Accountancy** book helps you to identify what intelligences you show more strongly and then details how you can tailor your study process to your preferences. It also includes handy hints on how to develop intelligences you exhibit less strongly, but which might be needed as you study accountancy.

Are you a **theorist** or are you more **practical**? If you would rather get to grips with a theory before trying to apply it in practice, you should follow the study sequence on page (viii). If the reverse is true (you like to know why you are learning theory before you do so), you might be advised to flick through Study Text chapters and look at examples, case studies and questions (Steps 8, 9 and 10 in the **suggested study sequence**) before reading through the detailed theory.

Step 2 **How much time do you have?**

Work out the time you have available per week, given the following.

- The standard you have set yourself
- The time you need to set aside later for work on the Practice & Revision Kit and Passcards
- The other exam(s) you are sitting
- Very importantly, practical matters such as work, travel, exercise, sleep and social life

		Hours
Note your time available in box A.	A	

Hours

Step 3 **Allocate your time**

- Take the time you have available per week for this Study Text shown in box A, multiply it by the number of weeks available and insert the result in box B. B [ ]
- Divide the figure in box B by the number of chapters in this text and insert the result in box C. C [ ]

Remember that this is only a rough guide. Some of the chapters in this book are longer and more complicated than others, and you will find some subjects easier to understand than others.

Step 4 **Implement**

Set about studying each chapter in the time shown in box C, following the key study steps in the order suggested by your particular learning style.

This is your personal **Study Plan**. You should try and combine it with the study sequence outlined below. You may want to modify the sequence a little (as has been suggested above) to adapt it to your **personal style**.

BPP Learning Media's **Learning to Learn Accountancy** gives further guidance on developing a study plan, and deciding where and when to study.

Suggested study sequence

It is likely that the best way to approach this Study Text is to tackle the chapters in the order in which you find them. Taking into account your individual learning style, you could follow this sequence.

Key study steps	Activity
Step 1 **Topic list**	Each numbered topic is a numbered section in the chapter.
Step 2 **Introduction**	This gives you the big picture in terms of the context of the chapter, the learning outcomes the chapter covers, and the content you will read. In other words, it sets your objectives for study.
Step 3 **Fast forward**	Fast forward boxes give you a quick summary of the content of each of the main chapter sections. They are listed together in the roundup at the end of each chapter to provide you with an overview of the contents of the whole chapter.
Step 4 **Explanations**	Proceed methodically through the chapter, reading each section thoroughly and making sure you understand.
Step 5 **Key terms and Assessment focus points**	• Key terms can often earn you *easy marks* (and they are highlighted in the index at the back of the text). • Assessment focus points state how we think the examiner intends to examine certain topics.
Step 6 **Note taking**	Take brief notes, if you wish. Avoid the temptation to copy out too much. Remember that being able to put something into your own words is a sign of being able to understand it. If you find you cannot explain something you have read, read it again before you make the notes.

Key study steps	Activity
Step 7 **Examples**	Follow each through to its solution very carefully.
Step 8 **Questions**	Make a very good attempt at each one.
Step 9 **Answers**	Check yours against ours, and make sure you understand any discrepancies.
Step 10 **Chapter roundup**	Work through it carefully, to make sure you have grasped the significance of all the fast forward points.
Step 11 **Quick quiz**	When you are happy that you have covered the chapter, use the Quick quiz to check how much you have remembered of the topics covered and to practise questions in a variety of formats.
Step 12 **Question(s) in the question bank**	Either at this point, or later when you are thinking about revising, make a full attempt at the Question(s) suggested at the very end of the chapter. You can find these at the end of the Study Text, along with the Answers so you can see how you did.

Short of time: Skim study technique?

You may find you simply do not have the time available to follow all the key study steps for each chapter, however you adapt them for your particular learning style. If this is the case, follow the **skim study** technique below.

- Study the chapters in the order you find them in the Study Text.
- For each chapter:
  - Follow the key study steps 1-2
  - Skim-read through step 4, looking out for the points highlighted in the fast forward boxes (step 4)
  - Jump to step 10
  - Go back to step 5
  - Follow through step 7
  - Prepare outline answers to questions (steps 8/9)
  - Try the Quick quiz (step 11), following up any items you can't answer
  - Do a plan for the Question (step 12), comparing it against our answers
  - You should probably still follow step 6 (note-taking), although you may decide simply to rely on the BPP Leaning Media Passcards for this.

Moving on...

However you study, when you are ready to embark on the practice and revision phase of the BPP Learning Media Effective Study Package, you should still refer back to this Study Text, both as a source of **reference** (you should find the index particularly helpful for this) and as a way to **review** (the Fast forwards, Assessment focus points, Chapter roundups and Quick quizzes help you here).

And remember to keep careful hold of this Study Text – you will find it invaluable in your work.

More advice on Study Skills can be found in BPP Learning Media's **Learning to Learn Accountancy** book.

Learning outcomes and Syllabus

Paper C04 Fundamentals of Business Economics

Syllabus overview

This paper primarily deals with the economic context of business and how competition, the behaviour of financial markets, and government economic policy can influence an organisation. It also provides the key microeconomic techniques underlying price determination and profit maximisation decisions.

The focus of this syllabus is on providing candidates with an understanding of the areas of economic activity relevant to an organisation's decisions.

Syllabus structure

The syllabus comprises the following topics and study weightings:

A	The macroeconomic context of organisations	25%
B	The goals and decisions of organisations	25%
C	The market system and the competitive process	25%
D	The financial system	25%

Assessment strategy

There will be a two hour computer based assessment, comprising 75 compulsory questions, each with one or more parts. In addition, a 15 minute tutorial is available before the start of the assessment to help familiarise yourself with the software and assessment environment.

A variety of objective test question styles and types will be used within the assessment.

Learning outcomes and syllabus content

Learning Outcomes On completion of their studies students should be able to:				
Lead		**Component**		**Indicative syllabus content**
A. The macroeconomic context of organisations (25%)				
1	Explain the factors affecting the level of a country's national income and the impact of changing growth rates on organisations.	(a)	Explain the determination of macroeconomic phenomena, including equilibrium national income, growth in national income, price inflation, unemployment, and trade deficits and surpluses:	• Changes to equilibrium level of national income using an aggregate demand and supply analysis • Types and consequences of unemployment, inflation and balance of payment deficits • The circular flow of income, the main injections and withdrawals and their determinants.
		(b)	Explain the stages of the trade	

			cycle, its causes and consequences for the policy choices of government;	• The trade cycle and the implications for unemployment, inflation and trade balances of each stage (recession, depression, recovery, boom). • Government macroeconomic policy goals: low unemployment, inflation, external equilibrium and growth. • Government policy for each stage of the trade cycle. • Impacts of recession and boom on forecast sales of capital and consumption goods, industry profitability and employment levels in the firm. • The main principles of public finance: the central government budget and forms of direct and indirect taxation, incidence of taxation (progressive, regressive) and potential impact of high taxation on incentives and avoidance. • The main principles of public finance: fiscal, monetary and supply side policies, including relative merits of each. • The effects on organisations of changes to interest rates, government expenditure and taxation. • The effects on organisations of direct government macroeconomic policies including prices and income policies, labour market regulation, regulation on trade and policies to encourage investment.
		(c)	Explain the consequences of the trade cycle for organisations;	
		(d)	Explain the main principles of public finance (i.e. deficit financing, forms of taxation) and macroeconomic policy;	
		(e)	Describe the impacts on organisations of potential policy responses of government, to each stage of the trade cycle.	
2	Explain the factors affecting the trade of a country with the rest of the world and its impact on business.	(a)	Explain the concept of the balance of payments and its implications for government policy;	• The main flows measured in the balance of payments accounts and the causes and effects of fundamental imbalances in the balance of payments. • Arguments for and against free trade and policies to encourage free trade (e.g. bi-lateral trade agreements, multi-lateral agreements, free trade areas, economic communities and
		(b)	Identify the main elements of national policy with respect to trade;	
		(c)	Explain the impacts of	

		exchange rate policies on business.	economic unions) and protectionist instruments (tariffs, quotas, administrative controls, embargoes). • The effect of changing exchange rates on the profits of firms and international competitiveness of national industry.
3	Explain the influences on economic development of countries and its effect on business.	(a) Explain the concept globalisation and the consequences for businesses and national economies; (b) Explain the role of major institutions promoting global trade and development.	• The nature of globalisation and factors driving it (improved communications, political realignments, growth of global industries and institutions, cost differentials). • The main trade agreements and trading blocks. • The social and political impacts of globalisation (e.g. widening economic divisions between countries) and its influence on business (e.g. off-shoring), industrial relocation, emergence of growth markets, enhanced competition, cross-national business alliances and mergers). • The impacts of modern information and communication technologies on international trade and patterns of development. • The principal institutions encouraging international trade (e,g. WTO/GATT, EU, G8).
B. The goals and decisions of organisations (25%)			
1	Distinguish between the economic goals of various stakeholders and organisations.	(a) Distinguish between the goals of profit seeking organisations, not-for-profit organisations (NPOs) and governmental organisations; (b) Explain shareholder wealth, the variables affecting shareholder wealth and its application in management decision making; (c) Identify stakeholders and their likely impact on the goals of organisations and the	• The forms of public, private and mutual ownership of organisations and their goals. • Concept of returns to shareholder investment in the short run (ROCE and EPS) and long run (NPV of free cash flows) and the need for firms to provide rates of return to shareholders at least equal to the firm's cost of capital. • Impact on share price of changes to a company's forecast cash flows or its required rate using perpetual annuity valuations.

		decisions of management; (d) Distinguish between the potential objectives of management and those of shareholders, and the effects of this principal-agent problem on decisions concerning price, output and growth of the firm;	• Role of stakeholders in setting goals and influencing decisions in organisations. • Types of not-for-profit organisations. • The status of economic considerations as constraints rather than the primary objectives of not-for-profit organisations. • The potential difference in objectives between management and shareholders. • The principal-agent problem, its likely effect on decision making in profit seeking organisations.
2	Describe the behaviour of the costs of a product and service provider as volume changes and the implications for prices, competition and industry structure.	(a) Distinguish between the likely behaviour of a firm's unit costs in the short run and long run; (b) Illustrate the potential effects of the likely behaviour on prices, the size of the organisation and the number of competitors in the industry; (c) Illustrate the potential impact on prices and competition of e-business and globalisation.	• Changing efficiency in the short run (eventually diminishing marginal returns) and the long run (increasing and diminishing returns to scale). • Graphical treatment of short run cost and revenue behaviour as output increases using curvilinear and total cost curves. • Long run cost behaviour and the long run average cost curve. • Increased competition and lower prices from the impact of e-business on costs of information search and by enabling low or zero variable cost. • Impact on competition of the ability of business to source products and services from low cost emerging economies.
3	Calculate the level of output and price to maximise profits.	(a) Demonstrate the point of profit maximisation graphically using total cost and total revenue curves; (b) Calculate the point of profit maximisation for a single product firm in the short run using data.	• Short-run profit maximisation using graphical techniques. • Profit maximising output using data on price, quantity and unit costs.

C. The market system and the competitive process (25%)			
1	Demonstrate the determination of prices by market forces and the impact of price changes on revenue from sales.	(a) Identify the equilibrium price in a product or factor markets likely to result from specified changes in conditions of demand or supply; (b) Calculate the price elasticity of demand and the price elasticity of supply; (c) Explain the determinants of the price elasticities of demand and supply; (d) Explain the effects of price elasticity of demand on a firm's revenues following a change in prices.	• The price mechanism, determinants of supply and demand and their interaction to form and change equilibrium price. • The price elasticity of demand and supply. Note: calculate using arc and point methods. • Influences on the price elasticity of demand and supply. • Consequences of different price elasticities of demand for total revenue, following price changes.
2	Explain the reasons for and effects of government intervention to stabilise prices.	(a) Identify causes of instability of prices in markets for primary goods; (b) Explain the impact of instability of prices on incomes of producers and the stability of the industry; (c) Explain the effects on prices, producer revenues and market equilibrium, of government policies to influence prices in markets; (d) Illustrate the impacts of price regulation in goods and factor markets.	• Impact of periodic variations in output, short run inelasticity of supply, inelastic demand and the cobweb (or hog cycle) on price stability in primary markets. • Implications of price fluctuations for producer incomes, industry stability and supply. • Government price stabilisation policies, deficiency payments, set-aside, subsidies. • Impact of employment costs. • Impact of minimum price (minimum wage) and maximum price policies in goods and factor markets.
3	Explain the main sources of market failures and the policies available to deal with them.	(a) Explain market concentration and the factors giving rise to differing levels of concentration between markets, including acquisitions and combinations; (b) Identify the impacts of the different forms of competition on prices, output and profitability;	• Measures of market concentration and the impacts of market concentration on efficiency, innovation and competitive behaviour. • Business integration including mergers, vertical integration and conglomerates. • Effect of monopolies and collusive practices on prices and output, and profitability.

		(c)	Explain the main policies to prevent abuses of monopoly power by firms;	• Competition policy and fair trading regulations. • Positive and negative externalities in goods markets, merit goods and demerit goods. • Government responses to market failure: indirect taxes, subsidies, polluter pays policies and regulation. • Government responses to market failure: public assurance of access to public goods, healthcare, education and housing. • Government responses to market failure: public versus private provision of services (nationalisation, privatisation, contracting out, public private partnerships).
		(d)	Explain market failures and their effects on prices, efficiency of market operation and economic welfare;	
		(e)	Explain the likely responses of government to market failures.	
D. The financial system (25%)				
1	Explain the causes of demand for finance and the assets used for borrowing.	(a)	Identify the factors leading to liquidity surpluses and deficits in the short, medium and long run in households, firms and governments;	• Finance for households: month to month cash flow management; short-term saving and borrowing; home buying; pension provision. • Finance for firms: cash flow management; finance of working capital and short-term assets; long term payment capital. • Finance for government: cash flow management; finance of public projects; long term management of the national debt. • Role of financial assets, markets and institutions: credit agreements, mortgages, bills of exchange, bonds, certificates of deposit, equities.
		(b)	Explain the role of various financial assets, markets and institutions in assisting organisations to manage their liquidity position and to provide an economic return to holders of liquidity.	
2	Explain the function of the main financial markets and institutions in facilitating commerce and development.	(a)	Explain the financial and economic functions of financial intermediaries.	• Role and functions of financial intermediaries: maturity transformation, risk management, aggregation, matching borrowers and lenders. • Role and influence of commercial banks on the supply of liquidity to the financial system through their activities in credit creation.
		(b)	Explain the role of commercial banks in the process of credit creation and in determining structure of interest rates;	

	(c) Explain the role of the 'central bank' in ensuring liquidity and in prudential regulation; (d) Explain the origins of the 2008 banking crisis and credit crunch; (e) Explain the role of the foreign exchange market and the factors influencing it, in setting exchange rates; (f) Explain the role of national and international governmental organisations in regulating and influencing the financial system; (g) Explain the role of supra-national financial institutions in stabilising economies and encouraging growth.	• Yield on financial instruments (i.e. bill rate, running yield on bonds, net dividend yield on equity), relation between rates, role of risk, the yield curve. • Role and common functions of central banks: banker to government, banker to banks, lender of last resort, prudential regulation. • Influence of central banks on yield rates through market activity and as providers of liquidity to the financial system as lenders of last resort, including by quantitative easing. • The 2008 banking crisis and credit crunch: exposure to sub-prime debt, poor regulation, excessive lending. • Role of foreign exchange markets in facilitating international trade and in determining the exchange rate. • Influences on exchange rates: interest rates, trade balance, currency speculation. • Governmental and international policies on exchange rates (exchange rate management, fixed and floating rate systems, single currency zones). • Role of major institutions (e.g. World Bank Group, International Monetary Fund, European Central Bank) in fostering international development and economic stabilisation.

The assessment

Format of computer-based assessment (CBA)

The CBA will not be divided into sections. There will be a total of seventy five objective test questions and you will need to answer **ALL** of them in the time allowed.

Candidates **may not** take a calculator into their assessment. Instead, an onscreen calculator will be available in the assessment environment.

Frequently asked questions about CBA

Q What are the main advantages of CBA?

A
- Assessments can be offered on a continuing basis rather than at six-monthly intervals
- Instant feedback is provided for candidates by displaying their results on the computer screen

Q Where can I take CBA?

A
- CBA must be taken at a 'CIMA preferred CBA Centre' or at a centre operated by Pearson Vue. For further information on CBA, you can email CIMA at cba@cimaglobal.com.

Q How does CBA work?

A
- Questions are displayed on a monitor
- Candidates enter their answers directly onto a computer
- The computer automatically marks the candidate's answers when the candidate has completed the examination
- Candidates are provided with some indicative feedback on areas of weakness if the candidate is unsuccessful

Q What sort of questions can I expect to find in CBA?

Your assessment will consist entirely of a number of different types of **objective test question**. Here are some possible examples.

- **MCQs.** Read through the information on page (xvi) about MCQs and how to tackle them.
- **Data entry.** This type of OT requires you to provide figures such as the correct figure for payables in a statement of financial position.
- **Multiple response.** These questions provide you with a number of options and you have to identify those which fulfil certain criteria.

This text provides you with **plenty of opportunities to practise** these various question types. You will find OTs **within each chapter** in the text and the **Quick quizzes** at the end of each chapter are full of them. The Question Bank contains exam standard objective test questions similar to the ones that you are likely to meet in your CBA.

Further information relating to OTs is given on page (xviii).

The **Practice and Revision Kit** for this paper was published in **December 2012** and is **full of OTs**, providing you with vital revision opportunities for the fundamental techniques and skills you will require in the assessment.

Tackling multiple choice questions

In a multiple choice question on your paper, you are given how many **incorrect** options?

A Two
B Three
C Four
D Five

The correct answer is B.

The MCQs in your assessment contain four possible answers. You have to **choose the option that best answers the question**. The three incorrect options are called distracters. There is a skill in answering MCQs quickly and correctly. By practising MCQs you can develop this skill, giving you a better chance of passing the exam.

You may wish to follow the approach outlined below, or you may prefer to adapt it.

Step 1 **Skim read** all the MCQs and **identify** what appear to be the easier questions.

Step 2 Attempt each question – **starting with the easier questions** identified in Step 1. Read the question thoroughly. You may prefer to work out the answer before looking at the options, or you may prefer to look at the options at the beginning. Adopt the method that works best for you.

Step 3 Read the four options and see if one matches your own answer. **Be careful with numerical questions**, as the distracters are designed to match answers that incorporate common errors. Check that your calculation is correct. Have you followed the requirement exactly? Have you included every stage of the calculation?

Step 4 You may **find that none of the options matches your answer**.

- Re-read the question to ensure that you understand it and are answering the requirement.
- Eliminate any obviously wrong answers.
- Consider which of the remaining answers is the most likely to be correct and select the option.

Step 5 If you are still **unsure** make a note **and continue to the next question**.

Step 6 **Revisit unanswered** questions. When you come back to a question after a break you often find you are able to answer it correctly straight away. If you are still unsure have a guess. You are not penalised for incorrect answers, so **never leave a question unanswered!**

Assessment focus. After extensive practice and revision of MCQs, you may find that you recognise a question when you sit the exam. Be aware that the detail and/or requirement may be different. If the question seems familiar read the requirement and options carefully – do not assume that it is identical.

BPP Learning Media's i-Pass for this paper provides you with plenty of opportunity for further practice of MCQs.

Tackling objective test questions

The vast majority of the questions in your assessment will be multiple choice questions. However, there may be a small number of objective test questions.

What is an objective test question?

An **OT** is made up of some form of **stimulus**, usually a question, and a **requirement** to do something.

(a) Multiple choice questions

(b) Filling in blanks or completing a sentence

(c) Listing items, in any order or a specified order such as rank order

(d) Stating a definition

(e) Identifying a key issue, term, figure or item

(f) Calculating a specific figure

(g) Completing gaps in a set of data where the relevant numbers can be calculated from the information given

(h) Identifying points/zones/ranges/areas on graphs or diagrams, labelling graphs or filling in lines on a graph

(i) Matching items or statements

(j) Stating whether statements are true or false

(k) Writing brief (in a specified number of words) explanations

(l) Deleting incorrect items

(m) Choosing right words from a number of options

(n) Complete an equation, or define what the symbols used in an equation mean

OT questions in CIMA assessment

CIMA has offered the following **guidance** about OT questions in the assessment.

- Credit may be given for **workings** where you are asked to calculate a specific figure.
- If you **exceed a specified limit on the number of words** you can use in an answer, you will **not be awarded any marks**.

Examples of OTs are included within each chapter, in the **quick quizzes** at the end of each chapter and in the **objective test question bank**.

BPP Learning Media's i-Pass for this paper provides you with plenty of opportunity for further practice of OTs.

Part A

The goals and competitive environment of organisations

1

Goals of organisations and their stakeholders

Introduction

Most major industrialised countries have mixed economies, with both a large private sector and also a substantial public (or government) sector.

In this chapter we will look more carefully at the kinds of organisations that undertake economic activity, their objectives, and some ideas about the way in which they should be run. As part of this we will look at the potential for a divergence of interests between the managers of an organisation and other stakeholders and the issue of assuring proper corporate governance.

Topic list	Learning outcomes	Syllabus references	Ability required
1. Forms of organisation	B1	B1(a)	Comprehension
2. Role of stakeholders in setting organisation goals	B1	B1(c)	Comprehension
3. Type of not-for-profit organisations	B1	B1(a)	Comprehension
4. Goal congruence between managers and shareholders	B1	B1(d)	Comprehension
5. The principal-agent problem	B1	B1(d)	Comprehension

1 Forms of organisations

FAST FORWARD

The economy can be divided into the **public and private sectors**. The public sector contains a range of organisations that **provide public services** and may also include some state-owned businesses.

1.1 The public and private sectors

The economy of a country can usually be divided into two sectors: the public sector and the private sector. Private sector organisations, also called firms, are owned and operated by private individuals or institutions, while organisations in the public sector are owned by the state.

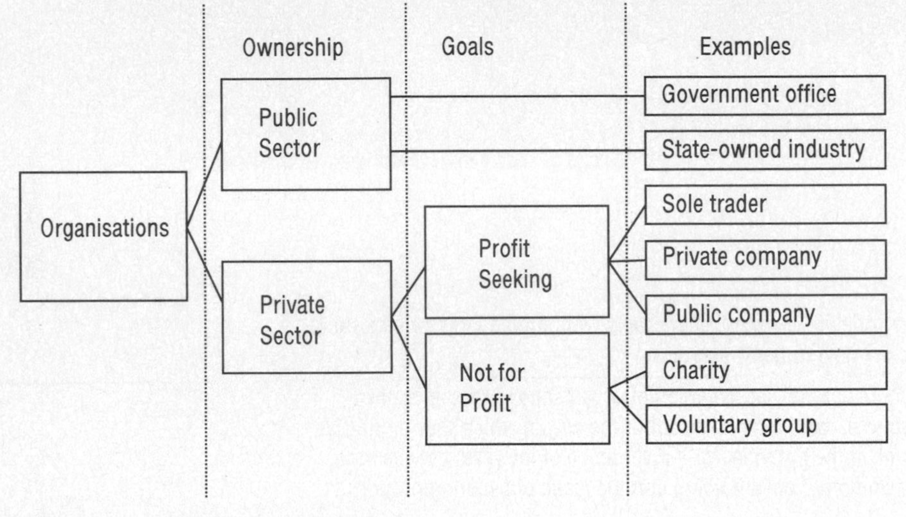

Figure 1 Types of organisation

1.2 Profit seeking organisations

These seek an **economic return** for their owners (eg profits for shareholders).

Businesses are of two main types

1. **Unincorporated:** an individual that has set up business on his or her own account, as a **sole trader** or in **partnership** with others. In either case, the law will not distinguish between the private assets and liabilities of the owners and those of the enterprise. The owners have **unlimited liability** for the debts of their businesses.

2. **Incorporated:** a separate legal entity is created in which the owners hold **shares**. The legal systems of most countries provide for some form of **limited liability** enterprise. Such businesses are referred to as corporations or **companies**.

In the UK, there are two forms of limited liability company. They differ in the extent to which they are permitted to solicit investment from the general public.

(a) **Private limited companies** may not offer their securities to the public;

(b) **Public limited company** (plc) may offer their securities to the public. When the shares of plcs are regularly bought and sold on a stock exchange, they may be referred to as **quoted companies.**

Key terms

> Note that **public limited companies** are owned by **private** investors (shareholders); they are **not** part of the **public sector**

1.3 Not-for profit organisations

1.3.1 Public sector bodies

Public sector bodies are all, ultimately, **responsible to government** for their activities. Their purposes are defined in the laws that established them. Public sector bodies' objectives will usually be defined in terms of the **provision of a service** that is deemed to be beneficial to society

Their managers are expected to exercise **good stewardship** and **prevent waste of resources**..

The main types of public sector organisations are:
Public service providers such as hospitals, schools, the police and the armed forces;

(a) **State owned industries** producing products or services sold for money such as energy, telecommunications and some heavy manufacturing industries.

(b) **Public private partnerships** (PPP) where an organisation is jointly owned by government and the private sector, usually with the private sector providing management and finance in return for a guaranteed annual fee from the government body. For example roads, hospitals and school buildings and social housing.

(c) **Quasi autonomous** non-governmental organisations (QUANGOs) are private organisations independent of the government but to which governments have devolved the authority for running public services.

1.3.2 Other not-for profit organisations

There is a wide range not-for-profit organisations. These usually exist to serve the interests of their members and subscribers. Examples include:

(a) Social clubs for members
(b) Charitable organisations to help the needy
(c) Professional bodies that regulate and represent members
(d) Trade associations and trade unions
(e) Political parties
(f) Some independent schools

2 Role of stakeholders in setting organisation goals

2.1 Types of stakeholder

FAST FORWARD

The stakeholder view holds that there are many groups in society with an **interest in the organisation's activities**. Stakeholders can be divided into internal, connected and external groups. The organisation's response to their priorities can be analysed according to their **power** (or influence) and their **interest**.

Key term

Stakeholders are those persons and organisations that have an interest in the strategy and behaviour of an organisation. CIMA *Official Terminology*

There are three broad types of stakeholder in an organisation.

- **Internal** stakeholders such as employees and management
- **Connected** stakeholders such as shareholders, customers, suppliers and financiers
- **External** stakeholders such as the community, government and pressure groups

Stakeholders:

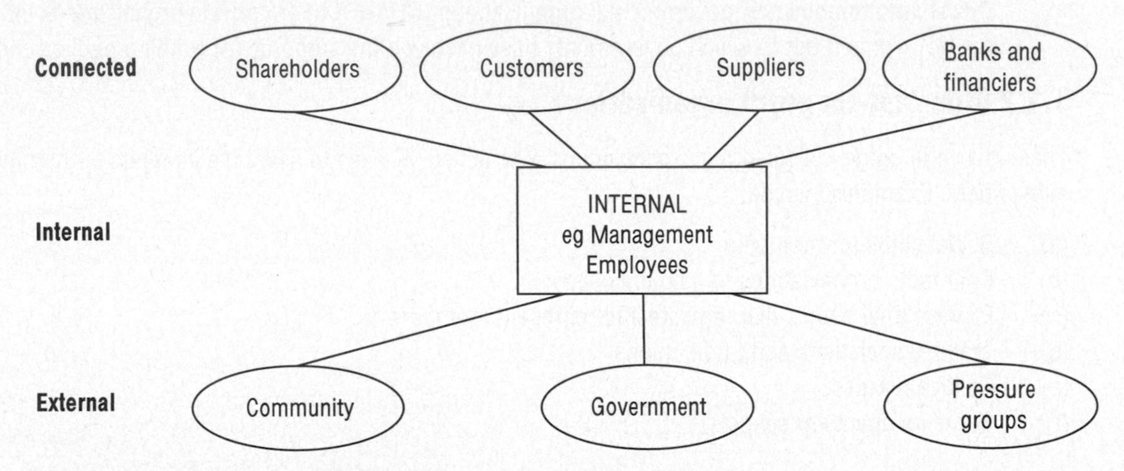

2.2 Influence of stakeholders

FAST FORWARD

Stakeholders can influence an organisation through their power to support, oppose or be consulted on its objectives.

Stakeholders can influence the objectives of an organisation in various ways:

(a) **Supporting** the actions of management through co-operation, providing funds, and agreeing to requests (such as for granting legal permissions)

(b) **Opposing** the actions of management such as through the law, industrial action or boycotting its products

(c) **Participation in decision-making**. Some stakeholders have a legal entitlement to be consulted. For example shareholders can vote on management proposals.

Stakeholders can be classified into three types. Their interests may sometimes conflict.

Internal stakeholders work for the organisation

Internal stakeholder group	Interest in the organisation	Potential conflicts with other stakeholders
Staff/employees	Wages, benefits and job security	Paying higher wages and having high staffing levels may reduce the profits of the firm and cause conflict with the interests of shareholders or owners
Management	Salaries, benefits, career progression, the chance to exercise power, the chance to do good in the wider community	Higher managerial pay and personal projects may reduce profits to shareholders and endanger the job security of employees

Connected stakeholders provide finance and income to the organisation

Connected stakeholder group	Interest in the organisation	Potential conflicts with other stakeholders
Shareholders	Dividends from their shares, rising share prices and the avoidance of excessively risky ventures by the organisation	Decisions by management to invest for long term growth may deprive the shareholders of dividend in the short run
Banks and other providers of finance	Regular interest payments and security that the debt will be repaid one day	Paying income to a bank will reduce the amount of money available to pay divided to shareholders
Suppliers	Revenues and profits from supplying the organisation, and prompt and sure payment of outstanding debts	Shareholders wanting higher profits may cause management to try to force down suppliers' prices
Customers	Reliable supply of good quality products and services at reasonable prices	Reducing prices may lead the organisation to make employees redundant by shifting production off-shore to a cheaper country

External stakeholders provide the social and legal context in which the organisation operates

External stakeholder group	Interest in the organisation	Potential conflicts with other stakeholders
The local community	Provision of jobs and business for local people and avoiding causing pollution and disruption	Decisions by management to transfer production to somewhere else will cause a decline in the local economy

External stakeholder group	Interest in the organisation	Potential conflicts with other stakeholders
Trade unions and employee organisations	Involvement in negotiation with management to ensure pay, fair treatment, job security and safety of their members	Actions to enforce their claims, such as strikes or refusal to co-operate will reduce supplies of products to customers and cut profits to shareholders
Interest groups	Less environmental damage, better treatment of minority groups, an end to supplying 'undesirable' goods and so on.	Threats of direct physical action, or legal action, against the organisation may increase costs, take up management time and endanger employees
Local and national government	Provision of jobs, exports and taxation revenues	Management decisions to increase profits by moving off-shore reduces jobs and taxation revenues and forces customers to import the product.

Mendelow classified stakeholders on a matrix whose axes are **power** (or influence) the stakeholder can exert and degree of **interest** the stakeholder has in the organisation's activities. These factors will help define the type of relationship the organisation should seek with its stakeholders.

Power/influence \ *Level of interest*	Low	High
Low	A	B
High	C	D

Figure 2 Mendelow's stakeholder mapping matrix

(a) **Minimal effort** is expended on segment A. An example might be a contractor's labour force.

(b) Stakeholders in segment B do not have great ability to influence strategy, but their views can be important in **influencing more powerful stakeholders**, perhaps by lobbying. They should therefore be **kept informed.** Community representatives and charities might fall into segment B.

(c) Stakeholders in segment C must be **treated with care**. While often passive, they are capable of moving to segment D. They should, therefore be **kept satisfied.** Large institutional shareholders might fall into segment C.

(d) **Key players** are found in segment D: any strategy the organisation wants to adopt must be *acceptable* to them, at least. An example would be a major customer. Key stakeholders may **participate** in decision-making.

Internal stakeholder groups are likely to have both more influence and more interest than external groups. This is because they are typically professional investment businesses that hold a significant percentage of the shares, and therefore votes. Coalitions of stakeholder groups are likely to have more influence than single stakeholders or small groups of stakeholders.

2.3 Stakeholder influence over profit seeking business

FAST FORWARD

Firms are assumed to **maximise profits** to give the best income to their owners. However stakeholder theory suggests that **other stakeholders** can influence the actions of a firm to satisfy their own **personal goals**.

Economists Cyert and March upset the conventional view that firms seek a single goal of maximising profits by stating 'organisations do not have objectives. Only people have objectives'. In other words organisations do not have a single mind and a single purpose. They are instead a **coalition of stakeholder groups** with each group pursuing its own interests.

(a) Shareholders and owners will require profits but may also seek other things such as prestige or avoidance of risks

(b) Management will pursue their salaries and careers and may also use the firms resources for pet projects

(c) Employees will seek wages but also job security, safe working conditions and promotions

(d) External stakeholders such as customers, suppliers and regulators will constrain what the firm is able to do, for example by resisting rising prices or behaviour that pollutes the environment.

For example commercial banks generally do not charge for customers to withdraw cash using Automated Teller Machines (ATMs) despite these being expensive pieces of equipment to install and maintain. Where banks have attempted to charge there is a public outcry that they are profiteering and customers and the government force the charges to be withdrawn.

This means that in setting objectives firms adopt the following approaches:

(a) Appease the dominant coalition of stakeholders such as a particular group of large investors or a significant group of key staff or managers. High pay to senior managers is an example of this.

(b) Seek to satisfy as many stakeholder groups as possible by giving each group something of what it wants. Paying higher dividends whilst also making charitable donations for instance.

(c) Give sequential attention to each stakeholder group, for example paying higher wages in one year to workers and then in the next year cutting costs to give higher profits to owners.

2.4 Stakeholders and not-for-profit organisations

FAST FORWARD

Stakeholders are particularly influential in not-for-profit organisations because of a **participative culture** and absence of an overriding profit goal.

Non-profit organisations do not have an over-riding responsibility to promote the interests of the owners: instead, they are subject to significant influence from more than one stakeholder group.

A **charity** set up to help the needy is a good example. There will be a class of **beneficiaries** whose requirements are the reason the organisation exists. However, there are also likely to be at least two other **important stakeholder groups,** volunteers and donors, whose views and requirements must be carefully considered too.

These organisations also have traditions of consultation due to being reliant on **members** or **volunteers.** A local sports club will have a committee of elected persons representing members and will rely on unpaid volunteers to assist at events and with administration. This creates a culture of **stakeholder participation** in decision-making.

In general, we may discern three areas in which stakeholders exercise influence in non-profit organisations.

(a) Objectives and goals are not based on profit, so there is scope for stakeholders to influence what the organisation sets out to do.

(b) Strategies cannot be aimed simply at profitability, so it can be developed to achieve other ends, such as doing things in a particular way. Many non-profit organisations will demand a particularly high standard of conduct in ethical terms.

(c) Management style and practices, particularly those elements that relate to the management of people, are highly likely to be of interest to some stakeholder groups.

3 Types of not-for-profit organisation

FAST FORWARD

The main types of not-for-profit organisations are **professional bodies**, **trade unions**, **charities**, **associations** and **mutual organisations**.

3.1 Non-financial goals of not-for-profit organisations

These are organisations whose primary goal is not profit. They may be called not-for-profit organisations or NPOs (sometimes NFPs). A group of friends socialising together at a barbeque does not seek to make a profit but it is not a not-for-profit organisation.

Key term

Organisations are 'social arrangements for the controlled performance of collective goals' (Buchanan and Huczynski)

To be included as a not-for-profit organisation it must have certain additional characteristics:

(a) Collective goals: there must be goals that the members of the organisation have agreed to in addition to their personal goals, ie it must have a purpose.

(b) Social arrangement: there need to be established hierarchies and ways of working.

(c) Controlled performance: systems and procedures to make sure the goals are achieved.

3.2 Examples of not-for-profit organisations

These differ according to their **aims** and how **formal** they are.

(a) Professional bodies: these seek to regulate the behaviour of members and represent their professional interests to legislators and others

(b) Trade unions: seek to establish collective bargaining to achieve pay, benefits and safe working conditions for members.

(c) Cause related charities: a wide range of organisations each with a specific interest ranging from the welfare of animals to the preservation of steam railway networks.

(d) Voluntary associations: these include amateur sports clubs, social clubs, and parent organisations to support a school.

(e) Educational establishments: many universities and schools are not-for-profit organisations established to provide schooling and research.

More formal and permanent not-for-profit organisations often adopt the legal form of a **Registered Charity** (or **charitable trust**). They are granted special concessions such as exemption from paying tax on earnings and donations. They are managed by **trustees** who must ensure the charity restricts itself to agreed areas of interest. Most professional accounting bodies are charitable trusts.

Mutual organisations ('mutuals') are a special case in the private sector. The essence of their nature is that they are commercial operations **owned by their customers** rather than having shareholders for whom they have to earn profit. This means that their customers benefit both from the **services** the mutuals provide to them and from the **trading surplus** they make by doing so. Mutuals thus resemble both non-profit making organisations and profit-seeking companies.

3.3 Financial constraints in not-for-profit organisations

FAST FORWARD

Money and finance are the **ends** (ie purpose) of a profit-seeking organisation and the product of service provides the **means** to do that. In not-for-profit organisations **means and ends are reversed**. The service is the end and the money is the means.

The essence of a 'non-profit' organisations is not seeking to generate a surplus of funds. The generation of wealth for their owners is **not the primary purpose** of their existence. Their purpose is to meet the **non-financial objectives** in their mission.

This leads to the following distinctive features:

(a) Providers of incomes may be different from the recipients of the service: a **donor** to a welfare charity is not likely to be the **recipient** of the helping hand. Governments frequently provide funds organisations with objectives in social welfare, education or artistic improvement.

(b) Demand not limited by price: not-for-profit organisations often provide services for free. A free health care organisation may have far more people demanding treatment than it has funds to buy medicines for.

Non-profit organisations must stay within their budgets to survive. But their stakeholders are primarily interested in how it contributes in its chosen field. This frequently leads to tensions between financial constraints and its objectives.

4 Goal congruence between managers and shareholders

FAST FORWARD

A **separation of ownership from control** occurs where the employment of **professional managers** means the firm is controlled by the managers rather than the owners. This means the firm may be **run in the interests of the management** instead of in the interests of the owners.

4.1 Separation of ownership from control

Few large businesses are managed by their owners. In the case of larger companies, there are large numbers of shareholders, and they are unlikely to wish to take part in the management of the company, viewing it simply as a vehicle for investment.

This leads to a **separation of ownership from control** because the limited liability structure does not give shareholders power to manage the company (unless they are also managers); their influence normally extends only to proposing and voting on resolutions at company meetings.

This separation of ownership from control is known as a principal-agent problem.

This problem is not confined to the management of companies: it is the general problem of the **agency relationship** and occurs whenever one person (the **principal**) gives another (the **agent**) power to deal with his affairs.

Key term

> The **principal-agent** problem arises where the owners or members of an organisation (principals) give authority to a manager (agent) to run the organisation. There is no assurance that the agent will run the organisation in the **best interests** of the principals.

4.2 Alternative managerial goals

Managers will not necessarily make decisions that will maximise profits.

(a) They may have no **personal interests** at stake in the size of profits earned, except in so far as they are accountable to shareholders for the profits they make.

(b) There may be a **lack of competitive pressure** in the market to be efficient, minimise costs and maximise profits, for example where there are few firms in the market.

Rather than seeking to **maximise** profits, managers may choose to achieve a **satisfactory** profit for a owners (called **satisficing**) and use the rest of the resources to pursue their own wealth or interests.

4.3 Baumol's sales maximisation model

Baumol's **sales maximisation model** – assumes that the firm acts to **maximise sales revenue** rather than profits. This could include allowing situations when the sale price is less than the costs (ie selling at a loss).

Managers benefit personally because of the prestige of running a large and successful company, and also because salaries and other perks are likely to be higher in bigger companies than in smaller ones.

5 The principal-agent problem

5.1 Agency theory and the principal-agent problem

The principal-agent problem is not restricted to profit-seeking organisations.

(a) A public servant may use their position in a hospital or state industry to pay themselves high salaries, advance their career or enjoy the privileges of travel and entertainment.

(b) The administrator of a charity may decide to favour particular causes that are close to their own hearts.

5.2 Resolving the principal-agent problem

FAST FORWARD

> The main ways to resolve the principal-agent problem are improved **scrutiny** of agents, **checks and balances** on their power, and appropriate **incentives**.

The real world solutions to the principal-agent problem have included the following:

(a) **Improved scrutiny**: Principals have kept a closer watch on agents through requiring clearer disclosure of decisions (eg at company meetings), appointing independent members to the management board, and appointing auditors to monitor decisions.

(b) **Checks and balances:** these avoid the particular manager to dominate the organisation. Measures include expanded management committees or boards, separation of duties (eg between chairman and chief executive), the requirement that more decisions be put to formal votes, and maximum periods of office for directors.

(c) **Incentives:** these tie the pay of the manager to the achievement of the goals of the agent. Thus, it is common for Chief Executives' **bonuses** to depend, at least in part, on satisfactory achievement in such matters as **profit and share price**. In a not-for-profit organisation managers' bonuses might be paid for achievement of **non-financial targets** such as increased membership numbers, or number of persons helped.

5.3 Corporate governance

Key term

Corporate governance is the systems by which companies and other organisations are directed and controlled.

CIMA *Official Terminology*

In a company, although the shareholders own the company, the responsibility for directing and controlling the company rests largely with the **board of directors**. The respective power and key responsibilities of shareholders and directors are summarised in the table below.

Shareholders	Board of directors
Appoint the directors	Determine the strategy of the company Oversee the management of the company and its performance in achieving strategy and objectives Report to shareholders on the performance of the company
Appoint the auditors	
Assure themselves that the system of corporate governance is appropriate and effective	Ensure suitable internal controls are in place and the company complies with laws and regulations.

5.4 Failures of corporate governance

Though mostly discussed in relation to large quoted companies, governance is an issue for all bodies corporate; commercial and not for profit.

5.4.1 Domination by a single individual

A feature of many corporate governance scandals has been boards dominated by a single senior executive doing what that executive wants with other board members merely acting as a rubber stamp. Sometimes the single individual may even bypass the board to action his own interests.

The presence of **non-executive directors** on the board is felt to be an important safeguard against domination by a single individual.

5.4.2 Lack of involvement of board

Boards that meet irregularly or fail to consider systematically the organisation's activities and risks are clearly weak. Sometimes the failure to carry out proper oversight is due to a **lack of information** being provided.

5.4.3 Lack of adequate control function

An obvious weakness is a **lack of internal audit,** since this is one of the most important aspects of internal control.

Another important control is **adequate technical knowledge** in key roles, for example in the audit committee or in senior compliance positions. A rapid turnover of staff involved in accounting or control may suggest inadequate resourcing, and will make control more difficult because of lack of continuity.

5.4.4 Lack of contact with shareholders

Often board members may have grown up with the company but lose touch with the **interests and views** of shareholders. One possible symptom of this is the payment of remuneration packages that do not appear to be warranted by results. Equally, the directors may choose to pursue their own interests and ignore the requirements of the shareholders.

5.5 Guidelines to improve corporate governance of companies

Around the world codes of practice have been laid down to compel management to take steps to ensure that firms are run in the interests of investors.

The recommendations include:

(a) **Separate roles of Chairman and Chief Executive**. The Chairman manages the Board and is independent of the influence of the Chief Executive. The Chairman ensures Board discussions are conducted properly and that all participants are listened to.

(b) **Independent appointment of directors**: to avoid the Chief Executive filling the Board with loyal supporters the Directors should be nominated by an independent **Nomination Committee** and approved by a meeting of shareholders.

(c) **Independent setting of directors pay**: pay is set independently by a Remuneration Committee and approved by a meeting of shareholders to prevent directors diverting excessive amounts to themselves.

(d) **Non-executive directors:** these are independent Board members who are there to bring expert judgement and to see governance is conducted properly. They are essential to staffing the committees on pay and nomination.

(e) **Participation by investors**. Shareholders should be given adequate information to judge the affairs of their firm and the shareholders meetings should encourage active questioning and scrutiny of the board.

Chapter roundup

- The economy can be divided into the **public and private sectors**. The public sector contains a range of organisations that **provide public services** and may also include some state-owned businesses.
- The stakeholder view holds that there are many groups in society with an **interest in the organisation's activities**. Stakeholders can be divided into internal, connected and external groups. The organisation's response to their priorities can be analysed according to their **power** (or influence) and their **interest**.
- Stakeholders can influence an organisation through their power to support, oppose or be consulted on its objectives.
- Firms are assumed to **maximise profits** to give the best income to their owners. However stakeholder theory suggests that **other stakeholders** can influence the actions of a firm to satisfy their own **personal goals**.
- Stakeholders are particularly influential in not-for-profit organisations because of a **participative culture** and absence of an overriding profit goal.
- The main types of not-for-profit organisations are **professional bodies**, **trade unions**, **charities**, **associations** and **mutual organisations**.
- Money and finance are the **ends** (ie purpose) of a profit-seeking organisation and the product of service provides the **means** to do that. In not-for-profit organisations **means and ends are reversed**. The service is the end and the money is the means.
- A **separation of ownership from control** occurs where the employment of **professional managers** means the firm is controlled by the managers rather than the owners. This means the firm may be **run in the interests of the management** instead of in the interests of the owners.
- The main ways to resolve the principal-agent problem are improved **scrutiny** of agents, **checks and balances** on their power, and appropriate **incentives**.

Quick quiz

1 Who proposed a model of business based on the objective of maximising sales?

A Drucker
B Williamson
C Ansoff
D Baumol

2 What does the term 'stakeholders' mean?

3 Which one of the following is not a stakeholder for a mutual organisation?

A Customers
B Staff
C Shareholders
D Directors

4 Which of the following denotes a stakeholder that should be Kept Informed in Mendelow's matrix?

A High power/low interest
B High interest/low power
C Low interest/low power
D High power/high interest

5 Which of the following is not a mechanism to improve corporate governance?

A Issue directors with long term employment contracts to improve their loyalty
B Separate the roles of Chairman and Chief Executive to avoid the board being dominated by an individual
C Provide incentives to directors that are based on the value they create for shareholders
D Employ non-executive directors to provide an independent viewpoint at board meetings

6 A director of a business division who does not own shares in the business can be termed

A A principal
B An agent
C A non-executive director
D None of the above

7 What does the term 'unincorporated' mean?

8 Which one of the following describes an organisation that is jointly owned by a state-owned organisation and a profit-seeking organisation ?

A Quango
B Mutual
C PPP
D Co-operative

Answers to quick quiz

1 D Baumol

2 The stakeholders of an organisation are people or organisations who have a legitimate interest in the strategy and behaviour of that organisation.

3 C By definition, mutual organisations do not have shareholders, because they are owned collectively by their customers.

4 B High interest/low power

5 A Most corporate governance codes encourage the opposite by putting directors on 3 year maximum term contracts and outlawing financial pay-offs if they are sacked earlier. This is deter directors from becoming complacent.

6 B Directors are agents of the shareholders. Response C is incorrect because a non-executive director would not be running a division.

7 Unincorporated means that the organisation does not have its own separate legal identity and therefore is no different in law from the people that own it

8 C This would be a Public Private Partnership

Now try the questions below from the Exam Question Bank

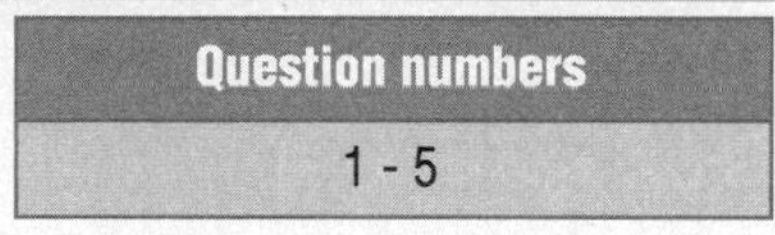

Question numbers
1 - 5

Measuring returns to shareholders

2

Introduction

The majority of private sector businesses are owned by shareholders. All but a few of the largest of these have issued shares on public stock markets and these shares are traded daily by investors.

Investors are very powerful stakeholders that are able to use their voting power and powers of scrutiny to influence the way firms behave. Understanding their interests is key to an economic analysis of business.

In this chapter we will look at the short and long run measures of financial performance monitored by shareholders and consider the factors that determine the minimum acceptable rate of profit for shareholders.

The chapter concludes with a discussion of the influence on share price of a firm's financial performance and prospects.

Topic list	Learning outcomes	Syllabus references	Ability required
1 Shareholders' interest	B1	B1 (a)	Comprehension
2 Short term measures of shareholder wealth	B1	B1 (a)	Comprehension
3 Long run measures of return	B1	B1 (b)	Comprehension
4 Risk and return – the required rate	B1	B1 (b)	Comprehension
5 Impact of financial performance on share price	B1	B1 (b)	Comprehension

1 Shareholders' interest

FAST FORWARD

Investors invest in companies by buying their shares. The companies are expected to maximise the wealth of their shareholders by generating **profit** from trading operations. Investors will only provide funds if they believe that the prospective returns are adequate.

1.1 Shares and share prices

A **company** (or corporation) is one of the commonest vehicles for carrying out a business. Funds are raised for the business activity by dividing up the ownership of the company into equal parts called **shares** that are then sold to investors for cash.

A **shareholder** is someone who owns shares in a company. The number of shares held by a shareholder represents his proportional ownership of the profits, losses and assets of the company. Any ownership interest is generally known as **equity**.

Ownership of shares represents ownership of equity in the company concerned: the term '**equities**' is often used to mean shares in companies.

Most theories of the firm begin from the basis that the main financial objective of a company is to **maximise the wealth of its shareholders**. It does this by **trading at a profit**.

Profits can then be paid to the shareholders as **dividends**, which are an immediate cash benefit, or they can be **retained** and re-invested in the company, which should **increase the value of the shareholders' equity**, generating wealth for the shareholder in the longer term.

Shares in quoted companies are usually bought and sold via an official **stock exchange market.** Leading world stock markets include the New York Stock Exchange/Euronext (combined), the on-screen market NASDAQ, the Tokyo Stock Exchange, the London Stock Exchange, the Shanghai Stock Exchange and the Hong Kong Stock Exchange.

If a company's shares are traded on a stock market, the wealth of the shareholder is increased when the share price goes up.

2 Short term measures of shareholder wealth

FAST FORWARD

Shareholders need **objective measures of company performance** if they are to make sensible investment decisions. Short-term measures include **ROCE**, **EPS** and **P/E** figures. ROCE and EPS are straightforward measures of current achievement; P/E number, however, reflects the market's view of the share's future prospects.

Shareholders use measures of company performance to make informed investment decisions on whether to **buy, hold or sell** shares in a firm. These measures can be divided into those suitable for the shorter term and those suitable for the longer term.

In this context, the limit of the shorter term may be taken to be the issue of the next set of financial statements.

2.1 Return on capital employed

Profits are the excess of revenues over costs for a given period, usually a year.

Simply measuring profit does not give a good measure of how well a firm is performing because it doesn't consider the investment shareholders has made. **Profitability is more important than profit**.

An example helps explain the reasoning behind measures of profitability. Suppose you were told that your bank account had earned $120 interest last year. You would very pleased if your bank balance had been only $500, but not pleased if the bank balance had been $50,000. In the first case the interest rate was 24% but in the second case is was only 0.24%. If it was a low rate you would take your money out and deposit it in a different bank to get a better return.

The same applies to investments in firms. If the rate of profit is too low then investors will **sell their shares** and invest their money in a more profitable firm.

Firms use capital to generate profit. This capital is the **assets** of the firm and **it belongs to the shareholders**. Assets can include non-current assets such as land, buildings and machinery, or current assets such as inventories of materials and finished goods, or trade debtors.

Return on capital employed (ROCE) measure of a company's current success by relating the *amount* of profit to the **value of the resources** employed in generating it. This reflects the efficiency with which the resources have been used.

Formula to learn

Return on capital employed (ROCE)

$$\text{ROCE} = \frac{\text{Profit before interest and tax (PBIT)}}{\text{Capital employed}} \times 100$$

Profit before interest and tax, or profit from operations, is profit available for all holders of capital (shares and loans). Capital employed is defined as total assets less current liabilities.

ROCE can also be defined as return on net assets.

Return on net assets

$$\text{Return on net assets} = \frac{\text{Operating profit (before interest and tax)}}{\text{Total assets minus current liabilities}} \times 100$$

For most companies, this will produce an answer that can be expressed as a percentage between zero and, say, 50%. Clearly if the company makes a loss, the ROCE figure will be negative.

Note that interest is deducted as a cost when the profit in the accounts is calculated. PBIT from a set of accounts, you would have to **add back to profit before tax the amount of any interest paid**.

2.1.1 Example: ROCE

In 20X8, Snoxall plc paid bank interest of $21,909 and earned profit before tax of $225,102. Total assets less current liabilities were $751,969. Calculate ROCE for 20X8.

If the corresponding figures for 20X9 were $18,115; $342,130 and $988,899, what would ROCE have been for 20X9?

	20X9	*20X8*
	$	$
Profit on ordinary activities before tax	342,130	225,102
Add back: Interest payable	18,115	21,909
PBIT	360,245	247,011

Solution

		20X9	20X8
ROCE	=	$\frac{360,245}{988,899}$	$\frac{247,011}{751,969}$
	=	36.4%	32.8%

This exercise illustrates a common use of measures such as ROCE: the making of comparisons between one year and another. We cannot really comment on the size of Snoxall plc's ROCE unless we know something about what is normal for its industry, but we can definitely say that it has improved between 20X8 and 20X9.

Assessment focus point

In the simple example above, we have calculated individual capital employed figures for each year. However, in your assessment, if you are asked to calculate ROCE and you are given two years' worth of capital employed figures, you should use an **average** capital employed figure for the later year.

So, based on the figures from our example above, ROCE for 20X9 would be calculated as:

PBIT = $360,245

Capital employed: average of $751,969 and $988,899 = $870,434

$$\text{ROCE} = \frac{\$360,245}{\$870,434} = 41.4\%$$

2.2 Earnings per share

ROCE is a general measure of the overall productivity of capital. **Earnings per share** (EPS) is a measure of how well the company has performed for its **equity shareholders specifically**, rather than providers of capital generally.

EPS is usually calculated as the profit available to equity shareholders divided by the number of equity shares **in issue**.

Formula to learn

Earnings per share

$$\text{EPS} = \frac{\text{Profit after tax and preference dividends}}{\text{Number of equity shares in issue}}$$

Here, because we are interested in the equity shareholders' point of view, we take the **profit after interest and tax** payments and we also deduct any dividends due to **preference shareholders**. Holders of preference shares receive a set amount of divided per share each year and therefore are regarded for this purpose as having more in common with lenders of debt such as a bank than they do with equity shareholders.

2.2.1 Example: EPS

Here is an extract from Monocular plc's income statement for 20X9.

	$
Profit before interest and tax	120,000
Interest	(20,000)
Profit before tax	100,000
Taxation	(40,000)
Profit after tax	60,000
Preference dividend	(1,000)
Profit available for ordinary shareholders (= earnings)	59,000
Ordinary dividend	(49,000)
Retained profits	10,000

The company has 80,000 ordinary shares and 20,000 preference shares.

Calculate earnings per share in 20X9.

Solution

EPS is $\frac{\$59,000}{80,000}$ = 73.75 cents

In practice, there are usually further complications in calculating the EPS, but fortunately these are outside your syllabus for this subject.

3 Long run measures of return

FAST FORWARD

The valuations based on **discounting forecast free cash flows** also relate the cost of equity to market share price.

3.1 Importance of long term earnings

Growing firms sometimes do not pay dividends: for example *Microsoft* was founded in 1975 but paid no dividends until 2003 and *Google* sold its shares for $23bn in 2004 but by 2010 had still not paid a dividend to the shareholders that bought these shares.

In these situations shareholders are prepared to wait for their investment to give a return. The consider the **long-term earnings** of the business.

There are several such models, but for the purposes of the C04 syllabus we are interested in a simple model based on **discounting the free cash flows**.

Once again, it is important for your consideration of the discounted cash flow model that you are familiar with the basic process of discounting as explained in your BPP C03 Business Mathematics Study Text.

However, here is a brief review of discounting.

3.2 Discounting

The **time value of money** means that $100 income received in one year's time is worth less in real terms to an investor than $100 received now. In order to make rational decisions about where to invest their money, investors need to adjust for the differences in the real value of income generated at different time periods in the future.

They can do this by **discounting** future income streams to convert them to their **net present value** (NPV). In other words, the value of the future flow of income must be reduced (discounted) to reflect the lower real value of income being received in future compared to the same amount being received now.

The future earnings are discounted by applying a **discount rate** to them. The discount rate (or discount factor) is calculated as:

$$\text{Discount factor} = = \frac{1}{(1+r)^t}$$

Where r = the rate of discount
t = time (years)

The figures for discount factors can be found on the present value tables which are provided by CIMA. (Note: these are rounded to 3 decimal places.)

The appropriate discount rate to use will depend on the specific circumstances of a calculation, but it is likely to be the **interest rate** or the **cost of capital**.

The discount rate will have an inverse relationship to the future value of the income stream. That is, the higher the discount rate, the lower the future value of the income stream, and vice versa.

When a discount rate has been applied to a stream of future earnings, the adjusted cash flows are known as the **discounted cash flow** (DCF).

The formula to calculate the discounted value of a cash inflow to be received at a future date is:

$$\text{Discounted value} = \frac{\text{Nominal value of the cash flow}}{(1+r)^t}$$

Where 'r' is the discount rate, and 't' is the year (time) when the inflow is received.

So if $1,000 is to be received for each of the next three years, and the discount rate is 10%, the calculation of the discounted cash flow will be as follows.

Year 1	*Year 2*	*Year 3*	*Total*
$\frac{1,000}{1.1}$	$\frac{1,000}{(1.1)^2}$	$\frac{1,000}{(1.1)^3}$	
= 909	= 826	= 751	2,486

The **discounted cash flows** for the three years are $909, $826 and $751 respectively.

The **present value** of the earnings is then obtained by adding together all the discounted cash flows. In this case the NPV would be $2,486.

The present value of the earnings that an investment project is expected to generate can be compared to the cost of the investment to see the overall **net present value** (NPV) of the project. If the **NPV is positive** the project should be regarded as **cash generating** and allowed to proceed. So, for example, let's say an investment of $2,000 was required to generate these discounted cash flows of $2,486, the net present value of the project would be $2,486 – $2,000 = $486 positive.

3.3 Free cash flows

Discounting and NPV are often used by businesses to assess whether to undertake investment projects, they can equally be used in the context of share values and company valuation as

Key term

> The **free cash flow to equity (FCFE)** represents the potential income that could be distributed to the **equity holders** of a company, as opposed to dividends which measures the actual cash disbursements to shareholders.

The free cash flow to equity (FCFE) is calculated in the same way as free cash flow to the firm (FCFF) except that interest payments due to debt holders have to be deducted as

FCFE = FCFF – INTEREST PAYMENTS TO DEBT HOLDERS.

3.4 Example

The following information is available on a company.

PBIT	5,000,000
Interest Expenses	500,000
Taxes	1,000,000
Capital Expenditure	300,000

The free cash flow to the firm (FCFF) is

FCFF = PBIT – Taxes – Capital Expenditure
= 5,000,000 – 1,000,000 – 300,000 = 3,700,000

The free cash flow to equity (FCFE) is

FCFE = FCFF – Interest Expenses
= 3,700,000 – 500,000 = 3,200,000

If we know what the equity shareholders' required rate of return is, we can use it as a **discount rate** to find the value of the company. Conversely, in principle, if we know the current market value of the company's shares and its **forecast free cash flows**, we can use this information to estimate the shareholders' required rate of return. However, this computation is outside your syllabus.

3.5 Example: discounting free cash flows

Flo plc's directors have forecast the company's expected levels of earnings in their medium term strategic plan. The earnings figures for the next three years are given below.

Time	$
Year 1	7,530,000
Year 2	7,980,000
Year 4	8,240,000

The company has 2,400,000 ordinary shares in issue. The equity shareholders require a rate of return on their investment of 17%. What should the company's current market value and ordinary share price be?

Solution

Year	*Cash flow*	*Discount factors*	*Present value*
	$	*@ 17%*	$
1	7,530,000	0.855	6,438,150
2	7,980,000	0.731	5,833,380
3	8,240,000	0.624	5,141,760
			17,413,290

The current market value on this basis is the sum of the present value column above, which is $17, 413,290. Dividing this figure by 2,400,000 (the number of shares in issue) will give us the current ordinary share price: this is $7.26.

Assessment focus point

Your syllabus requires you to be able to carry out both types of valuation calculation illustrated above.

4 Risk and return – the required rate

FAST FORWARD

Before deciding whether to buy, hold or sell shares in a firm the investor will consider whether the returns from the firm are adequate to **compensate them for the risks** of investing in the firm. The **minimum rate of return** that is acceptable to shareholders is called the **required rate.**

4.1 The risks incurred by shareholders

In normal times a depositor who puts money into a bank account enjoys **certainty of return.** They will receive a specified rate of interest and also can rely on getting their initial capital sum back.

Investing in shares involves several risks:

(a) The annual return on the share will **vary according to the profits** of the businesses.

(b) The value of their shareholding will rise and fall according to **market sentiment** about the business

(c) Their shares could become worthless if the firm becomes **bankrupt** because ordinary shareholders rank for a pay-out from the proceeds of selling off the assets of the firm.

These risks are often classified into **systematic risk** and **unsystematic risk.**

Key terms

Systematic risk is the risk associated with investing in any equities in a particular section of the market. For example shares in pharmaceutical industries may have greater systematic risks than shares in bakeries.

Unsystematic risk (or specific risk) is the risk associated with investing in a particular firm. For example a firm's shares may have high unsystematic risk due to the firm's high dependence on the sales of a single line of product.

4.2 Shareholders risk-return curve

FAST FORWARD

A shareholders' **risk return curve** shows the **minimum rate of return** that shareholders will accept as compensation for higher risks to their investments.

Figure 1 shows a shareholders' risk-return curve (also called a shareholders indifference curve).

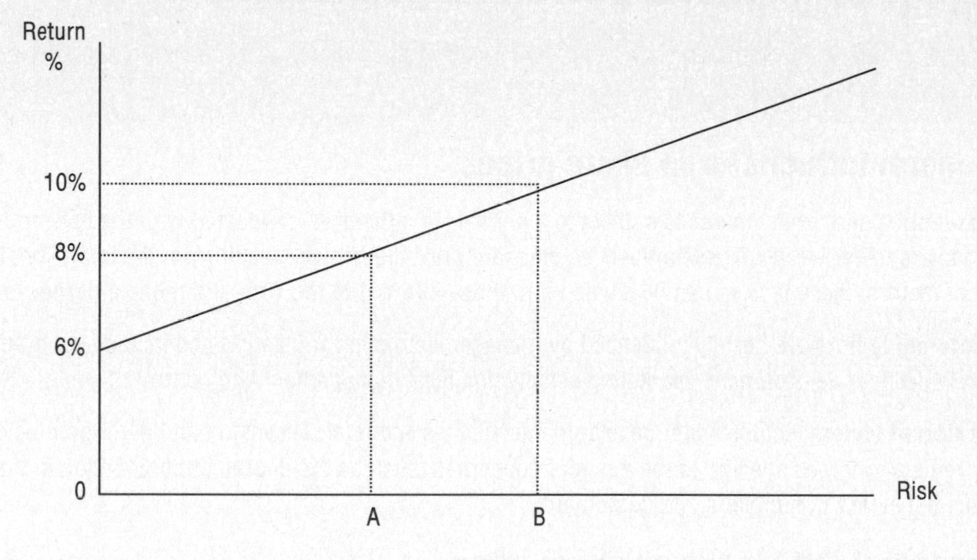

Figure 1 Investors risk-return curve

In Figure 1 if risk is 0 the investor regards 6% as the minimum return they will take for investing. This is sometimes called the **risk free rate.** If investors are asked to invest the in the shares of Firm A they will require a return of at least 8% before they will do so. Firm B is seem as more risky and so the investors would require at least 10% return.

The higher the risk, the higher the required return.

The risk free rate is determined by two factors:

(a) **The time value of money**: investing money now means that the investor must delay buying goods and services for a while. They will require some compensation for this as a minimum return on their money.

(b) **The rate of inflation**. if prices are rising at 5% it would mean that $100 invested at the start of the year could only buy $95 worth of goods at the end of the year. Investors need to receive a minimum return to compensate for this.

4.3 Influences on the required rate

The main factors influencing the required rate are:

(a) General economic conditions (which affects the risk-free rate)

(b) The specific strategies of the firm itself and whether they increase or reduce commercial risk.

(c) The rates of return available elsewhere from other investments

(d) The rate of inflation in the economy

(e) The marketability of the investment – can the investor find a buyer willing to pay full price for the share when they want to get their money back?

If these change there will a change in the required rate.

5 Impact of financial performance on share price

FAST FORWARD

An **increase** in forecast dividends or free cash flows will lead to an **increase** in current market price, as will a **reduction** in the cost of equity.

5.1 General influences on share prices

The market price of a firm's shares is subject to a number of influences connected with the investment's likely effect on shareholder wealth. These influences on share price themselves result from the interplay of a large number of factors; these factors can be divided into those **internal to the firm** and those **external** to it.

(a) **Internal factors** are heavily influenced by management policy and action and include such things as rate of new product development, marketing activity, financial management and control of costs.

(b) **External factors** include wider developments such as economic recession and demographic change; and events and forces specific to the industry concerned, such as the degree of competition in the market and the behaviour of suppliers and customers.

5.2 Financial influences on share price

FAST FORWARD

The causes of share price variation can be analysed as changes in **reported profits**, changes in **forecast profits**, and changes in **required rate of return**.

(a) If the expected cash flows **increase**, predictably enough, the current market value will **increase** and *vice versa*. Changes in the immediate future will have a larger effect than those in the more distant future.

(b) An **increase** in the **cost of equity** will **reduce** the current market value and *vice versa*. Returning to the data from paragraph 3.1 above, we can demonstrate this effect by recomputing Flo plc's current value assuming that investors have increased their required return to 20%.

Year	*Cash flow*	*Discount factors*	Present value
	$	*@ 20%*	$
1	7,530,000	0.833	6,272,490
2	7,980,000	0.694	5,538,120
3	8,240,000	0.579	4,770,960
			16,581,570

The current market value is now $16,581,570. Actually, examination of the discount factors themselves $[1/(1 + r)^t]$ will demonstrate the basic principle involved. The higher the discount rate is, the smaller the discount factors are and so, logically, the smaller are the present values of the discounted cash flows.

Question — **Changing the cost of equity**

Flo plc has for many years been involved in dangerous and speculative activities involving prospecting for radio-active ores in politically unstable parts of the world. The company's directors have stated that the company effectively ceased its participation in these activities at the end of the end of the last accounting period; the funds released have been invested in a portfolio of commercial properties in European capital cities. Remarkably, the net effect of this change on forecast profits is zero.

Required

Explain the effect this change is likely to have on the market value of the company's shares.

Answer

The effect of this change in business focus is a significant reduction in the riskiness of Flo plc's activities overall. This should have the effect of reducing the cost of equity, since investors no longer need high returns to compensate them for a high level of risk. Since the forecast cash flows are unchanged, but the cost of equity has fallen, we would expect the market value of Flo plc's shares to rise.

In practical market terms, Flo plc has become a much more attractive investment, offering high returns at low risk. Demand will increase, but the current owners of the shares will be reluctant to sell at the existing market price. Increased demand will drive the price up to a point at which the current investors are prepared to sell.

Chapter roundup

- Investors invest in companies by buying their shares. The companies are expected to maximise the wealth of their shareholders by generating **profit** from trading operations. Investors will only provide funds if they believe that the prospective returns are adequate.
- Shareholders need **objective measures of company performance** if they are to make sensible investment decisions. Short-term measures include **ROCE**, **EPS** and **P/E** figures. ROCE and EPS are straightforward measures of current achievement; P/E number, however, reflects the market's view of the share's future prospects.
- The valuations based on **discounting forecast free cash flows** also relate the cost of equity to market share price.
- Before deciding whether to buy, hold or sell shares in a firm the investor will consider whether the returns from the firm are adequate to **compensate them for the risks** of investing in the firm. The **minimum rate of return** that is acceptable to shareholders is called the **required rate**
- A shareholders' **risk return curve** shows the **minimum rate of return** that shareholders will accept as compensation for higher risks to their investments
- An **increase** in forecast dividends or free cash flows will lead to an **increase** in current market price, as will a **reduction** in the cost of equity.
- The causes of share price variation can be analysed as changes in **reported profits**, changes in **forecast profits**, and changes in **required rate of return**.

Quick quiz

1 How do shares give wealth to shareholders?

   A By paying annual dividends only
   B By rising in price only
   C By a combination of annual dividends and share price rises
   D By entitling the shareholder to votes

2 Which of the following, in theory, determines the price of a share

   A It will be the same as its EPS

   B It will be the same as the price it was sold at when the share was issued

   C The discounted present value of the expected future earnings of the firm divided by the number of shares in issue

   D The value of this years dividend

3 What is the name given to the risks of investing in the shares of firms from a particular industrial sector?

4 What is the formula for return on capital employed?

5 What is the formula for earnings per share?

6 Which of the following best describes the risk free rate?

   A The rate of interest on a loan

   B The rate of dividend on a preference share

   C The minimum return that a shareholder will accept on a company's shares

   D The minimum return a shareholder will accept to compensate for tying their money up and suffering loss of value due to inflation.

7 The present value of Megalith's forecast future cash flows is now $267 million. What will happen to this value if Megalith plc's cost of equity rises?

   A It will rise
   B It will fall
   C It will remain the same
   D It is impossible to say

8 What is the name of the process through which future income streams are given a present value?

Answers to quick quiz

1 C Shares give wealth as income from dividends and also by the profit the shareholder will enjoy if they rise in price

2 C

3 Systematic risk

4 ROCE $= \frac{\text{PBIT}}{\text{Capital employed}} \% = \frac{\text{Profit from operations}}{\text{Total assets less current liabilities}} \%$

5 EPS $= \frac{\text{Profit after tax and preference dividends}}{\text{Number of equity shares in issue}}$

6 D

7 B It will fall. The cost of equity is the discount rate for this calculation. An increase in the discount rate used for a present value calculation will inevitably produce a fall in the present value computed.

8 Discounting.

Now try the questions below from the Exam Question Bank

Question numbers
6 - 10

The market system 1 – demand and supply analysis

3

Introduction

In this chapter, we look in more depth at the microeconomic level of the individual firm, individual markets and consumers (or households). This means looking at what influences the amount of a product which is demanded or supplied and analysing how price and output are determined through the interaction of **demand** and **supply**.

We start by examining the concept of a market which, in economics, goes beyond the idea of a single geographical place where people meet to buy and sell goods.

Topic list	Learning outcomes	Syllabus references	Ability required
1 Definition of a market	C1	C1 (a)	Comprehension
2 The demand curve	C1	C1 (a)	Comprehension
3 The supply curve	C1	C1 (a)	Comprehension
4 Formation of equilibrium price	C1	C1 (a)	Comprehension
5 Momentary, short run and long run equilibrium price	C1	C1 (a)	Comprehension

1 The definition of a market

FAST FORWARD

Markets are where exchanges take place and market prices are established. In practice few markets are actual physical places. Instead exchange is carried out in many locations and on-line.

1.1 What is a market?

Key term

A **market** can be defined as a situation in which potential buyers and potential sellers (*suppliers*) of a good or service come together for the purpose of exchange.

The term 'market' is used as an **abstract concept** to refer to any process where exchange takes place.

Examples of markets include:

(a) **Product markets**: this could include a street market selling fresh vegetables and the market for used furniture conducted in the back pages of the local newspaper

(b) **Commodity markets**: this includes the global market for copper, conducted between mine owners and users, or between dealers on the floor of the London or Shanghai Metal Exchanges or the New York Commodity Exchange (COMEX)

(c) **Financial markets**: this includes stock markets where shares in companies are traded, or money markets where banks trade loans using computer screens

(d) **Factor markets:** such as the labour market for qualified accountants, or the market for office accommodation.

In practice markets can be **differentiated**. For example although we read about the **property market** in reality it breaks down into **market segments** such as the local market for luxury homes . This implies the market within a restricted geographical radius, ie local, and particular types of property, ie luxury homes.

1.2 Markets for products

The discussion in this chapter will be restricted to product markets. A market involving the **buyers and sellers of a good who influence its price**.

Key term

Goods is the term used in economics to mean both tangible items like cars, furniture and food, and intangible services like motor insurance or window cleaning.

Suppliers and potential suppliers are referred to in economics as **firms**. The potential purchasers of consumer goods are known as **households**.

Price theory is concerned with how market prices for goods are arrived at, through the interaction of demand and supply.

2 The demand curve

FAST FORWARD

The demand curve (or schedule) shows how much of a good consumers are willing and able to purchase at any given price.

The position of the **demand curve** is determined by the demand conditions, which include consumers' tastes and preferences, and consumers' incomes.

2.1 The concept of demand

Key term

Demand for a good or service is the quantity of that good or service that potential purchasers would be willing and able to buy, or attempt to buy, at any possible price.

Demand refers to the total volume of a product that buyers are **willing and able to buy** at a particular **price**.

(a) **Willing to buy**: means that if the good were available at that price they would buy it.

(b) **Able to buy**: mean they have the money needed to buy the good. It does not mean that the good is actually available at that price.

(c) **At a particular price**: means that demand is price determined

2.2 The demand schedule and the demand curve

The relationship between demand and price can be shown graphically as a **demand curve**. The demand curve of a single consumer or household is derived by estimating how much of the good the consumer or household would demand at various hypothetical market prices. Suppose that the following **demand schedule** shows demand for biscuits by households over a period of one month.

Price per kg	*Quantity demanded*
$	Kg
1	9.75
2	8.00
3	6.25
4	4.50
5	2.75
6	1.00

Notice that we show demand falling as price increases. This illustrates the **law of demand.** The law of demand is a **general law** of economic behaviour of markets. It is used in the same way as general laws of mechanics are used to describe the working of our solar system.

Key term

Law of demand: as the price of a good falls, other factors remaining constant, the quantity demanded will increase.

Because purchasers have a limited amount of money to spend and must choose between goods that compete for their attention. When the price of one good rises, it is likely that other goods will seem relatively more attractive and so demand will switch away from the more expensive good to the cheaper alternative. This is called a **substitution effect.**

We can show this schedule graphically, with **price on the 'y' axis** and **quantity demanded on the 'x' axis.** If we assume that there is complete divisibility, so that price and quantity can both change in infinitely small steps, we can draw a demand curve by joining the points represented in the schedule by a continuous line (Figure 1). This is the **demand curve** for biscuits in the particular market we are looking at.

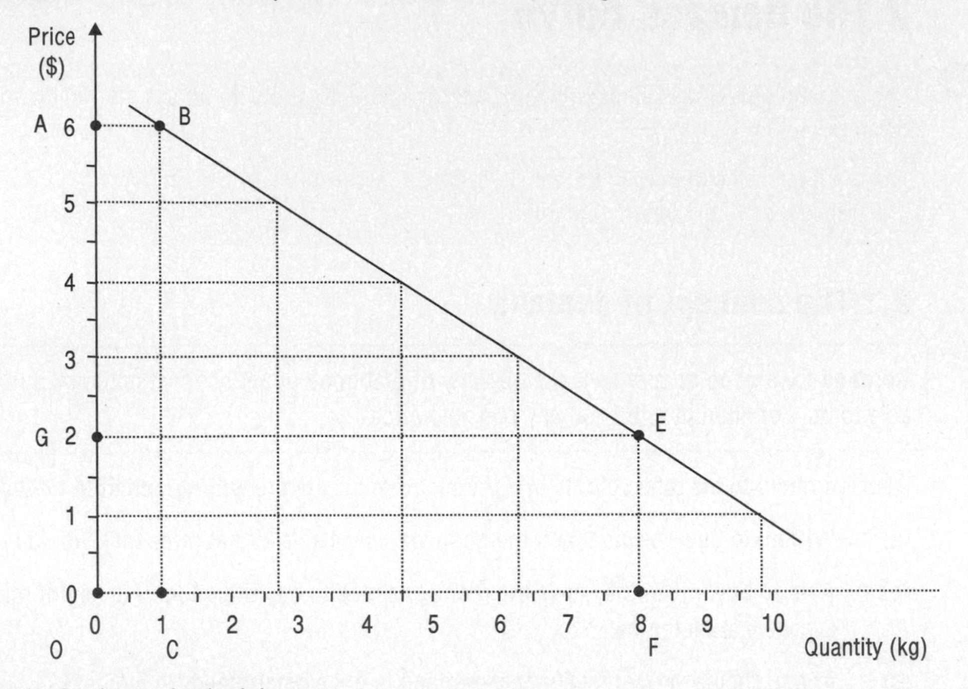

Figure 1 Graph of a demand schedule

The **area of each rectangle** in Figure 1 represents the **total money outlay** by consumers at the price in question. For example, at a price of $6, demand would be 1 kilogram and total spending would be $6, represented by rectangle ABCO. Similarly, at a price of $2, demand would be 8 kilograms and the total spending of $16 is represented by rectangle GEFO.

Put another way, the area of each rectangle shows the **revenue the supplier will earn** from selling the product at each price.

Assessment focus point

Sketching demand and/or supply curves may be a useful way of analysing an assessment question.

In Figure 1, the demand curve happens to be a straight line. In reality, a demand curve is more likely to be a curved line convex to the origin. As you will be able to appreciate, such a demand curve means that there are progressively larger increases in quantity demanded as price falls (Figure 2).

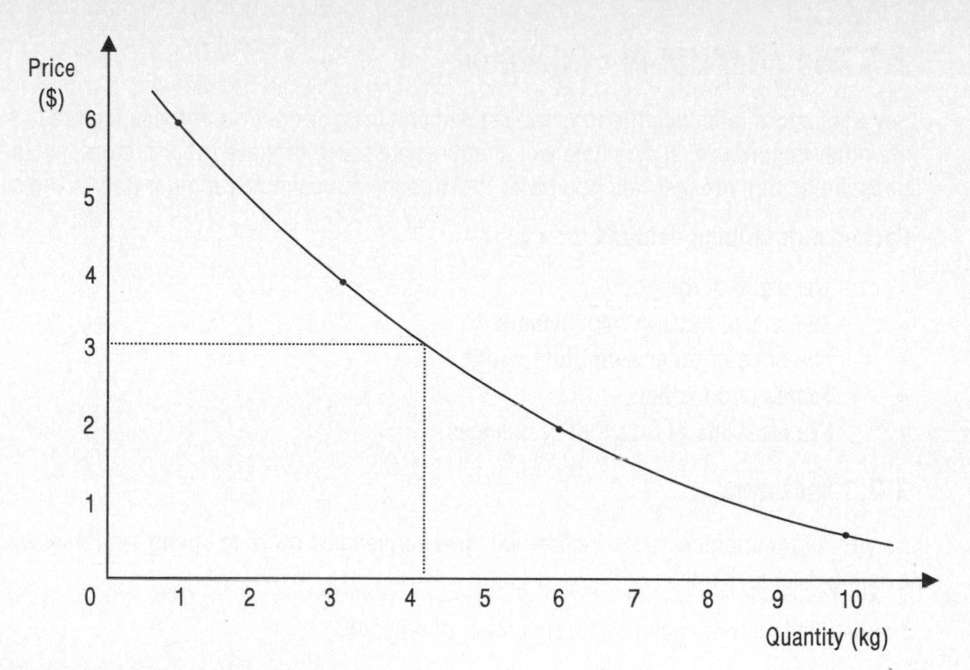

Figure 2 Demand curve convex to the origin

Question

Demand curve

Refer to Figure 2. The price of the commodity is currently $3 per kilo, and demand is approximately 4 kilograms at that price. What would be the (approximate) demand for the commodity if the price fell to $2 per kilo? And what would be the demand if the price rose to $4 per kilo?

Answer

Quantity demanded increases to (approximately) 6 kilos at the reduced price of $2 per kilo. If price rises to $4 per kilo, demand falls to (approximately) 3 kilos.

Note that changes in demand caused by changes in price are represented by movements **along the demand curve,** from one point to another. These changes in quantity demanded in response to a change in price are called **extensions** or **contractions** in demand. The price has changed, and the quantity demanded changes (prompting a movement along the curve), but **the demand curve itself remains the same.**

Key terms

Extensions of demand refer to the increases in quantity demand due to the price of the good falling. **Contractions of demand** are the effects of the price of the good rising.

Market demand is the total quantity of a product that all purchasers would want to buy at each price

A market demand schedule and a market demand curve are therefore simply the sum of all the individual demand schedules and demand curves put together.

2.3 The conditions of demand

Several factors influence the total market demand for a good. One of these factors is obviously its price, but there are other factors too, and to help you to appreciate some of these other factors, you need to recognise that households buy not just one good with their money but a whole range of goods and services.

Factors determining demand for a good

- The **price** of the good
- The size of **households' income**
- The price of other **substitute goods**
- **Tastes** and fashion
- **Expectations** of future price changes

2.3.1 Incomes

As you might imagine, more income will give households more to spend, and they will want to buy more goods at existing prices.

Household incomes may rise for a number of reasons:

(a) Rises in **gross income:** due to rises in salaries, interest, dividends or other sources of income

(b) Rises in **disposable income:** due to reduction in the rates of tax on these incomes leaving more for the household to spend

(c) Rises in **discretionary income:** due to reduction in costs of fixed commitments such as mortgage payments, property taxes and so on.

Demand and the level of income may be related in different ways.

(a) We might normally expect a rise in household income to lead to an increase in demand for a good, and goods for which demand rises as household income increases are called **normal goods**.

(b) Demand may rise with income up to a certain point but then fall as income rises beyond that point. Goods whose demand eventually falls as income rises are called **inferior goods**: examples might include 'value' or 'basics' ranges of own-brand supermarket foods (which could be substituted for more expensive ranges), and bus or coach travel (which could be substituted for rail or air travel). The reason for falling demand is that as incomes rise, customers can afford to switch demand to superior products.

Key terms

Normal goods: goods for which demand increases as household incomes increase.

Inferior goods: goods for which demand decreases as household incomes increase.

2.3.2 Substitutes and complements

Key terms

Substitute goods are goods that are alternatives to each other, so that an **increase** in the demand for one is likely to cause a **decrease** in the demand for another. Switching demand from one good to another 'rival' good is **substitution**

Complements are goods that tend to be bought and used together, so that an **increase** in the demand for one is likely to cause an **increase** in the demand for the other.

A change in the price of one good will not necessarily change the demand for another good. For example, we would not expect an increase in the price of televisions to affect the demand for bread. However, there are goods for which the market demand is inter-connected. These inter-related goods are referred to as either **substitutes** or **complements**.

Examples of substitute goods and services

- Rival brands of the same commodity, like Coca-Cola and Pepsi-Cola
- Tea and coffee
- Some different forms of entertainment

Substitution takes place when the price of one good rises relative to a substitute good.

By contrast, complements are connected in the sense that demand for one is likely to lead to demand for the other.

Examples of complements

- Cups and saucers
- Bread and butter
- Motor cars and the components and raw materials that go into their manufacture

Question

Substitutes and complements

What might be the effect of an increase in the ownership of domestic deep freezers on the demand for perishable food products?

Answer

(a) Domestic deep freezers and perishable products are complements because people buy deep freezers to store perishable products.

(b) Perishable products are supplied either as fresh produce (for example, fresh meat and fresh vegetables) or as frozen produce, which can be kept for a short time in a refrigerator but for longer in a freezer. The demand for frozen produce will rise, while the demand for fresh produce will fall.

(c) Wider ownership of deep freezers is likely to increase bulk buying of perishable products. Suppliers can save some packaging costs, and can therefore offer lower prices for bulk purchases.

Sometimes the invention of a better substitute, even at a higher price, will cause a fall in demand for the established good due to its **technical obsolescence**. For example the arrival of digital players and downloadable songs has lead to significant year on year declines in demand for CDs.

2.3.3 Demand, fashion and expectations

A change in **fashion or tastes** will also alter the demand for a product. For example, if it becomes fashionable for middle class households in the UK to drink wine with their meals, expenditure on wine will increase. There may be passing fads, such as particular styles of clothing

And tastes can be **affected by advertisers** and suppliers trying to 'create' demand for their products. However, the effect of a product becoming fashionable will be that demand for it rises without its price having to be reduced.

Expectations work in advance on price changes. If consumers believe that prices will rise, or that shortages will occur, they may attempt to stock up on the product before these changes occur. Again, this could lead to increases in demand despite the price of the good remaining unchanged.

2.4 Shifts of the demand curve

So far, we have been looking at the way a change in price affects the quantity demanded, depicted as a movement **along** the demand curve. However, when there is a **change in the conditions of demand**, the quantity demanded will change even if price remains constant. In this case, there will be a different price/quantity demand schedule and so **a different demand curve**. We refer to such a change as a **shift of the demand curve**.

Figure 3 depicts a rise in demand at each price level, with the demand curve shifting to the right, from D_0 to D_1. For example, at price P_1, demand for the good would rise from X to Y. This shift could be caused by any of the following **conditions of demand**.

- A rise in **household income** (including a reduction in direct taxes)
- A rise in the price of **substitutes**
- A fall in the price of **complements**
- A change in **tastes** towards this product
- An **expected rise** in the price of the product
- An **increase** in population.

Figure 3 shows an outward shift in the demand curve, but conversely a fall in demand at each price level would be represented by a shift in the opposite direction: a shift to the left of the original demand curve. Such a shift may be caused by the opposite of the conditions of demand shown above.

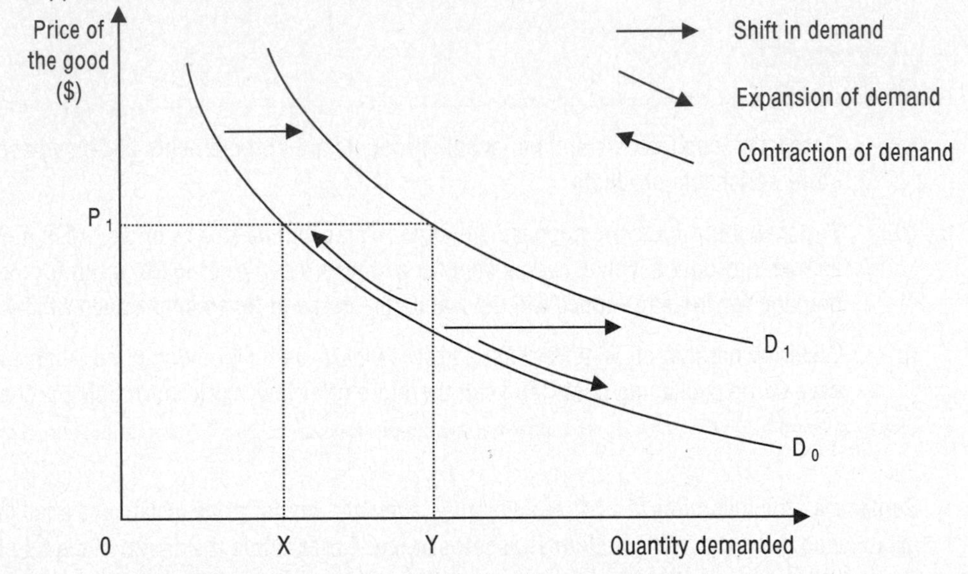

Figure 3 Changes in quantity demanded and outward shift of the demand curve

Assessment focus point

The difference between a change in demand and a shift of the demand curve is of fundamental importance. Remember:

(a) Movements along a demand curve (contractions or expansions) for a good are caused solely by changes in its price

(b) Variations in the conditions of demand create shifts in the demand curve

Question

Substitutes and complements

In County X, a recent fall in the price of DVDs has seen demand for DVDs increase significantly. However, cinema operators have reported a decline in customer numbers, and they believe this is due to people preferring to buy DVDs to watch rather than going to the cinema.

What effect is the fall in the price of DVDs likely to have on the demand curves for:

(a) DVD players
(b) cinema tickets.

Answer

(a) There is likely to have been an outward shift in the demand curve for DVD players. DVD players are complements to the DVDs themselves because people will need to buy the DVD players in order to watch their DVDs. So, the increased demand for DVDs will lead to an increase in demand for DVD players even though their price may be unchanged. This results in an **outward shift** in their demand curve (an expansion of demand).

(b) There is likely to be an inward shift in the demand curve for cinema tickets (a contraction of demand). Even though the price of cinema tickets has not changed, people are demanding less of them because they are choosing to watch DVDs instead. Cinema tickets are a substitute product to DVDs, and a fall in the price of a substitute leads to an inward shift of the demand curve for a product.

3 The supply curve

FAST FORWARD

The **supply curve** shows the quantity of a good which would be supplied by producers at a given price.

3.1 The concept of supply

Key term

Supply refers to the quantity of a good that existing suppliers or would-be suppliers are willing and able to produce for the market at a given price.

The quantity supplied shows what firms will supply at a range of prices:

(a) **Willing to supply**: the price is high enough to provide a profit to the supplier

(b) **Able to supply:** the firm has the resources to supply the product. This does not mean that there are sufficient customers willing to buy the whole quantity supplied of the product at this price

(c) **At a given price:** firms are incentivised to produce products by the prospect of higher profits from higher priced products.

As with demand, a distinction needs to be made.

(a) An **individual firm's supply schedule** is the quantity of the good that the individual firm would want to supply to the market at any given price.

(b) **Market supply** is the total quantity of the good that all firms in the market would want to supply at a given price.

3.2 The supply curve

A **supply schedule** and **supply curve** can be created both for an individual supplier and for all firms which produce the good.

Key terms

The law of supply: as price rises, other factors remaining constant, the quantity supplied of the good will increase.

A supply curve is constructed in a similar manner to a demand curve (from a schedule of quantities supplied at different prices) but shows the quantity suppliers are willing to produce at different price levels. It is an **upward sloping curve from left to right**, because greater quantities will be supplied at higher prices.

We usually assume that suppliers aim to maximise their profits, and the upward slope of the supply curve reflects this desire to make profit (ie they are prepared to supply more of something the higher the price that customers will pay for it).

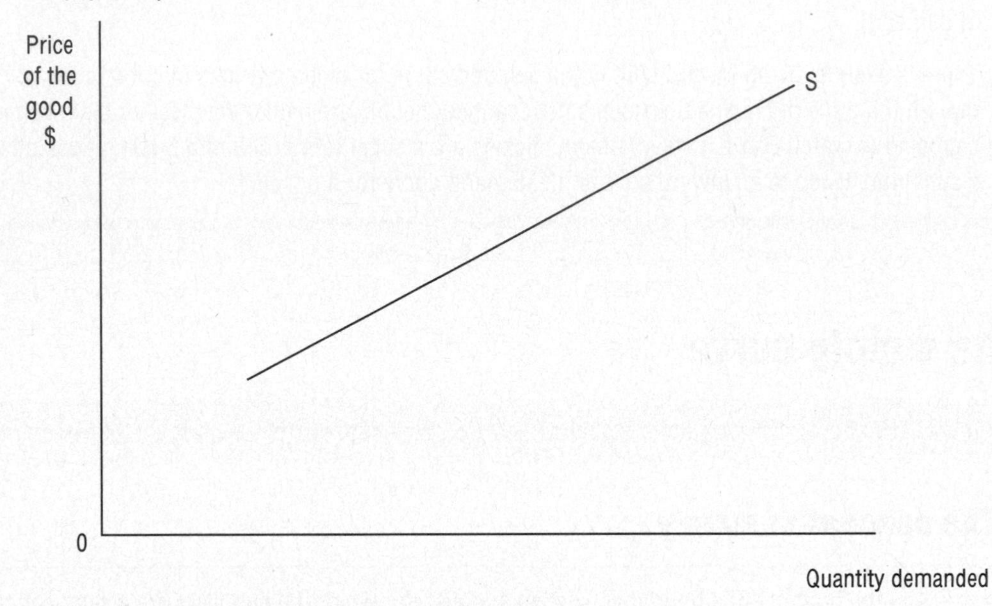

Figure 4 The market supply curve for a product

3.3 Factors influencing the supply quantity

The quantity supplied of a good depends, as you might expect, on prices and costs. More specifically, it depends on the following factors.

(a) The **costs of making the good**. These include raw materials costs, which ultimately depend on the prices of factors of production (wages, interest rates, land rents and profit expectations)

(b) The **prices of other goods**. When a supplier can switch readily from supplying one good to another, the goods concerned are called **substitutes in supply**. An increase in the price of one such good would make the supply of another good whose price does not rise less attractive to suppliers. When a production process has two or more distinct and separate outputs, the goods produced are known as **goods in joint supply** or **complements in production**. Goods in joint supply include, for example, meat and hides. If the price of beef rises, more will be supplied and there will be an accompanying increase in the supply of cow hide.

(c) **Expectations of price changes**. If a supplier expects the price of a good to rise, he is likely to try to reduce supply while the price is lower so that he can supply more of his product or service once the price is higher.

(d) **Changes in technology**. Technological developments which reduce costs of production (and increase productivity) will raise the quantity of supply of a good at a given price

(e) **Other factors**, such as changes in the weather (for example, in the case of agricultural goods), natural disasters or industrial disruption

The supply curve shows how the quantity supplied will change in response to a change in price. If **supply conditions** alter, a different supply curve must be drawn. In other words, a change in price will cause a change in supply **along the supply curve**. A change in other supply conditions will cause a **shift in the supply curve itself**.

Assessment focus point

This distinction between a movement along the supply curve and a shift in the supply curve is just as important as the similar distinction relating to the demand curve.

3.4 Shifts of the market supply curve

The **market supply curve** is the aggregate of all the supply curves of individual firms in the market. A shift of the market supply curve occurs when supply conditions (other than the price of the good itself) change. Figure 5 shows a shift in the supply curve from S_0 to S_1. A **rightward** (or **downward**) shift of the curve shows an expansion of supply and may be caused by the factors below.

(a) A fall in the cost of factors of production, for example a reduction in the cost of raw material inputs

(b) A fall in the price of other goods. The production of other goods becomes relatively less attractive as their price falls. Firms are therefore likely to shift resources away from the goods whose price is falling and into the production of higher priced goods that offer increased profits. We therefore expect that the supply of one good will rise as the prices of other goods fall (and vice versa)

(c) Technological progress, which reduces unit costs and also increases production capabilities

(d) Improvements in productivity or more efficient use of existing factors of production, which again will reduce unit cost

A shift of the supply curve is the result of changes in costs, either in absolute terms or relative to the costs of other goods. If the price of the good is P_1, suppliers would be willing to increase supply from Q_0 to Q_1 under the new supply conditions (Figure 5).

Conversely, we might see a **leftward** (or **upward**) shift in the supply curve if the cost of supply increases. This would mean that at the existing price, a firm's output will decrease and less will be supplied.

This is also illustrated on Figure 5: at price P_1, the quantity supplied now falls from Q_0 to Q_2, as the supply curve shifts from S_0 to S_2.

In order for the supplier to restore output levels to the original Q_0, price would have to increase to P_2.

An upward (leftward) shift ($S_0 \rightarrow S_2$) in supply could be caused by:

(a) An increase in the cost of factors of production (eg a rise in wages and salaries, which are the costs of labour)

(b) A rise in the price of other goods which would make them relatively more attractive to the producer

(c) An increase in indirect taxes, or a reduction in a subsidy, which would make supply at existing prices less profitable.

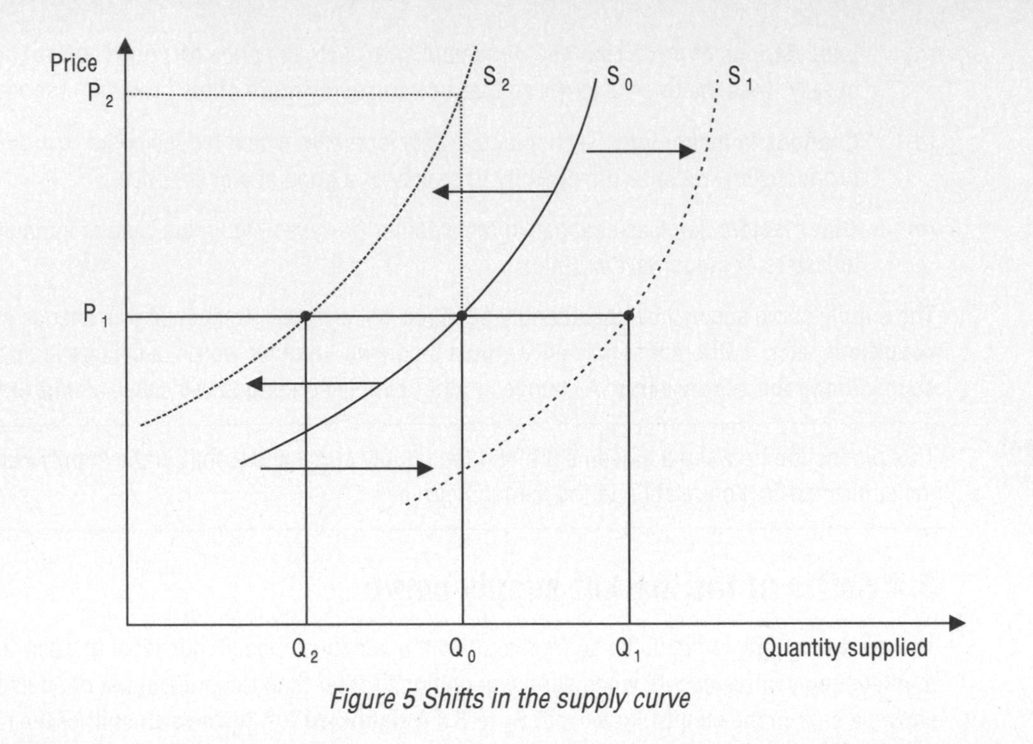

Figure 5 Shifts in the supply curve

Question

Quantity supplied

What effect will higher grain prices have on the supply curve of a cereal manufacturer who makes cereals from grain?

Answer

The higher price of grain will cause the supply curve to shift leftwards (or upwards). The increase in grain prices increase the cereal manufacturer's production costs, making supply at existing prices less profitable.

4 Formation of equilibrium price

FAST FORWARD

The competitive market process results in an **equilibrium price**, which is the price at which market supply and market demand quantities are in balance. In any market, the equilibrium price will change if market demand or supply conditions change.

4.1 The price mechanism and the equilibrium price

Key terms

The **price mechanism** brings demand and supply into equilibrium, and the **equilibrium price** for a good is the price at which the volume demanded by consumers and the volume that firms would be willing to supply is the same. This is also known as the **market clearing price**, since at this price there will be neither surplus nor shortage in the market.

The way demand and supply interact to determine the equilibrium price can be illustrated by drawing the market demand curve and the market supply curve on the same graph (Figure 6).

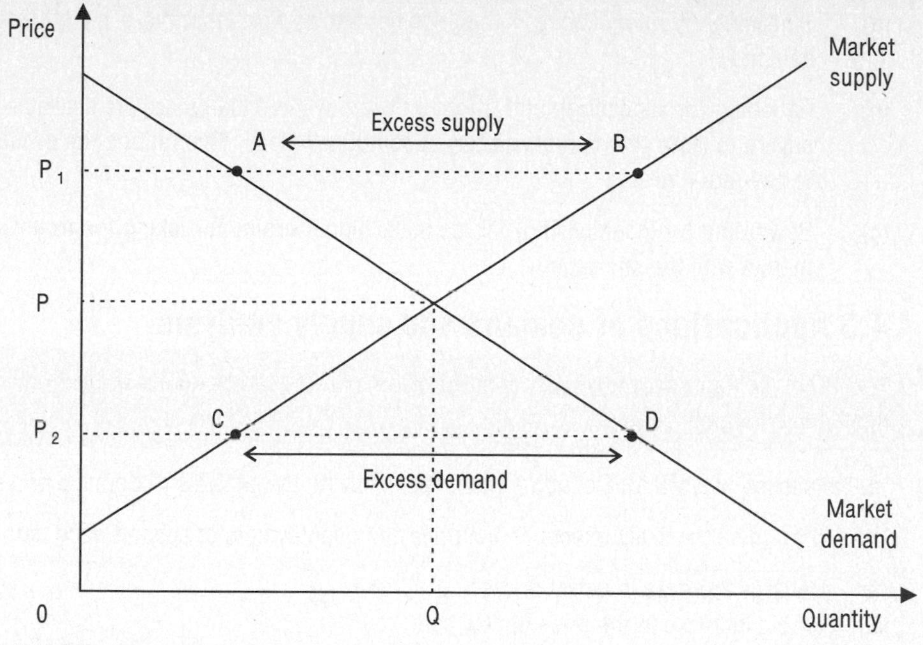

Figure 6 Market equilibrium

At price P_1 in Figure 6, suppliers want to produce a greater quantity than the market demands, meaning that there is excess supply, equal to the distance AB. Suppliers would react as the stock of unsold goods accumulates:

(a) They would cut down the current level of production in order to sell unwanted inventories.
(b) They would also reduce prices in order to encourage sales.

The opposite will happen at price P_2 where there is an excess of demand over supply shown by the distance CD. Supply and price would increase. Faced with an excess of demand, manufacturers would be able to raise their prices. This would make supplying the good more profitable and supply would increase.

At price P the amount that sellers are willing and able to supply is equal to the amount that customers are willing and able to buy. Consumers will be willing to spend a total of $(P \times Q)$ on buying Q units of the product, and suppliers will be willing to supply Q units to earn revenue of $(P \times Q)$. P is the **equilibrium price**.

The forces of supply and demand push a market to its equilibrium price and quantity. Note carefully the following key points.

(a) If there is no change in conditions of supply or demand, the **equilibrium price will prevail** in the market and will remain stable.

(b) If price is not at the equilibrium, the market is in **disequilibrium** and supply and demand will push prices towards the equilibrium price.

(c) In any market there will only be one equilibrium position where the market is cleared.

(d) Shifts in the supply curve or demand curve will change the equilibrium price (and the quantity traded).

4.2 Functions of the price mechanism

FAST FORWARD

The three functions of the price mechanism are to **signal** where there are shortages or surpluses, to **ration** scarce supply amongst potential buyers, and to **reward** firms and households for alleviating shortages or surpluses.

Figure 6 shows that at low prices like P_2 the quantity demanded will exceed the quantity supplied. It also shows that price will rise. In this situation of an initial shortage price has performed **three functions**:

(a) Signalling: by rising above P_2 the price has shown firms that there is a market in which supply is less than demand

(b) Rationing (or allocating): at P_2 more units are wanted than there are available. The rising price causes some buyers to leave the market and buy substitutes instead. This rations the product out to the people prepared to pay more for it

(c) Rewarding (or incentivising) **:** firms make higher profits for taking the trouble to transfer resources to the market with the shortage.

4.3 Applications of demand and supply analysis

FAST FORWARD

> The effects of **demand and supply conditions** on markets can be analysed by studying the behaviour of both demand and supply curves.

In this section, we will look at some examples involving the analysis of demand and supply conditions.

We will examine the likely effects on the price and quantity sold of second hand cars in the event of:

(a) A large increase in petrol prices
(b) A big increase in the price of new cars
(c) A massive investment in public transport

Assessment focus point

> The CBA will feature questions asking you to identify the effects on price of a change in a condition of demand and/or supply

4.4 Analysis

Petrol and cars are **complementary** products; demand for one is likely to affect demand for the other. Hence, any change in the market for petrol (part (a) of this example) would be expected to affect the market for second-hand cars. The demand for petrol, however, is likely to be relatively unresponsive to a change in price, so a change in price will only have a small impact on the quantity demanded. Consequently, a major change in its price will be necessary to affect the demand for any complementary product. Figure 7 assumes that there is a large increase in the price of fuel (petrol) as stated above.

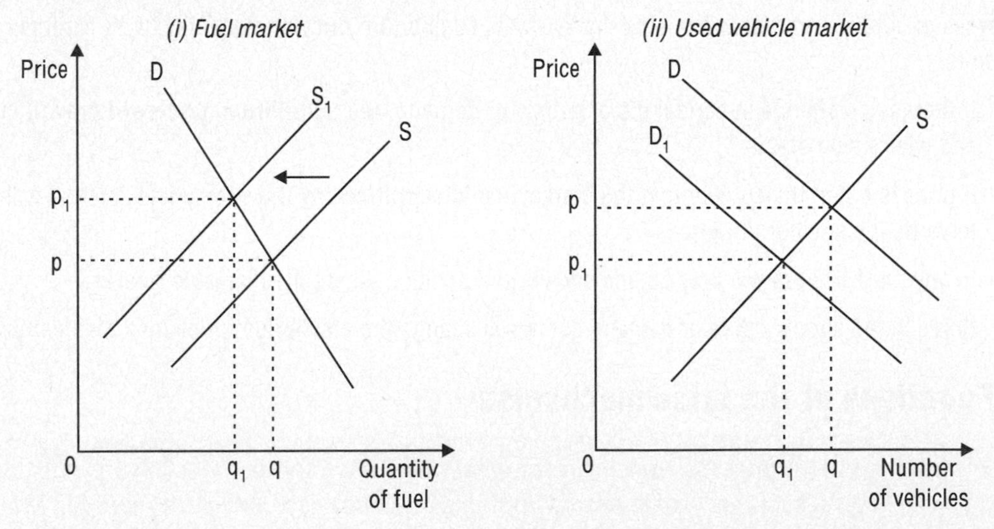

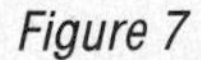
Figure 7

In this instance, we have assumed that the rise in the price of fuel results from a change in the conditions of supply. This is the basis of the new supply curve S_1 shifting to the left of the existing one (Figure 7 (i)). A rise in the price of fuel is a rise in the cost of owning and running a car. There will thus be a fall in the demand for second-hand cars and a fall in the price and quantity sold (Figure 7 (ii)).

Part (b) of the example involves new vehicles and used vehicles, which are **substitute** products. A consumer has a choice to buy either a new car or a used car. The consumer is likely to buy one or the other, not both.

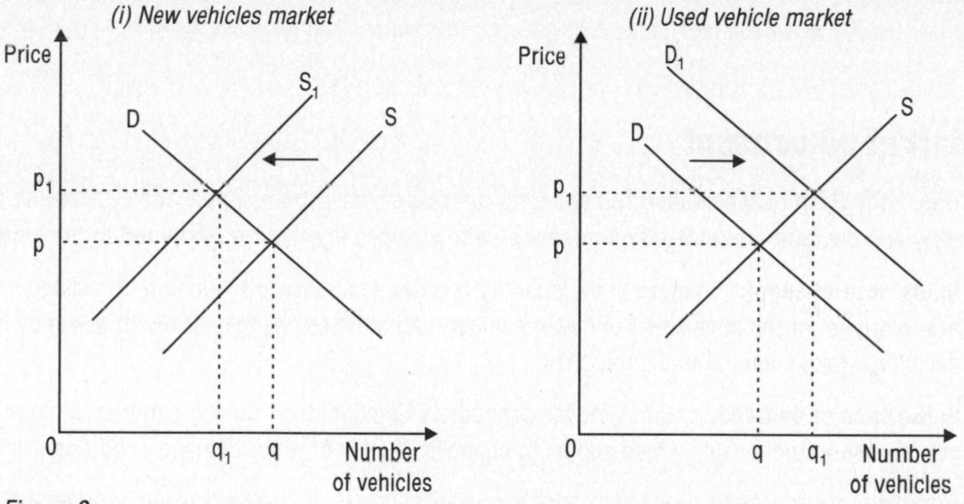

Figure 8

It is assumed that the increase in the price of new cars is the result of a major increase in supply costs. The rise in price causes a switch of demand into second-hand vehicles, so pushing up their price and leading to an increase in the number sold (Figure 8(ii)).

The increased price of new vehicles could alternatively result from an increase in the demand for them.

Part (c) of the example involves another 'product' which is in competition with second-hand cars. If there is a reduction in the price of public transport services following the outward shift in supply, the result is likely to be as shown in Figure 9.

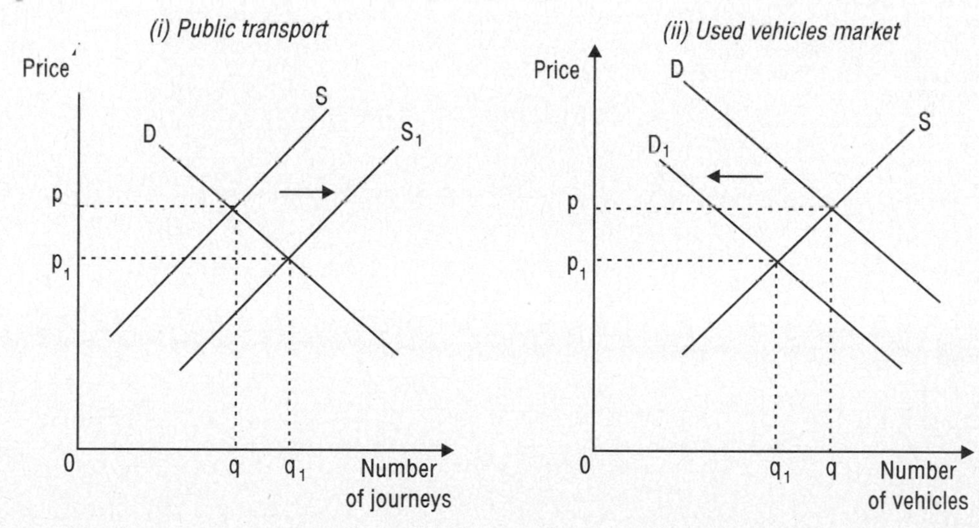

Figure 9

In part (c) of our example, the fall in public transport prices leads to an expansion in demand for public transport (Figure 9(i)) while the demand for second-hand cars falls (with a new demand line D_1 in Figure 9(ii)) together with a fall in price. However, the relationship between public transport and the market for second-hand cars is likely to be a highly complex and indeterminate one. Thus, people might make greater use of public transport while the ownership of cars (including second-hand cars) could continue to increase.

5 Momentary, short-run and long run equilibrium price

FAST FORWARD

Market price and quantities take time to adjust to changes. Therefore price will adjust through momentary stage, immediately following the change, short run, a state of transition, and long run, where the market settles down finally.

5.1 Market adjustment

We need to distinguish between short run and long run responses of both supply and demand. **In the short run** both supply and demand are **relatively unresponsive** to changes in price, as compared to the **long run**.

(a) **In the case of supply**, changes in the quantity of a good supplied often require the laying off or hiring of new workers, or the installation of new machinery. All of these changes, brought about by management decisions, take some time to implement.

(b) **In the case of demand**, it takes time for consumers to adjust their buying patterns, although demand will often respond more rapidly than supply to changes in price or other demand conditions.

In some markets, responses to changes in price are relatively rapid. In others, response times are much longer. In stock markets for example, the supply and demand for company shares respond very rapidly to price changes, whereas in the markets for fuel oils or agrichemicals response times are much longer.

5.2 The three market stages of adjustment

Figure 10 below analyses the impact of a change in demand.

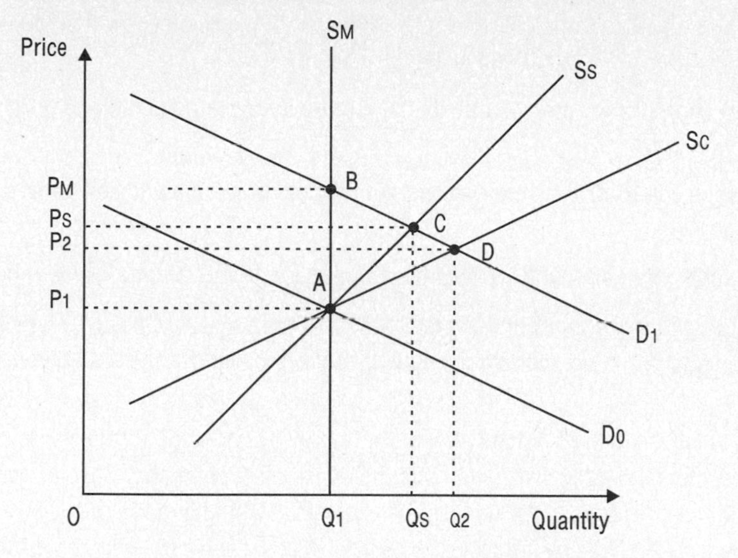

Figure 7 Momentary, short run, long run equilibrium prices

This shows the market for an imported exotic vegetable used in cooking. The market is initially in equilibrium at price P1 with quantity Q1 bought and sold each day. This is shown by point A.

Demand rises from D0 to D1 following a popular television cookery show that featured recipes for the exotic vegetable.

(a) In the momentary (or market) period supply is fixed at Q1 per day, shown by the momentary supply curve Sm. This forces price to rise to Pm and establishes a momentary equilibrium at point B.

(b) The high price leads importers to order more of the vegetable and within a few days the level of supply increases. This causes the short run supply curve to shift around to S_S and establishes a short run equilibrium price of Ps at point C.

(c) In the long run importers will have fully responded to the increased popularity of the exotic vegetable and the long run supply curve S_L will be established, drawing market price down to P2 at point D.

This shows that markets adjust **dynamically over time** to changes in the conditions of demand and supply rather than leap from one long run equilibrium price to another long run equilibrium price. This can sometimes take many years to happen where markets are characterised by **time lags** in expanding production or reducing consumption.

Chapter roundup

- Markets are where **exchanges take place** and market prices are established. In practice few markets are actual physical places. Instead exchange is carried out in many locations and on-line.
- The **demand curve** (or schedule) shows how much of a good consumers are willing and able to purchase at any given price.
- The position of the demand curve is determined by the demand conditions, which include consumers' tastes and preferences, and consumers' incomes.
- The **supply curve** shows the quantity of a good which would be supplied by producers at a given price.
- The competitive market process results in an **equilibrium price**, which is the price at which market supply and market demand quantities are in balance. In any market, the equilibrium price will change if market demand or supply conditions change.
- The three functions of the price mechanism are to **signal** where there are shortages or surpluses, to **ration** scarce supply amongst potential buyers, and to **reward** firms and households for alleviating shortages or surpluses.
- The effects of **demand and supply conditions** on markets can be analysed by studying the behaviour of both demand and supply curves.
- Market price and quantities **take time to adjust** to changes. Therefore price will adjust through **momentary** stage, immediately following the change, **short run**, a state of transition, and **long run**, where the market settles down finally.

Quick quiz

1 What factors influence demand for a good?

2 What are (a) substitutes and (b) complements?

3 What factors affect the supply quantity?

4 What is meant by equilibrium price?

5 A demand curve is drawn on all *except* which of the following assumptions?

A Incomes do not change.
B Prices of substitutes are fixed.
C Price of the good is constant.
D There are no changes in tastes and preferences.

6 The diagram shown relates to the demand for and supply of Scotch whiskey. The market is initially in equilibrium at point X. The government imposes a specific tax on Scotch whilst at the same time, the price of Irish Whiskey (a substitute for Scotch Whisky) rises. Which point, A, B, C or D represents the new market equilibrium?

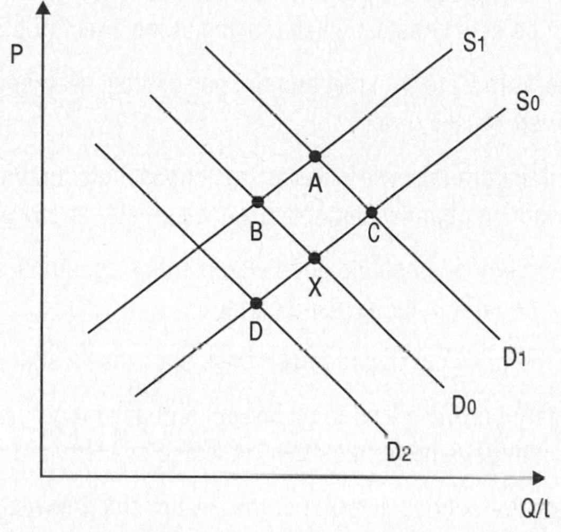

7 Which one of the following would normally cause a rightward shift in the demand curve for a product?

A A fall in the price of a substitute product
B A reduction in direct taxation on incomes
C A reduction in price of the product
D An increase in the price of a complementary product

8 What is an inferior good?

A A good of such poor quality that demand for it is very weak
B A good of lesser quality than a substitute good, so that the price of the substitute is higher
C A good for which the cross elasticity of demand with a substitute product is greater than 1
D A good for which demand will fall as household income rises

Answers to quick quiz

1 The price of the good
The price of other goods
Household income
Taste and fashion

2 Substitutes are goods that are alternatives to each other (for example, Coca-Cola and Pepsi)
Complements are goods which are bought and used together (for example, cars and petrol)

3 The price obtainable for the good
The prices obtainable for other goods, particularly goods in joint supply
The costs of making the good
Disruptions such as bad weather and strikes

4 The price at which the volume of demand and the volume of supply are equal; there is neither surplus nor shortage.

5 C Demand curves express the quantity demanded at each given market price. Non-price determinants such as income must be held constant when looking at the effect of price movements in isolation.

6 A Supply shifts from S_0 to S_1, reflecting the per-unit tax. Demand shifts from D_0 to D_1 as the price of a substitute (Irish whiskey) rises.

7 B A reduction in income tax will increase 'real' household income, and so demand for normal products will shift to the right, ie quantity demanded will be greater at any given price.

A fall in the price of a substitute good would entice consumers away from the original good. This would cause a leftward shift in the demand curve.

A change in the price of the good itself does not cause a shift in the curve but a movement along it.

Complementary products tend to be bought and used together, so an increase in the price of one will lead to a reduction in demand for the other, reflected in a leftward shift in the demand curve.

8 D Inferior goods are defined in terms of the relationship between quantity demanded and income. The issue of substitutes is not relevant.

Now try the questions below from the Exam Question Bank

Question numbers
11 - 13

The market system 2 – price elasticity

4

Introduction

We have discussed in the previous chapter the direction of changes in demand and supply when prices change. When price of a good goes up, the quantity demanded will fall, and the quantity suppliers will be willing to supply will go up.

But if prices are increased or reduced, how much will this affect the amount of revenue from selling a good?

How much will supply of a good change if the price changes?

In this chapter, we consider such questions, and introduce the key concept of elasticity. You need to have a good understanding of this concept, because it could be relevant in a number of different contexts in assessment questions.

Topic list	Learning outcomes	Syllabus references	Ability required
1 Calculation of price elasticity of demand	C1	C1 (b)	Application
2 Impacts of price elasticity of demand	C1	C1 (d)	Comprehension
3 Influences on price elasticity of demand	C1	C1 (c)	Comprehension
4 Calculation of price elasticity of supply	C1	C1 (b)	Application
5 Influences on price elasticity of supply	C1	C1 (c)	Comprehension

1 Calculation of price elasticity of demand

FAST FORWARD

Demand for a good depends largely on **price**, **household income** and the relative **price of substitutes or complementary goods**. Changes in any of these will cause either a movement along the demand curve or a shift in the demand curve. **Price elasticity of demand** indicates the **responsiveness** in the quantity demanded of a good to a change in the price of that good.

1.1 The price elasticity of demand

Assessment focus point

Elasticity is a common assessment topic. It is also of great practical importance in the real world of business (for example, in pricing decisions) and you will need to use it later in your CIMA studies. Make sure you have a good understanding of the concept of elasticity.

Elasticity, in general, refers to the relationship between two variables. Price elasticity of demand explains the relationship between the **change in quantity demanded** and the **change in price**.

If prices went **up** by 10%, would the quantity demanded **fall** by the same percentage?

Key term

Price elasticity of demand (PED) is a measure of the extent of change in the market demand for a good in response to a change in its price.

The coefficient of PED is measured as:

$$\frac{\text{Percentage change in quantity demanded}}{\text{Percentage change in price}}$$

Since demand usually increases when the price falls, and decreases when the price rises, elasticity has a negative value. **However, it is usual to ignore the minus sign**, and just describe the absolute value of the coefficient.

This can be expressed as:

$$\frac{\frac{\Delta Q}{Q} \times 100}{\frac{\Delta P}{P} \times 100}$$

where Δ is the symbol for 'change in'
Q is the quantity demanded of the good
P is the price of the good

If we are measuring the responsiveness of demand to a large change in price, we can measure elasticity between two points on the demand curve, and the resulting measure is called the **arc elasticity of demand**. We calculate the arc elasticity of demand from the percentage change in quantity relative to **average** quantity for the relevant range of output and from the percentage price change relative to the **average** of the corresponding price range.

If we wish to measure the responsiveness of demand at one particular point in the demand curve, we can calculate a **point elasticity of demand**, without averaging price and quantity over a range. In doing so, it is convenient to assume that the demand curve is a straight line unless told otherwise.

1.2 Example: arc elasticity of demand

The price of a good is \$1.20 per unit and annual demand is 800,000 units. Market research indicates that an increase in price of 10 cents per unit will result in a fall in annual demand of 70,000 units.

What is the price elasticity of demand measuring the responsiveness of demand over this range of price increase?

Solution

Annual demand at \$1.20 per unit is 800,000 units.
Annual demand at \$1.30 per unit is 730,000 units.

Average quantity over the range is 765,000 units.
Average price is \$1.25.

% change in demand $\frac{70,000}{765,000} \times 100\% = 9.15\%$

% change in price $\frac{10c}{125c} \times 100\% = 8\%$

Price elasticity of demand = $\frac{-9.15}{8} = -1.14$

Ignoring the minus sign, the arc elasticity is 1.14.

The demand for this good, over the range of annual demand 730,000 to 800,000 units, is **elastic** because the price elasticity of demand is greater than 1. Now try the following exercise yourself.

Question

Arc price elasticity of demand

If the price per unit of X rises from \$1.40 to \$1.60, it is expected that monthly demand will fall from 220,000 units to 200,000 units.

What is the arc price elasticity of demand over these ranges of price and output?

Answer

Monthly demand at \$1.40 per unit = 220,000 units

Monthly demand at \$1.60 per unit = 200,000 units

Average quantity = 210,000 units

Average price = \$1.50

% change in demand $\frac{20,000}{210,000} \times 100\% = 9.52\%$

% change in price $\frac{20}{150} \times 100\% = 13.33\%$

Arc price elasticity of demand = $\frac{-9.52}{13.33} = -0.71\%$

Ignoring the minus sign, the arc elasticity is 0.71.

Demand is **inelastic** over the demand range considered, because the price elasticity of demand (ignoring the minus sign) is less than 1.

1.3 Example: point elasticity of demand

The price of a good is $1.20 per unit and annual demand is 800,000. Market research indicates that an increase in price of 10 cents per unit will result in a fall in annual demand for the good of 70,000 units.

Required

Calculate the elasticity of demand at the current price of $1.20.

Solution

We are asked to calculate the elasticity at a particular price. We assume that the demand curve is a straight line.

At a price of $1.20, annual demand is 800,000 units. For a price rise:

% change in demand $\frac{70{,}000}{800{,}000} \times 100\% = 8.75\%$ (fall)

% change in price $\frac{10c}{120c} \times 100\% = 8.33\%$ (rise)

Price elasticity of demand at price $1.20 = $\frac{-8.75}{8.33} = -1.05$

Ignoring the minus sign, the price elasticity at this point is 1.05. Demand is **elastic** at this point, because the elasticity is greater than 1.

Question

Point price elasticity of demand

If the price per unit of x rises from $1.40 to $1.60, it is expected that monthly demand will fall from 220,000 units to 200,000 units.

What is the point price elasticity of demand when the price is $1.40?

Answer

We assume that the demand curve is a straight line.

At a price of $1.40, demand is 220,000 units.

For a price rise of 20 cents to $1.60:

% change in demand $\frac{20{,}000}{220{,}000} \times 100\% = 9.09\%$ (fall)

% change in price $\frac{20c}{140c} \times 100\% = 14.29\%$ (rise)

Price elasticity of demand = $\frac{9.09}{-14.29} = -0.64$

or 0.64 ignoring the minus sign.

Demand is **inelastic** at this point, because it is less than 1.

Assessment focus point

If it is not clear from the details of an assessment question whether you need to calculate arc or point elasticity, then calculate the **point** elasticity.

Question

Range of elasticity

A shop sells 100 shirts each month at a price of \$20. When the price is increased to \$24, the total sales revenue rises by 14%. Within which range does the price elasticity of demand lie?

A Under 0.15
B Greater than 0.15 and less than 0.5
C Greater than 0.5 and less than 1.0
D Greater than 1.0

Answer

B Total revenue of \$20 = 100 × \$20 = \$2,000
Total revenue at \$24 = \$2,000 × 1.14 = \$2,280
Number sold at \$24 = \$2,280 ÷ 24 = 95

Price elasticity of demand

Point method

$$\frac{\frac{5}{100}\times 100}{\frac{4}{20}\times 100} = \frac{5\%}{20\%} = 0.25$$

Arc method

$$\frac{\frac{5}{97\frac{1}{2}}\times 100}{\frac{4}{22}\times 100} = \frac{5.13\%}{18.2\%} = 0.28$$

1.4 Elastic and inelastic demand

The value of demand elasticity may be anything from zero to infinity.

- Demand is **inelastic** if the absolute value is less than 1
- Demand is **elastic** if the absolute value is greater than 1

Think about what this means if there is an increase in price. Where demand is **inelastic**, the quantity demanded falls by a **smaller** percentage than the rise in price. Where demand is **elastic**, demand falls by a **larger** percentage than the rise in price.

1.5 Price elasticity and the slope of the demand curve

Generally, demand curves slope downwards. Consumers are willing to buy more at lower prices than at higher prices. Except in certain special cases (which we look at below), **elasticity will vary in value along the length of a demand curve.**

It is therefore not possible to state the comparative elasticities of any two curves over different price ranges simply by looking at the slopes of the curves. However, it is possible to say that if a downward sloping demand curve shifts to become **steeper** over a particular range of quantity, then demand is becoming more **inelastic**. Conversely, a demand curve becoming **shallower** over a particular range indicates more **elastic** demand.

The ranges of price elasticity (η) at different points on a downward sloping straight line demand curve are illustrated in Figure 1.

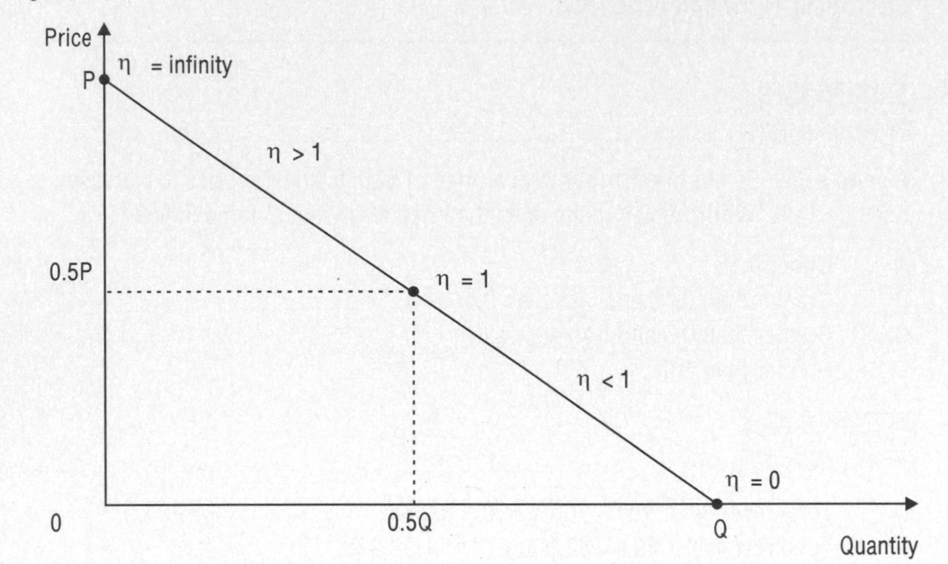

Figure 1 Ranges of price elasticity of demand

At **higher prices** on a straight line demand curve (the top of the demand curve), small percentage price reductions can bring **large percentage** increases in quantity demanded. This means that demand is **elastic** over these ranges.

At **lower prices** on a straight line demand curve (the bottom of the demand curve), **large percentage** price reductions can bring small percentage increases in quantity. This means that demand is **inelastic** over these price ranges.

1.6 Special values of price elasticity of demand

There are three special values of price elasticity of demand: 0, 1 and infinity.

(a) **Demand is perfectly inelastic**: $\eta = 0$. There is no change in quantity demanded, regardless of the change in price. In this case, the demand curve is a **vertical straight line**.

(b) **Perfectly elastic demand**: $\eta = \infty$ (infinitely elastic). Consumers will want to buy an infinite amount, but only up to a particular price level. Any price increase above this level will reduce demand to zero. In this case, the demand curve is a **horizontal straight line.**

(c) **Unit elasticity of demand**: $\eta = 1$. Total revenue for suppliers (which is the same as total spending on the product by households) does not change regardless of how the price changes. The demand curve of a good whose price elasticity of demand is 1 over its entire range is a **rectangular hyperbola** (Figure 2).

This means that in Figure 2, rectangles OABC, ODEF and OGHJ all have the same area, since the areas of these rectangles represent total spending by customers at each price.

(i) If the selling price were D, total demand would be F and total spending on the product would be D × F (rectangle ODEF).

(ii) If the selling price were A, total demand would be C, and total spending on the product would be A × C (rectangle OABC).

(iii) If the selling price were G, total demand would be J and total spending on the product would be G × J (rectangle OGHJ).

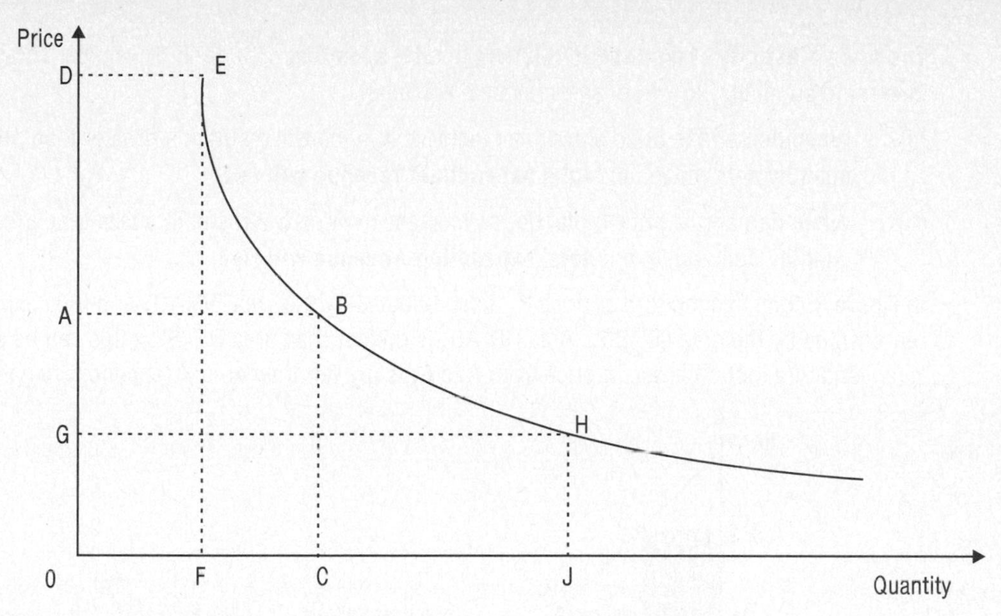

Figure 2 Unit elasticity of demand

Table 1 summarises the different price elasticities of demand

Level of elasticity	Coefficient value	Type of good	Actual examples
Perfectly inelastic	0 (zero)	–	–
Relatively inelastic	Between 0 – 1	Necessity	Medicines; basic foodstuffs (bread, water)
Unit elasticity	1	–	–
Relatively elastic	> 1	Luxury	Holidays; luxury cars
Perfectly elastic	∞ (infinity)	–	–

Table 1: Summary of price elasticity of demand

2 Impacts of price elasticity of demand

2.1 Price elasticity of demand and revenue

FAST FORWARD

For the assessment, you need to be able:

- To understand the **factors influencing elasticity**
- To **measure** price elasticity from given price and demand data, and to draw appropriate conclusions from such information
- To draw the correct implications for the **total revenue** of the producer of changes in the price of the product

The price elasticity of demand is relevant to total spending on a good or service. Total expenditure is a matter of interest to suppliers, to whom sales revenue accrues.

(a) When demand is price **elastic,** an increase in price will result in a greater than proportional fall in the quantity demanded, and **total expenditure/revenue will fall**.

(b) When demand is price in**elastic,** an increase in price will result in a less than proportional fall in the quantity demanded, and **total expenditure/revenue will rise**.

In Figure 3, total expenditure at price P_A is represented by the area OP_AAQ_A and total expenditure at price P_B is represented by the area OP_BBQ_B. Area OP_AAQ_A is greater than area OP_BBQ_B: this can be seen by observing that area Y (expenditure lost on a rise in price from A to B) is greater than area X (expenditure gained).

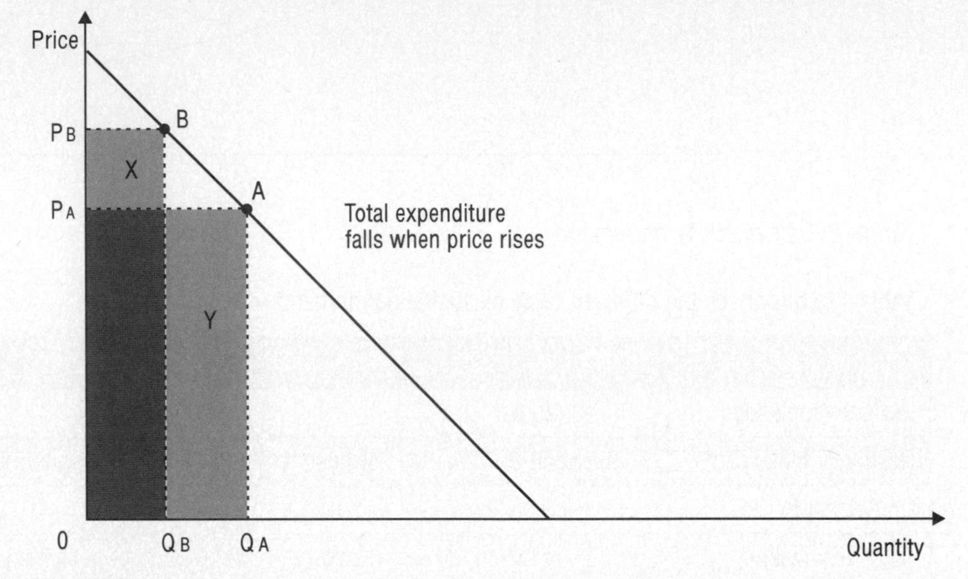

Figure 3 Elastic demand

When demand is **inelastic,** an increase in price will still result in a fall in quantity demanded, but the fall in quantity demanded will be less than proportional to the rise in price so **total expenditure will rise**. In Figure 4, area X (expenditure gained) is greater than area Y (expenditure lost).

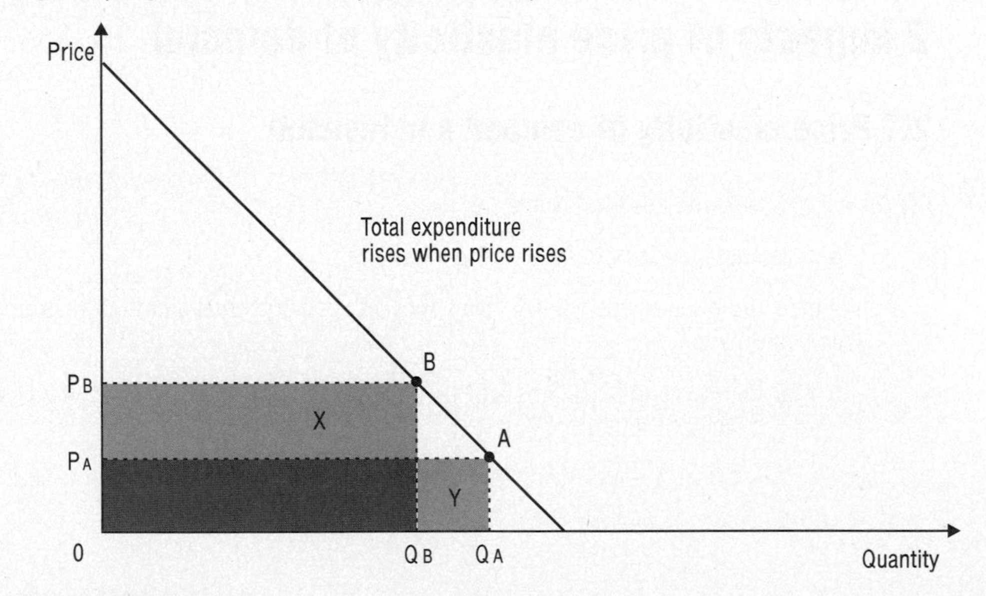

Figure 4 Inelastic demand

With **unit elasticity, expenditure will stay constant** regardless of a change in price. In Figure 5, area X and area Y are the same.

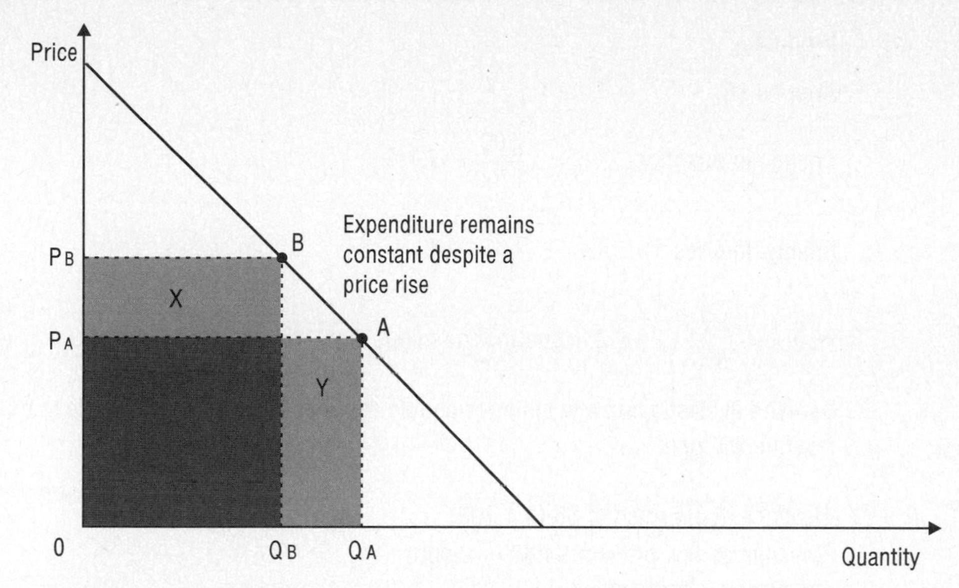

Figure 5 Unit elasticity

2.2 Uses of information on price elasticity of demand

Information on price elasticity of demand indicates how **consumers can be expected to respond to different prices**.

Business people can make use of information on how **consumers will react to pricing decisions** as it is possible to trace the effect of different prices on total revenue and profits.

Information on price elasticities of demand will be useful to a business which needs to know the price decrease necessary to clear a surplus (excess supply) or the price increase necessary to eliminate a shortage (excess demand). Elasticity is also useful, more generally, for a firm if it is considering changing the price of a good or service, and considering the impact this change will have on revenues.

Question — Elasticity and total revenue

Suppose that there are two products, A and B.

Product A currently sells for $5, and demand at this price is 1,700 units. If the price fell to $4.60, demand would increase to 2,000 units.

Product B currently sells for $8 and demand at this price is 9,500 units. if the price fell to $7.50, demand would increase to 10,000 units.

In each of these cases (and using the 'point' method), calculate:

(a) The price elasticity of demand (PED) for the price changes given

(b) The effect on total revenue, if demand is met in full at both the old and the new prices, of the change in price.

Answer

(a) Product A

At price $5:

Change in quantity $\frac{300}{1{,}700} = 17.7\%$

Change in price $\frac{40c}{\$5} = 8\%$

PED $= -\frac{17.7\%}{8\%} = -2.2$. (Ignoring the minus sign = 2.2, and so > 1.)

Demand is elastic and a fall in price should result in such a large increase in quantity demanded that total revenue will rise.

	$
Revenue at old price of $5 (× 1,700)	8,500
Revenue at new price of $4.60 (× 2,000)	9,200
Increase in total revenue	700

(b) Product B

At price $8:

Change in quantity $\frac{500}{9,,500} = 5.3\%$

Change in price $\frac{50c}{\$8} = 6.25\%$

PED $= -\frac{5.3\%}{6.25\%} = -0.85$. (Ignoring the minus sign = 0.85, and so < 1.)

Demand is inelastic and a fall in price should result in only a relatively small increase in quantity demanded. Total revenue will fall.

	$
Revenue at old price of $8 (× 9,500)	76,000
Revenue at new price of $7.50 (× 10,000)	75,000
Fall in total revenue	1,000

3 Influences on the price elasticity of demand

3.1 Factors influencing price elasticity of demand for a good

Factors that determine price elasticity of demand (PED) are similar to the factors other than price that affect the volume of demand. The PED is really a measure of the strength of these other influences on demand.

FAST FORWARD

The **main factors affecting PED** are the **percentage of income** spent on the good, the availability of substitutes, whether the good is a **necessity** or a luxury, the **time horizon**, and whether the good is a **habitual** purchase.

3.1.1 Percentage of income spent on the good

If expenditure on a good only constitutes a **small proportion of a consumer's income**, then a change in the price of that good will not have much impact on the consumer's overall income and demand will be **relatively inelastic**.

Therefore demand for low price goods (such as safety matches) is likely to be inelastic. By contrast, demand is likely to be price elastic for expensive goods like cars.

3.1.2 Availability of substitutes

The more substitutes there are for a good, especially close **substitutes**, the **more elastic** the price elasticity of demand for the good will be.

For example the elasticity of demand for a particular brand of breakfast cereals will be much greater than the elasticity of demand for breakfast cereals as a whole, because the former have both more, and also closer, substitutes. A rise in the price of a particular brand of cereal is likely to result in customers switching their demand to a rival brand.

3.1.3 Degree of necessity

Demand for goods which are **necessary for everyday life** (for example, basic foodstuffs) tends to be **relatively inelastic** while demand for luxury goods tends to be elastic. If a good is a luxury and its price rises, the rational consumer may well decide he or she no longer needs that good and so demand for it will fall. However, if a good is a necessity, the consumer will have to continue buying it even though its price has increased.

3.1.4 The time horizon

Elasticity tends **to increase as the time period increases**

The time horizon influences elasticity largely because the longer the period of time which we consider, the greater the **knowledge** of substitution possibilities by consumers and the **provision** of substitutes by producers. If the price of a good is increased, there might initially be little change in demand because the consumer may not be fully aware of the increase, or may not have found a suitable substitute for the product. Then, as consumers adjust their buying habits in response to the price increase, demand might fall substantially.

3.1.5 Habitual purchasing

Goods which are **habit-forming tend to be inelastic**, because the consumer 'needs' the goods despite their increase in price. This pattern can be seen with addictive products such as cigarettes.

4 Calculation of price elasticity of supply

FAST FORWARD

Elasticity of supply measures the responsiveness of the quantity of a good supplied following a change in the price of that good.

4.1 Price elasticity of supply

Key term

The **price elasticity of supply** indicates the responsiveness of supply to a change in price.

$$\text{Elasticity of supply} = \frac{\%\text{ change in quantity supplied}}{\%\text{ change in price}}$$

Where the supply of goods is **fixed** whatever price is offered, for example in the case of antiques, vintage wines and land, supply is **perfectly inelastic** and the elasticity of supply is **zero. The supply curve is a vertical straight line**.

Where the supply of goods **varies proportionately** with the price, **elasticity of supply equals one** and the supply curve is a straight line **passing through the origin**. (Note that a demand curve with unit elasticity along all of its length is **not** a straight line, but a supply curve with unit elasticity **is** a straight line.)

Where the producers will **supply any amount at a given price** but none at all at a slightly lower price, elasticity of supply is infinite, or **perfectly elastic. The supply curve is a horizontal straight line**.

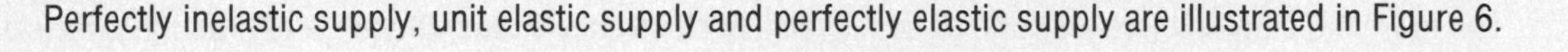

Perfectly inelastic supply, unit elastic supply and perfectly elastic supply are illustrated in Figure 6.

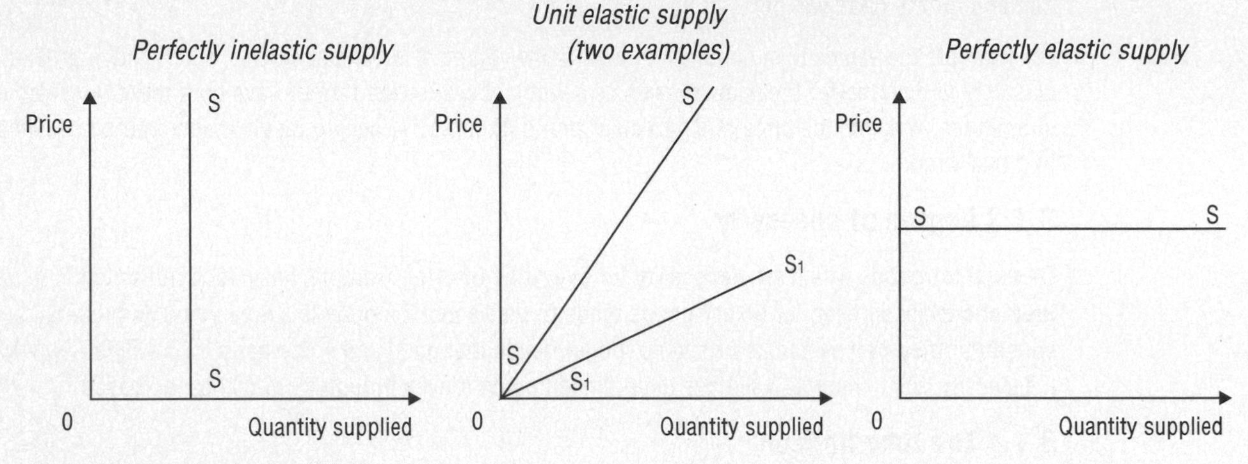

Figure 6 Elasticity of supply (i)

Note that a supply curve with unit elasticity can have many different gradients. The key feature that identifies unitary elasticity is not the gradient of the curve, but the fact that it passes through the origin.

Supply is **elastic** (greater than 1) when the percentage change in the amount producers want to supply is greater than proportional to the percentage change in price.

Supply is **inelastic** (less than 1) when the amount producers want to supply changes by a smaller percentage than the percentage change in price.

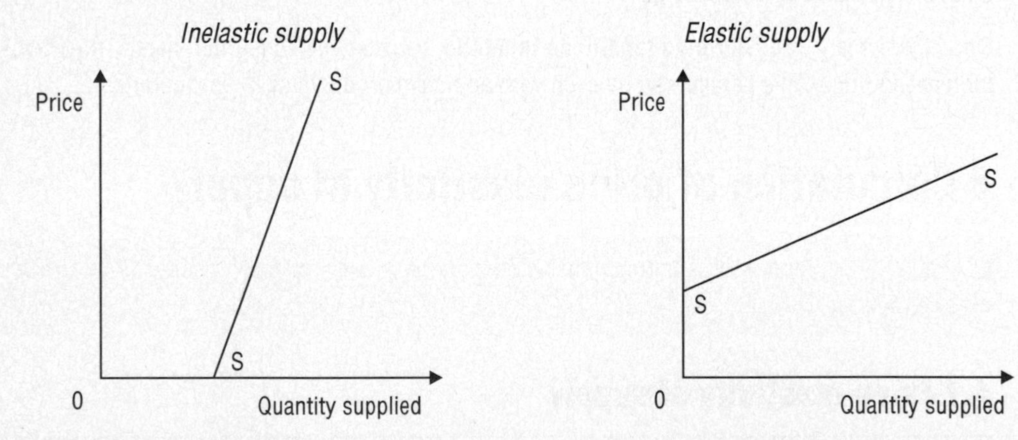

Figure 7 Elasticity of supply (ii)

Note: If the supply curve 'cuts' across the quantity supplied axis, supply is inelastic (< 1). If the supply curve 'cuts' across the price axis, supply is elastic (> 1).

5 Influences on price elasticity of supply

5.1 Factors affecting elasticity of supply

Elasticity of supply is a measure of firms' ability to adjust the quantity of goods they supply. This depends on a number of constraints.

(a) **Existence of inventories of finished goods**: if a firm has large inventories of finished goods then it can draw on these to increase supply following an increase in the price of the good. So supply will be relatively elastic. Perishability or shelf life are important considerations here though.

(b) **Availability of labour**: when unemployment is low it may be difficult to find workpeople with the appropriate skills.

(c) **Spare capacity**: if a firm has spare capacity (eg machinery which is not being fully utilised) it can quickly and easily increase supply following an increase in price. In this way, spare capacity is likely to increase elasticity of supply.

(d) **Availability of raw materials and components**. The existence and location of inventories is important, just as they are for finished goods.

(e) **Barriers to entry**. Barriers to entry are covered in more detail later in this Study Text. Here it is sufficient to point out that if firms can move into the market easily and start supplying quickly, elasticity of supply in that market will be increased.

(f) The **time scale**. This is dealt with in the next paragraph.

5.2 Elasticity of supply and time

As with elasticity of demand, **the elasticity of supply of a product varies according to the time period over which it is measured**. For analytical purposes, three lengths of time period may be considered.

(a) **The momentary (or market) period** is so short that supplies of the commodity in question are limited to existing inventories. In effect, supply is fixed.

(b) **The short run** is a period long enough for supplies of the commodity to be altered by increases or decreases in current output, but not long enough for the fixed equipment (plant, machinery and so on) used in production to be altered. This means that suppliers can produce larger quantities only if they are not already operating at full capacity; they can reduce output fairly quickly by means of redundancies and laying-off staff.

(c) **The long run** is a period sufficiently long to allow firms' fixed equipment to be altered. There is time to build new factories and machines, and time for old ones to be closed down. New firms can enter the industry in the long run.

In general, supply tends to be more elastic in longer time periods.

5.3 Response to changes in demand

The price elasticity of supply can be seen, in effect, as a measure of the readiness with which an industry responds following a shift in the demand curve.

Suppose that there is an increase in the demand for restaurant meals in a city, shown by the rightward shift in the demand curve in Figure 8 from D_1 to D_2. The capacity of the industry is limited in the short run by the number of restaurants in operation. The restaurants can be used more **intensively** to a certain extent, and so supply (S_1) is not perfectly inelastic, but there is a limit to this process. As a result, in the short run there is a large increase in the price from P_1 to P_2.

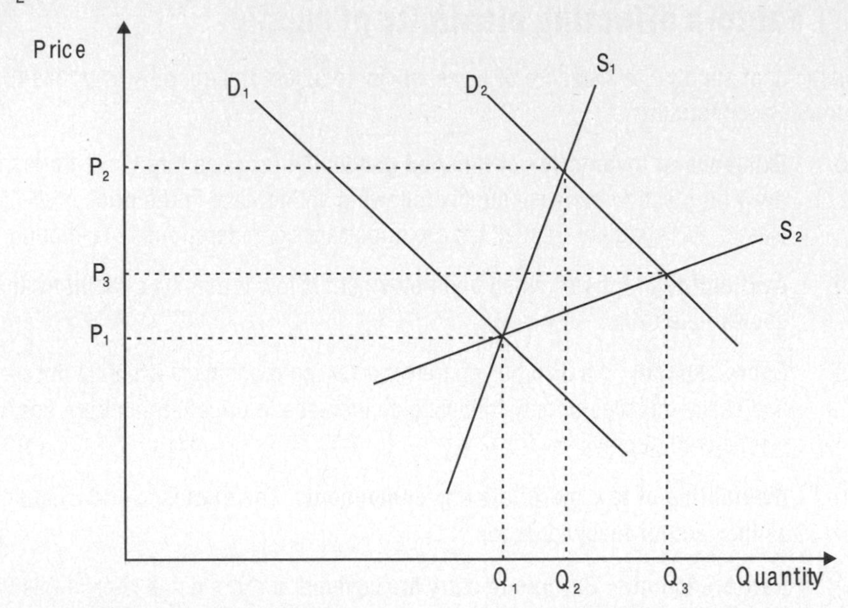

Figure 8 Response to a shift in the demand curve

The rise in price in the **short run** will encourage entrepreneurs to open new restaurants to take advantage of the profits to be earned. In the **long run**, supply is consequently **more elastic** and is shown by supply curve S_2. The expanded output in the industry leads to a new equilibrium at a lower price P_3 with the new level of output being Q_3.

Question

Elasticity of supply

Which diagram shows perfectly elastic supply?

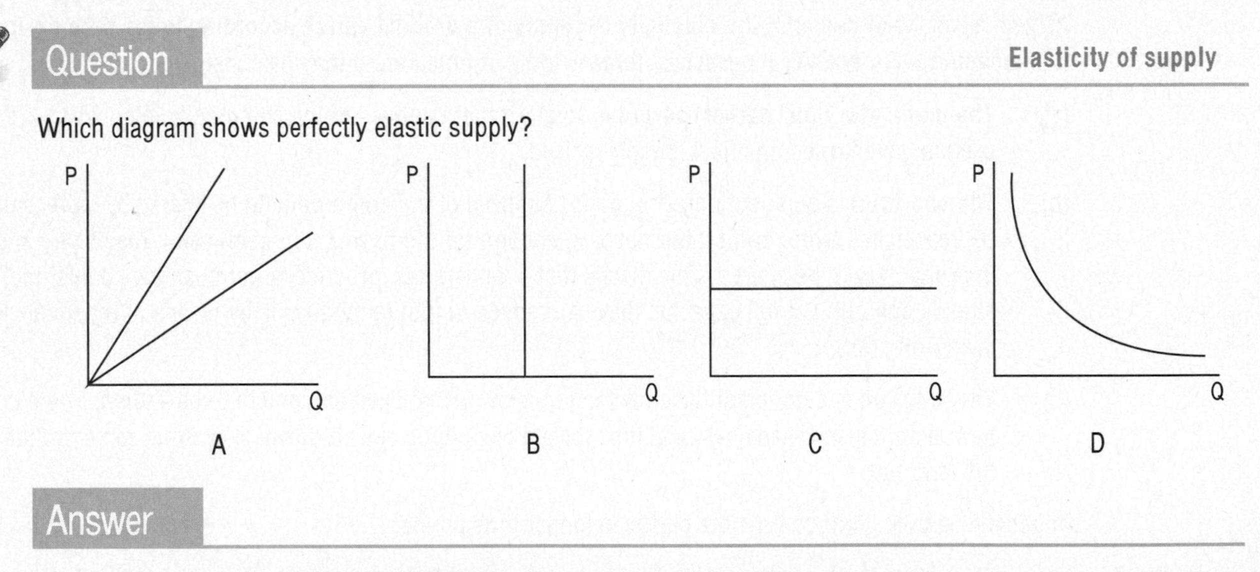

Answer

C A is unit elastic supply (two examples). B is perfectly inelastic supply (or demand), D is unit elastic demand. C shows perfectly elastic supply.

Chapter roundup

- Demand for a good depends largely on price, household income and the **relative price of substitutes or complementary goods**. Changes in any of these will cause either a movement along the demand curve or a shift in the demand curve.
- **Price elasticity of demand** indicates the responsiveness in the quantity demanded of a good to a change in the price of that good.
- For the assessment, you need to be able t0 understand the **factors influencing elasticity**, to **measure** price elasticity from given price and demand data, and to draw appropriate conclusions from such information, and to draw the correct implications for the **total revenue** of the producer of changes in the price of the product
- The **main factors affecting PED** are the **percentage of income** spent on the good, the availability of **substitutes**, whether the good is a **necessity** or a luxury, the **time horizon**, and whether the good is a **habitual** purchase.
- Elasticity of supply measures the responsiveness of the quantity of a good supplied following a change in the price of that good.

Quick quiz

1 What is meant by the price elasticity of demand (PED) for a commodity?

2 What is the significance of PED to a manufacturer?

3 If the absolute value of the price elasticity of demand for dry white wine is greater than one, a decrease in the price of all wine would result in:

A A more than proportional decrease in the quantity of dry white wine purchased
B A less than proportional decrease in the quantity of dry white wine purchased
C A less than proportional increase in the quantity of dry white wine purchased
D A more than proportional increase in the quantity of dry white wine purchased

4 Which combination of demand and supply curves would be appropriate for a firm attempting to increase its profits by increasing its market share?

A Inelastic demand, inelastic supply
B Elastic demand, elastic supply
C Inelastic demand, elastic supply
D Elastic demand, inelastic supply

5 Fish and chips are considered complementary products. If the price of fish rises, what will the impact be in demand for chips?

A Rises
B Stays the same
C Falls
D Doubles

6 Using the point method, what is the price elasticity of demand of product X as price falls from its current price of \$20 to \$15?

	Old	*New*
Price	20	15
Quantity	10	15

A 0.5
B 1
C 1.5
D 2

7 Elasticity is not constant along a straight line demand curve.

Put the correct values for elasticity in the boxes on this diagram.

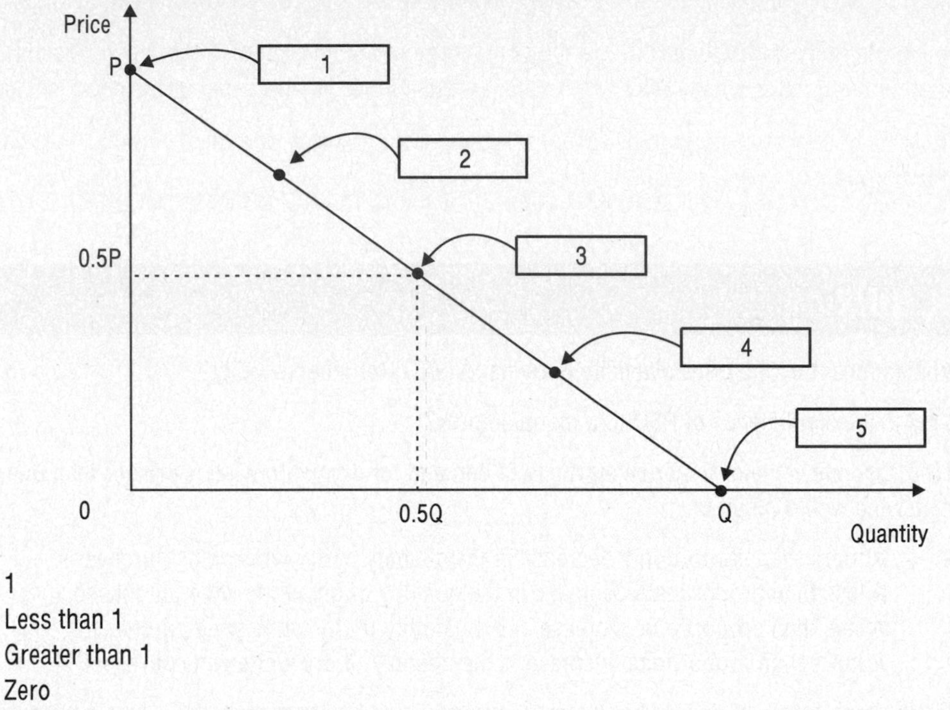

A 1
B Less than 1
C Greater than 1
D Zero
E Infinity

8 Which diagram shows perfectly inelastic supply?

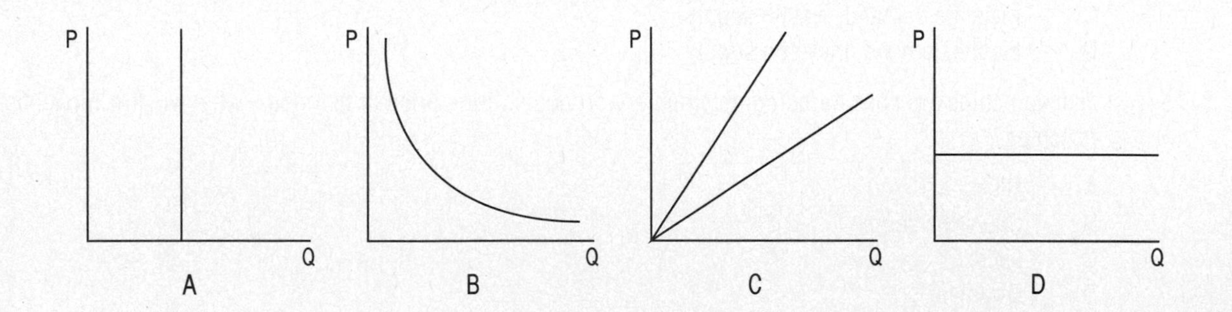

Answers to quick quiz

1 PED is a measure of the extent to which the demand for a commodity changes proportionately in response to a change in its price.

2 If a good has low elasticity of demand, the manufacturer can increase the price without losing much sales revenue. If demand is inelastic, people will buy almost the same amount of the good even if its price goes up.

3 D Assuming a normal good, a decrease in price results in a greater quantity being demanded. Given that demand is price elastic, the increase in quantity will be proportionally greater than the price fall.

4 B To increase market share requires greater quantities of the firm's products to be both demanded and supplied. To sell more, a firm needs to lower price. For this to be profitable, demand must be elastic. To produce more, supply must also be elastic.

5 C Because chips are a complementary product to fish, a rise in the price of fish will lead to a fall in the demand for chips.

6 D Percentage change in quantity = 50%. Percentage change in price = 25%.

7
- 1 E Change in quantity from or to zero is infinitely large.
- 2 C % change in quantity is larger than % change in price.
- 3 A % change in quantity and price are identical.
- 4 B % change in price is larger than % change in quantity.
- 5 D Change in price from or to zero is infinitely large.

8 A B is a demand curve and could show unit elastic **demand**, C is unit elastic supply (two examples), D is perfectly elastic supply (or demand). A shows perfectly inelastic supply (or demand).

Now try the questions below from the Exam Question Bank

Question numbers
14 - 18

5

The market system 3 – price instability and government intervention

Introduction

So far our discussion of the market system has been within the context of a free market. In this chapter we will consider the role of government in modifying markets.

Most markets for agricultural products feature attempts at price regulation to protect supplies and preserve the incomes of farmers.

Some goods and factor markets feature statutory price regulation by governments to achieve particular social policies.

Topic list	Learning outcomes	Syllabus references	Ability required
1 Causes of price instability in markets for primary goods	C2	C2 (a)	Comprehension
2 Implications of price instability for producer incomes and supply	C2	C2 (b)	Comprehension
3 Price stabilisation policies	C2	C2 (c)	Comprehension
4 Minimum and maximum pricing policies in goods markets	C2	C2 (d)	Comprehension
5 Minimum and maximum pricing policies in factor markets	C2	C2 (d)	Comprehension

1 Causes of price instability in markets for primary goods

FAST FORWARD

Inelasticity of both **supply** and **demand** is an important feature of some markets, particularly in the primary sector. Agricultural markets illustrate two important effects especially well: these are the **cyclic variation** in supply and the paradox that farmers' incomes tend to vary inversely with levels of production.

1.1 Primary goods

Primary goods include:

(a) Basic foodstuffs eg wheat, maize, rice, milk, coffee, orange juice
(b) Primary raw materials eg cotton, rubber, hemp
(c) Minerals and metals eg oil, copper, bauxite, iron ore

Producers of primary goods are frequently **highly dependent** on incomes from these products and therefore their incomes are exposed to any declines in price.

1.2 Causes of cyclic variation in supply

The characteristics of some goods are such that adjustments to levels of production take **significant periods** to have any effect. This is particularly true of agricultural products, many of which are subject to long delays between the decision to produce and eventual delivery to market. In temperate climates, for example, many crops can only be grown on an annual cycle, so a farmer can only change production levels once a year.

1.2.1 The 'hog cycle'

The effect of such long time lags in adjusting supply is to create **linked cyclic variations in both price and output**.

A very good example of this cyclic variation is found in the production of pork. In the USA, the production of 'hogs' (pigs), has been observed to be highly cyclic, with a complete cycle taking, on average, about four years. The reproductive biology of pigs is such that there is a time lag of about 10 months between the decision to increase output and the delivery of increased numbers of animals to market. This delay drives the cycle.

The 'hog cycle' is illustrated in Figure 1.

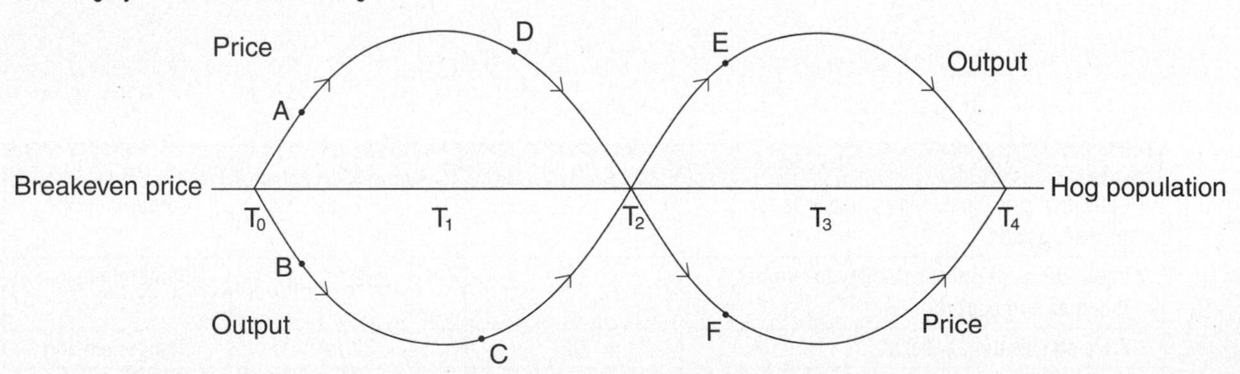

Figure 1 The Hog Cycle

In the diagram, the horizontal axis represents both the break-even price and the average national total number of hogs. The cycle begins with a small rise in price that takes it above the break-even level. As the price rises towards point A, producers decide to **increase output**. To do this, they need more breeding stock, so they **send fewer animals to market**. This is, effectively, a *reduction* in output towards point B, so prices continue to rise. Approximately a year later, the decision to increase breeding stock starts to have effect and output rises past point C. As a result, **price starts to fall** past point D.

At about the end of year 2 (T_2), price has fallen to the break-even level and farmers decide to **reduce production**. This cannot be done immediately and, in the short term, the decision leads to an *increase* in the number of animals sent to market in order to reduce breeding stock numbers. The production curve rises towards point E, while **price falls** towards point F. Production then actually declines during year 4, while price rises back to the break-even point and the cycle begins again.

A similar cycle has been observed in the production of potatoes.

1.2.2 The cobweb effect

The implications of a delayed supply response to changing prices can be explored further using the kind of supply and demand diagrams you have become familiar with. These particular illustrations are known as **cobweb diagrams**, for reasons that will become obvious if you extrapolate the trajectory of market price in the diagrams below.

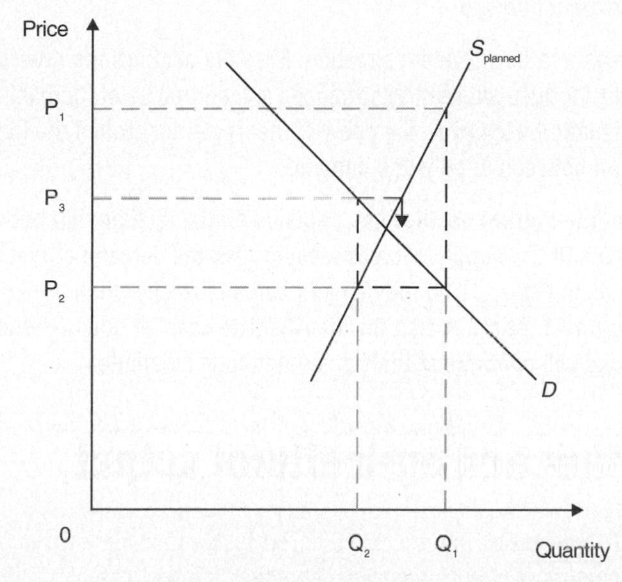

Figure 2 Convergent cobweb

Figure 2 shows a situation that starts in the same way as the hog cycle: the market in the first time period is in **disequilibrium** because the current price is P_1, not the market clearing price. This price leads producers to plan to supply Q_1 in the second time period. When this amount of the good eventually reaches the market, the producers are disappointed to find that price has fallen to P_2 due to the excess of supply over demand. They decide that they will only produce quantity Q_2 in the third time period. This restriction in supply inevitably leads to a rise in price to P_3.

It is easy to see what will happen in subsequent time periods: price and quantity will continue to **oscillate**, though, in this case, the market will approach equilibrium at the market clearing price.

However, while in this instance we have shown price gradually converging on the market clearing price, this is not always the case.

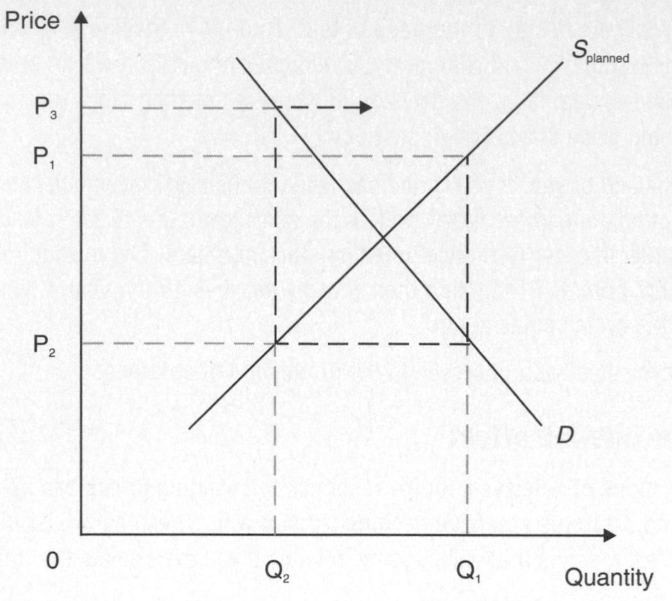

Figure 3 Divergent cobweb

Figure 3 shows a rather different situation. Here the **oscillations diverge** and equilibrium is never attained. Such a market would produce alternating surpluses and shortages of increasing size. Fortunately, this is an entirely theoretical situation. However, the cobweb theory demonstrates the instability of price in the market once there is a disequilibrium between supply and demand.

The nature of the **market oscillations** depends on the relationship between the gradients of the **supply** and **demand** curves. If the supply curve is steeper than the demand curve, the oscillations will decay towards equilibrium, as in Figure 10. If the demand curve is steeper than the supply curve, the oscillations will expand, as shown in Figure 11. There is also the intermediate case, of course, where the gradients are identical: in this case the oscillations will continue at the same magnitude indefinitely.

2 Weather and agricultural output

FAST FORWARD

Agriculture is affected by unpredictable harvests due to climate variations. Price inelastic demand for output means that increased supply often reduces the revenues of producers

2.1 Influence of climate on farm incomes

Agriculture is particularly subject to the influence of the weather. Levels of production can vary quite markedly from year to year.

Paradoxically, a good growing season does not usually mean a good trading year for farmers and *vice versa*. This is because demand for agricultural produce is quite **inelastic** overall: people's choices of individual foodstuffs are affected by their relative prices, but their total consumption does not vary very much.

In the previous chapter we discussed **the effect of a rise in price when demand is inelastic** and we showed that total revenue would rise. This is the situation farmers find themselves in when harvests generally are bad: the supply curve shifts to the left, with less being offered at any price, and **prices go up**.

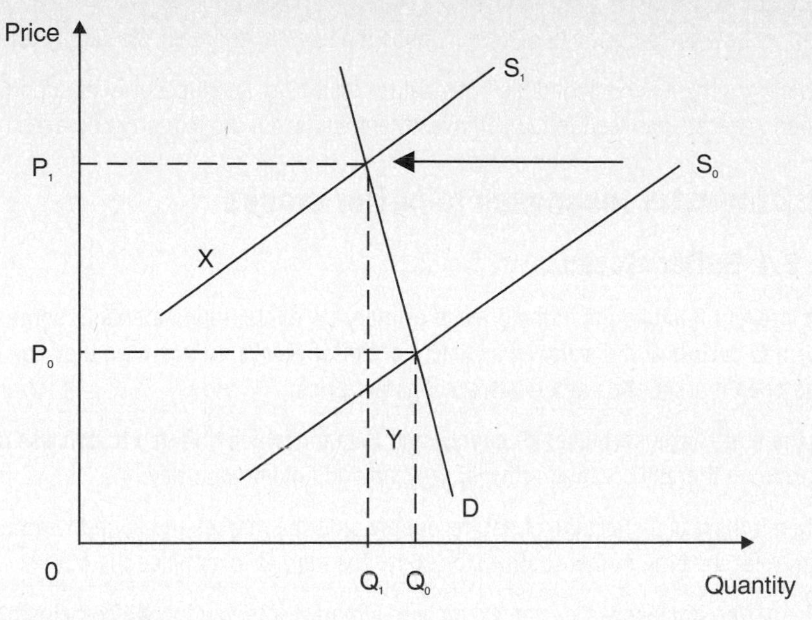

Figure 4 The effect of a poor harvest

Figure 4 shows the effect of the overall shift in the supply curve resulting from a poor harvest. At time 0, supply was at S_0 and price was at P_0. The next harvest was poor and by time 1, the supply curve has shifted to the left. The quantity sold, Q_1, is not very much reduced below Q_0, but there has been a marked increase in price from P_0 to P_1. Total revenue equal to area Y has been lost, but this is more than compensated for by extra revenue equal to area X.

Note also that customers have to pay a high price for the product. Given this is food the extra costs may lead to a **significant decline in living standards** amongst poorer populations.

However if harvests are plentiful the situation in Figure 5 below will occur.

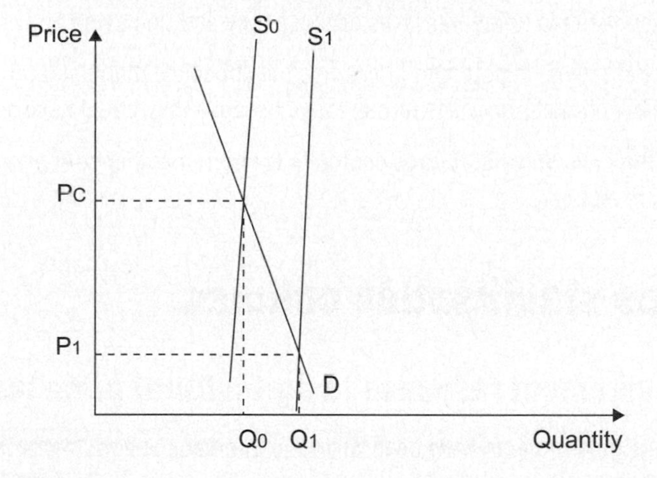

Figure 5 The effect of a good harvest

Initial equilibrium is at price P0 with Q0 bought and sold.

The effect of the good harvest is to shift market supply from S0 to S1. The fall in price is significant due to the combination of two effects:

(a) Low price elasticity of demand: because this is a basic foodstuff and therefore a necessity, the fall in price will not stimulate much additional demand

(b) Low price elasticity of supply: once the harvest is grown the supply for the season is fixed.

Therefore there is considerable potential for instability and insecurity of supply in agriculture, in that a series of good harvests can lead to lack of investment, exit from the industry and even financial failure among farmers.

2.2 Industry responses to buffer stocks

2.2.1 Buffer stocks

To prevent fluctuations in the price of primary products (raw materials), some of the world's main suppliers have formed **cartels** and developed a system of **buffer stocks**. In this way, they can intervene in the markets and control the open market price at a relatively constant price.

If there are large surpluses of supply over demand which threaten to depress prices, the cartel will buy up the surplus – thereby creating artificial demand and holding up price.

Then if there is a shortage of natural supply onto the market and such that prices are likely to rise, the suppliers can release some of their buffer stock onto the market to stabilise the market.

The buffer stock scheme is an example of a market intervention which helps to stabilise price for both consumers and producers.

2.2.2 Futures markets

Producers can use **commodities markets** to guarantee their income by selling their crop in advance before the harvest is gathered and taken to market. For example a cocoa producer may contract to sell a guaranteed quantity of cocoa beans to a chocolate manufacturer in a year's time at a price agreed today. This contract is called a **contract for futures** (or futures contract).

The **risk is then shared** between the chocolate manufacturer and the cocoa farmer.

(a) If the harvest is good and prices fall the farmer wins because they get a better price under the future and the chocolate manufacturer loses because they end up paying above market price

(b) If the harvest is poor and prices rise the chocolate manufacturer gains because they buy their cocoa at below market price. The farmer loses because they could have sold their crop for more.

However the main value of futures contracts for both manufacturer and farmer is to gain **certainty** over future costs and revenues.

3 Price stabilisation policies

3.1 Government response to agricultural price instability

Historically, governments have been willing to intervene in agricultural markets.

FAST FORWARD

Government stabilisation schemes for agricultural markets include **direct payments** to producers, **subsidies** for set-aside or for producing particular crops, and **government purchase of surpluses.**

3.1.1 Direct payments schemes

The government pay a sum to farmers based on the amount they produce. For example a beef farmer would receive an amount of money per head of cattle.

This is amount is usually based on the difference between the average market price for the crop and the income that the government wish the farmer to receive.

3.1.2 Subsidies and set aside

This is a payment **not to produce** the product. It is used where market prices have been depressed by excess supply. The government will pay a subsidy per area of farm land to produce an alternative crop or a price to set-aside the land and grow nothing on it.

3.1.3 Government purchase of surplus

In some cases the government agrees to buy unsold crop at a guaranteed minimum price. This surplus is then stored and released in future years to push prices down if the harvest has been poor and prices are rising.

3.1.4 Consequences of government intervention in agricultural markets

There are also disadvantages to all forms of intervention and critics make the following case against it.

(a) It is extremely difficult to decide the price at which the market should be stabilised.

(b) Intervention has costs, to public funds, to consumers or to both.

(c) Intervention tends to protect inefficient producers against efficient ones and domestic producers against foreign ones: the effects on less-developed countries are particularly harmful.

(d) Purchase of surpluses represents a shift of the demand curve to the right: as a result, production expands, tending to produce very large surpluses. The European Union has a bad record for dumping its surpluses on the world market, further depressing the prospects of producers in less developed countries.

4 Maximum and minimum pricing policies in goods markets

FAST FORWARD

Where **maximum prices** are imposed, there will be **excess demand**: rationing may be necessary, and black marketeers may seek to operate. Where **minimum prices** are imposed, producers will make **excess supply**.

4.1 Price regulation

Governments might try to control prices in two ways.

(a) They might set a **maximum price** (or **price ceiling**) for a good, perhaps to **encourage its consumption** or to prevent **exploitation of buyers**

(b) They might set a **minimum price** (or **price floor**) for a good. This is designed to ensure that producers receive at least the minimum prices for their produce.

4.2 Maximum prices

The government may try to prevent prices of goods rising by establishing a price ceiling **below** the equilibrium price.

Assessment focus point

> Assessment questions often ask about the effects of a price ceiling that is higher than the equilibrium price. Setting a price ceiling above market price will have no effect at all on quantities or prices

If the maximum price M is below what the equilibrium price would be, there will be an excess of demand over supply (Figure 6). The low price attracts customers, but deters suppliers. Because the price ceiling M is below the equilibrium price P, producers will reduce the quantity of goods supplied to the market place from Q to A. However, the quantity demanded will increase from Q to B because of the fall in price. The excess quantity demanded is AB.

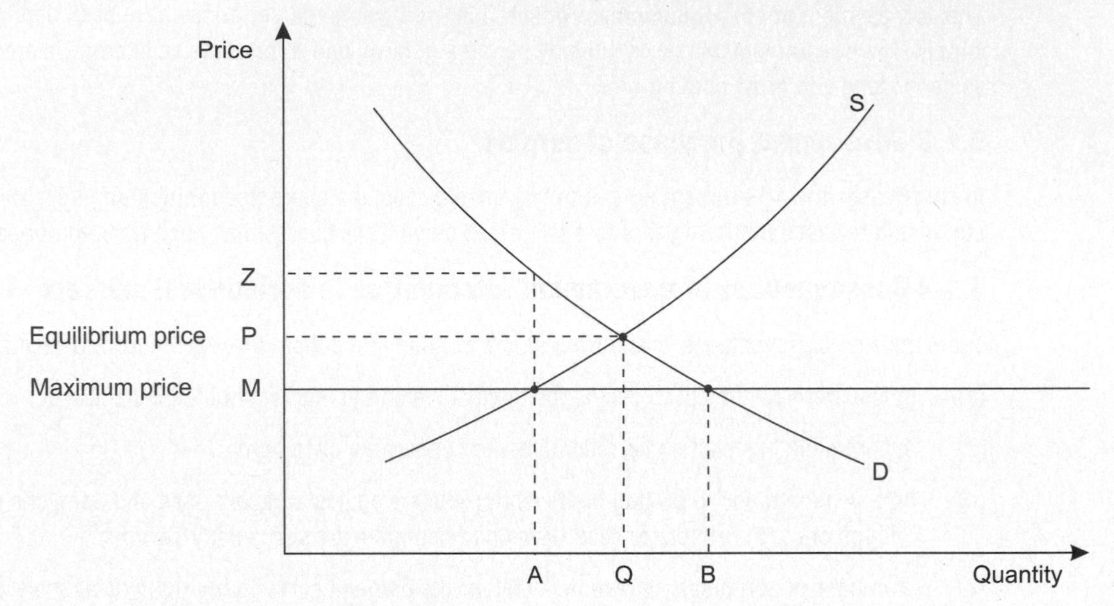

Figure 6 Maximum price below equilibrium price

Setting a maximum price in this way means the price mechanism **cannot perform its three functions**:

(a) It cannot rise above M and so cannot **signal** to producers that there is a shortage

(b) It is too low to **incentivise** supply greater then A

(c) It cannot **ration** the limited quantity of goods, A, amongst the greater volume of demand, B

This leads to **alternative rationing mechanisms**

(a) **Formal rationing** such as coupons or basing allocation on administrative decisions

(b) **Time** such as queues or a **waiting list** (as for local authority housing).

(c) **Racketeering**: in Figure 6 consumers demand quantity B but can only get A. However, for quantity A they are prepared to pay price Z, which is well above the official price M. The racketeer stepx in to exploit the gap. The commodity may be sold on ration at the official price M, but racketeer may sell illicit production at price Z.

Question

Supply of and demand for good Q are initially in equilibrium as shown in the diagram below.

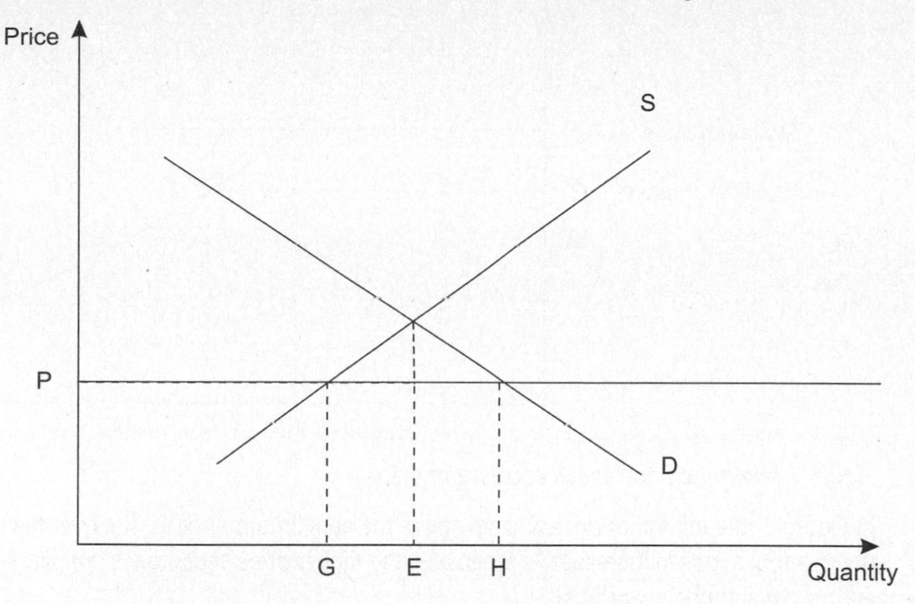

The government introduces a maximum price P. What effect will this have on the quantity of good Q purchased?

A It will rise from G to E
B It will rise from E to H
C It will fall from H to G
D It will fall from E to G

Answer

D The initial equilibrium quantity is E (where the supply and demand curves intersect). Quantity demanded at the controlled price P will be H. However, only quantity G will be supplied and purchases will therefore be limited to this amount. Therefore, the quantity purchased will fall from E to G due to the shortage of supply available.

4.3 Minimum prices

Minimum price legislation aims to ensure that suppliers earn at least the minimum price (or floor price) for each unit of output they sell.

Assessment focus point

If the minimum price is set below the market equilibrium there is no effect. But if it is set above the market price, it will cause an excess supply (see surplus 'AB' in Figure 7).

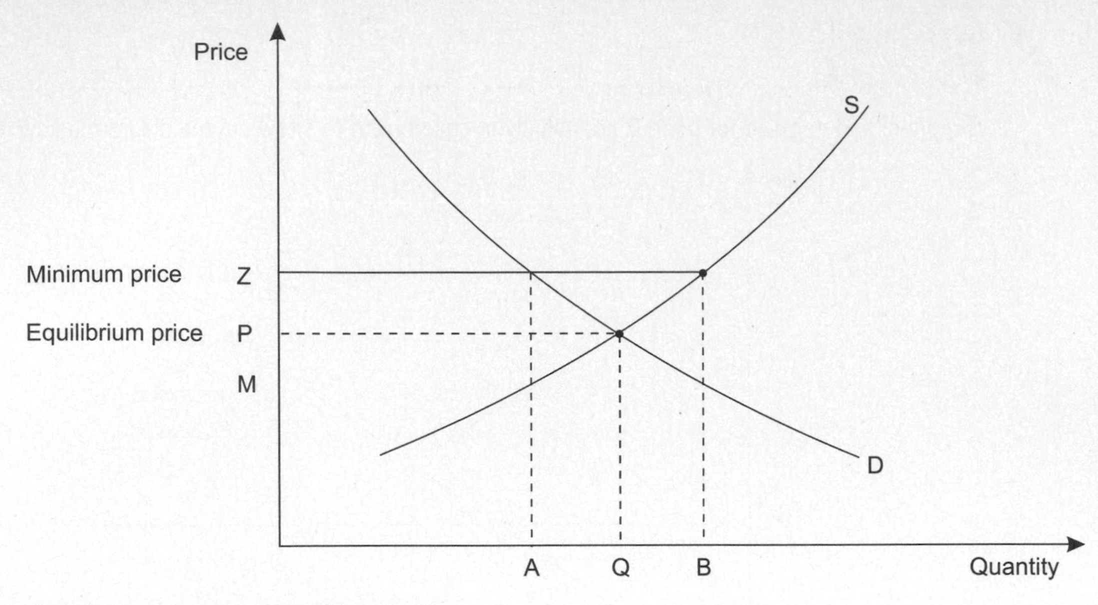

Figure 7 Minimum price above equilibrium price

In Figure 7, the minimum price Z is set above the equilibrium price P. The quantity demanded falls from Q to A but the quantity supplied increases to B because the higher price encourages suppliers to supply more. There is excess supply equal to the quantity AB.

The impacts of minimum price policies are:

(a) **Creation of surplus product:** more of the good will be produced than can be sold at the minimum price, and so **surplus quantities** will build up, which have to be either stored or destroyed.

(b) **Higher incomes to producers:** in Figure 7 the producers' incomes would be the rectangle Z x B which is greater than the income they would receive under the free market (P x Q)

(c) **Administrative controls:** these are needed to prevent over-supply and 'dumping' of excess supply at low prices. A system of **production quotas** might be introduced whereby each supplier is only allowed to produce up to a maximum quantity and no more.

5 Minimum and maximum pricing policies in factor markets

FAST FORWARD

Minimum and maximum pricing can be applied in factor markets including the **labour market** and the market for **capital**.

5.1 Minimum wages

A minimum wage is an application of floor pricing in the labour market.

The **purposes** of a minimum wage are:

(a) To ensure that low-paid workers earn enough to have an acceptable standard of living

(b) To encourage workers to train in the skills needed to join the industry

Minimum wages can be set in various ways:

(a) By **legislation**, for example a **statutory minimum wage**

(b) Negotiated for an industry by a trade union

The minimum wage will probably be above the current wage level for the jobs concerned. This would have two consequences.

(a) To raise wage levels for workers employed to a level above the 'equilibrium' wage rate
(b) To reduce the demand for labour and so cause job losses

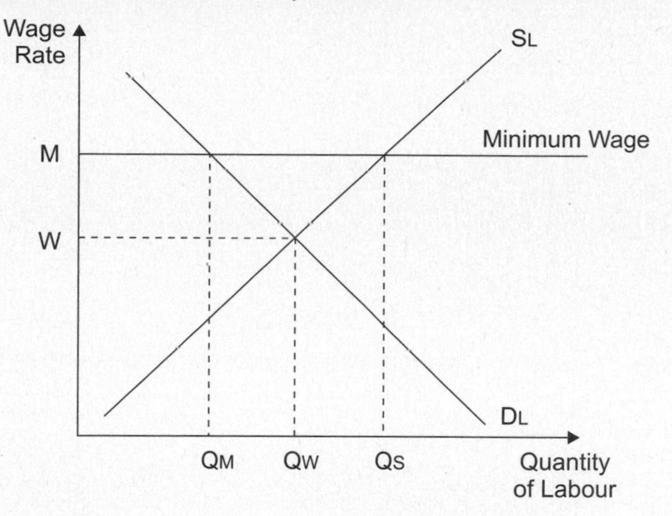

Figure 8 Minimum wage

In Figure 8 the free market would be W and Q_W workers would be employed

The imposition of a minimum wage of M has the following effects:

(a) The level of employment falls to Q_m

(b) The incomes of the workers left in work rise from W to M

(c) The higher wage encourages a labour supply of Q_s and therefore excess supply of labour in the industry of Q_s minus Q_m

(d) Attempts to undercut the minimum wage by firms establishing informal arrangements with workers prepared to work for less than the minimum wage.

5.2 Price regulation in capital markets

Governments may use minimum and maximum pricing in capital markets. The price of capital is the interest rate paid for it.

5.2.1 Maximum pricing for capital

Governments may seek to place a maximum price on the cost of capital in order to encourage firms to borrow to undertake investment to improve efficiency and create jobs.

The methods used to do this include:

(a) Direct supply of capital to firms at the maximum price

(b) Instructions to or persuasion of lenders to lend at the maximum rate

(c) Manipulation of the financial markets by using the country's central bank to increase the supply of funds (this will be returned to in Chapter 10)

5.2.2 Minimum pricing for capital

This is quite rare and is used where a government disapproves of a particular line of business, such as importing, or is seeking to ration out scare investment funds.

Chapter roundup

- **Inelasticity** of both **supply** and **demand** is an important feature of some markets, particularly in the primary sector. Agricultural markets illustrate two important effects especially well: these are the **cyclic variation** in supply and the paradox that farmers' incomes tend to vary inversely with levels of production.
- Agriculture is affected by unpredictable harvests due to climate variations. Price inelastic demand for output means that increased supply often reduces the revenues of producers
- Government stabilisation schemes for agricultural markets include **direct payments** to producers, **subsidies** for set-aside or for producing particular crops, and **government purchase of surpluses**.
- Where **maximum prices** are imposed, there will be **excess demand**: rationing may be necessary, and black marketeers may seek to operate. Where **minimum prices** are imposed, producers will make **excess supply**.
- Minimum and maximum pricing can be applied in factor markets including the **labour market** and the market for **capital**.

Quick quiz

1 What does the hog cycle refer to?

2 Which of the following gives rise to unstable farm prices and incomes

A Susceptibility to variations in harvest
B Low price elasticity of demand for agricultural goods
C Low price elasticity of supply of agricultural goods
D All of the above

3 What role does a futures market play in stabilising farm incomes?

4 Which of the following is a *disadvantage* of government guaranteed prices to farmers?

A Encourages a stable supply of the product
B Ensures a minimum income to farmers which enables them to stay in the industry
C Encourages excess supply of the product
D Stabilises prices if used in conjunction with a buffer stock scheme

5 What impact would a minimum price set above market price have on the market for a product

A No impact as the market price would take precedence
B It would cause shortages and lead to alternative rationing mechanisms
C It would leave a lot of product unsold and encourage secret undercutting of the price
D It would increase producer incomes providing demand was price elastic

6 Which functions of price are frustrated by the setting of maximum prices

A Signalling
B Rationing
C Rewarding
D All of the above

7 Country X has a policy to stabilise farm incomes. Each year an effect of this policy is that the government has to destroy large quantities of farm produce. Which policy is Country X operating?

A A direct payments scheme

B A set aside scheme

C A maximum pricing scheme

D A scheme in which the government offers to buy product at a minimum market price above free market price

8 If the demand for labour were wage inelastic what would be the effect of introducing a minimum wage above market wage rate

A It would reduce employment but increase total earnings in the industry
B It would reduce employment and reduce total earnings in the industry
C It would increase employment and increase total earnings in the industry
D It would increase employment and decrease total earnings in the industry

Answers to quick quiz

1 The hog cycle shows that the supply and price of livestock such as hogs (pigs) will fluctuate through time due to time lags between prices changing and supply changing.

2 D

3 A futures market allows the farmer to guarantee a price for their produce by selling it in advance of its harvest. This protects against price falls in years of generally good harvests

4 C all the other statements refer to advantages of the scheme

5 C this would cause a contraction of demand and a surplus

6 D

7 D the schemes in A and B allow market prices to prevail and so stocks do not build up. Option C would not guarantee farm incomes

8 A The rise in wages will cause a contraction of demand (which means options C and D are incorrect). If demand is inelastic then spending on a product rises. This is the same in labour markets where the higher wage would increase total wage bill of the industry, it increase earnings (revenues) of the workforce.

Now try the questions below from the Exam Question Bank

Question numbers
19 - 22

Decision making 1 – cost behaviour

6

Introduction

In this chapter we will be looking at the costs of production for an individual firm, and how these are affected by both short run and long run factors.

However, we will also look at how individual firms look to grow in order to benefit from cost savings and efficiencies.

Topic list	Learning outcomes	Syllabus references	Ability required
1 Types of cost	B2	B2 (a)	Comprehension
2 Short run cost behaviour	B2	B2 (a)	Comprehension
3 Long run cost behaviour	B2	B2 (a)	Comprehension
4 Impact of long run costs on industry structure	B2	B2 (b)	Comprehension

1 Types of cost

FAST FORWARD

For profit seeking organisations the unit price received for a product should exceed the unit cost of making the product.

Although we have identified that there are a range of organisations with differing objectives, we will focus now on organisations which seek to make a profit.

The basic condition for profitability is very simple: **overall revenues must exceed overall costs**.

Key term

Profit is equal to total revenue minus total cost of any level of output.

1.1 Fixed costs and variable costs

FAST FORWARD

The distinction between **fixed costs** and **variable costs** is recognised in economic theory and in the practice of management accounting,

In most industries the decision to produce more of a product will lead to the **total costs** of production rising.

Total costs are made up of two elements, **fixed costs** and **variable costs**.

Key terms

Fixed costs: costs that do not rise with output

Variable costs: costs that rise with output

1.2 Example

A proprietor of an hotel might distinguish between fixed and variable costs as follows:

Fixed costs	Variable costs
Monthly lease payments to the landlords that own hotel	Costs of laundry for towels and bedding which are changed when guests leave
Costs of insurance	Costs of food and drinks consumed by guests
Costs of heating the hotel	Costs of electricity used in guest bedrooms
Wages of permanent staff working in reception and in restaurants	
Costs of advertising in tourist publications	
Costs of electricity to light common areas in the hotel (reception, stairways, restaurants)	

1.3 Basis for distinguishing variable and fixed costs

Note that the hotel proprietor regards costs as varying according to the number of guests staying at the hotel.

This means that variable costs are costs that vary with the **volume of production**. To produce more product entails more cost for the firm.

Fixed costs are costs that do not increase as the volume of production increases.

The following data shows the costs of providing meals in a restaurant

Number of meals produced per hour	Total costs per hour $
0	20
1	30
2	40
3	50

This table gives the following cost estimates:

(a) Variable cost is $10 per meal. This can be seen by subtracting the total cost of 2 meals from the total cost of 1 meal (ie £40 minus $30 = $10 per meal)

(b) Variable cost per meal is constant at $10. This can be seen by calculating the rise in costs due to producing 1 meal instead of 0 meals (£30 minus $20 = $10) or increasing production from 2 meals to 3 meals ($50 minus $40 = $10)

(c) Fixed costs of the restaurant are $20. This can be calculated in two ways: either as the total costs of 0 meals, or as the total costs of 1 meal minus the variable costs of the meal (ie $30 minus $10 = $20)

Assessment focus point

Be sure to note that fixed and variable costs are defined with respect to volume. Fixed costs may vary though time as prices of materials rise but this does not make them into variable costs.

Some conventional economics texts will define costs according to time periods and whether various classes of resource (called factors of production) can be varied or not. CIMA does not require you to have knowledge of that approach.

1.4 Total cost curves

Figure 1 shows the simple example of the restaurant above as a diagram.

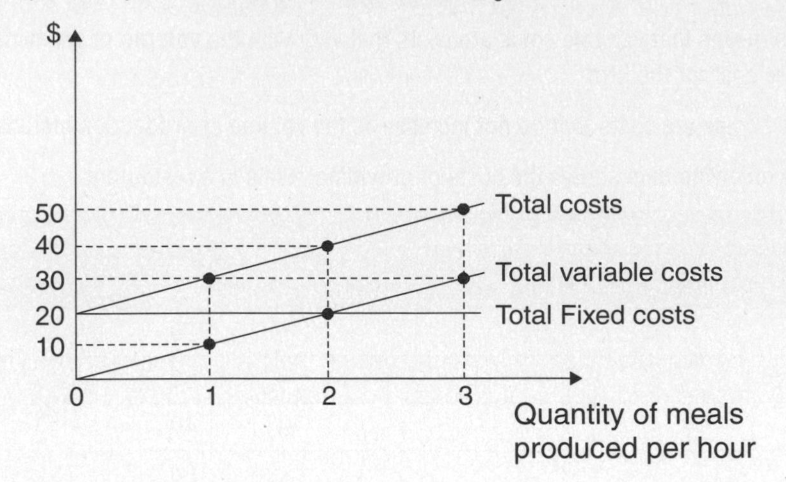

Figure 1 Total cost curves

Notice the following things about Figure 1:

(a) At 0 quantity variable cost is $0 and total cost is $20.

(b) The total fixed cost schedule is horizontal from $20 showing that as the quantity of meals produced increases the total fixed costs do not rise

(c) If one meal is produced total variable cost is $10 which, added to fixed cost of $20, gives the total cost of $30

(d) The slope of the total variable cost curve is determined by the variable cost per meal

(e) The total cost curve is parallel to the variable cost curve and above it by the amount of fixed cost. This means that the total variable cost curve is unnecessary in this diagram because it is always reflected in the total cost curve.

Figure 2 shows the effect of a rise in variable cost per meal from $10 to $15

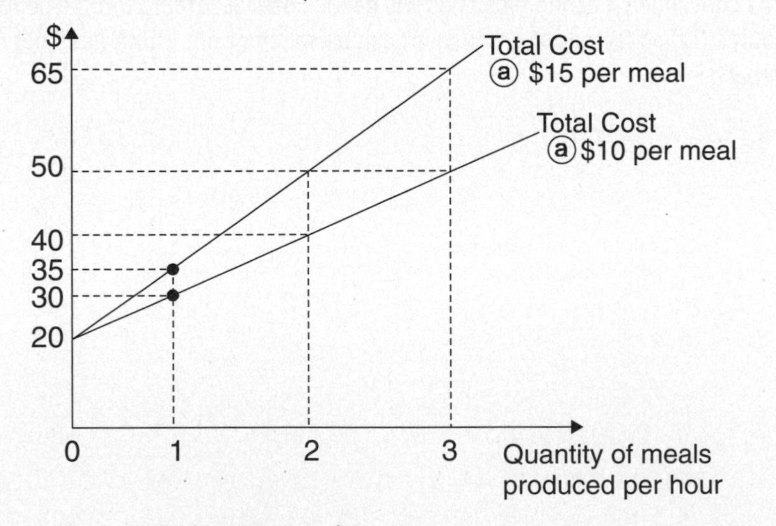

Figure 2 Impact of a rise in variable cost per unit

Notice the following things about Figure 2:

(a) The total fixed cost curve has been removed. This is because the fixed costs are shown adequately by the intercept of the total cost curve with the vertical axis. This shows that at 0 output total costs are $20 and it follows that these are the fixed costs

(b) The total variable cost curve has been removed. This is because the total cost curve shows the level of variable cost clearly. For example if at 3 meals per hour the total costs are $50, and fixed costs as $20, then it follows that the total variable costs must be $30 (ie $50 minus $20)

(c) The effect of a rise in variable cost per unit is to make the total cost curve steeper.

1.5 Slopes of the total cost curves

FAST FORWARD

The slope of a total cost curve shows the rate at which cost rises as output rises. Therefore a **total fixed cost curve** has a **slope of zero** because fixed costs do not rise as output rises. **Total variable cost curves** have a **positive slope** because total variable costs rise as output rises. **Steeper gradient** curves illustrate **higher the variable cost per unit**.

The cost curves in Figures 1 and 2 are straight lines (*ie linear*). A straight line cost curve reflects the assumption that **the rate of increase of cost is constant.** In the example above the original cost of serving an extra meal each hour is $10, and that fixed costs also rise at a constant rate of zero.

Changes in costs are shown as movements of the cost curve.

Question

Short run linear cost curves

Learning outcome: B 2 a)

Identify the cost changes responsible for the change in the total cost curve from TC to TC1 in the diagrams below

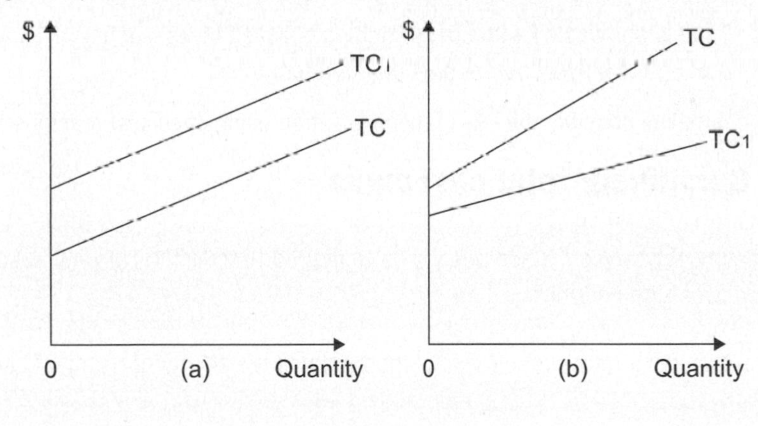

Answer

Diagram (a) shows the effect of a rise in fixed costs. This is shown by the total cost at 0 output having risen. Because TC1 has the same slope at TC this demonstrates that variable costs per unit have not risen.

Diagram (b) shows two cost changes. There has been a fall in fixed costs, shown by the total costs at zero output having become lower. There has also been a fall in variable costs per unit, shown by the slope of the total cost curve having become shallower.

2 Short run cost behaviour

FAST FORWARD

Straight line total cost curves are unlikely to occur in practice due to **changing levels of efficiency** as output increases.

Straight line total cost curves reflect the assumption that variable **cost per unit stays constant** regardless of whether the firm produces a small or a large quantity of the good. This is a **simplifying assumption** that ignores the possibility of changing levels of efficiency.

2.1 Benefits of specialisation

In business it is assumed that larger businesses are likely to be more efficient than smaller business due to the benefits of specialisation and division of labour.

A firm that produces only small quantities of a given product will need to have staff who can combine tasks. For example a shop with only a small level of sales will employ one or two staff and will expect them to combine the tasks of unloading deliveries, stacking shelves, advising customers, taking money, inventory checking and so on.

A large supermarket will have a higher volume of sales and can benefit from specialisation. It will have staff who unload, whilst others work on the check-outs taking money, and another group advise customers.

Key term

Division of labour: the breaking down of jobs into individual tasks that can each be assigned to different individuals

As a firm increases its output in the short run it can employ a division of labour. This increases productivity and therefore reduces unit costs in the following ways:

(a) Staff need less time to learn the job because they are being trained for only one task and not all the tasks

(b) Tasks can be allocated to the staff member with the greatest aptitude for the task

(c) Learning effects will be enjoyed as staff members learn and find ways to perform their task more quickly

(d) Time is not wasted with staff switching between tasks, such as in moving from machine to machine or in putting tools away before selecting different tools

(e) It makes possible the use of mechanisation using specialist machinery dedicated to each task

2.2 Curvilinear total cost curve

FAST FORWARD

Short run cost curves are assumed to be **S-shaped** to reflect initially increasing efficiency followed by declining efficiency at high volumes.

Figure 3 shows a total cost curve that incorporates the effects of rising efficiency due to specialisation

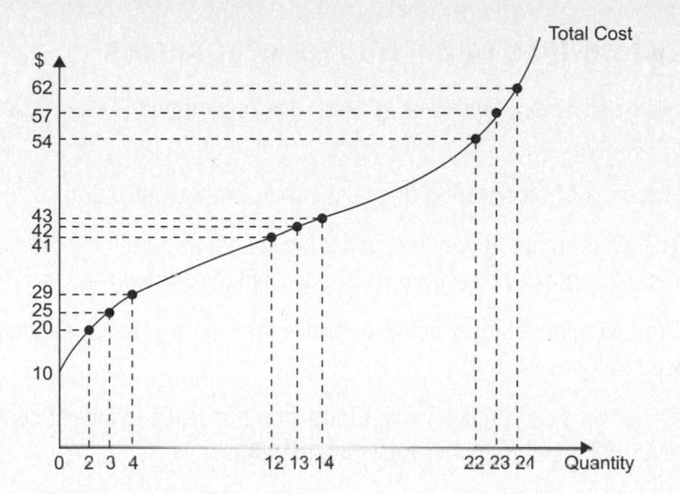

Figure 3 *Curvilinear short run cost curve*

Figure 3 shows the impact on total cost of changing levels of efficiency as output increases. This shows the variable cost per unit changing as output increases:

Unit number	Variable cost of unit	Calculation
3	\$5	Total cost of 3 units minus total cost of 2 units \$25 - \$20 = \$5
4	\$4	\$29 - \$25 = \$4
13	\$1	\$42 - \$41 = \$1
14	\$1	\$43 - \$42 = \$1
23	\$3	\$57 - \$54 = \$3
24	\$5	\$62 - \$57 = \$5

This shows the three stages of the S shaped curvilinear cost curve

(a) Units 3 and 4 are produced with **increasing efficiency** causing falling variable cost per unit. The total cost curve becomes shallower

(b) Units 13 and 14 are produced with **constant efficiency** and therefore lead to constant variable cost per unit. The total cost curve has a constant slope and is a straight line

(c) Units 23 and 24 are produced with **reduced efficiency** and this leads to rising variable cost per unit. The total cost curve becomes steeper.

2.3 Causes of falling efficiency at higher volumes

Figure 3 shows total cost per unit rising at higher production levels. The reason for this is a loss of productive efficiency from factors including:

(a) Bottlenecks in the production process due to running the business too hard

(b) Higher costs of labour such as paying premium rates for overtime working and using contract staff

2.4 Implications of curvilinear cost curves

Figure 1 showed straight line cost curves. This assumption is often used in management accounting to assist with decision making.

The implications of recognising that cost curves are S shaped are:

(a) The assumption of constant variable cost per unit can only be made for changes in production volumes in the mid-range of the curve. This is termed the *relevant range*.

(b) Producing at volumes below or above the relevant range will incur higher variable costs per unit and could lead to loss of profits

(c) There will be a single level of production that leads to lowest cost per unit. Producing below or above this level will result in higher total cost per unit.

Question

Point of lowest unit cost

Learning outcome: B2(a)

Consider Figure 3 above. Which level of output allows the firm to produce at the lowest total cost per unit?

Answer

If you answered 12, 13 or 14 units you misread the question. These are the outputs with the lowest *variable* cost per unit ($1) but the question specifies lowest *total* cost per unit.

The following table shows the total cost per unit is lowest at total production of 22 units

Total production	Total cost per unit	Calculation
2	$10	Total cost divided by total quantity $20/2 = $10
3	$8.33	$25/3 = $8.33
4	$7.25	$29/4 = $7.25
12	$3.41	$41/12 = $3.41
13	$3.23	$42/13 = $3.23
14	$3.07	$43/14 = $3.07
22	$2.45	$54/22 = $2.45
23	$2.47	$57/23 = $2.47
24	$2.58	$62/24 =$2.58

The example above illustrates an important principle in understanding cost behaviour. Increasing output beyond the relevant range means falling efficiency will cause variable cost per unit to rise.

However the total cost per unit will continue to fall due to the fact that **fixed costs are being spread over a larger volume of output**. This has the effect of offsetting the rising variable cost per unit.

2.5 Marginal cost

FAST FORWARD

Marginal cost is the **rise in total cost** resulting from producing an **extra unit** of the product. This will be the **same as the rise in variable cost** because fixed costs do not rise as output rises. Marginal cost can be depicted as the **slope of a tangent** touching the total cost curve at the given level of output.

Key term

Marginal Cost (MC): the addition to total costs resulting from increasing total output by one unit.

The variable costs of producing an extra unit can be referred to as **marginal costs**. The analysis of Figure 3 above calculated marginal costs.

The slope of the total cost curve at a given point depicts the marginal cost.

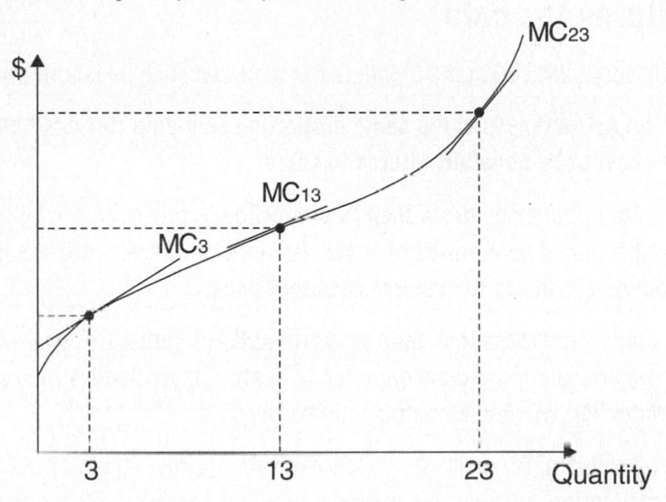

Figure 4 Marginal cost

In Figure 4 shows tangents drawn touching the total cost curve at output levels 3, 13 and 23.

(a) The slope of this tangent MC_3 is the rate of increase of total cost for producing unit 3. This was calculated as $5

(b) The slope of this tangent MC_{13} is the rate of increase of total cost for producing unit 13. This was calculated as $1

(c) The slope of this tangent MC_{23} is the rate of increase of total cost for producing unit 23. This was calculated as $3 earlier.

The steeper the slope of the tangent, the higher the marginal cost.

3 Long run cost behaviour

FAST FORWARD

Long run costs describe the behavour of unit costs as the firm makes **significant changes to its volume of production** involving significant investment in **new capacity** and **adaptation** of its organisational **structure and production processes**.

3.1 Costs in the long run

In the short run the firm's output was constrained by its scale of operation. Consequently inefficiencies arose when volume was increased.

In the long run a firm can adjust permanently to higher production volumes by investing in new resources, such as plant and machinery, IT systems, staff, and premises in order to gain greater efficiency.

There are two direct consequences of this.

(a) Since all resources can be scaled-up there are **no fixed costs in the long run**.
(b) A firm can change its **scale of production** significantly.

3.2 Returns to scale

Output will vary with variations in inputs of resources such as labour and capital equipment.

(a) If output increases in the **same proportion** as inputs (for example doubling all inputs doubles output) there are said to be **constant returns to scale**.

(b) If output increases **more than in proportion** to inputs (for example doubling all inputs trebles output) there are beneficial **economies of scale**. Economies of scale mean that the long run unit costs of production will continue to fall as the volume of output rises.

(c) If output increases **less than proportionally** to inputs (for example trebling all inputs only doubles output) there are said to be **diseconomies of scale**. Diseconomies of scale mean that the long run unit costs of production will rise as output volume rises.

Returns to scale are, for example, concerned with improvements or declines in productivity **by increasing the scale of production**, for example by mass-producing instead of producing in small batch quantities.

3.3 Economies of scale

Key term

Economies of scale: factors which cause unit cost to decline in the long run as output increases.

Figure 5 shows how unit costs may change as a firm scales up production volumes in the long run

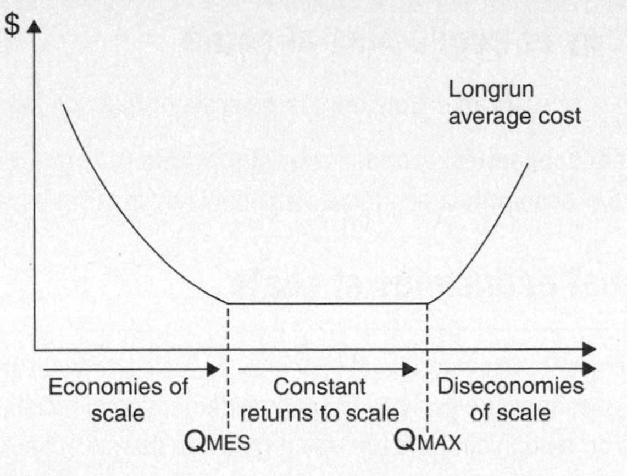

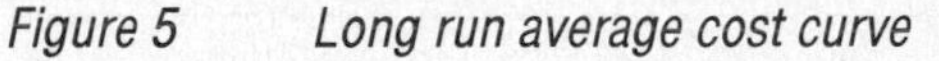
Figure 5 Long run average cost curve

Key term

Average cost: the unit cost of producing a product at a given volume of output.

Calculated as Total Cost / Total Output

Figure 5 shows the long run average cost behaviour for a firm.

As production scale increases towards Q_{MES} the average cost falls progressively. This is the effect of **economies of scale.**

If the firm increases production above Q_{MES} towards Q_{MAX} it will enjoy no further reduction in average costs because the potential for further economies of scale have been exhausted. This is the range of **constant returns to scale**.

If the firm increases output beyond Q_{MAX} it begins to suffer inefficiencies and rising average costs. These are **diseconomies of scale.**

Question

Growth of large supermarkets

Learning outcome: B2 (a) and (b)

A feature of the past 50 years of retailing in most countries has been the growth of large supermarkets at the expense of smaller family run grocery and provisions shops. The supermarkets are more profitable despite seeming to charge lower prices. This suggests they enjoy economies of scale that are not available to smaller shops.

Identify potential sources of economies of scale for supermarkets.

Answer

Using your business understanding you probably suggested some of the following economies of scale:

- Ability to use bargaining power to obtain lower prices from producers
- Spreading of fixed costs over longer opening times than offered by smaller shops
- More efficient use of staff due to customers being required to select, wrap and check out their purchases
- Cheaper advertising by spreading the cost of the campaign across a large number of stores

3.4 Sources of economies of scale

The economies of scale attainable from large scale production fall into two categories.

(a) **Internal economies**: economies **arising within** the firm from the organisation of production
(b) **External economies**: economies attainable by the firm because of the **growth of the industry as a whole**

3.5 Internal economies of scale

Assessment focus point

There are many potential sources of economy of scale and you can't be expected to have learned them all. In the assessment questions are likely to focus on whether you can distinguish between internal and external economies of scale, and on recognising the four main types of internal economy of scale below.

3.5.1 Technical economies

Technical economies arise in the production process. They are also called **plant economies of scale** because they depend on the size of the factory or piece of equipment.

(a) Large undertakings can make use of **larger and more specialised machinery**. This is because their high volumes of production of the same item will justify purchasing specialist machines. For example a large printing firm could justify buying presses and guillotines for making books that a small general purpose printer would not.

(b) A large firm can overcome **indivisibilities**. For example a small logistics firm will need a minimum network of depots and vehicles to provide a service, but the shelves and vehicles would be operating half full. The firm could not halve the depots and vehicles because this would destroy its network. A larger logistics firm would have the same network but be using it to full capacity at no extra cost.

(c) **Dimensional economies of scale** arise from the relationship between the volume of output and the size of equipment (eg storage tanks) needed to hold or process the output. The cost of a container for 10,000 gallons of product will be much less than ten times the cost of a container for just 1,000 gallons. Sometimes called the **cube law** this can apply to buildings. For example building a warehouse of double the cubic capacity requires only a small increase in the size of two walls

3.5.2 Commercial or marketing economies

(a) **Buying economies** may be available, reducing the cost of material purchases through bulk purchase discounts

(b) **Inventory holding** becomes more efficient. The most economic quantities of inventory to hold increase with the scale of operations, but at a lower proportionate rate of increase

(c) **Bulk selling** will enable a large firm to make relative savings in **distribution** costs, and **advertising** costs

(d) **Economies of scope** refer to the cost savings available by offering a wider range of products. For example supermarkets have added clothing, music and films, and electrical goods to their ranges . But by piggy-backing these on to their existing stores and logistics systems they pay much lower additional costs than are paid by specialist retailers of these products.

3.5.3 Organisational economies

These are the costs of running the business.

(a) Centralisation of functions such as administration, R&D and marketing may reduce the burden of overheads (ie the indirect costs of production) on individual operating locations

(b) More efficient use of management because the numbers of management and supervisory staff does not increase at the same rate as output, for example a hotel with 100 bedrooms and a hotel with 1000 bedrooms would each have a single General Manger, Head Chef and so on.

(c) Specialist staff save money because large firms can justify employing specialist staff in IT, HR, accountancy etc and their skills can be fully utilised in their specialist areas.

3.5.4 Financial economies

A large cost of many firms is the interest they must pay on borrowing capital from banks. Large firms will generally enjoy the following financial economies of scale.

(a) **Better asset turnover ratio**: larger firms may have less assets relative to their sales revenue due to the technical economies described above. Therefore they need to pay less interest relative to turnover because they have needed to borrow less

(b) **Cheaper finance:** Chapter 2 showed that investors require higher returns for higher risk. Larger firms are perceived to be less risky due to having more valuable assets to pledge as security and their greater market power giving them stability. Quoted firms can also raise finance by selling shares to the public via a stock exchange.

Question — **Economies of scale**

The above list of sources of economies of scale is not exhaustive. Can you add to it?

Answer

(a) Large firms attract *better quality employees* if the employees see better career prospects than in a small firm. These staff save money by being more efficient and effective.

(b) Specialisation of labour applies to management, and there are thus *managerial economies*; the cost per unit of management will fall as output rises.

(c) *Marketing economies* are available, because a firm can make more effective use of advertising, specialist salesmen, and specialised channels of distribution.

(d) Large companies are able to devote more resources to *research and development* (R & D). In an industry where R & D is essential for survival, large companies are more likely to prosper.

3.6 External economies of scale

Whereas internal economies of scale accrue to an individual firm, it is also possible for general advantages to be enjoyed by all of the firms in an industry. These are known as external economies of scale.

External economies of scale occur as an **industry** grows in size. Here are two examples.

(a) **A large skilled labour force is created** and educational services can be geared towards training new entrants. This saves the firms the costs of training.

(b) **Specialised ancillary industries will develop** to provide components, transport finished goods, trade in by-products, provide special services and so on. For instance, law firms may be set up to specialise in the affairs of the industry and save the firms the costs of maintaining in house legal teams.

(c) **Government assistance** may be granted to industries that promise large amounts of jobs or export earnings. In recent years information technology, green energy and biotechnology industries have benefited from this.

3.7 Diseconomies of scale

Economic theory predicts that there will be **diseconomies of scale** in the long run costs of a firm, once the firm gets beyond an ideal size. The main reasons for possible diseconomies of scale are managerial, human and behavioural problems of a large firm. In a large firm employing many people, with many levels in the hierarchy of management, there may be a number of undesirable effects.

(a) Communicating information and instructions may become difficult.

(b) Chains of command may become excessively long, and management will become too remote, and lose control over operations.

(c) Morale and motivation amongst staff may deteriorate, and there may be conflicts between different departments which have different objectives.

(d) Senior management may have difficulty in assimilating all the information they need in sufficient detail to make good quality decisions.

(e) There may be increased levels of bureaucracy.

A firm may also experience **technical** diseconomies of scale. For example, increasing the size of the plant and equipment may create large administrative overheads thereby increasing total average costs, even though the direct production cost itself is lowered.

These are all **internal** diseconomies of scale. However, there may also be **external diseconomies of scale** which affect all firms in an industry as the industry grows. For example, if a natural resource such as oil or gas is over-used then shortages may result. In turn, this would increase the average cost of production.

The implication of diseconomies of scale is that companies should achieve a certain size to benefit fully from scale economies, but should not become too big, because if they do cost controls might slacken and organisational inefficiency may be likely to result.

4 Impact of long run costs on industry structure

FAST FORWARD

In competitive industries where sales are determined by prices the existence of economies of scale will lead to industry competition becoming reduced to the small number of large firms able to achieve minimum costs.

4.1 The impact of competition on the survival of firms

In order to survive firms must make adequate profits. Failure to do so can lead to the disappearance of the firm from one or more of the following reasons:

(a) **Run out of cash**: profits are related to the difference between the amounts of cash the firm is spending and the money it is earning. A loss making firm will be one that has too little cash to pay its costs. Unless it can borrow cash to cover the shortfall it will be unable to pay its staff and suppliers and will have to cease business due to **insolvency**.

(b) **Investor pressure**: if profits are not adequate to satisfy shareholders they will demand that the firm be sold to other owners such as a rival firm in a **takeover or merger**. This will enable the shareholders to **liquidate their investment** in the firm by taking cash in return for parting with their shares. If this is not possible the investors will demand the **breaking up** of the firm through it selling off its businesses and assets for cash.

(c) **Leave the industry**: management may decide that the assets and staff of the business can be more profitably used in serving a different market where competition is less or the firm is better able to compete. This is sometimes termed a **diversification.**

In general competition reduces profits of firms in two ways:

(a) **Reducing prices**: to gain sales and market share aggressive rivals will **discount their prices.** Large buyers will exploit this competition by playing one firm against another to obtain bigger discounts

(b) **Increasing costs**: some firms may seek to gain sales and market share by offering the customer a better product or service, or promoting more heavily. This forces other firms to do the same and drives up the **costs of participation** in the industry.

4.2 Minimum efficient scale

Key term

> Given the idea of economies of scale, it is generally accepted that in any industry there is a **minimum efficient scale** of production which is necessary for a firm to achieve the full potential economies of scale.

Minimum efficient scale is the lowest level of output at which the firm can achieve minimum average cost. If a firm is producing at quantities below the minimum economic scale, its unit costs of production may be higher than the unit costs of its bigger competitors. This means it will not compete successfully and it will make lower profits, or even losses.
Figure 6 shows the impact of this.

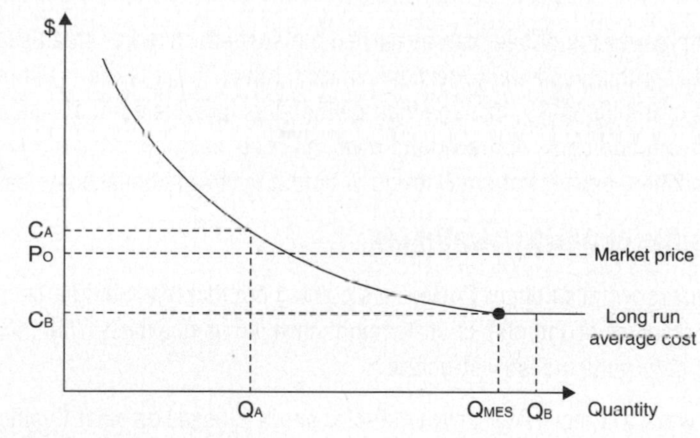

Figure 6 Impact of MES on profits of firms

Figure 6 is drawn using the simplifying assumption that all firms in the industry have similar long run average cost curves.

If Firm A is producing at Q_A it will have unit costs of C_A. It has not reached minimum efficient scale. Firm B is producing at Q_B and has unit costs of C_B, the minimum feasible cost in the industry.

Firm B might seek to set market price at P_0 to inflict losses of $C_A - P_0$ per unit on Firm A whilst making profits of P_0-C_B itself. This would have the effect of driving Firm A from the industry.

The level of the **minimum efficient scale** (MES) will vary from industry to industry. In the paint manufacturing industry, for example, it might be necessary to have a 15% share of the market in order to achieve maximum scale economies, whereas in frozen food production, a 25% share of the market might be necessary, and so on.

In some industries the MES may occur at levels of output in excess of 50% of total industry sales. This leads to a situation of **natural monopoly** in which the forces of competition drives all but one firm from the industry. Examples of this are public utilities (piped gas, mains electricity and water, and fixed line telephones) and rail transport where the costs of building and maintaining the network need a significant market share of sales to repay them.

4.3 Alternative strategies for firms

FAST FORWARD

The existence of significant economies of scale in an industry leads to only the largest firms surviving. Some firms **deliberately increase fixed costs** in an industry to drive out rivals. However alternative strategies such as **differentiation,** the **outsourcing** of high cost activities, or **off-shoring** can enable smaller firms to survive.

There are few economies of scale available in industries such as hairdressing, plumbing services or replacement windows. This allows these industries to have many firms competing in each. But there are relatively few aircraft manufacturers, IT network services providers, or providers of home video game consoles. This indicates that economies of scale may affect the structure of industries.

4.3.1 Deliberate increasing of industry fixed costs

Some industries have few technical economies of scale available. This would normally lead to a large number of suppliers being able to share the market.

To exclude competition firms may deliberately create high cost operations to force other firms to do the same and render themselves unprofitable.

For example brewing of beer can be carried out cost effectively at small scale and the industry was once very fragmented with independent breweries in each town. Today larger firms use saturation marketing campaigns to establish brand identities, manage their own outlets, provide point of sale assistance to retailers, and invest in alternative technologies of brewing to raise the costs of being in the market and ensure that smaller firms cannot get established, because at small levels of output these additional costs can't be recovered.

4.3.2 Differentiation strategies

The business writer **Michael Porter** has pointed out that many industries are not dominated by a small number of low cost firms as economies of scale might have led us to expect. This means there must be other factors beside cost that determine industry structure.

Porter's work will recur later in your studies and it is based on clear business economics principles. If a firm can't reduce costs to make profits then it must find a way to charge a higher price.

Porter identified **three generic strategies** by which a firm can compete profitably. He uses the term generic to mean 'basic type of' or 'roots of' strategy.

(a) Cost leadership: provide the product at the lowest cost in the industry. This is the same as achieving MES and is based on the ability of the cost leading firm to undercut and force out smaller rivals.

(b) Differentiation: provide a product of higher benefit or value to the buyer. This enables the firm to avoid becoming trapped in a low-price section of the market where cost efficiency determines which firm will survive.

(c) Focus: avoid going into competition with large firms in the market as a whole. Instead find a niche section of the market that the large firms cannot easily serve or have overlooked. Here price may not be such an issue if the firm can give customers exactly what they want.

The use of Differentiation and Focus strategies can help smaller firms survive profitably despite their lack of economies of scale.

4.3.3 Outsourcing

Key term

Outsourcing refers to transferring an activity previously conducted by the firm itself to an outside contractor.

When supplying a market a firm undertakes a chain of activities. For example a catalogue or internet shopping firm must develop websites, purchase inventory, provide warehousing, operate contact centres to deal with customers, employ and pay its staff, operate a home delivery service and so on.

Each activity will have its own MES. This means the firms costs will be as high as the highest cost activity in its chain of activities.

Where a firm is being made uncompetitive due to the high costs of one of its activities it can reduce its costs by outsourcing that activity to a contractor. The contractor can do the activity at lower cost because it pools the work of the firm with the work of other clients and so achieves the MES.

4.3.4 Off-shoring

Key term

Off-shoring is the practice of shifting a business activity, or the firm as a whole, to another country where costs are lower.

The costs of operation vary widely from country to country due to factors such as

(a) Lower general pay rates

(b) Better skills available

(c) Better support services such as transportation, information systems or education and training

(d) More favourable regulatory environment such as lower taxation, less costs of complying with government regulations.

A firm may decide to outsource some of its activities to off-shore locations in order to gain cost efficiencies needed to compete in its market.

4.4 Review of industry structure

FAST FORWARD

Industry structure analysis considers the **number of firms** in the industry and, in particular, whether the industry has **competition** amongst many firms, or limited competition between a few. It also considers whether firms compete directly or avoid competition through differentiation, the **use of networks** of outsourcing and also the **geographical location** and use of off-shoring.

Industry structure analysis considers how an industry is made up and how it operates.

Conventionally this analysis has been restricted to considering merely the number of firms in the industry and the competition between them.

However the discussion above has included more contemporary themes in structure analysis such as the competitive strategies used by firms, the use of outsourcing and the use of off-shoring within the context of the firm's need to remain profitable.

There are several implications for industry structure:

(a) **Non-competing groups within an industry:** it is not sensible to define an industry in terms of the product that is being made. For example, not all car makers are in the same industry. The use of differentiation and focus strategies mean that there is little competitive overlap between a niche sports car manufacturer like Aston-Martin, a luxury car producer like Lexus, and a volume car producer like Ford Motor Company

(b) **Network organisations:** it is misleading to think of a single firm supplying a good to a market. Frequently the supply of a good involves the efforts of several firms in partnership due to the high degree of outsourcing to achieve cost efficiency.

(c) **Global operations:** the use of off-shoring means that firms now co-ordinate across several countries, time-zones and cultures.

These issues will recur in your future studies.

Chapter roundup

- For profit seeking organisations the unit price received for a product should exceed the unit cost of making the product
- The distinction between **fixed costs** and **variable costs** is recognised in economic theory and in the practice of management accounting
- The slope of a total cost curve shows the rate at which cost rises as output rises. Therefore a **total fixed cost curve** has a **slope of zero** because fixed costs do not rise as output rises. **Total variable cost curves** have a **positive slope** because total variable costs rise as output rises. **Steeper gradient** curves illustrate **higher the variable cost per unit**.
- Straight line total cost curves are unlikely to occur in practice due to **changing levels of efficiency** as output increases.
- Short run cost curves are assumed to be **S-shaped** to reflect initially increasing efficiency followed by declining efficiency at high volumes.
- **Marginal cost** is the **rise in total cost** resulting from producing an **extra unit** of the product. This will be the same **as the rise in variable cost** because fixed costs do not rise as output rises. Marginal cost can be depicted as the **slope of a tangent** touching the total cost curve at the given level of output.
- **Long run costs** describe the behaviour of unit costs as the firm makes **significant changes to its volume of production** involving significant investment in **new capacity** and **adaptation** of its organisational structure and **production processes**.
- In competitive industries where sales are determined by prices the existence of economies of scale will lead to industry competition becoming reduced to the small number of large firms able to achieve minimum costs.
- The existence of significant economies of scale in an industry leads to only the largest firms surviving. Some firms **deliberately increase fixed costs** in an industry to drive out rivals. However alternative strategies such as **differentiation**, the **outsourcing** of high cost activities, or **off-shoring** can enable smaller firms to survive.
- **Industry structure analysis** considers the **number of firms** in the industry and in particular whether the industry has competition amongst many firms, or limited competition between a few. It also considers whether firms compete directly or avoid it through differentiation, the **use of networks** of outsourcing and also the **geographical location** and use of off-shoring.

Quick quiz

1 Which of the following best defines a fixed cost?

A A cost that does not change from year to year

B A cost that does change when output rises

C A cost that does not change when output changes

D A cost that has been laid down in a contract

2 A firm with a straight line total cost curve reports that its total costs for producing one unit are $50 and for producing 10 units are $140. What is its variable cost per unit?

A $9.90

B $10

C $14

D $50

3 Why might there be diseconomies of scale?

4 What is the name given to section of a total cost curve over which fixed costs can be assumed to be fixed, and variable costs to be at a constant amount per unit ?

5 Which of the following is not an advantage of the division of labour

A Less training costs and time for workers to learn the job

B Opportunity to use specialist tools and equipment

C Repetition of same task leads to boredom and errors

D Workers can do tasks suited to their natural abilities

6 Define marginal cost

7 Which of the following terms describes a situation where a firm can reduce unit costs by offering a wider selection of products

A External economy of scale

B Economy of increased dimensions

C Financial economy of scale

D Economy of scope

8 Which of the following is an example of an external economy of scale?

A Increased wage costs due to falling unemployment in the region.

B The employment of specialist managers by a firm to cope with higher output levels.

C The extension of low-cost telecommunication links to an area of the country not previously served by such links.

D Cheaper finance in recognition of the firm's increased share of the market and therefore its stability.

Answers to quick quiz

1 C This is a deliberately tricky question because B looks correct. However C is better because fixed costs are fixed for both rise and falls in output.

2 B The additional costs of producing 9 units is $90 ($140-$50). Given that the only costs that rise with output are variable costs this equates to $10 per unit ($90/9 units)

3 Diseconomies of scale are problems of size and tend to arise when the firm grows so large that it cannot be managed efficiently. Communications may become difficult, motivation may deteriorate because of alienation and senior management may find it difficult to identify the information they need in the vast volumes available.

4 It is called the *relevant range*

5 C This is a disadvantage of the division of labour

6 Marginal cost is the addition to total costs resulting from increasing output by one unit

7 D Economy of scope due to spreading fixed costs across a wider range of products

8 C This is an external economy of scale.

A is a diseconomy of scale.
B is an internal economy of scale.
D is an internal economy of scale.

Now try the questions below from the Exam Question Bank

Question numbers
23 - 27

7

Decision making 2 – profit maximisation

Introduction

A key decision for a firm is how much to produce in order to maximise its profits. This decision will depend on the firm's revenues and costs.

The level of output at which profits will be maximised can be demonstrated graphically and calculated numerically using the cost and revenue concepts from earlier chapters.

The new economy has its origins in the development of digital technologies and Advanced Communications Technologies (ACT), e-business and the internet. This new economy is characterised by different cost behaviour from conventional commerce.

Globalisation has made an impact on the cost structures of many industries and its implications for decision making are explored.

Topic list	Learning outcomes	Syllabus references	Ability required
1 Cost, volume, profit analysis	B3	B3 (a)	Application
2 Profit maximisation – graphical approach	B3	B3 (a)	Application
3 Profit maximisation – numerical approach	B3	B3 (b)	Application
4 Influence of e-business on cost and market behaviour	B2	B2 (c)	Comprehension
5 Influence globalisation on cost and market behaviour	B2	B2 (c)	Comprehension

1 Cost, volume, profit analysis

FAST FORWARD

Cost, volume, profit analysis (CVP) is a **fundamental technique** used in **management accounting**. It provides a good introduction to an economic analysis of a firm's **short-run profit maximisation** decisions

1.1 CVP diagram

Cost, volume, profit analysis (CVP) is also called **breakeven analysis**. It shows how costs and profits will change as volume changes.

Figure 1 shows a basic CVP diagram

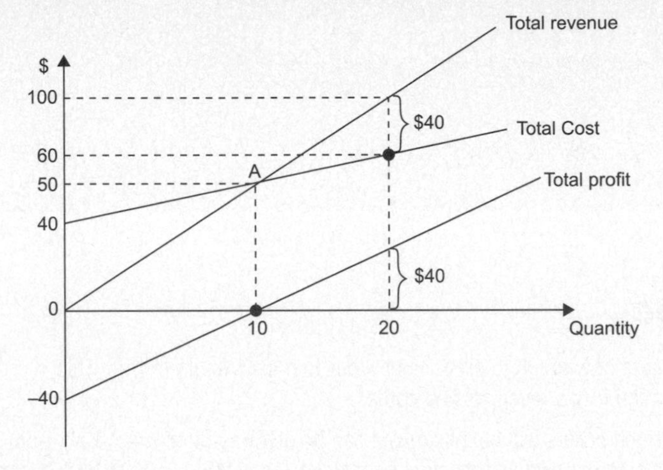

Figure 1 Cost, volume, profit analysis

Figure 1 shows the following features:
Total revenue is zero at zero output but rises as output rises. Given that total revenue is \$50 when 10 units are sold this means the slope of the total revenue curve is \$5 per unit. This is the same as saying the sales price of the product is \$5 per unit

(a) Fixed costs are \$40. The total cost curve shows total cost is \$40 at zero output. There would be no variable costs associated with producing zero output and therefore it follows that this \$40 must be fixed costs

(b) The breakeven point is where the firm makes neither a profit nor a loss. This is shown as Point A where total revenue and total costs intersect and both are \$50. The breakeven quantity is 10 units

(c) The variable costs are \$1 per unit. This is because the total cost of producing 10 units is shown as \$50. Total costs are made up of fixed costs + variable costs. Given that fixed costs are \$40 this means total variable cost for 10 units is \$10 (\$50 - \$40), which equates to \$1 of variable cost per unit (\$10/10 units)

(d) The total profit at 20 units will be \$40. This can be calculated as total revenue of \$100 (20 x \$5 per unit) less total costs of \$60 made up of fixed costs of \$40 plus variable costs of \$20 (20 x \$1 per unit)

(e) The distance between the total revenue curve and the total costs curve at a given output is the profit or loss at that level of output. This amount is summarised in the total profit curve.

1.2 Limitations of CVP analysis

CVP analysis is an established and useful management accounting technique. However it has several limitations.

(a) **Linear short run cost curve:** the approach assumes that variable cost per unit doesn't change as output changes. This ignores the likely change in efficiency as output rises

(b) **Linear total revenue curve:** the approach assumes that sale price will remain the same regardless of how much is supplied. This is contradicted by the law of demand that states that as volume supplied rises the price will need to fall in order to sell the additional output.

(c) **Fixed costs are assumed to be fixed:** the approach encourages the belief that output can keep rising and incur further variable costs only. In practice a significant rise in scale of operation may lead to a need for additional premises, administrative staff and so on. These would have been regarded as fixed costs but now they have risen. In practice CVP is modified to include **stepped fixed costs** showing the rise in fixed costs as volume produced passes particular milestone quantities.

2 Profit maximisation – graphical approach

FAST FORWARD

A graphical approach to profit analysis features a **curvilinear** total revenue curve and total cost curve. The curve of the total revenue curve is determined by the **price elasticity of demand** for the product. The curvilinear total cost curve reflects the **changing levels of efficiency** in the production process.

2.1 The total revenue curve

The law of demand states that quantity demanded extends as price is reduces. This tells us the firm that in order to sell a greater quantity of a product the firm will need to reduce its price to attract customers.

Figure 2 demonstrates how the total revenue curve is determined by the demand curve facing the firm.

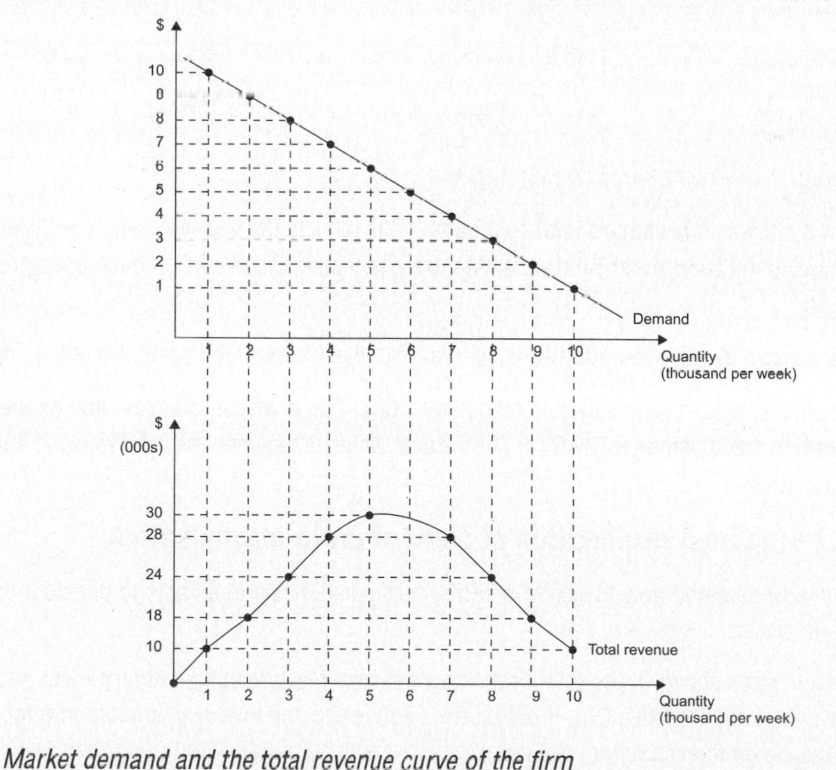

Figure 2 Market demand and the total revenue curve of the firm

Figure 2 shows a firm facing a downward sloping demand curve. The firm is a **price maker** because the market price falls if the firm tries to sell more of the product.

If the firm charges $10 per unit it can sell 1,000 units a week and receive a revenue of $10,000.

As it increases output above 1,000 units up to 5,000 units the price falls but total revenue rises. This shows the demand curve is **price elastic** over this range.

If the firm increases sales from 6,000 units to 7,000 units the total revenue falls from $30,000 to $28,000. This shows the demand curve is **price inelastic** beyond 6,000 units. The fall in total revenue happens because the revenue the firm gets from selling an extra 1,000 units at $4 per unit, ie $4,000 does not compensate for the loss of potential revenue it lost by selling 6,000 for $1 less than it used to, ie $6,000.

If the firm increases sales from 5,000 to 6,000 the total revenue remains at $30,000. This means there is **unit price elasticity of demand** between 5,000 and 6,000 units.

2.2 The point of profit maximisation

2.2.1 Diagram

Figure 3 shows a version of CVP analysis with curvilinear revenue and cost curves.

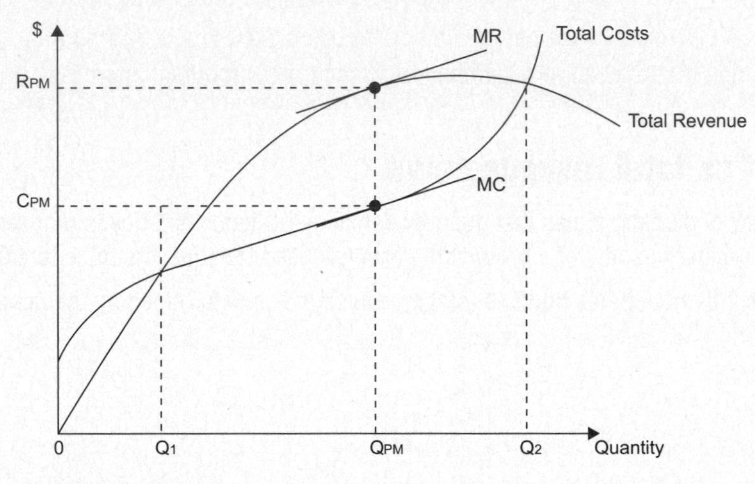

Figure 3 Point of profit maximisation

Figure 3 shows an **S-shaped total cost curve**. This reflects the varying levels of efficiency as output is increased. It also shows the **curvilinear total revenue curve**, reflecting the need to reduce price progressively to sell greater outputs.

There are **two break-even quantities**, where total revenue and total costs are equal. These are at Q_1 and Q_2

The point of profit maximisation is output level Q_{PM}. This is where **total revenue exceeds total costs by the greatest amount**, by the distance $R_{PM} - C_{PM}$. The vertical distance between the total revenue and total cost curves measures the total profit.

2.2.2 Graphical explanation of point of profit maximisation

A way to understand how the point of profit maximisation is arrived at is to consider the slopes of the total cost and revenue curves.

As output rises above Q_1 the total cost curve and total revenue curves **diverge** and become further apart from each other until output reaches Q_{PM}. If output rises above Q_{PM} the total cost curve and total revenue curves **converge** and become closer to each other.

Therefore at Q_{PM} they are at their **furthest distance apart**. At levels of output below Q_{PM} the curves will still getting further apart and so an increase in output would increase profits. At levels of output above Q_{PM} the curves get closer together which means total profits will be less.

Based on the assumption that firms seek to maximise their profits firms should produce at point Q_{PM}

2.2.3 Marginal cost equals marginal revenue at point of profit maximisation

Key terms

Marginal cost (MC): the addition to total cost resulting from increasing output by one unit.

Marginal revenue (MR): the addition to total revenue resulting from increasing total sales by one unit

The slope of the total revenue curve illustrates the rise in total revenue as total sales volume increases. Figure 3 shows a tangent touching the total revenue curve at output level Q_{PM}. The slope of this tangent it identical to the slope of the total revenue curve at this point. This slope is the **marginal revenue** derived from selling the final unit of the product.

The slope of the total cost curve shows the rise in costs for each extra unit produced. The tangent drawn against the total cost curve at Q_{PM} shows the additional cost resulting from increasing output by the final unit. This is the **marginal cost.**

The two tangents in Figure 3 have the same slope, in other words, marginal cost equals marginal revenue. This is because this is the precise point at which the total cost and revenue curves cease to diverge and begin to converge. It is the point of profit maximisation, where **marginal revenue equals marginal cost (MR=MC)**.

At output level Q_{PM} the addition to total revenue from selling the most recent unit, the marginal revenue, is equal to the addition to total cost resulting from making it, the marginal cost.

Therefore the following statements can be made:

(a) At Q_{PM} the addition to total costs from producing the extra unit is equal to the addition to total revenue resulting from selling it

(b) At output levels below Q_{PM} the addition to total revenue from selling the extra unit is greater than the addition to total costs resulting from making it (**MR>MC**) and so the firm would **increase profits by increasing the quantity produced**

(c) At output levels above Q_{PM} the addition to total costs from producing the extra unit is greater than the addition to total revenue resulting from selling it (**MC>MR**) and so the firm would **increase profits by reducing the quantity produced**.

2.3 Applying graphical analysis in business

Few managers will draw graphs to establish the point of profit maximisation for their business. The graphical approach is a shorthand to help explain how costs and revenues behave, and the implications of this for the total profits of the business.

Management accountants will use numbers to show the profit resulting from production decisions.

3 Profit maximisation – numerical approach

3.1 Calculating total profit

Completing the following simple table demonstrates one way to calculate the point of maximum profit.

Question — **Calculating total profit**

The following data refer to the revenue and costs of a firm.

Output	*Total revenue*	*Total costs*
	$	$
0	–	110
1	50	140
2	100	162
3	150	175
4	200	180
5	250	185
6	300	194
7	350	229
8	400	269
9	450	325
10	500	425

Required

(a) Calculate the Total profit (loss) at each level of output and insert the figure in the Total profit column (bearing in mind that Total profit = Total revenue minus Total costs)

(b) Identify the profit maximising level of output and the amount of profit the firm will make at this level.

Answer

Output	*Total revenue (TR)*	*Total costs (TC)*	*Total profit TR – TC*
	$	$	$
0	–	110	(110)
1	50	140	(90)
2	100	162	(62)
3	150	175	(25)
4	200	180	20
5	250	185	65
6	300	194	106
7	350	229	122
8	400	269	131(max)
9	450	325	125
10	500	425	75

(b) The firm will maximise profits by producing at a level of output at which total revenue exceeds total cost by the largest amount. It can be seen from the table that this occurs at output level 8.

3.2 Calculating profit maximisation using marginal cost and marginal revenue

FAST FORWARD

The point of profit maximisation can also be found by identifying the point at which **marginal cost** equals **marginal revenue**.

The limitations of using a total profit calculation in practice is that the firm needs data on all its costs to be able to arrive at the right figure.

Management accountants are called on to **project** the impact of changes to quantities on total profits. Providing the management accountant has data on the prices and the variable costs that will arise from producing extra output they will be able to identify the profit maximising output.

Question — Calculating marginal cost and marginal revenue

The following data refer to the revenue and costs of a firm.

Output	*Projected price*	*Projected total variable costs*
	$	$
0	-	
1	50	30
2	49	52
3	48	65
4	47	70
5	46	75
6	45	84
7	44	109
8	43	159
9	42	215
10	41	315

Required

(a) Calculate the marginal revenue for the firm at each level of output
(b) Calculate the firm's marginal cost at each level of output
(c) Identify the level of output at which the firm will maximise profits
(d) Calculate the total profit at the profit maximising level of output where fixed costs are $110.

Answer

Output	Total revenue (TR) $	(a) Marginal revenue $TR_n - TR_{(n-1)}$ $	(b) Marginal costs $TC_n - TC_{(n-1)}$ $
0	–	–	–
1	50	50	30
2	98	48	22
3	144	46	13
4	188	44	5
5	230	42	5
6	270	40	9
7	308	38	35
8	344	36	40
9	378	34	56
10	410	32	100

(c) The firm will maximise profits by producing at a level of output at which marginal cost equals marginal revenue. Inspection of the table shows this will occur between 7 and 8 units of output.

(d) The total profit is calculated as total revenue minus total costs.

At 7 units of output total revenue is $308 and total costs will be $219 ($110 + $109) giving a total profit of $89.

At 8 units of output total revenue will be $344 and total costs will be $269 ($110 +$159) giving a total profit of $75.

Therefore the firm should produce 7 units to make a maximum profit of $89.

4 Influence of e-business on cost and market behaviour

This topic has been introduced into the syllabus to demonstrate the application of business economic analysis to a key 21st Century phenomenon, the growth of e-business.

FAST FORWARD

e-business uses **Advanced Communications Technologies (ACT)** to provide products and services. This has the potential to **radically change the prices** and **competitive structures** of markets.

4.1 The impact of ACT

Advanced Communication Technologies (ACT) is a collective term used to describe the Internet, mobile telephone and data systems, digital television, and network communications between firms using extranets and electronic data interchange. They are accessed and supported by a new generation of hardware, such as web-books, smart-phones, digital players, and home entertainment systems, and supported by smart applications software ('apps').

These technologies permit households, firms and other organisations to transmit and to receive high volumes of data very quickly and over substantial distances.

This is sometimes called the 'third industrial revolution' because it is having a profound effect on industries.

4.2 Reduced search costs for buyers

FAST FORWARD

By reducing **search costs** for buyers the availability of e-commerce **increases the price elasticity of demand** for products by permitting **wider sharing of price information** and providing **more substitutes.**

Key term

Search costs: the costs incurred by buyers in locating suitable products and finding the best prices.

4.2.1 Origin of search costs

Compare buying some music or booking a holiday using conventional shopping with buying the same thing using ACT. Someone seeking better prices for something incurs **search costs** such as time spent, telephone calls, and journey times

ACT reduces search costs in several ways:

(a) Buyers and sellers can compare a wider range of prices using search engines and price comparison websites

(b) It reduces the costs of gathering additional information on the item by providing on-line samples of movies, music and books, pictures and customer reviews of hotels and restaurants, and answers to frequently asked questions

4.2.2 Impact on price elasticity of demand

The reduction of search costs by the introduction of ACT will **increase the price elasticity of demand**:

(a) The demand curve an individual firm faces will often become more price elastic because information on price cuts is cheaper to obtain due to reduced search costs. The number of customers spotting the lower price and responding to it will be greater than under conventional commerce. Price comparison sites and auction sites facilitate this.

(b) The market demand curve will also become more price elastic due to the greater availability of substitutes. A new release DVD or CD now faces the competition from downloads which are potentially cheaper and more convenient.

This is summarised in Figure 4

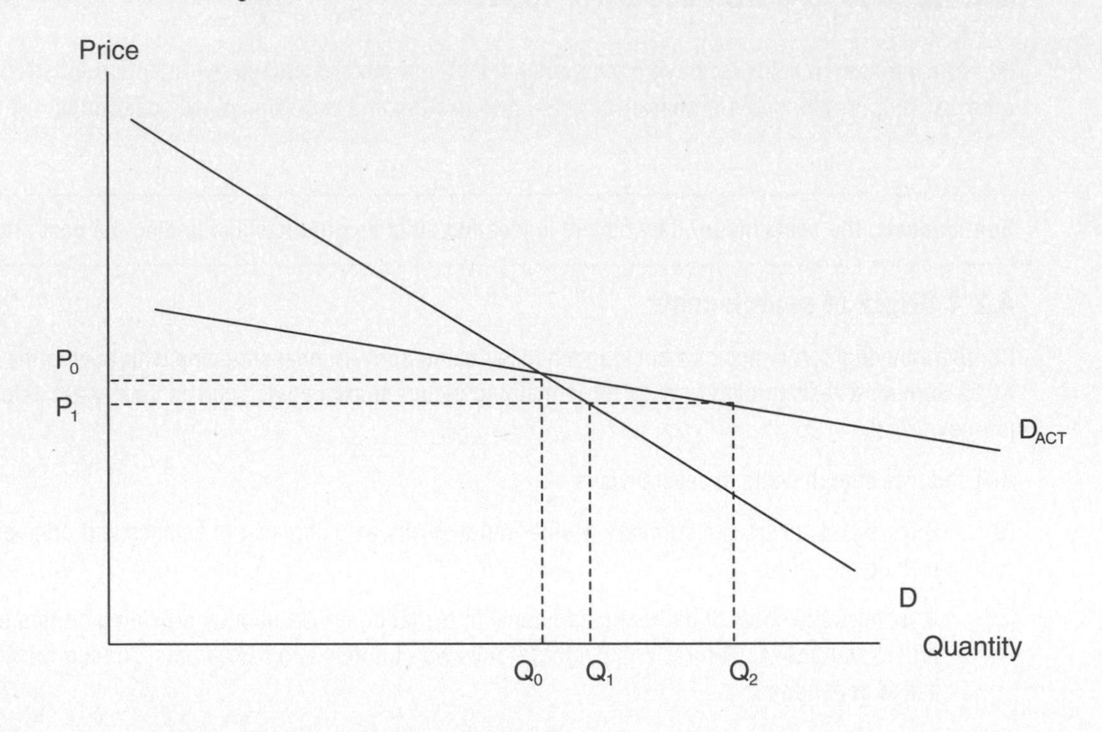

Figure 4 Impact of ACT on price elasticity of demand

In Figure 4 the conventional demand curve is shown as D. A supplier who cuts price from P_0 to P_1 enjoys only a small extension of demand from Q_0 to Q_1. This is because the search costs the customer incurs in finding the lower priced product outweigh the saving from buying at a cheaper price.

The demand curve when the market is served by ACT is shown by D_{ACT}. A supplier who cuts price from P_0 to P_1 in this market enjoys a larger extension of demand from Q_0 to Q_2. This is because more customers will be able to spot the lower price and switch to the supplier with the lower price.

This helps explain the price competitiveness in the markets for insurance premiums, airline travel and contact lenses amongst other markets.

4.3 Zero variable costs

FAST FORWARD

Because providing more downloads doesn't increase variable costs for the firm, the supply curve becomes **perfectly price elastic**.

In a conventional market, selling twice as much of something means the supplier must pay additional variable costs to make the increased volumes required.

ACT allow extra units of a product to be sold in digital format by download. This doesn't require much or any increase in variable costs at all.

For example the costs of downloading books, newspaper, music, films or software are born as data charges by the customer.

Suppliers incur high fixed costs to establish the content and download sites, but across fairly large increases of output, costs do not rise as output rises and **supply becomes perfectly price elastic**.

Figure 5 shows the likely impact on price.

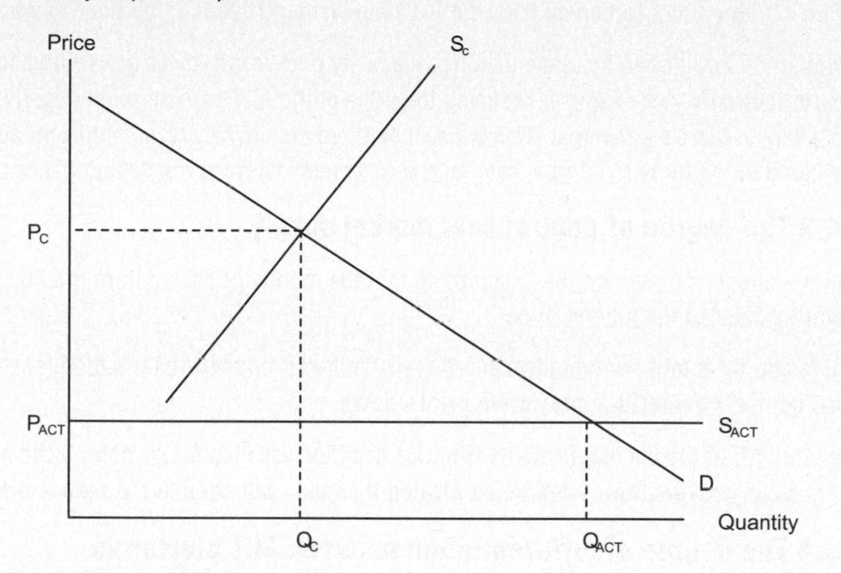

Figure 5 *Impact of ACT on market price*

The demand curve in Figure 5 is drawn using the simplifying assumption that consumers are equally happy with the conventional product and its digital version.

The supply curve Sc denotes the supply curve of the conventional producer. It is upward sloping reflecting the rising total variable costs of a conventional production process. Market price is established at Pc with quantity sold at Qc.

The supply curve S_{ACT} denotes the supply curve of the producer using ACT. It is flat because variable costs are zero and hence costs do not rise with output. Market price is established at P_{ACT} with quantity sold at Q_{ACT}.

4.4 Influence of e-business on market prices

The general effect of ACT will be to reduce market prices.

The extent to which ACT brings about the fall in price and rise in consumption denoted will depend on a number of factors:

4.4.1 The nature of the product

ACT reduces prices more where the product is a 'commodity product' ie where it is a standard product of known specification such as a CD or book. It is less effective if the product is differentiated such as a wedding dress or a piece of fine art.

4.4.2 The price elasticity of demand for the product

For an ACT producer to benefit from cutting price demand needs to be price elastic.

Although ACT will often increase the price elasticity of demand, there are some situations where price elasticity **will remain inelastic**. For example, reducing the price of the ACT version of an eagerly awaited novel or music release is unlikely to increase revenue. This is because there are unlikely to be sufficient additional readers buying a download of the book to compensate for the revenues lost from not selling the book at a higher price to fans.

4.4.3 The degree of control over market supply

Figure 5 above is drawn on the assumption that the market price is determined by one producer and that this producer decides the market price.

Where supply is more competitive and there is limited product differentiation, such as competing magazines or video games, **competition may drive prices down**.

The strength of Intellectual Property Right protections will be a factor here. If the owner of the rights to a recording or book can **prevent their work being pirated** then they will not need to reduce prices to compete.

4.4.4 The degree of differentiation between ACT platforms

The demand for some products is **affected by complements**. The video game market features a small number of console producers (Sony, Nintendo, and Microsoft). These consoles play the same video games as each other but the console software means that software producers have to develop a special version for each console and a version of the game software, say for a Nintendo, cannot then be played on a Sony PlayStation.

This has the effect of increasing the ability of the platform owner to decide price and supply.

5 Influence of globalisation on cost and market behaviour

FAST FORWARD

Globalisation refers to the development of markets and production operations spanning the globe. One effect of this has been availability of considerably lower costs of production in developing economies than in established economies.

5.1 Origins of globalisation

Key terms

Globalisation: the increasing unification of the world's economic order through reduction of such barriers to international trade as tariffs, export fees, and import quotas. The goal is to increase material wealth, goods, and services through an international division of labour by efficiencies brought about by international relations, specialisation and competition.

Globalisation is described further in Chapter 14. In summary the origins of globalisation are:

(a) Improved communications across the globe, including telecommunications and air transport

(b) Elimination of trade barriers between country as nations give up protectionist behaviour to enjoy the potential gains from trade

(c) Political change that has moved more economies away from tribal or state-planned economies towards a market system.

5.2 Impacts of globalisation on costs of the firm

The costs of materials and labour vary significantly from country to country due to a number of influences:

(a) Sizes of population: some countries have abundant population that drives wages to low levels

(b) Better skill base: certain countries have designed an education system to produce large numbers of people with skills that are scarce and expensive in developed countries

(c) Legal differences: costs in some countries are low because business is not expected to pay for things like annual leave entitlements, employee health and welfare, or guaranteed minimum wages

(d) Special assistance: to attract business national governments may give gifts of free land, build infrastructure, and give loans or grants for investment on generous terms (these are examples of external economies of scale).

(e) Lower costs of materials and other services: setting a factory up in a low cost economy leads to savings on wages but also allows the firm to obtain cheaper metal, power and other inputs because these industries are also enjoying lower costs.

The effect of these factors are to lower both fixed and variable costs of production.

A domestic firm can take advantage of the lower costs available globally in one of two ways:

(a) It can relocate production to the low cost economy by building a factory there, and perhaps closing its domestic factory

(b) It can contract-out production to an independent firm in the low cost country.

Figure 6 shows the impact of globalisation on a firms costs.

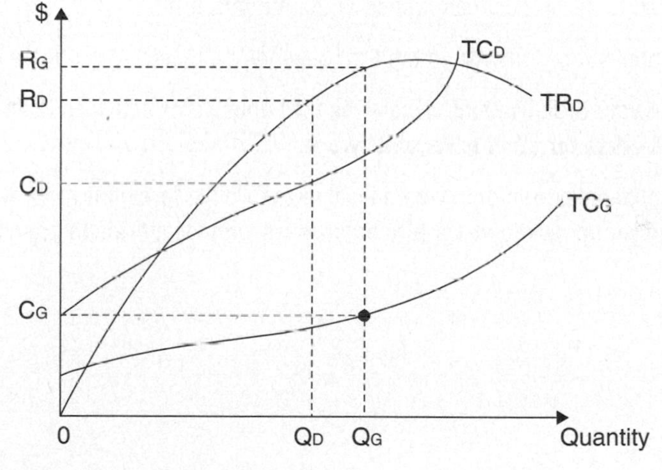

Figure 6 Impact of globalisation on costs and output

Figure 6 shows the situation of a representative firm before and after the opening up of lower cost production facilities through globalisation. To make explanation simpler we can assume it is a clothes manufacturer.

The total revenue curve remains the same at TR_D, reflecting that the domestic customer does not care whether the product is made domestically or in a foreign country.

Initially the firm faces the domestic total cost curve TC_D. It maximises profit at output Q_D and makes a total revenue of R_D, costs of C_D and total profit of R_D minus C_D .

The costs of producing the same products in a low cost global location is shown by the total cost curve TC_G. Note that this curve shows lower fixed costs, shown by the fact that it has shifted down, and lower variable costs, shown by the fact that it is shallower than TC_D.

If the firm takes advantage of the lower costs it will over to output Q_G and make a profit equal to R_G minus C_G. Note that the total sales of the product have increased due to a fall in price.

Firms that do not undertake global production will normally be forced into low profit positions if markets become price-competitive with competitors sourcing low cost product from global suppliers.

This is because other firms will have the incentive to shift production to the low cost location and expand output and reduce prices.

In Figure 6 the situation can be shown as the domestic firm still seeking to produce at Q_D with costs of C_D but facing the lower prices shown at R_G. It would be producing at a marginal revenue, set by the global producers, substantially below its marginal cost of production. It would be making losses on marginal units and, possibly, a loss overall.

This combination of lower costs, expanded market volumes, and lower prices can be seen in the clothing markets of many high income economies. It is also exhibited in markets such as bicycles, electrical goods, musical instruments, sports goods, and plastic toys.

5.3 Globalisation of production in practice

In practice firms tend to **off-shore** particular parts of their production processes to the countries that can perform them most cheaply. For example the customer contact centre (call-centre) to one location, transactions processing to another, and manufacture to a third country.

This has led to several characteristics of the modern firm:

(a) Global supply chains: as the firm depends on receiving products or components from around the world

(b) Network organisations: where the firm does some activities itself but contracts with other lower-cost providers for other parts of its work

(c) Global collaborations: where local laws forbid a foreign firm to own factories in a country the foreign firm will set up new joint-venture businesses with local firms to open factories together.

Chapter roundup

- Cost, volume, profit analysis (CVP) is a fundamental technique used in management accounting. It provides a good introduction to an economic analysis of a firm's short-run profit maximisation decisions
- A graphical approach to profit analysis features a curvilinear total revenue curve and total cost curve. The curve of the total revenue curve is determined by the price elasticity of demand for the product. The curvilinear total cost curve reflects the changing levels of efficiency in the production process.
- The point of profit maximisation can also be found by identifying the point at which marginal cost equals marginal revenue
- E-business uses Advanced Communications Technologies (ACT) to provide products and services. This has the potential to radically change the prices and competitive structures of markets.
- By reducing search costs for buyers the availability of e-commerce increases the price elasticity of demand for products by permitting wider sharing of price information and providing more substitutes.
- Because providing more downloads doesn't increase variable costs for the firm the supply curve becomes perfectly price elastic.
- Globalisation refers to the development of markets and production operations spanning the globe. One effect of this has been availability of considerably lower costs of production in developing economies than in established economies. Investors invest in companies by buying their shares. The companies are expected to maximise the wealth of their shareholders by generating profit from trading operations. Investors will only provide funds if they believe that the prospective returns are adequate.

Quick quiz

1. Which one of the following statements is *false* about the breakeven point on a CVP chart?

   A Profit will be zero
   B Profits can be increased by reducing output
   C Profits will be increased if output is increased
   D It is the volume where total cost equals total revenue

2. Which one of the following statements is *true* about breakeven points on curvilinear cost and revenue charts?

   A There is only one breakeven point
   B Profits can be increased by reducing output
   C Profits will always be increased if output is increased
   D It is the volume where total revenue is at a maximum

3. True or false? There is no incentive for a firm to increase output beyond the point at which price elasticity of demand = 1

4. Which of the following statements is *false* about the point of profit maximisation

   A Marginal cost will equal marginal revenue
   B The firm made no profit on the final unit it made
   C The distance between the total cost curve and the total revenue curve will be at its greatest
   D Reducing fixed costs will shift the point of profit maximisation to a different level of output

5. What is meant by the term 'globalisation'?

6. Which of the following statements explains why lower search costs enabled by e-commerce reduce prices in a market?

   A E-commerce reduces the costs of producing some products
   B Firms have lower fixed costs due to replacing shops with websites
   C Consumers can locate lower prices without incurring high costs to do so
   D The intellectual property of suppliers is no longer protected

7. Which of the following would *reduce* price elasticity of demand in the market for a video game?

   A The game is designed to be played on only one brand of games console
   B There are many similar sorts of game available
   C The game has a high price
   D There are no extra variable costs associated with supplying additional copies of the video game

8 In the diagram below the music provider initially produced CDs and sold at point B. Which of the following points denotes its position following the decision to cease selling CDs and instead to sell music solely as downloadable files.

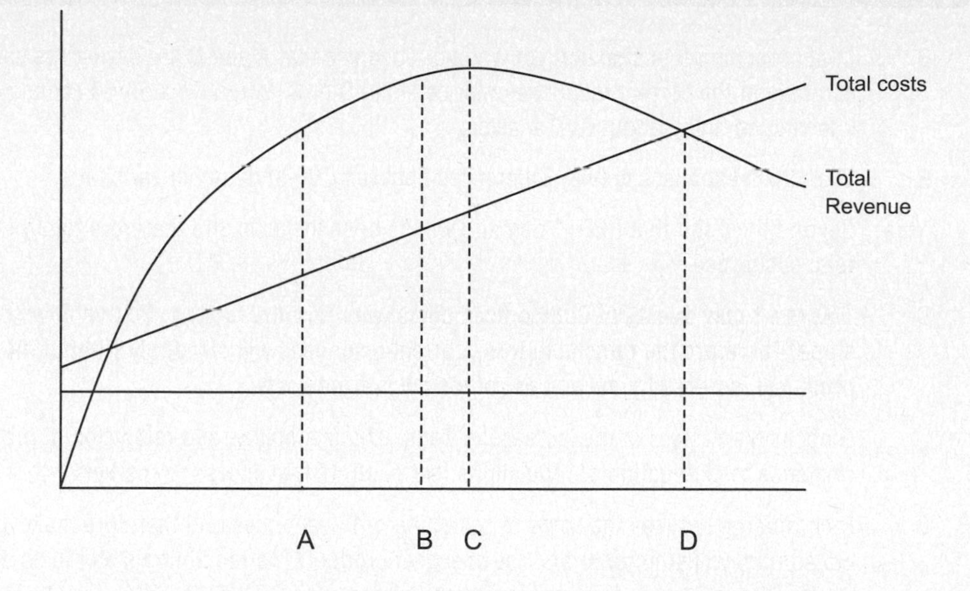

A
B
C
D

Answers to quick quiz

1	B	In approaching this question you should recognise that A and D are saying the same thing. So by elimination the correct response must be either B or C. You have a 50/50 chance of being correct without knowing anything about CVP analysis
2	B	The other responses are key differences between CVP and curvilinear charts
3	True	Beyond the point that PED=1 demand will be price inelastic and therefore total revenue would fall whilst total costs rose
4	D	This is a tricky question. Cutting fixed costs will move the total cost curve down but it will not change its slope. Therefore the remaining three correct responses will still apply without the volume changing. Total profit will increase by the amount of the fall in fixed costs
5		Globalisation refers to the increase in trade, labour mobility, and relocation of production across nations in response to elimination of regulations that obstruct free access to markets
6	C	E-commerce reduces the costs of searching out rival prices and therefore make it more likely that consumers will attempt to find the cheapest product. The remaining statements are true but they do not explain the link between search costs and prices.
7	A	A unique video game console means that if the price of the game was reduced its extra sales would be limited by the number of people owning the console. A rise in its price would not lead to a big contraction in demand because of a lack of cheaper substitutes. Option B is wrong because more substitutes increases price elasticity of demand. Option C is also wrong because high prices increase the proportion of income spent on the good and this in turn *increases* price elasticity of demand. D is incorrect because it affects the supply curve, not the demand curve.
8	C	At point C the firm will maximise its profits because it will be selling at the peak of its total revenue curve. Another way to see this is that at point B the firm maximised profit where its marginal revenue, shown by the slope of its total revenue curve, equalled marginal cost, shown by the slope of its total cost curve. Its new total cost curve has marginal costs of zero and therefore it will increase output until its marginal revenue is also zero, ie at the highest point of its total revenue curve.

Now try the questions below from the Exam Question Bank

Question numbers
28 - 31

Competition, market failures, and government intervention

8

Introduction

In this chapter, we examine some of the motives for, and effects of, government regulation of particular markets.

The **growth of large businesses** can lead to abuse of **monopoly power.** Government use **competition policy** to regulate the growth of firms and to intervene to stop abuses of market position.

Other **market failures** include situations where the **social and environmental effects** of production and consumption are not fully accounted for in the prices paid in the market. These are **externalities** and are the reason for various forms of **market intervention** by governments.

In some cases the government may take over **direct provision** of essential goods and services, such as by **state enterprise** and through **nationalisation**. In recent years this has given way to **privatisation** and **Public Private Partnerships.**

Topic list	Learning outcomes	Syllabus references	Ability required
1 Methods of business integration	C3	C3(a)	Comprehension
2 Measures of market competition and concentration	C3	C3(a)	Comprehension
3 Effects of monopoly and collusive practices	C3	C3(b)	Comprehension
4 Competition policy	C3	C3(c)	Comprehension
5 Nature of externalities	C3	C3(d)	Comprehension
6 Government intervention in market to deal with externalities	C3	C3(e)	Comprehension
7 Government provision of goods and services	C3	C3(e)	Comprehension

1 Methods of business integration

FAST FORWARD

Firms seek to grow in order to improve their relationship with their owners and to achieve **economies of scale**. If there are significant economies of scale to be earned, there is a strong argument in favour of growth by firms. The two methods of growth are **organic** and by **mergers and acquisitions**. Growth may take the form of **vertical** or **horizontal integration** or **conglomerate diversification**.

1.1 Business integration

Key term

Business integration refers to the process by which two or more separate businesses combine to form a larger business entity.

1.1.1 Directions of business growth

In order to increase profits firms seek to increase sales revenues by selling more. The choices of **growth direction** open to a business is summarised in Figure 1. This is called the **Ansoff Growth Matrix** and is named after its author, Professor Igor Ansoff.

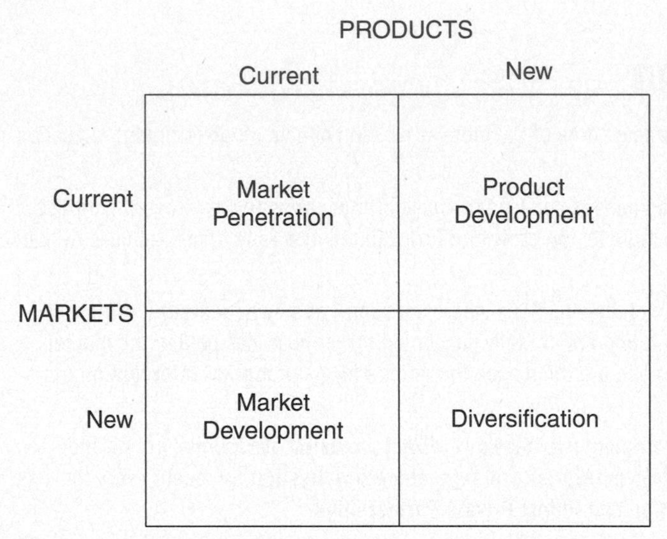

Figure 1: Ansoff Growth Matrix

The four quadrants in Figure 1 show four potential directions of growth for a firm.

(a) **Market penetration:** the firm seeks to sell greater quantities of is present range of products. This generally means it seeks to take market share away from rival firms

(b) **Product development:** the firm offers its existing customers a wider range of products by adding new product lines to its output

(c) **Market development:** the firm seeks new sorts of customers for its products by repositioning the product for different sorts or people, or by expanding into new geographical markets

(d) **Diversification:** the firm joins entirely new industries. Sometimes this may involve **vertical integration** in which the firm becomes its own supplier or customer, for example a film production studio launching its own television channel. This is also called **related diversification**. Sometimes firms will enter an entirely new industry, in which case this is called **unrelated diversification** of which an example might be an aeroplane manufacturer setting up an automobile manufacturer (as Saab did) or a musical instrument maker beginning to produce motorcycles (as Yamaha did).

Question

Directions of growth

Learning outcome: B3(a)

Using the Ansoff matrix, identify which directions of growth each of the following initiatives would be for a supermarket operator that presently sells just food and drink

(a) Opening supermarkets in a new country
(b) Buying a furniture retailer
(c) Launching a low-price promotion campaign
(d) Selling clothes in the supermarket
(e) Buying a firm that produces processed foods
(f) Opening additional stores in its home county

Answer

(a) This would be market development

(b) This would be diversification as the market and products have both changed

(c) This should increase sales and is therefore market penetration

(d) This is a new range and so is product development

(e) Here the supermarket has become its own supplier. Therefore this is diversification (or backward vertical integration)

(f) This is probably market penetration because it will increase sales. If the new stores are in a region of the country that the supermarket has not operated in before it would be market development.

1.1.2 Forms of growth

The possibility of achieving economics of scale through expansion should encourage firms to try to grow in size. There are two broad methods of obtaining growth.

(a) **Organic growth,** which is growth through a gradual build-up of the firm's own resources: developing new products, acquiring more plant and machinery, hiring extra labour, opening new stores, and so on. Organic growth is often a slow but steady process.

(b) **Growth through mergers and acquisitions,** which is the combination of two or more firms into one. An acquisition is often a **hostile form** of takeover, in which one business acquires ownership of another without the agreement or full approval of the target firm's directors. A **merger** is usually a **mutual agreement**, where the two firms agree to form a new company.

1.2 Mergers and acquisitions

Key terms

Acquisition: where one firm approaches the shareholders of another firm and buys their shares from them to gain control of the business and its assets.

Merger: where the shareholders of two or more firms agree to exchange their shares for shares in a new firm that have been set up to combine the activities of previously separate firms.

The nature of a merger or acquisition can be categorised according to which firms are coming together: are they in exactly the same line of business? Are they in very similar businesses? Are they in related businesses, but operating in different stages of the production and selling process? Are they in unrelated lines of business?

Key terms

Horizontal integration. When two firms in the same business merge, there is horizontal integration. Horizontal integration tends to create monopolies. For example, if The Chocolate Co with a 15% share of the chocolate market were to merge with Splendid Choc Co which has a 20% share of the market, the enlarged company might expect to hold a 35% share of the market.

Vertical integration. Two firms operating at different stages in the production and selling process might merge. When they do, vertical integration occurs. For example a company which operates exclusively in oil refining might take over an oil shipping company, and perhaps an oil extraction company too. This would be **backward vertical integration**, moving back through stages in production towards the raw material growing/extracting stage. The same company might take over a company with a distribution fleet of petrol tanker lorries, and perhaps a chain of petrol stations too. This would be **forward vertical integration**: integrating forward through stages in production and selling towards the end consumer sales stage.

Conglomerate diversification. A company might take over or merge with another company in a completely different business altogether. This form of merger is diversification, and a group of diversified companies is referred to as a conglomerate organisation.

The advantages and disadvantages of these different types of business expansion are summarised in the table below.

<table>
<tr><th colspan="2">Horizontal expansion or integration</th></tr>
<tr><td>Advantages
• Economies of scale from larger production quantities, ie lower costs.
– Technical economies (use of larger machines or more specialised machines)
– Managerial economies (greater specialisation of middle managers)
– Commercial economics (bulk buying and selling)
– Financial economies (ability to borrow money more cheaply)
– Risk-bearing economies (some greater spread of products made within the same general market should help the firm to spread its risks)
– Knowledge economies (consolidating research and development facilities to advance technical knowledge)
• To increase market share with the possibility of achieving monopoly greater control over prices and quantities in the market</td><td>Disadvantages
• Top management might be unable to handle the running of a large firm efficiently, ie there might be management diseconomies of scale.
• The creation of a monopoly will be unacceptable to government.</td></tr>
<tr><th colspan="2">Vertical integration</th></tr>
<tr><td>Advantages
• Gives the firm greater control over its sources of supply (backward vertical integration) or over its end markets (forward vertical integration).
– This should improve cost efficiency between the various stages of production, because there are no longer third parties trying to make a profit
– It should also increase the reliability of supplies (which is an important requirement for flexible manufacturing techniques)
• By increasing control over the sources of supplies and/or the sales and distribution network, a firm can increase barriers to entry stopping new entrants joining the industry.
• Achieves financial economies of scale and possibly some commercial economies. Otherwise few economies of scale unless production now becomes better co-ordinated through its various stages.</td><td>Disadvantages
• Possible management diseconomies of scale, owing to lack of familiarity with businesses acquired.</td></tr>
</table>

Diversification	
Advantages	**Disadvantages**
• Risks are spread by operating in several industries. If one industry declines, others may thrive. • Economies of scope by having a larger product range and possibly economies of scale in finance and administration. • Expertise can be shared across areas which would previously have been unconnected.	• No technical or commercial economies of scale. • Possible management diseconomies of scale, owing to lack of familiarity with businesses acquired.

2 Measures of market competition and concentration

2.1 Market concentration

FAST FORWARD

Market concentration describes the extent to which a market is controlled by a few large firms. It can be measured by a **concentration ratio**, which only considers a few firms, or by the **Herfindahl index** and the **Gini coefficient**, both of which consider them all. The Gini coefficient is supplementary to the Lorenz curve graphical depiction of concentration.

Very large suppliers are able to exert influence over market price. This is because they limit the availability of substitutes and therefore **reduce the price elasticity of demand**. Faced with a relatively price inelastic demand curve the firm then raises the price to increase revenue.

Monopoly describes the extreme case of this where there is a **sole supplier** of the product. But it is not necessary to achieve monopoly in order to exert significant market power.

Key terms

Market concentration is the extent to which supply to a market is provided by a small number of firms. **Industry concentration** is a similar concept, dealing with a complete industry (or group of related markets) rather than a single market.

The **degree of concentration in an industry**, and thus the potential for uncompetitive price-fixing, is of interest to both customers and suppliers and to government regulatory bodies.

2.2 Measuring market concentration

2.2.1 The market concentration ratio

A simple measure of concentration is the proportion of output (or employment, if that is easier to measure) accounted for by the largest producers: this is called the **concentration ratio**. Concentration ratios for single markets might be calculated for the top three, four or five producers.

In 2004 the Office for National Statistics (ONS) used a five-firm concentration ratio to calculate competition as follows

Most heavily concentrated industries (Five firm concentration ratio ranked by % of total industry value)	Least heavily concentrated industries (Five firm concentration ratio ranked by % of total industry value)
Sugar: 99%	Metal forging, pressing etc.: 4%
Tobacco products: 99%	Plastic products: 4%
Gas distribution: 82%	Furniture making: 5%
Oils and fats: 88%	Construction: 5%
Confectionery: 81%	Structural metal products: 6%
Man-made fibres: 79%	Wholesale distribution: 6%
Coal extraction: 79%	General purpose machinery: 8%
Soft drinks and mineral waters: 75%	Wood and wood products: 9%
Pesticides: 75%	
Weapons and ammunition: 77%	

2.2.2 The Herfindahl index

The **Herfindahl index** reflects the degree of concentration in an entire industry by including data **on all the firms in it**, rather than just that relating to a small number of large firms.

The construction of the index is based on **squaring the market share percentages** of all the firms in the market; the process of squaring tends to emphasise the position of the larger firms in the market. The squares are summed to find the index. The higher the index, the less competitive and more concentrated the market is.

2.2.3 Example: Herfindahl index

Consider two industries: both have forty small firms, each with one percent of the total turnover in its market. Market A also has four slightly larger firms that each have two percent of the market and a single very large firm that controls the remaining fifty two percent of turnover. Market B is completed by five large firms, each controlling twelve percent of the market. It is reasonably clear that Market A is likely to be much less competitive than Market B. Nevertheless, the two markets' five firm concentration ratios are identical, since in both markets the top five firms have sixty percent of the total turnover.

The Herfindahl indices for the two markets are calculated as below.

Index A = $52^2 + 4(2^2) + 40(1^2) = 2704 + 16 + 40 = 2{,}760$
Index B = $6(12^2) + 40(1^2) = 864 + 40 = 904$

The difference in size of the two indices reflects the degree of concentration in the two markets much more effectively than does the market concentration ratio. Market A has the higher index, and is likely to be the less competitive market because one firm controls 52% of turnover.

2.2.4 Regulation and the Herfindahl index

A Herfindahl index of zero indicates a perfectly competitive market in which there is a huge number of firms of equal size. An index of 10,000 indicates pure monopoly where all sales are under the control of one firm.

2.2.5 The Lorenz curve and Gini coefficient

The **Lorenz curve** and **Gini coefficient** may also be used to show market concentration.

2.2.6 The Lorenz curve

A Lorenz curve of market concentration would be drawn on a horizontal axis representing the cumulative percentage of the total number of firms in the industry or market, starting with the smallest, and a vertical axis showing the cumulative percentage of industry or market turnover attributable to the firms.

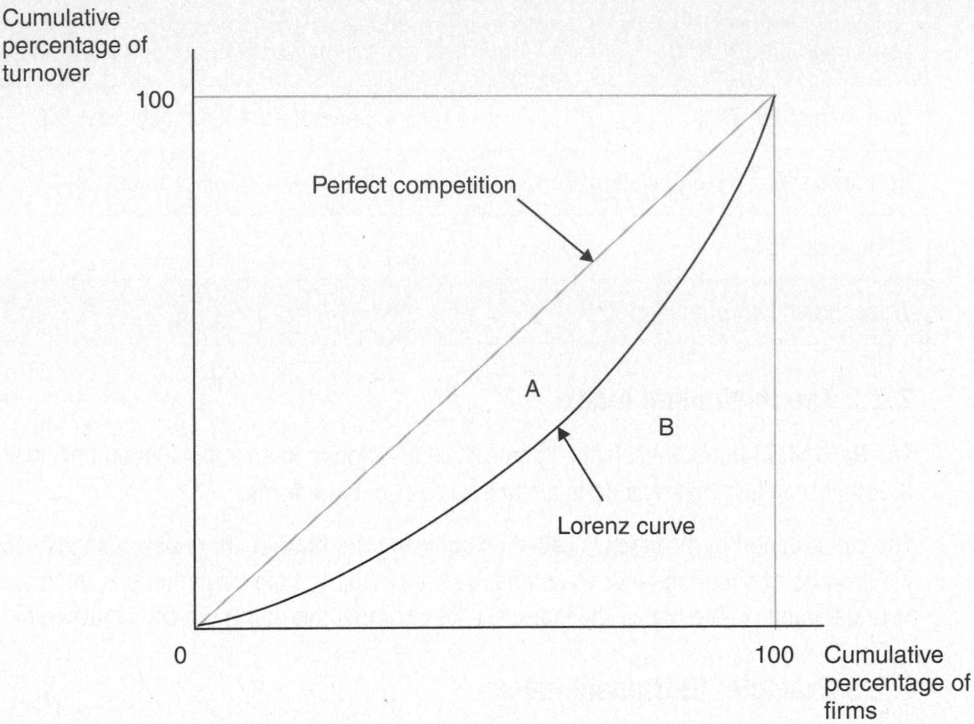

Figure 2 Lorenz curve

A straight line at forty five degrees from the origin would show a perfectly competitive market because it would indicate that cumulative market share increases at exactly the same rate as the cumulative number of firms, since all have the same turnover.

Lorenz curves typically display **increasing gradients** as the horizontal coefficient increases towards one hundred percent. This is because the smaller firms by definition, have less than an average share of the market. As the cumulative percentage increases, the larger firms come into consideration and when the firm with the exact average market share is reached, the gradient of the curve reaches forty five degrees. Larger firms are then included and since they have above average market shares, the gradient increases until the largest is reached.

2.2.7 The Gini coefficient

The construction of the Lorenz curve is such that the greater the area between the curve and the forty five degree line, the greater is the concentration in the market.

The **Gini coefficient** measures the deviation of the Lorenz curve from the forty five degree line. It is the ratio of the area between the curve and the forty five degree line to the whole area below the forty five degree line. In Figure 5, this is the ratio of area A to (area A + area B). The Gini coefficient of a **perfectly competitive** industry would thus be **zero**: that is to say, the Lorenz curve would not deviate from the forty five degree line, as explained above. The Gini coefficient of a pure **monopoly** would be **unity**: area B would disappear completely, since the Lorenz curve would run along the horizontal axis until the one hundred percent market share point was reached and then would rise vertically. Thus, any Gini coefficient will be between zero and one: **the higher it is, the greater the degree of market concentration**.

2.3 Problems with measures of market concentration

2.3.1 Defining the market

An important problem for all measures of market concentration is the way in which the market or industry is defined, since firms tend to **specialise**. A broad definition of a market might show limited concentration, but this might conceal a high degree of market power within specialised aspects of the market. Take, for example, the market for screwdrivers: this might show up as highly competitive, with several medium sized firms trading in it. However, closer inspection might reveal that one of these firms has specialised in very long screwdrivers and has achieved a near monopoly in supplying them.

2.3.2 New entrants

The entry of a new firm into a market should reduce concentration. However, it will not affect the concentration ratio unless it immediately seizes a significant market share and it may not affect either the Lorenz curve or the Gini coefficient.

3 Effects of monopolies and collusive practices

FAST FORWARD

Monopolies refer to markets where a sole supplier, or at least a very small number of firms, provide the product. It is believed that they will **exploit customers'** lack of substitutes by **pushing price up**.

Collusive practices occur when several firms in an industry **work together** to co-ordinate price and output to push prices up to increase their profits in a **cartel** arrangement.

3.1 Impact of monopoly on market price

FAST FORWARD

Monopolies can raise prices in a market by **restricting supply** below the level it would be if the market were instead supplied by a large number of competitive firms.

3.1.1 Conditions for effective monopoly

For a market to be characterised as a monopoly the following **three conditions** must be present:

(a) The market must be supplied by a **sole supplier**.
(b) The product must have **no close substitutes**
(c) There must be **barriers to entry** to prevent competitors joining the market.

These are the conditions necessary to enable the firm to exercise market power.

The maker of a branded soft drink, like Coca Cola, or a branded car, like Ford, could claim to be the sole supplier of the product. In practice this does not lead to monopoly power because there are other soft drinks and cars available.

Because monopolists use their market power to raise their profits this creates an incentive for other firms to join. The monopolist must have a way to stop this otherwise they will not be able to sustain high prices in the long run. These will be discussed in more detail later.

3.1.2 Impact of monopoly on price

Monopolists are said to be **price-makers.** This is because they face the entire market demand curve and if they can set price by how much they supply.

Figure 3 shows the effect of a monopoly on a market

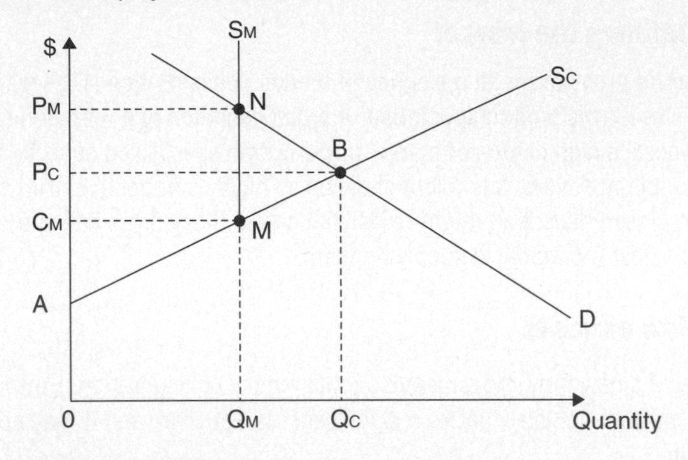

Figure 3 Impact of monopoly on market price

The easiest way to understand Figure 3 is to imagine an industry which moved from being competitive to being a monopoly by one firm buying up all the other firms through acquisitions.

When the market was **competitively supplied** the industry supply curve was S_C. The equilibrium market price settled at P_C and quantity Q_C was bought and sold.

The total profits enjoyed by the competitive industry are equivalent to the triangle ABP_C. This is because the supply curve is assumed to be the lowest price at which the firms would produce the product, ie where total revenue equals total cost. Therefore any price above the supply curve would yield a profit.

The **monopolist supplied** market has the supply curve SM and a market price of PM. Because it is a price-maker this may have been arrived at by the monopoly supplier in one of two ways:

(a) The monopoly decided to restrict output to QM, thereby causing a shortage that allowed price to rise up to PM; or

(b) The monopoly decided to set price at PM and to avoid a surplus it then restricted output to QM.

The price rises to P_M and the quantity consumed falls to Q_M.

The profits of the monopolist are shown by the area AMN P_M

This seems to suggest that markets served by monopolies may be less beneficial to society than markets served by competitive firms.

3.2 Arguments against monopolies

FAST FORWARD

It may be that monopolies encourage **complacency about costs** and may charge exploitative prices. Goals other than profit maximisation pursued in large companies could also result in **inefficiencies**.

Arguments against monopolies include the following.

(a) The profit-maximising output of a monopoly is at a point where **total market output is lower and prices are higher** than they would be under a more competitive market structure. This suggests that the owners of the monopolist are benefiting at the expense of society as a whole.

(b) **Monopolies do not use resources in the most efficient way possible.** Figure 3 shows that the monopoly restricts output below the level that it could make with its resources. Efficient producers seek to cut costs and use all the resources they have in order to stay profitable. A monopoly does not need to do this because they rely on higher prices to achieve their profits

(c) Because they are not threatened by competition and can earn supernormal profits, **monopolies might become slack about cost control**, so that they fail to achieve the lowest unit costs they ought to be capable of. They may also adopt a **complacent attitude to innovation** as it has less need to innovate than a firm operating in a more competitive market would have.

(d) Monopolies might **stifle competition**, by taking over smaller competitors who try to enter the market or by exploiting barriers to entry against other firms trying to enter the market.

(e) There might be **diseconomies of scale** in a large monopoly firm.

In a global competitive market a country may find that having key industries in the hands of monopolies can lead to a **loss of international competitiveness** for the reasons above.

3.3 Arguments in favour of monopolies

FAST FORWARD

Arguments to **support monopolies** usually focus on the ability of larger firms to enjoy **economies of scale** and **fund new products** than can smaller, competitive firms

Many countries operate **competition policies** and regulatory regimes to prevent monopolies being created, or to limit the power of those that do exist. Firms wishing to grow or be allowed to acquire others can use several arguments in defence of their size:

(a) A firm might need a monopoly share of the market if it is to achieve maximum economies of scale. Economies of scale mean lower unit costs. Therefore its can argue monopoly provides a better utilisation of resources. The consumer is likely to benefit from these cost efficiencies through lower prices from the monopoly supplier.

(b) Monopolies can afford to spend more investment and on research and development, and are able to exploit innovation and technological progress much better than small firms and they can safeguard the rewards of their risks through securing patent rights.

(c) Monopolies provide order to a market such as by promoting common technical standards for other industries to work with. This argument is often used in software and technology industries

(d) Monopolies need the cushion of high profits and assured sales to take on the risks of innovation and new lines of business

(e) The firm needs to be large to be able to compete with large global players in the same industry

(f) Monopolies may find it easier than small firms to raise new capital on the capital markets, and so they can finance new technology and new products. This may help a country's economy to grow.

3.4 Barriers to entry

FAST FORWARD

Monopolies may shelter behind **barriers to entry** such an unique products, exclusive licenses and economies of scale to **protect their long-run profits**

Key term

Barriers to entry: factors which make it difficult for suppliers to enter a market, and therefore allow supernormal profits to be maintained in the long run.

Barriers to entry can be classified into several groups.

(a) **Product differentiation barriers**. An existing monopolist would be able to exploit its position as supplier of an established product so that the consumer can be persuaded to believe it is a top quality product. A new entrant to the market would have to design a better product, or convince customers of the product's qualities, and this might involve spending substantial sums of money on research and development, advertising and sales promotion.

(b) **Exclusive control barriers**. These exist where an existing monopolist (or oligopolist) has access to, and exclusive control over, cheaper raw material sources or know-how that the new entrant would not have. This gives the existing monopolist an advantage because his input costs would be cheaper in absolute terms than those of a new entrant.

(c) **Economies of scale**. These exist where the long run average cost curve for firms in the market is downward sloping, and where the minimum level of production needed to achieve the greatest economies of scale is at a high level. New entrants to the market would have to be able to achieve a substantial market share before they could gain full advantage of potential scale economies, and so the existing monopolist would be able to produce its output more cheaply.

(d) The amount of **fixed costs** that a firm would have to sustain, regardless of its market share, could be a significant entry barrier.

(e) **Legal barriers**. These are barriers where a monopoly is fully or partially protected by law. For example, there are some legal monopolies (nationalised industries perhaps) and a company's products might be protected by patent (for example computer hardware or software).

(f) **Cartel agreements**. If firms work together and agree to co-operate rather than compete they can, in effect, form a monopoly. Such collusion can take the form of **price fixing**.

(g) **Geographical barriers**. In remote areas, the transport costs involved for a supplier to enter a market may prevent it from entering that market. For example, in the UK, local village shops have historically had a local monopoly, although the barriers to entry to such a market have been weakened by the growth of the internet and online shopping.

3.5 Collusive practices

FAST FORWARD

In industries with a **small number of firms** there have been cases of deliberate **collusion** in **price rings** or in **cartels** to allow the firms to act as if they were a monopoly.

In an industry each firm could increase its profits if all the firms together control prices and output as if the market were a monopoly, and split the output between them. This is known as **collusion.**

In most economies such **collusion is generally illegal** because it usually leads to higher prices and lower outputs than the free market equilibrium. However on a **global level they are more common** because of the lack of international laws under which to bring prosecutions against them.

A **price cartel** or **price ring** is created when a group of oligopoly firms combine to **agree** on a price at which they will sell their product to the market. The market might be willing to demand more of the product at a lower price, while the cartel attempts to impose a higher price (for higher unit profits) by restricting supply to the market.

Figure 4 shows that in a competitive market, with a market supply curve S_1 and demand curve D, the price would be P_1 and output Q_1. A cartel of producers might agree to fix the market price at P_2, higher than P_1. But to do so, the cartel must also agree to cut market supply from Q_1 to Q_2, and so fix the market supply curve at S_2.

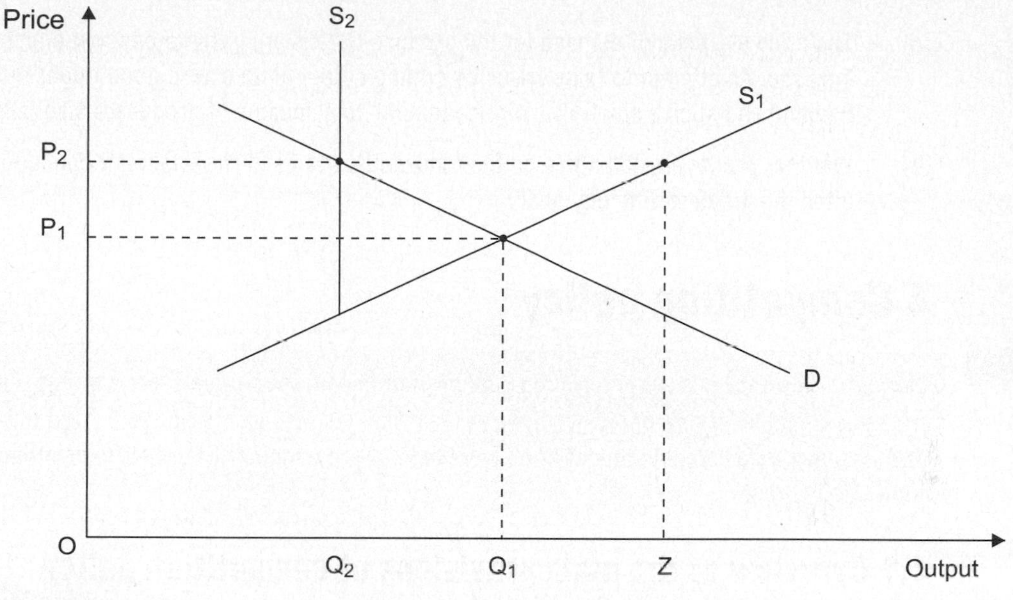

Figure 4 Price cartel

3.6 Establishing a cartel

FAST FORWARD

Effective cartels are ones that **control supply** to the industry and whose members can **agree on price** and the **sharing of available sales** between them.

Establishing a cartel depends on three things.

(a) The firms in the cartel must be able to **control supply** to the market.

(b) The firms must **agree on a price and on the output** each should produce

(c) There should be **barriers to entering the industry** against new suppliers

In Figure 4, if the market price is fixed at P_2, firms would want to supply output Z in a free market. This cannot be allowed to happen; otherwise market price P_2 could not be sustained.

The main **weakness** with cartels is that each firm is still seeking the best results for itself, and so there is an incentive for an individual firm to break the cartel agreement by secretly increasing its output and selling it at the fixed cartel price. However, if all firms increased their output in this way, the cartel would collapse because the high price could not be sustained without a restricted output, and excess supply on the market would force down the price.

This has been the common experience of the oil-producing countries of the Organisation of Petroleum Exporting Countries (OPEC). Attempts to agree on a restricted output quota for each country in order to push up oil prices have often broken down because some member countries exceeded their quota, or sold below the cartel's agreed price.

The **success** of a price cartel will depend on several factors.

(a) Whether it consists of most or all of the producers of the product.

(b) Whether or not there are close substitutes for the product. For example, a price cartel by taxi drivers might lead to a shift in demand for buses and trains, because these are possible substitutes for taxis.

(c) The ease with which supply can be regulated. In the case of primary commodities, such as wheat, rice, tea and coffee, total supply is dependent on weather conditions and even political events in the producing country.

(d) The price elasticity of demand for the product. Cartels are likely to be most effective for goods which are inelastic. An attempt to raise prices by cutting output of an elastic good might result in such a large a fall in demand and such a small rise in price that the total income of producers also falls.

(e) Whether producers can agree on their individual shares of the total restricted supply to the market. This is often the greatest difficulty of all.

4 Competition policy

FAST FORWARD

Competition policy is a set of legal regulations stemming from **competition law** that seeks to prevent firms from engaging in abuse of monopoly positions in their markets. It is also called **anti-trust law** (or trust-busting) in the USA because the shareholdings of firms were held in anonymous trusts that made it difficult to see who was controlling whom.

4.1 Overview of the main provisions of competition policy

Competition policy refers to the **enforcement of laws** against anti-competitive behaviour by firms. Governments, or regulators working on their behalf, apply to the courts to **levy fines** on firms that break these laws, or demand that the firms are **broken up** or that they **share their trade secrets** with others to promote competition. The policy may also **prevent mergers and acquisitions** that would create significant reductions in competition.

In some jurisdictions the **directors and officers** of a firm may be fined or jailed if it is found they participated in anti-competitive practices.

All competition policy starts from the assumption that large firms that are able to dominate a market are likely to be able to use their market power to the disadvantage of customers and the economy as a whole.

Because laws are **specific to countries**, such as USA, Japan, UK, or jurisdictions, such as the European Union, the approaches vary widely from place to place. Some attempts have been made to co-ordinate competition law through the **International Competition Network** established in 2001 as a co-ordination body for 107 of the World's main competition agencies.

FAST FORWARD

The main goals of competition policy are to **prohibit restrictive trade practices**, to **ban abuse of market power**, and to **regulate mergers and acquisitions**.

Most competition policy has three goals:

(a) **Prohibiting restrictive trade practices:** these are agreements between firms, or practices that restrict free trading and competition between business or exclude new entrants from the market. A particular target of this is cartels or attempts to rig the outcome of tenders, such as in construction or public services contracting

(b) **Banning abuse of position by market leading firms:** this includes the use of predatory pricing such as selling product at below production cost to bankrupt rivals, overcharging for products needed by rivals, or refusing to deal with rivals, such as in the supply of car parts to independent service stations

(c) **Supervising mergers and acquisitions:** using powers under the law to forbid consolidations where it would eliminate effective competition or, at least, demanding that some parts of the combined businesses be sold off to enable effective competition to continue.

4.2 The approaches to competition policy

FAST FORWARD

Approaches to competition policy vary between **rule-based** and **discretionary** approaches

Most approaches to competition policy fall on a spectrum between two broad approaches, **rule-based** and **discretionary**.

4.2.1 Rule-based approaches to competition policy

These start from the assumption that a dominant share of the market, in practice defined as 25%+, will lead to anti-competitive practices. The firm is presumed guilty unless it can demonstrate otherwise.

This approach was dominant in the USA following the passage of the Sherman and Clayton Acts in the late 19th and early 20th Centuries. This led to the break up of firms like Standard Oil and AT&T, and attempts to break up US Steel.

The problems with this approach are:

(a) **Narrow focus**: it is concerned only with the effect of the firm on the consumer market and overlooks other adverse effects such as exploitation of weak suppliers, labour, or local communities. It also fails to consider the broader national interest that might be served by having a larger firm.

(b) **Problems defining a market**: most firms provide more than one sort of product and operate in more than one region. A nationwide firm may have a large share of the overall car rental market in a country but actually be in second or third place behind local monopolies in each region.

(c) **Competitive disadvantage:** firms from a rule-based competition regime may be prevented from gaining the cost advantages of scale and research that are enjoyed by rivals from a discretionary regime. This was the argument used by the **Chicago School** in the USA that led federal government to modify its approach after late 1980's.

(d) **Burden on firms:** the presumption of guilt means that firms must pay the costs of proving that they are not abusing their position. This is expensive and encourages irresponsible attacks from regulators seeking political advantage or wishing to appear busy.

4.2.2 Discretionary approach

This approach accepts the broad argument that large firms are potentially harmful to competition but **judges each case on its effects** rather than on the size of the business.

Indicators that may be used to judge effects of market power include:

(a) **Relative prices**: if it can be shown that the large firm charges lower prices due to cost savings than would smaller firms it is likely to be allowed to continue

(b) **Profitability**: if the firm has very high rates of return on capital compared to the rest of the industry this may be seen as a sign of misuse of position

(c) **Quality of service**: this considers whether the firm is using market power to save costs by providing an inferior service

(d) **Stability**: in some markets the larger firms are more reliable suppliers than small firms

(e) **Impacts on suppliers and the community**: a large firm may be found to have exploited weak suppliers or abused its welcome in the community through pollution or unsightly buildings which are tolerated due to lack of an alternative employer

(f) **Public interest**: the broader contribution of the business to research, export earnings, support for the community and so on.

These criteria are sometimes referred to as **gateways** because they are gateways through which a firm may be permitted to merge or to escape from fines or directives.

The discretionary approach is more common in Europe. Generally the government will employ a regulator to whom it can refer firms or industries for investigation. For example in the UK the competition policy is overseen by the **Competition Commission** and the investigations passed over to be carried out by the **Office of Fair Trading** or specific **sector regulators** such as the Gas and Electricity Markets Authority.

The discretionary approach has a number of drawbacks:

(a) **Arbitrary**: firms are no longer clear on when they may be investigated because appearing to under perform on one of the criteria above may be sufficient to spark an investigation. For example in the UK the large supermarkets have submitted to several investigations in the past 10 years

(b) **Political interference**: although investigations may be independent the political climate and wishes of government may put weight put on issues such as public interest. There have been decisions in cross-media ownership and defence contracting that have attracted criticism on this basis.

5 The nature of externalities

Key terms

Market failure: the failure of a market to produce socially acceptable outcomes

Social costs: the total costs to society as a whole of using economic resources

Social benefits: the total gains to society as a whole flowing from an economic decision

Externalities: the differences between private and social costs

Public goods: goods which cannot be provided privately because if they are, everyone will benefit from them; regardless of whether they have paid for them or not. As a result, individuals would have no incentive to pay for these goods

Merit goods: goods which need to be provided in the long-term public interest.

5.1 Social costs and private costs

In a free market, suppliers and households make their output and buying decisions for their own private benefit. Private costs and private benefits therefore determine what goods are made and bought in a free market.

FAST FORWARD

Governments may seek to **regulate or intervene** where they feel that the social costs or benefits from an activity or product are **not properly taken into account** by the actions of the market on its own.

Private costs and benefits are not necessarily the same as the social costs and benefits from using the resources (ie the costs and benefits to society as a whole).

(a) **Private cost** measures the cost to the firm of the resources it uses to produce a good

(b) **Social cost** measures the cost to society as a whole of the resources that a firm uses

(c) **Private benefit** measures the benefit obtained directly by a supplier or by a consumer

(d) **Social benefit** measures the total benefit to society from a transaction.

For example, suppose a private firm pays to have its employees trained in health and safety procedures:

(a) Private cost is the cost of the train course and the output lost due to staff needing to attend the training

(b) Social cost would be the lost output from the firm and the pollution or disruption caused by the training and transporting the staff to where the training takes place

(c) Private benefit to the firm is the avoidance of costly claims for injury, fines and so on. The private benefit to the worker would be any extra pay they might get from being a health and safety officer

(d) Social benefit would the reduction in injuries at work, costs of hospital treatments and possibly the need to pay welfare benefits to families that have been affected by industrial accidents.

When private benefit is **not** the same as social benefit, or when private cost is **not** the same as social cost, an allocation of resources which only reflects private costs and benefits **may not be socially acceptable**.

Here are some examples of situations where **private cost** and **social cost** differ.

(a) A firm produces a good and, during the production process, pollution is discharged into the air. The private cost to the firm is the cost of the resources needed to make the good. The social cost consists of the private cost plus the additional 'costs' incurred by other members of society, who suffer from the pollution.

(b) The private cost of transporting goods by road is the cost to the haulage firm of the resources to provide the transport. The social cost of road haulage would consist of the private cost plus the cost of repairs and maintenance of the road system (which sustains serious damage from heavy goods vehicles) plus any environmental costs, such as harm to wildlife habitats from road building or pollution emitted by the transport lorry.

5.2 Private benefit and social benefit

Here are some examples of situations where **private benefit** and **social benefit** differ.

(a) Customers at an open air café benefit from the entertainment provided by professional musicians, who are hired by the café. The customers of the café are paying for the service in the prices they pay, and they obtain a private benefit from it. At the same time, other people passing by, who are not customers of the café, might stop and listen to the music. They will obtain a benefit, but at no cost to themselves. They are **free riders**, taking advantage of the service without contributing to its cost. The social benefit from the musicians' service is greater than the private benefit to the café's customers.

(b) Suppose that a large firm pays for the training of employees as accountants, expecting a certain proportion of these employees to leave the firm in search of a better job once they have qualified. The private benefits to the firm are the benefits of the training of those employees who continue to work for it. The total social benefit includes the enhanced economic output resulting from the training of those employees who go to work for other firms.

Question

Think of some situations other than those mentioned above in which private costs differ from social costs and private benefits differ from social benefits. How might these differences be prevented or compensated for in each situation?

5.3 Externalities

FAST FORWARD

Externalities occur when an exchange in a market **has impacts on other people** and society that go **beyond the costs and benefits** to the **original trading parties**

Key term

Externalities are the spill-over effects of a transaction which extend beyond the parties to the transaction and affect society as a whole. In other words, externalities are the differences between the **private** and the **social** costs, or benefits, arising from an activity.

An 'externality' is a cost or benefit which the market mechanism fails to take into account, because the market responds purely to private signals.

Demand and supply analysis can illustrate the consequences of externalities. If an adverse externality exists, (the social cost of supplying a good is greater than the private cost to the supplier firm), then a supply curve which reflects total social costs will be above the (private cost) market supply curve.

Figure 5 shows two possibilities.

(a) If a free market exists, the amount of the good produced will be determined by the interaction of demand (curve D) and supply curve S. Here, output would be Y, at price P_y

(b) If social costs are taken into account, and the market operated successfully, the supply curve should shift leftwards, and the amount of the good produced should be X, at price P_x.

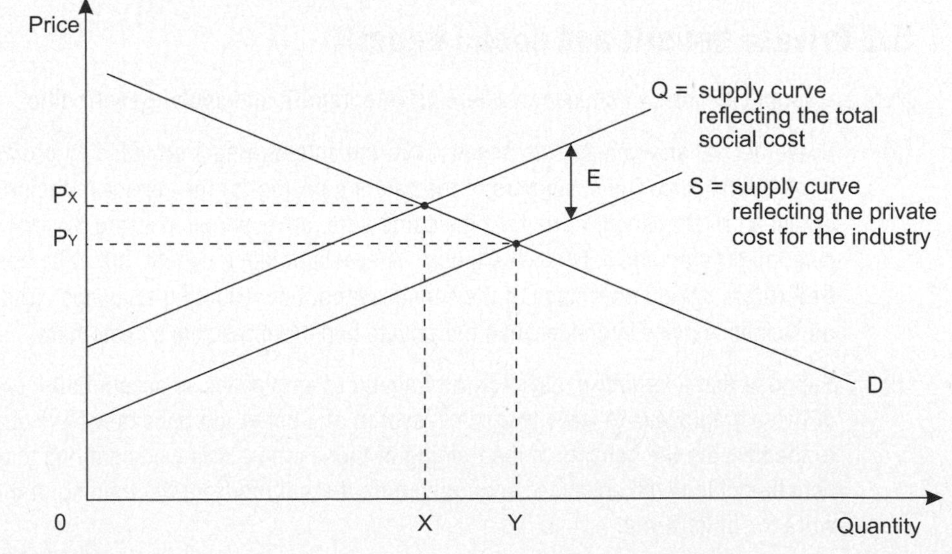

Figure 5 Externalities

Given a free market, output of the good will exceed what it ideally should be (by Y – X in Figure 5 above), and so resources will have been over-allocated to production of this particular good.

Externalities can be of four sorts:

(a) Positive externality in consumption: where the benefits of consumption extend beyond the original purchaser. For example a newspaper which is bought and read but then left in a public place for others to read.

(b) Positive externality in production: the production process generates benefits to people beyond those involved in the original buying and selling. For example farmers working the land for crops also provide an attractive landscape to walk through.

(c) Negative externality in consumption: occurs when the buyer's consumption of the product reduces the welfare of others. For example the noise from someone riding a large motorcycle through a quiet village

(d) Negative externality in production: the social costs of production exceed the private costs. For example the pollution falling on a town from a factory chimney.

5.4 Public goods

Key term

Public goods: goods which by their nature are hard to exclude the general public from enjoying without having voluntarily paid for them.

5.4.1 Conditions for public goods

The classic example of a public good is a **lighthouse.** The beam from a lighthouse has the **two conditions for a public good:**

(a) **Non- diminishable**(or non-rivalrous): the consumption of the good (or service) by one individual or group **does not significantly reduce the amount available for others**

(b) **Non-exclusive:** it is impossible to **exclude** anyone from its benefits, once the good has been provided.

If one shipping firm builds a lighthouse it is a benefit to all shipping.

Assessment focus point

Public goods are public in consumption, not public in production. The conditions for public goods are non-diminishability (or non-rivalrous) and non-exclusivity. Beware of questions that suggest they are provided by the public sector, or that they are free to everyone.

Other examples of public goods include street-lighting, public gardens, defence and police services, and roads.

5.4.2 The free-rider problem

Because the good is **non-exclusive** individuals can benefit from the good without paying for it.

This means that unless non-payers can be compelled to pay, or can be excluded from consuming the good, there would be no economic incentive for firms to make the good because they would get no revenue.

This has been overcome in practice by:

(a) **Compulsory payment:** this includes licenses to use roads and televisions, or compulsory payment through taxation for defence and police services

(b) **Exclusion on non-payers:** the use of smart cards to allow decoding of satellite television broadcasts, or pay gates on websites

(c) **Public provision:** the government may choose to provide the service direct and levy a charge from the population via taxation

5.5 Merit and demerit goods

FAST FORWARD

Merit goods are things that **society benefits** from a market producing. However the market may **under produce** these.

Key terms

Merit goods are considered to be worth providing to everyone irrespective of whether everyone can afford to pay for them, because their consumption is in the long-term public interest. Education is one of the chief examples of a merit good.

Demerit goods are goods that create social harm in their production or consumption

5.5.1 Merit goods

There is a danger that merit goods would be **under-consumed** if left to a market mechanism. For example education is a merit good because it permits society to enjoy a higher level of culture, arts and discoveries.

However a family might decide to pay to provide its children with the minimum level of education needed to read and write and get a job because there would be no financial justification for paying more.

Therefore the government will encourage consumption of merit goods by:

(a) Providing the service free to the user, such as state schooling

(b) Providing subsidy payments to firms willing to provide the service, such as tax reduction and grants to firms which provide training

(c) Make consumption of the service compulsory, such as a minimum school leaving age and fining of parent that do not send their children to school.

5.5.2 Demerit goods

Demerit goods are 'social bads' which governments may wish to discourage.

For example many governments want to see less consumption of certain demerit goods, such as tobacco, liquor and high fuel consumption cars. The methods used are:

(a) Prohibitions on production and marketing of the the product
(b) Taxation levied on the product to deter demand by making it more expensive to buy
(c) Subsidisation and publicity for preferable alternative products

Question — **Pollution**

An industrial company alters its production methods to reduce the amount of waste discharged from its factory into the local river. What will be the effect (increase or decrease) on:

(a) Private costs
(b) External benefits

Answer

(a) Private costs of the company will presumably increase: the anti-pollution measures will have involved a financial outlay.

(b) External benefits will presumably increase: the public will benefit from a cleaner river.

5.6 Pollution policy

One area often discussed in relation to externalities is that of pollution. Pollution can occur in the production chain or during the consumption process.

For example a car creates pollution during the making of its components, during its assembly, whilst it is being driven and finally once the car is dumped at the end of its life cycle.

The reason for products polluting arise from the fact that the social costs of the product exceed the private costs. For example the price paid for a car doesn't take into account the social costs of the pollution and resource depletion created during its manufacture and, ultimately, its disposal. The price paid to drive the car doesn't take account of the exhaust pollution, noise and congestion it causes.

Polluter pays policies are designed to make the persons responsible for the pollution to pay the costs of it. This creates an incentive to minimise the amount of pollution they cause and perhaps to reduce consumption of the good.

Examples of polluter pays charges are:

(a) Tradable permits to pollute: factories are given permits to produce a certain volume of emissions, say carbon dioxide gas, each year. They can buy additional ones. A firm that invests in clean technologies can sell its unused permits to other firms for money and so pay for its investment

(b) Charges for dumping waste product: these are often based on the amount of potentially disposable materials that are in the product and are called 'landfill taxes'. They encourage the firms to recycle where possible and to cut down the amount of waste they generate, for example by reducing the packaging in the goods they sell.

(c) Fines for breaching regulations: governments may set minimum limits for recyclable or recoverable materials in a product, or require that firm prove they have used the most environmentally friendly technology. The government levy charges and fines when they discover firms have not done what they were expected to do.

6 Government intervention in market to deal with externalities

FAST FORWARD

Demand and supply analysis can be used to examine the effects on a market of imposing an **indirect tax** or a **subsidy** to influence the consumption or production of goods with externalities

6.1 Indirect taxes

Key term

Indirect taxes are levied on expenditure on goods or services as opposed to direct taxation which is applied to incomes. A **selective** indirect tax is imposed on some goods but not on others (or is imposed at a higher rate on some goods than on others).

Indirect taxation may be used to improve the **allocation of resources** when there are damaging externalities.

If an indirect tax is imposed on a good, the tax will shift the supply curve **upwards** (leftwards) by the amount the tax adds to the price of each item. This is because although the price to **consumers** includes the tax, the revenue the suppliers receive is only the **net-of-tax price**. For example, in Figure 6:

- The supply curve without any tax is S_0
- The supply curve including the cost of the tax is S_1
- The tax is equal to $P_1 - P_2$ or the distance A – B.

Before the tax was imposed, quantity supplied and demanded was X_0, but once the tax has been imposed, the equilibrium quantity is only X_1.

At this point (demand = X_1), the price the **consumer pays** is P_1, but the amount that the **supplier receives** is only P_2.

$P_1 - P_2$ is the amount of tax payable.

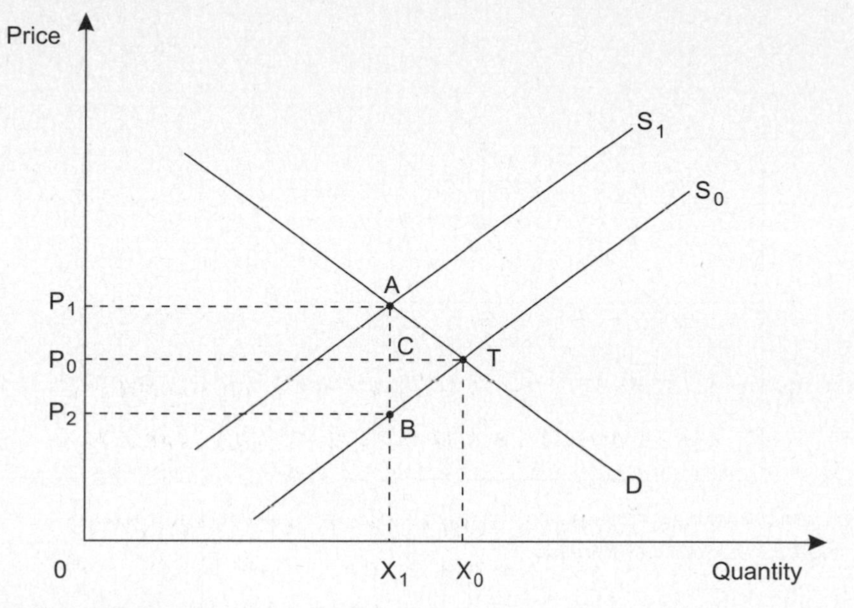

Figure 6 The effect of an indirect tax

Without the tax, output would be X_0 and price P_0. Total expenditure (before the tax was imposed) can be shown by the rectangle OP_0TX_0.

(a) After the tax has been imposed, output falls to X_1 and price with tax rises to P_1. Total expenditure is OP_1AX_1, of which P_2P_1AB is tax revenue and OP_2BX_1 is producers' total revenue.

(b) A new price equilibrium arises at point A.

(i) Price to the customer has risen from P_0 to P_1.

(ii) Average revenue received by producers has fallen from P_0 to P_2.

(iii) The tax burden is **shared** between the producers and consumers, with CB borne by the supplier and AC borne by consumers.

Consumers pay P_0P_1AC of total tax revenue and producers pay P_2P_0CB.

There is less of this product being produced and also the government has the tax revenue to help it clear up the bad effects.

6.2 Elasticity effects

FAST FORWARD

The **incidence** of a tax or subsidy refers to who pays it or receives it. This **depends on the price elasticities** of demand and supply.

The proportion of the tax which is passed on to the consumer rather than being borne by the supplier depends upon the elasticities of demand and supply in the market.

Figures 7(a) and 7(b) illustrate the extreme cases of perfectly elastic demand and perfectly inelastic demand respectively.

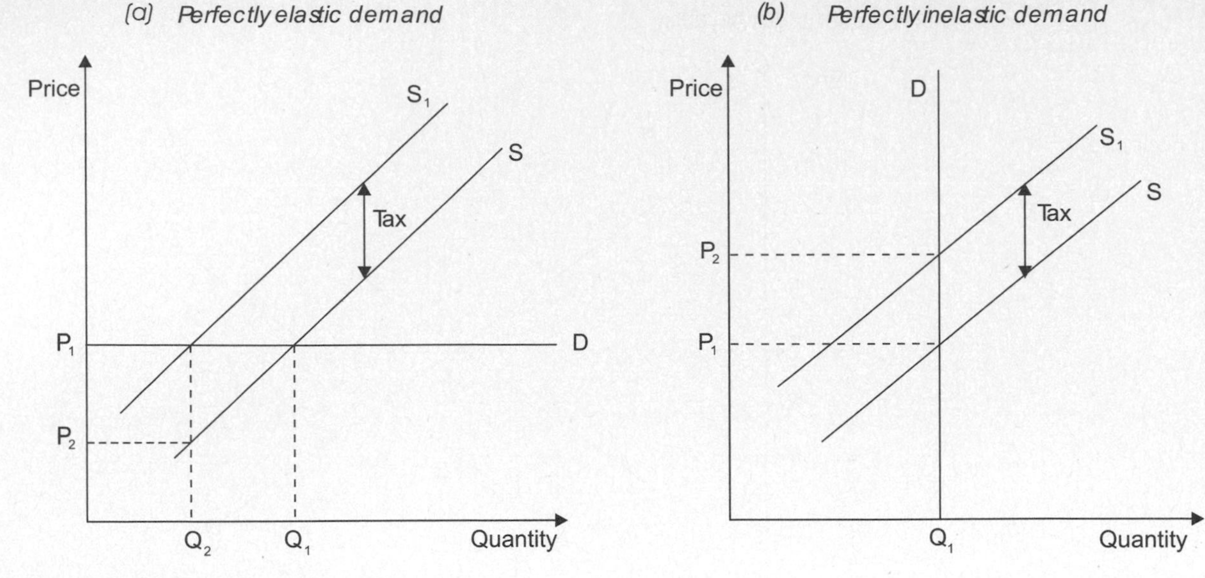

Figure 7 Elasticity of demand

Question

Burden of taxation

Try to work out yourself (from general principles, or from study of Figure 7) who bears the burden of taxation in each of these extreme cases.

Answer

In Figure 7(a), with perfectly elastic demand, demand falls to zero if the price is raised. Consequently, the supplier must bear the full burden of the tax. In spite of the imposition of the tax, the market price remains the same but there is a fall in the quantity supplied from Q_1 to Q_2. The supplier only receives P_2 after paying $P_1 - P_2$ in tax.

In the case of perfectly inelastic demand (Figure 7(b)), the supplier can pass on the full amount of the tax to the consumer by increasing the price from P_1 to P_2. Demand is not reduced at all by the increase in price. Because the supplier can charge a higher amount to compensate for the tax payable, the quantity supplied remains unchanged.

The elasticity of supply is also relevant. Figure 8 shows that for a given demand curve, the more inelastic the supply curve, the greater the proportion of the tax that is borne by the supplier.

(a) Figure 8(a) shows a relatively inelastic supply curve (S). Imposition of the tax shifts the supply curve vertically upwards to S_1 and the equilibrium price rises from P_1 to P_2. The price to the consumer rises by AB per unit, while the supply price to the producer falls by BC per unit. Thus, the greater burden is borne by the supplier (because the distance BC is greater than the distance AB).

(b) By contrast, Figure 8(b) shows a relatively elastic supply curve S. With the imposition of the tax, the supply curve shifts to S_1 and the equilibrium price rises to P_2. The price to the consumer rises by AB per unit, and the supply price to the producer falls by BC per unit. The greater burden is borne by the consumer (because AB is greater than BC).

So, Figure 8 shows that the consumer bears a greater proportion of the tax burden the more elastic is the supply curve. Figure 8 also shows that, for any given demand curve, the price rise and the fall in the equilibrium quantity will also both be greater when the supply curve is elastic than when it is inelastic.

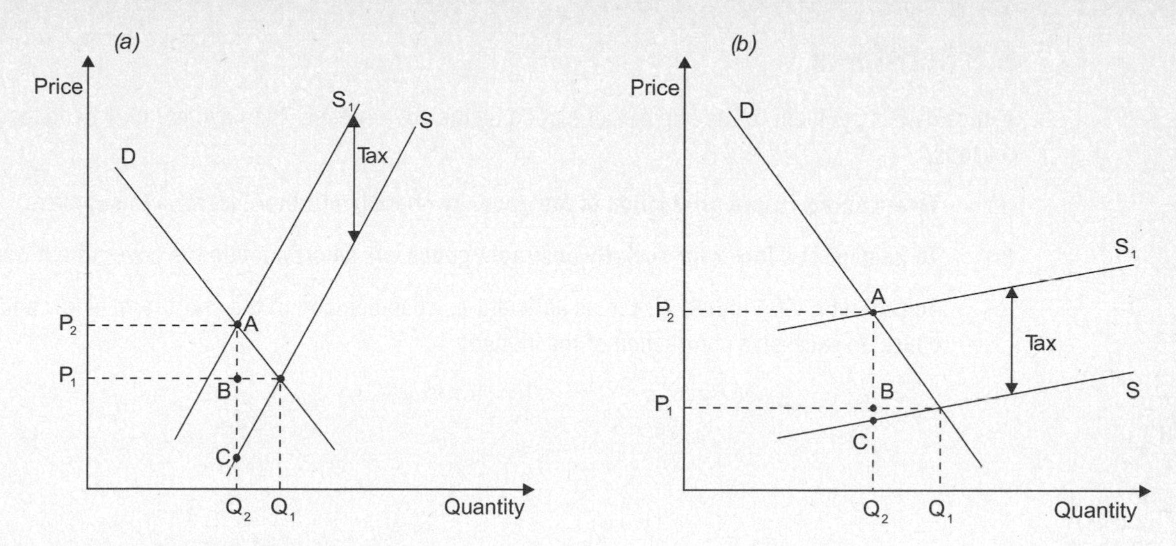

Figure 8 The effect of elasticity illustrated

It is also important to consider the relationship between the elasticity of demand and the elasticity of supply when assessing how the burden of tax will be split between producer and consumer.

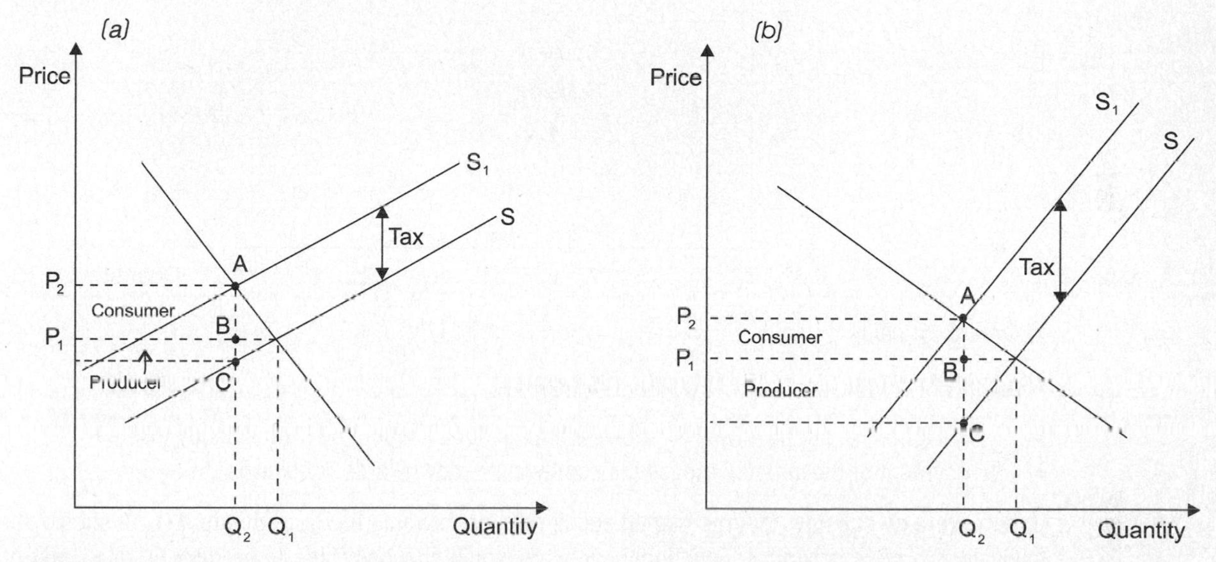

Figure 9 (a) Inelastic demand, elastic supply

Figure 9 (b) Elastic demand, inelastic supply

Figure 9: The effect of the relative elasticities of supply and demand

If demand is less elastic than supply – Figure 9(a) – the consumer will bear the greater proportion of the tax burden.

If demand is more elastic than supply – Figure 9(b) – the producer will bear the greater proportion of the tax burden.

Assessment focus point

Make sure you know how the relative elasticities of supply and demand affect the way the burden of tax is distributed between producers and consumers.

6.3 Subsidies

A subsidy is a payment to the supplier of a good by the government. The payment may be made for a variety of reasons.

(a) **To encourage more production of the good**, by offering a further incentive to suppliers

(b) **To keep prices lower for socially desirable goods** whose production the government wishes to encourage

(c) **To protect a vital industry** such as agriculture, when demand in the short term is low and threatening to cause an excessive contraction of the industry.

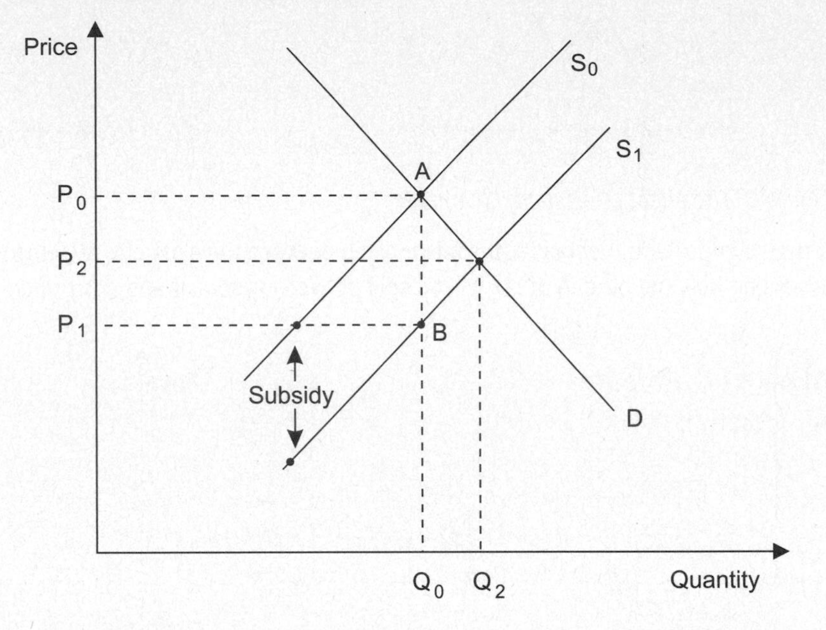

Figure 10 Subsidy

A subsidy is rather like indirect taxation in reverse.

- In Figure 10, supply curve S_0 shows what the supply would be if no subsidy existed.
- Payment of the subsidy moves the supply curve downwards (outwards) to S_1.

If there were no subsidy, the free market equilibrium price would be P_0, and output Q_0. A subsidy per unit equivalent to AB is introduced, such that suppliers would now be willing to produce Q_0 at a lower price (P_1 rather than at P_0). In other words, the supply curve shifts outwards from S_0 to S_1. As a result, there will be a shift in the equilibrium quantity produced to Q_2, which can be sold on the market for P_2. Thus, the subsidy will have two effects.

- The amount supplied in equilibrium will increase (from Q_0 to Q_2).
- The price will fall (from P_0 to P_2), but the decrease in price will be less than the value of the subsidy itself ($P_0 - P_1$).

Question — **Subsidy**

By reference to Figure 10, analyse the extent to which the benefit of the subsidy falls to:

(a) The consumer
(b) The supplier

Who bears the cost of the subsidy?

Answer

The benefit of the subsidy will be shared between the consumer and the supplier.

(a) Consumers benefit by the lowering of prices from P_0 to P_2.

(b) Suppliers benefit because although they receive a lower price, P_2, they receive the subsidy AB per unit.

The cost of the subsidy is borne by the **government** (in effect, the taxpayer).

7 Government provision of goods and services

FAST FORWARD

The **state can provide services** and good by using government **departments**, setting up **state enterprises**, or by **nationalising** existing private businesses.

7.1 State provision and state ownership of production

7.1.1 Methods of public provision

The state may undertake direct responsibility for provision of a service in a number of ways:

(a) **Government department or agency**: in most countries services such as police, and defence are provided by the state. In some countries other services such as education and environmental services such as refuse collection and street cleaning are provided the same way. These are paid for from taxation.

(b) **State enterprise**: a separate business is created, owned by the state, and which sells the product on the market with the aim to break-even rather than make a profit. This commonly includes energy, telecommunications and postal services.

Nationalisation: the state decides to buy up previously private businesses and to run them as a state enterprise.

7.1.2 Arguments for public provision

The arguments used to justify state provision of a product or service include:

(a) To **regulate a monopoly**: the private monopoly would exploit customers and be inefficient whereas the state will run it to break even and with the interests of the society in mind

(b) To **ensure necessary investment** takes place: where the industry is essential to the growth of the country the state will invest in it providing the state also gets all the benefits

(c) Greater **efficiency and co-ordination**: the large state owed operation will enjoy better co-ordination and greater economies of scale than would lots of competing small firms

(d) To **stabilise a sinking business**: where the private firms would otherwise go bankrupt the state may take them over to avoid this. Many banks were nationalised or taken under government control in the global banking crisis of 2007 to 2010.

(e) To **assure the provision of a key service**: the government will not cease production if profits fall

(f) To **accommodate externalities** better: the state will take these into account better because it is focused on social goals and not just profit

(g) To allow the **population to share the benefits**: this is often the justification for nationalisation of primary industries like oil and mining where the assets are felt to belong to the people

(h) Ethically and **morally superior**: effectively the political argument that the state is a better judge than private firms of what society needs, and will be fairer in how it distributes output

7.1.3 Reasons for decline of public provision

Attitudes to public provision vary widely between countries and to a large extent reflect the political and social history of the respective countries. In general there seems to be a trend away from widespread state provision due to:

(a) **Lack of available funding**: state provision requires government taxation and borrowing to finance it. In recent years many governments have sought lower taxation and to restrict their borrowing to avoid crowding-out private enterprise and initiative

(b) **Political meddling**: some industries have suffered as the government of the day use them for other purposes such as to soak up unemployment, or provide services that have low demand

(c) **Poor efficiency**: without a motive to control costs or to meet demand some state provided services seemed to gather levels of administration and planning that soaked-up resources without adding significant value to the operation

(d) **Failures in planning**: in practice it proved very difficult to plan and manage such large organisations and this led to diseconomies of scale

(e) **International treaties**: many countries signed up to free trade agreements and received funding from organisations like the World Trade Organisation and parts of the World Bank. A condition of this membership and funding was the abandonment of state enterprise which, the donor countries argued, was holding back the development of these economies

7.2 Privatisation and denationalisation

FAST FORWARD

Privatisation has been a response to some of the **difficulties of funding** state enterprises and also an attempt to **improve efficiency**

Key term

Privatisation is the transfer by government of state owned activities to the private sector.

Privatisation as originally envisaged takes three broad forms.

(a) The **deregulation of industries**, to allow private firms to compete against state owned businesses where they were not allowed to compete before (for example, deregulation of public transportation, postal services, telecommunications and so on).

(b) **Contracting out** work to private firms, where the work was previously done in-house by government employees – for example, computer services, health care, refuse collection

(c) **Transferring the ownership of assets** from the state to private shareholders or to other forms of organisation, for example mining and energy assets, manufacturing plants, rail infrastructure

7.3 For and against privatisation generally

The following are **possible advantages of privatisation**.

(a) Privatised firms may be **more efficient** than state monopolies and private sector managers are likely to try to reduce costs and strip out unproductive labour. Private firms may also provide **better quality** because they will have to compete to survive. The threat of competition may also lead to innovation.

(b) Denationalisation provides an immediate **source of money** for the government, through the sale of assets or businesses.

(c) Privatisation **reduces bureaucratic and political meddling** in the industries concerned.

(d) Privatised companies may have a **more flexible** and **profit-oriented management culture**.

(e) There is a view that **wider share ownership** should be encouraged. If workers and the general population own shares in their company, they are more likely to want it to be successful.

There are arguments against privatisation too.

(a) State owned industries are more likely to respond to the **public interest**, ahead of the profit motive. For example, state owned industries are more likely to cross-subsidise unprofitable operations from profitable ones.

(b) Encouraging private competition to state-run industries might be inadvisable where **significant economies of scale** can be achieved by monopoly operations.

(c) Government can **provide capital more cheaply** than the market to industries whose earning potential is low, but which are deemed to be of strategic importance, such as aircraft manufacture.

(d) State-owned industries can be run in a way that **protects employment.** The problem with this is that the taxpayer is effectively **subsidising technical inefficiency**.

(e) Surpluses from state-run industries can be used for **public welfare** rather than private wealth. However, the problem here is that points (a) and (d) above tend to preclude the creation of surpluses.

7.4 Criticisms of privatisation

There are also a number of criticisms of privatisation in practice.

(a) Critics argue that privatisation **has not enhanced competition**, and in some cases it has merely transferred a public monopoly to a **private monopoly**

(b) **Quality of service has diminished** where privately owned companies have tried to cut costs on services previously provided centrally

(c) The assets sold by governments have been **undervalued** and this allowed private investors to make large capital gains by acquiring the assets

(d) In some industry sectors, privatisation has been **selective**, and only the profitable parts of the sector have been sold off. This means the unprofitable areas remain in the public sector, and are a drain on public funds

(e) Top executives of privatised companies have been granted very **large salaries and share options**, which looks insensitive in the context of trying to improve employee efficiency and competitiveness.

Question

Can you identify three possible benefits of privatisation?

Answer

Any three of:

- Improved efficiency of production in privatised companies
- Reduces bureaucracy and political interference in the industries concerned, so producers have greater economic freedom
- Private companies have a more profit-oriented management culture
- Encourages wider share ownership

7.5 Public Private Partnerships (PPP)

FAST FORWARD

Public Private Partnerships (PPP) are a **compromise** between the **benefits of state provision** and the need to **private sector funding and efficiency**.

7.5.1 Nature of a PPP

Public Private Partnerships (PPP) have become increasingly common throughout the World from their UK origins in the 1990's as the **Private Finance Initiative** (PFI).

The government enlists private sector **capital** and **management expertise** to provide public services at reduced cost to the public sector budget. The capital aspect of the scheme has been particularly welcome to government as it allows for expansion of public services **without an increase in taxes or government borrowing.**

A typical PPP contract involves a consortium of private companies which undertake to design, finance, build and manage a facility such as a school, hospital, road, airport or rail network over a long term contract, typically 30 years. The consortium accepts the **risk** of the project and takes its **returns** in the form of **periodic fees**. Because they usually involve the provision of services, PPP contracts tend to be very complex in order to ensure that performance standards are rigorously defined.

7.5.2 Perceived advantages of PPP

(a) Government is able to finance improved provision of goods and services for the public without increasing its borrowing.

(b) Risks are transferred to the private sector.

(c) Private sector qualities of efficiency and innovation are brought into the public sector.

7.5.3 Criticisms of PPP

(a) Public projects will be more expensive because a private company cannot borrow as cheaply as the government.

(b) There is often no real transfer of risk, as the government will be forced to support projects that suffer financial failure, or bail out the private companies which are managing them.

(c) Cost savings have been made to the detriment of quality of service.

Chapter roundup

- **Firms** seek to grow in order to improve their relationship with their owners and to achieve **economies of scale**. If there are significant economies of scale to be earned, there is a strong argument in favour of growth by firms. The two methods of growth are **organic** and by **mergers and acquisitions**. Growth may take the form of **vertical** or **horizontal integration** or **conglomerate diversification**.
- Market concentration describes the extent to which a market is controlled by a few large firms. It can be measured by a **concentration ratio**, which only considers a few firms, or by the **Herfindahl index** and the **Gini coefficient**, both of which consider them all. The Gini coefficient is supplementary to the Lorenz curve graphical depiction of concentration.
- **Monopolies** refer to markets where a sole supplier, or at least a very small number of firms, provide the product. It is believed that they will **exploit customers'** lack of substitutes by **pushing price up**.
- **Collusive practices** occur when several firms in an industry **work together** to co-ordinate price and output to push prices up to increase their profits in a **cartel** arrangement.
- **Monopolies** can raise prices in a market by **restricting supply** below the level it would be if the market were instead supplied by a large number of competitive firms.
- It may be that monopolies encourage **complacency about costs** and may charge exploitative prices. Goals other than profit maximisation pursued in large companies could also result in **inefficiencies**.
- Arguments to **support monopolies** usually focus on the ability of larger firms to enjoy **economies of scale** and **fund new products** than can smaller, competitive firms
- Monopolies may shelter behind **barriers to entry** such an unique products, exclusive licenses and economies of scale to **protect their long-run profits**
- In industries with a **small number of firms** there have been cases of deliberate **collusion** in **price rings** or in **cartels** to allow the firms to act as if they were a monopoly.
- **Effective cartels** are ones that **control supply** to the industry and whose members can **agree on price** and the **sharing of available sales** between them.
- **Competition policy** is a set of legal regulations stemming from **competition law** that seeks to prevent firms from engaging in abuse of monopoly positions in their markets. It is also called **anti-trust law** (or trust-busting) in the USA because the shareholdings of firms were held in anonymous trusts that made it difficult to see who was controlling whom.
- The main goals of competition policy are to **prohibit restrictive trade practices**, to **ban abuse of market power**, and to **regulate mergers and acquisitions**.
- **Approaches to competition policy** vary between **rule-based** and **discretionary** approaches
- Governments may seek to **regulate or intervene** where they feel that the social costs or benefits from an activity or product are **not properly taken into account** by the actions of the market on its own.
- **Externalities** occur when an exchange in a market **has impacts on other people** and society that go **beyond the costs and benefits** to the **original trading parties**
- **Merit goods** are things that **society benefits** from a market producing. However the market may **under produce** these

- **Demand and supply analysis** can be used to examine the effects on a market of imposing an **indirect tax** or a **subsidy** to influence the consumption or production of goods with externalities
- The **incidence** of a tax or subsidy refers to who pays it or receives it. This **depends on the price elasticities** of demand and supply.
- The **state can provide services** and good by using government **departments**, setting up **state enterprises**, or by **nationalising** existing private businesses.
- **Privatisation** has been a response to some of the **difficulties of funding** state enterprises and also an attempt to **improve efficiency**
- **Public Private Partnerships (PPP)** are a **compromise** between the **benefits of state provision** and the need to **private sector funding and efficiency**.

Quick quiz

1 Which of the following describes diversification by a firm?

A The firm is making new products for its current customers
B The firm is finding new markets for its current products
C The firm is exploring new industries
D The firm is increasing its share of its current market

2 What is an externality?

3 List the various forms of government intervention in markets.

4 Which of the following are imperfections in a market?

1 Consumer brand loyalty to a firm's branded goods, regardless of price;
2 The lack of completely accurate information for consumers about all goods and services available;
3 The slow response of firms to price changes and the relatively inelastic supply of a good in the short run.

A Items 1 and 2 only
B Items 2 and 3 only
C Items 1 and 3 only
D Items 1, 2 and 3

5 Which of the following are weaknesses of a completely free market?

1 It only reflects private costs and private benefits;
2 It may lead to serious inequalities in the distribution of income and wealth;
3 It may lead to production inefficiencies and a wastage of resources.

A 1 and 2 only
B 2 and 3 only
C 1 and 3 only
D 1, 2 and 3

6 Muddy Waters Co is an industrial company which has altered its production methods so that it has reduced the amount of waste discharged from its factory into the local river. Which of the following is most likely to be reduced?

A Total private costs
B Social costs
C External benefit
D Variable costs

7 Much Wapping is a small town where a municipal swimming pool and sports centre have just been built by a private firm, Builder Co. Which of the following is an external benefit of the project?

A The increased trade of local shops
B The increased traffic in the neighbourhood
C The increased profits for the sports firm
D The increased building on previous open land

8 The government has just increased the tax on tobacco. Assuming that the demand for cigarettes is completely inelastic, who pays the tax?

A It is shared between supplier and consumer in proportions equal to the relative prices before and after the increase.

B The supplier

C The consumer

D It is shared between supplier and consumer in proportions equal to the relative quantities sold before and after the increase.

9 Which of the following statements is *always* true if an indirect tax is imposed on a good or service:

A The price will rise by an amount equal to the tax
B The producer will bear more of the tax than the consumer
C The price rise will be smaller the greater the price elasticity of demand is
D The price rise will be greater the greater the price elasticity of demand is

Quick quiz answers

1 C The best way to approach this was to recognise that the remaining three statements described the remaining three quadrants in Ansoff's matrix. Therefore the rather vague 'new industries' was bound to be the right answer.

2 An externality is an effect caused by an economic transaction which extends beyond the parties to the transaction.

3 Controlling the means of production
Legal regulation of products and prices
Indirect taxation
Subsidies
Redistributing income via taxation and welfare payments

4 D Brand loyalty can make consumers pay more for a good, without getting any greater total satisfaction from consuming it. Lack of information to consumers will result in 'bad' purchasing decisions. The slowness to price changes is a further market imperfection.

5 D The need to limit or avoid these weaknesses is the chief argument in favour of some government involvement in the allocation of economic resources – ie in favour of a mixed economy or even a command economy.

6 B Social cost is the sum of the private cost to a firm *plus* the external cost to society as a whole. Here, social cost is the sum of production costs (private costs) plus the cost of pollution (external cost). The firm's private costs might have been increased by the measures to reduce pollution, but the external costs will have fallen, so that total social costs should have fallen too.

7 A This is correct because the benefits to local shops are additional to the private benefits of the sports firm and as such are external benefits.

B is an external *cost* of the project, since increased volumes of traffic are harmful to the environment.

C is a private benefit for the firm.

D would only be an external benefit if a building is better for society than the use of open land, which is unlikely.

8 C As the consumer's consumption is not altered by the price rise, the supplier can pass the price rise on in full.

9 C The price rise will be lower for products with a higher price elasticity of demand. In the extreme case, if demand is perfectly elastic, there will be no increase in the price at all.

Option A would be true if the good or service had a perfectly inelastic demand, but that is the only condition under which it would be true. Equally, Option B would be true if demand was relatively more elastic than supply, but it will not always be true.

Now try the questions below from the Exam Question Bank

Question numbers
32 - 38

Part B
The financial system

Financial systems 1 – functions of the financial system

9

Introduction

So far in this Text we have concentrated on the way businesses, consumers, and governments operate in particular markets. However, we will now turn to look at how financial system and institutions help meet the financial needs of these businesses and consumers.

A national economy depends on a vast network of economic relationships. Among the most important are those that facilitate the flow of value between households, firms and governments. This chapter looks as the financial needs of these units.

The role of **financial intermediaries** such as banks in an economy is to provide the means by which funds can be transferred from **surplus units** in the economy to **deficit units**. Financial intermediaries develop the facilities and **financial instruments** which make lending and borrowing possible

Topic list	Learning outcomes	Syllabus references	Ability required
1 Finance for households	D1	D1(a)	Comprehension
2 Finance for firms	D1	D1(a)	Comprehension
3 Finance for government	D1	D1(a)	Comprehension
4 Roles and functions of financial intermediaries	D2	D2(a)	Comprehension

1 Finance for households

FAST FORWARD

Within an economy, some people, firms and organisations will have money which is surplus to their needs, and others will have less money than they need for their spending requirements. **Credit** involves lending money, and the transfer (usually in return for interest payments) of money from surplus units to deficit units. **Financial intermediaries**, such as banks, make the provision of credit much easier, by taking deposits from savers and re-lending to borrowers.

1.1 The flow of funds

The flow of funds is the movement of money between people or institutions in the economic system.

If we begin by ignoring imports and exports and foreign investments, we can start to build up a picture of the flow of funds by identifying three main sectors in the economy that make payments and receipts.

(a) Households and individuals or the **personal sector**

(b) Firms or the **business sector** – ie companies and other businesses

(c) Governmental organisations or the **government sector** – ie central government, local government and public corporations

Within each of these three sectors, there is a continual movement of funds, payments and receipts on a short-term, medium and long-term basis.

1.2 The need for financial intermediation

In a barter economy, income and expenditure are simultaneous because they are two sides of the same transaction. However, in a money-based economy, a flow of income no longer has to be the same as a flow of expenditure, and they do not have to occur at the same time either.

This means that individuals, businesses and governments can all have cash inflows which are not the same as their cash outflows in any given time period. In other words, there can be a **lack of synchronisation between receipts and payments**. This applies equally to the short, medium and long term, although the nature of the receipts and payments will vary according to the time period involved.

An important consequence of this is that in any one period there will be net **savers** (whose inflows exceeds their expenditures) and net **borrowers** (who have expenditures which exceed incomes).

As a result, market economies need to have effective mechanisms to enable the surplus funds of net savers to be transferred to the net borrowers in a way which is appropriate to their requirements.

This is the rationale for the **financial intermediaries** (such as banks) who provide the link which enables money to be transferred from savers to borrowers. This transfer process is known as **financial intermediation**.

1.3 Households

FAST FORWARD

Households suffer a **lack of synchronisation** in a year between **monthly pay cheques** and **continuous expenditure** and some **peak spending** on holidays, celebrations and unexpected repairs. Over the **lifetime** of the individual there are periods of **earning** and periods of **home buying** and of **retirement** that also require **financial planning** to cope with them.

Households and individuals receive income from employment, savings and investments, and social security and pensions. They will need to use these to finance both their short term needs for food, shelter and clothing and also their longer term needs such as buying a house or buying a car.

However, the timings of the inflows are unlikely to match the expenditures. Therefore households will need to develop ways of dealing with this lack of synchronisation.

They can do this in a number of ways.

Time Frame	Ways to deal with lack of synchronisation
Short term (routine transactions)	• Retain cash in hand to meet day-to-day expenditure needs • Use short term credit functions, such as credit cards and bank overdrafts • Make savings in periods of net surplus (when receipts exceed payments) in order to finance periods of net deficit
Medium term (infrequent purchases of more expensive items, such as cars or holidays)	• Save over a period of time prior to expenditure, for example using a deposit account at a bank • Borrow money to fund the purchase and then repay over a period of time, for example through taking out a bank loan, or through hire purchase or lease finance arrangements.
Long term (for example, buying a house, or retirement planning)	• Need very long-term financial instruments, for example mortgages or pension funds • Mortgages are loans used to acquire an asset, typically a property. The asset is conveyed to the lender as security for the loan and ownership only passes to the buyer once the mortgage is repaid in full.

In all of the time frames, the households use financial intermediaries to provide the facilities they need to match their income with their expenditure.

2 Finance for firms

FAST FORWARD

The financial needs of firms can be separated into needs for **short term working capital** and needs for **longer term investment finance**. Firms will use **retained earnings**, **equity** and **debt** to provide it with finance.

2.1 Flow of funds in business

Businesses, like households, will find that flows of payments and receipts rarely match.

A business will have **receipts** from several sources, which might include sales, investment income and proceeds from the disposal of non-current assets.

A firm's **outlays** include the need to finance working capital, pay wages and salaries, rent and utility bills. For its medium and long term needs the company will need to purchase assets such as premises, machinery and equipment.

In order to achieve profit and function as a going concern, most companies will need funding over and above the contribution by shareholders.

The need for finance for firms arises for two reasons.

(a) **Short term working capital needs:** production takes place before products are sold. A firm has to finance production (labour, raw material, inventory) before any receipts accrue and therefore needs funds in the form of working capital in order to operate. This type of finance is a bridging type and is short term

(b) **Long term investment capital needs:** a firm to need funds is for investment purposes. Like individuals, businesses that need to expand or replace their plant and equipment may need funds far in excess of the income that the company earns from its activities. These types of funds are typically long-term.

2.2 Sources of finance for firms

FAST FORWARD

Businesses have **three main sources** of long-term finance: **equity capital** (through issuing shares), **internally generated funds** (retained profits), and **debt capital** (such as bank loans and corporate bonds)

New capital enables the firm to expand its activities and achieve the advantages of large-scale production.

2.2.1 The matching concept

Credit may be short-term, medium-term or long-term. The **length of credit ought to match the life of the assets** they finance, and should not exceed the asset's life.

(a) The amount of short-term credit taken by a firm should be limited by considerations of liquidity. The firm must have the cash to pay creditors on time, and so short-term credit should not become excessive in relation to current assets, which are short-term sources of cash.

(b) The amount of long-term credit is effectively measured by the **capital gearing ratio**, the ratio of debt to total capital funds which should remain at an acceptable level to avoid the shareholders sacrificing too much of their earnings to the interest demands of lenders.

2.2.2 Principal sources of short-term capital

(a) **Credit agreements** allow businesses to borrow money for the immediate purchase of goods or services and to pay for them over an extended period of time. These agreements take a variety of forms including bank loans, overdraft facilities, credit card, trade credit, hire purchase and lease finance.

(b) **Bank overdrafts** are a short-term facility which allow businesses to borrow money up to an agreed limit. The bank will charge interest on the amount overdrawn, but the overdraft can be a valuable means of overcoming a short-term cash flow problem or working capital shortage.

(c) **Bills of exchange** are a means of one business providing credit to another business for a short period, usually for 3 months. The lender makes up the bill for a specified sum payable at a future date and the borrower accepts the bill by signing it. Once the loan has been made there may be secondary trading in the bill, that is the loan will be sold on to a third party. The bill will be bought from the drawer at a discount form the face value of the loan, this discount representing an interest charge on the amount owed.

(d) **Commercial Paper** Banks and companies with good credit ratings raise funds by issuing unsecured promissory bearer notes that can be interest-bearing or discounted. These notes usually have short lives of up to 270 days.

(e) **Retained cash**. A business can also solve the short term mismatch of payments and receipts (the cash flow problem) by retaining a reserve of cash in its bank accounts to use in periods where expenditure exceeds income.

2.2.3 Principal sources of long-term capital

(a) **Issued share capital**. Share capital might be in the form of ordinary shares (**equity**) or preference shares. Bear in mind that only the ordinary shareholders are owners of the company, and preference shares are comparatively rare.

(b) **Retained profits and other reserves**. Retained profits are profits that have been kept within the company, rather than paid out to shareholders as dividends. These provide a source of **internally generated funds**.

(c) **Borrowing and long-term loans**. Companies borrow from banks and from private or institutional investors. Investors might purchase debt securities issued by the company. The company promises to repay the debt at a date in the future, and until then, pays the investors interest on the debt. **Debt capital** includes debentures and, for larger companies, eurobonds and commercial paper.

Debentures and other loan stock are **long-term loans**, the terms of which are set out in a debenture trust deed. Debentures issued by large companies are traded on the stock market.

Bonds are financial securities issued by government or businesses to provide them with long-term borrowing. The bonds bear a fixed nominal (or coupon) rate of interest. The market in secondary dealings for bonds involves selling the bonds at various prices in order to keep the effective interest rate in line with current interest rates. **Eurobonds** are bonds sold outside the jurisdiction of the country in whose currency the bond is denominated.

(d) **Venture capital (private equity)**. Venture capitalists are prepared to finance risky ventures such as start ups. Because they accept a high degree of risk (with many of their ventures producing little or no return) they require a very high return from the ones that do succeed. They also require a clear exit route that allows them to realise their capital, such as a public flotation issue of shares.

(e) **Mezzanine finance:** this in effect, combines aspects of both debt and equity finance. Although the financing is initially given as a loan (debt capital), the lender has the rights to convert to an equity interest in the company if the loan is not paid back in time and in full.

2.2.4 Difficulties in raising finance

Despite the existence of various capital markets and money markets, it is not necessarily easy for firms to raise new capital, except by drawing on retained profits. Small firms in particular find it difficult to attract investors without surrendering a measure of **control**, with the banks remaining the major source of funds for such companies. The capital markets are dominated by institutional investors who have tended to channel their funds into safe investments such as 'blue chip' stocks and shares which are traded on the major stock markets (such as the London Stock Exchange or the New York stock exchange), as well as government securities. The venture capital providers take a more adventurous approach, although it should be noted that some of the venture capital organisations have been set up by the large institutional investors.

3 Finance for government

FAST FORWARD

Governments have a **fiscal budget** consisting of **taxation** and other revenues to balance against **government spending** on capital items, employing staff, and welfare payments. They often undertake **government borrowing** in the short and long terms to provide sufficient funds.

3.1 Government payments and receipts

3.1.1 Government payments

Governments need to spend money on a number of outlays of a current or long term nature. These can be analysed into the following categories:

(a) **Government purchases of goods and services**

Short term: Expenditure on current goods and services such as:

(i) Salaries of government employees
(ii) Repairs, maintenance of public buildings
(iii) Payments for goods and services needed to carry on daily government activities (eg heat and light)

Medium and long term: Investment on infrastructure such as building roads, schools and hospitals.

(b) **Transfer payments**

These are payments made for which the government received no goods or services in return. Examples include:

(i) Unemployment and welfare payments
(ii) Other social security payments
(iii) State pension

3.1.2 Government receipts

To pay for expenditure governments collect revenues, mainly taxes. There are four main types of government revenues.

(a) **Taxes on income and capital gains**

(i) Taxes paid by individuals (income tax)
(ii) Taxes paid by companies such as corporation tax

(b) **Indirect taxes on expenditure** or **sales taxes** whereby consumers pay a tax on their consumption of goods and services. Sales taxes are **excise duties** on tobacco, alcohol and petrol and **value added tax**.

(c) **Social security contributions**

These are payments by the employer and firm to provide for state health care and pensions. They are a fixed percentage of a worker's salary up to a certain ceiling and they are matched by contributions from the employer (national insurance contributions).

(d) **Other revenues**

One of the main elements of this category is income from government enterprises and also from its investments in other businesses.

3.2 Matching government payments and receipts

FAST FORWARD

Government borrowing may be **short term**, to deal with **timing mismatches** between receiving tax payments periodically and making payments monthly, or , **longer term** such as when the government needs to finance a **military engagement** or is trying to **stimulate the economy** during a recession.

Governments, like households and businesses, find that their payments are not synchronised with their receipts. Receipts from tax can be very uneven during a year, but social security payments to unemployed people are required regularly throughout the year.

Governments may also have to spend more in some years than others, for example, an increase in government spending may be required to boost demand in the economy during a recession. In such cases, it is also likely that government spending will increase while government receipts from taxation are decreasing.

Therefore governments also have to find ways of dealing with the problem of synchronisation.

Time Frame	Consequence
Short term (Social security payments and pensions; payment of wages and salaries to government employees; payments to providers of routine goods and services).	• If expenditure exceeds revenue, government needs short term credit, which is usually provided by the **central bank**. • One of the central bank's functions is to act as banker to government.
Medium term (public sector investment activities, such as construction of schools, hospitals or roads)	• Governments may allocate more funds to one year rather than another as part of their fiscal policy to manage economic growth. In this case, government spending is likely to be counter-cyclical with the economic cycle, and will be highest in those years when tax revenues are lowest. • Governments may run **budget deficits**, to be funded by borrowing from the private sector. • Governments can raise funds by **issuing bonds** and securities.
Long term (investment projects to develop infrastructure)	• Governments can continue to borrow in the long term provided there is sufficient taxation revenue to fund the resulting debt. • Amounts borrowed through budget deficits aggregate to form the **national debt**. • In practice, the national debt will never be entirely repaid.

3.3 Government deficits/surpluses

Key terms

> A **fiscal year** is the period over which the government revises its revenue and expenditure plans

Government expenditure is very unlikely to be equal to government revenues in each \b, and so a government is likely to have either a budget surplus or a budget deficit.

When revenues exceed outlays there is a **budget surplus**. When outlays exceed revenues there is a **budget deficit**.

The deficit can therefore be represented as

Budget deficit = government expenditures – government revenues

= government purchases (P) + transfers (TR) + net interest (INT) – government revenues (T)

= $P + TR + INT - T$

When governments spend more than they raise in taxes and therefore incur a budget deficit, they have to borrow.

FAST FORWARD

> The **main instruments** of government borrowing are short-dated **Treasury Bills** or longer dated **Treasury Bonds**.

Governments borrow by issuing debt. This debt is of two forms

(a) **Treasury Bills**: short term promissory notes, usually for 90 days, that promise the pay the holder a set amount on their **maturity.** To give the buyer a profit on their loan to the government they are sold at a **discount** to their maturity value.

(b) **Treasury Bonds**: these promissory notes can be short term (less than a year), medium or long term (15 years +) and they offer the holder a set payment every year until they mature, called the **coupon rate.** In the UK, government bonds are referred to as gilt edged securities.

3.3.1 Government deficit and government debt

It is important to understand the distinction between government deficit and government debt.

The government **deficit** represents the excess of government spending over government revenues in any one period. As such, the government deficit is a flow concept, just like the profit and loss is a flow concept in the financial statements of a company.

In any one year, the budget deficit represents the amount of **new borrowing** that the government must undertake.

Government **debt** is the accumulation of government deficits over time and represents all the debt issued to fund the deficits. Since deficits by governments are funded by issuing government bonds, government debt is the total outstanding amount of bonds presently in issue.

4 Role and functions of financial intermediaries

4.1 The flow of funds

We discuss now how **surplus units** are able to transfer surplus funds to **deficit units**, and how the deficit units can raise the requisite funds.

There are two ways in which the transfer of funds takes place. First, there is the direct way, in which economic units transact directly in an organised market. There are many markets that cater for all the needs of the economic units in terms of maturity or currency. A schematic approach of the flow of funds is shown as

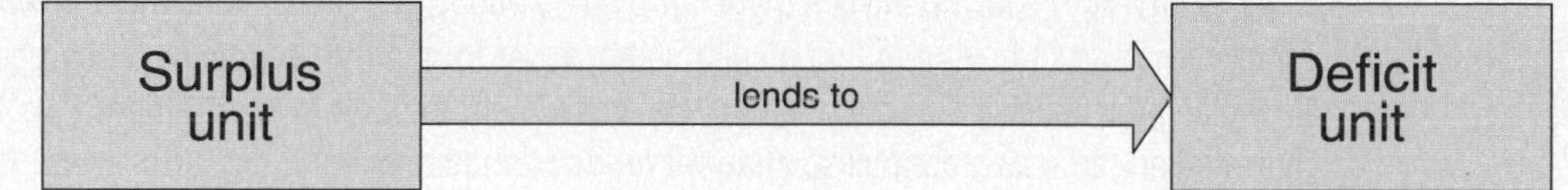

The second way of bringing together surplus and deficit units is through a **financial intermediary**. The intermediary provides a service to both the surplus unit and the deficit unit, by accepting surplus funds and making these funds available to a deficit unit.

The main advantage of financial intermediation is that it provides a way of channelling funds for large and small economic units. For example, a person might deposit savings with a bank, and the bank might use its collective deposits of savings to provide a loan to a company.

The two methods of channelling funds are shown schematically below.

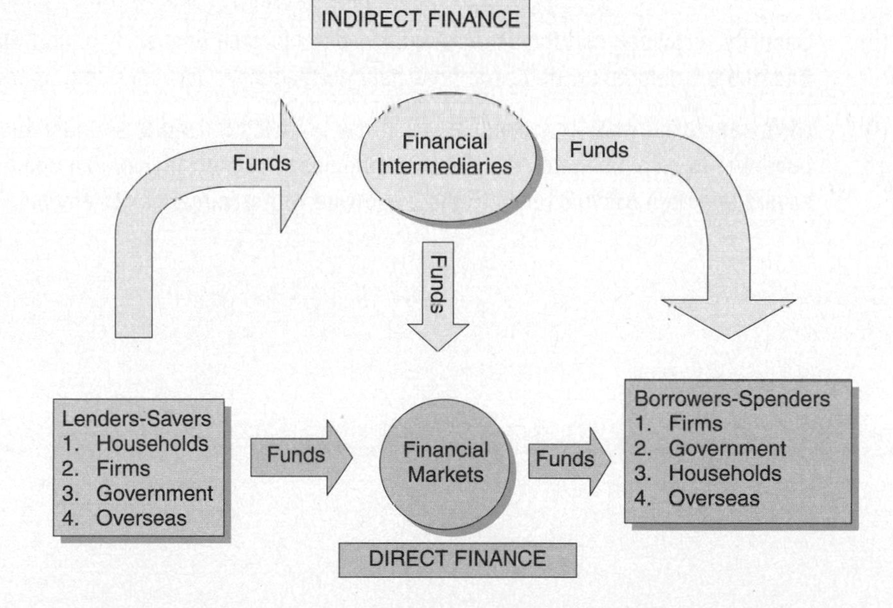

Figure 1 Flow of funds in an open economy, showing the role of financial intermediation

In the next sections we shall discuss the main financial intermediaries and financial markets in the financial system.

4.2 Financial intermediaries

FAST FORWARD

Financial intermediaries are institutions which channel funds from savers to borrowers

Financial intermediaries are institutions which channel funds from savers to borrowers. In doing so, the intermediaries provide a link between savers and borrowers, meaning that individual savers and borrowers do not have to make individual arrangements between themselves.

4.3 Advantages of financial intermediaries

(a) **Ease of saving**. Financial intermediaries provide obvious and convenient ways in which a saver can **save money**. Instead of having to find a suitable borrower for his money, the saver can deposit his money with a financial intermediary that offers a financial instrument to suit his requirements. So the financial intermediary acts as a conduit to **channel funds** from net savers to net borrowers. It also pays interest on the savings so the saver earns a return on his money.

(b) **Provide liquidity:** they are a **ready source of funds for borrowers**. Even when money is in short supply, a borrower will usually find a financial intermediary prepared to lend some. Intermediaries are an efficient, and often cost-effective, source of money for borrowers.

(c) **Aggregation**. They can package up the amounts lent by savers and lend on to borrowers in bigger amounts. Without aggregation, a borrower would either have to find a lender who is prepared to lend the amount he wants to borrow, or else would need to use a number of different lenders in order to raise the amount of funds he wants to borrow.

(d) **Maturity transformation**. Financial intermediaries bridge the gap between the wish of most lenders for liquidity and the desire of most borrowers for loans over longer periods. They do this by providing investors with financial instruments which are liquid enough for the investors' needs and by providing funds to borrowers in a different longer term form (for example, mortgages).

(e) **Security.** Provided that the financial intermediary is itself financially sound, **the lender's capital is secure**. Bad debts would be borne by the financial intermediary in its re-lending operations.

(f) **Risk transformation**. An individual saver may not wish to lend to an individual borrower, considering that borrower to be a bad debt risk. However, the financial intermediary can borrow from a number of different savers and then provide funds to the borrowers with minimal risk to any single saver.

Chapter roundup

- Within an economy, some people, firms and organisations will have money which is surplus to their needs, and others will have less money than they need for their spending requirements. **Credit** involves lending money, and the transfer (usually in return for interest payments) of money from surplus units to deficit units. **Financial intermediaries**, such as banks, make the provision of credit much easier, by taking deposits from savers and re-lending to borrowers.
- Households suffer a **lack of synchronisation** in a year between **monthly pay cheques** and **continuous expenditure** and some **peak spending** on holidays, celebrations and unexpected repairs. Over the **lifetime** of the individual there are periods of **earning** and periods of **home buying** and of **retirement** that also require **financial planning** to cope with them.
- The financial needs of firms can be separated into needs for **short term working capital** and needs for **longer term investment finance**. Firms will use **retained earnings**, **equity** and **debt** to provide it with finance.
- Businesses have **three main sources** of long-term finance: **equity capital** (through issuing shares), **internally generated funds** (retained profits), and **debt capital** (such as bank loans and corporate bonds)
- Governments have a **fiscal budget** consisting of **taxation** and other revenues to balance against **government spending** on capital items, employing staff, and welfare payments. They often undertake **government borrowing** in the short and long terms to provide sufficient funds.
- **Government borrowing** may be **short term**, to deal with **timing mismatches** between receiving tax payments periodically and making payments monthly, or , **longer term** such as when the government needs to finance a **military engagement** or is trying to **stimulate the economy** during a recession.
- The **main instruments** of government borrowing are short-dated **Treasury Bills** or longer dated **Treasury Bonds**.
- **Financial intermediaries** are institutions which channel funds from savers to borrowers

Quick quiz

1 What is a financial intermediary?

2 Which of the following means of borrowing is *unlikely* to be used by a household

3 A Equities
B A mortgage agreement
C A loan agreement
D A credit card

3 List the main sources of credit available to businesses.

4 What is meant by the 'matching concept'?

A That borrowing and lending should be at the same rate of interest
B The process by which banks introduce lenders to borrowers
C Ensuring loans and repayments are in the same currency
D Ensuring that the length of credit is similar to the life of the asset being bought with it

5 What is meant by 'maturity transformation'?

6 What is a government budget surplus ?

7 A person receives their salary on the 1st day of the month and aims to spend the last part of it on the last day of the month. What term describes this person for all but the last day of the month?.

8 The functions of commercial financial intermediaries include all the following except:

A Maturity transformation
B Reduction of transactions costs
C Aggregation
D Issuing of government debt

Answers to quick quiz

1 A financial intermediary is any organisation that stands between borrowers and lenders and facilitates transactions

2 A Equities are issued by firms. Incorporation means that even a family-owned business is legally distinct from the household and therefore it is the business, not the household, that issues the shares.

3 D

4 Short term credit may be had in the form of overdraft, trade credit and the issue of bills of exchange. Medium term credit often takes the form of term loans from banks, hire purchase and finance leases. Longer term credit may be obtained by issuing debentures and mortgages.

5 Maturity transformation describes the way financial intermediaries bridge the gap between lenders' desire for liquidity and borrowers' desires for loans over longer periods.

6 A government budget surplus is where the revenues of the government over a year are greater than its expenditure.

7 They are a surplus unit for all but the last day of the month, assuming no borrowings elsewhere.

8 D Issuing of government debt is the role of a central bank.

Now try the questions below from the Exam Question Bank

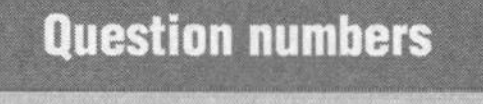

Question numbers
39 - 44

BPP
LEARNING MEDIA

10

Financial systems 2 – domestic institutions and markets

Introduction

In this chapter, we look more closely at several issues. First, we discuss the **role of the banks** in the **financial system** and in particular how they create **credit** and provide **liquidity**. Secondly we discuss the structure of **yields** of the various instruments that trade in the financial markets . Next we discuss the role of the **central bank**, and how it influences the functioning of the financial system. Finally we consider how this system came close to collapse in the **global banking crisis** that began in 2007.

The areas are intertwined because the monetary policy of a government, operated through its central bank, influences the behaviour of banks by influencing their credit creation activities, and affects the level and structure of financial yields by setting short run interest rates. As both banks and financial markets are the major sources through which firms and individuals raise capital, the **central bank** can have a potent **impact on the financial markets** and the **real economy**. The influence on the real economy became evident when the global banking crisis lead to a **credit crunch** that tipped most countries in the World into a **recession**.

Topic list	Learning outcomes	Syllabus references	Ability required
1 Commercial banks and credit creation	D2	D2 (b)	Comprehension
2 Yield on financial instruments	D2	D2 (b)	Comprehension
3 Role of central banks	D2	D2 (c)	Comprehension
4 Influence of central banks over financial markets	D2	D2 (b)	Comprehension
5 The global banking crisis	D2	D2 (d)	Comprehension

1 Commercial banks and credit creation

FAST FORWARD

Commercial banks can be separated into clearing banks, retail banks, and investment banks.

1.1 The banks and the banking system

Banks are major financial intermediaries in a financial system. There are different types of bank:

(a) **Clearing banks** operate the clearing system for settling payments (eg payments by cheque by bank customers).

(b) The terms **retail banks** or **commercial banks** are used to describe the traditional 'High Street' banks, such as HSBC and Barclays. The term **wholesale banks** refers to banks which specialise in lending in large quantities to major customers.

(c) **Investment banks** (which used to be referred to as **merchant banks**) offer services, often of a specialised nature, to corporate customers.

1.2 The functions of the commercial banks

(a) **Providing a payments mechanism**. The **bank clearing system** is a way of transferring money between accounts within a branch of a bank, between different branches, and between different banks. The **clearing system** enables individuals and firms to make payments by cheque, and therefore acts as a system for **transferring money**. Banks also enable individuals and firms to make payments by using direct debits, standing order, and electronic transfers. Again, in these ways, the banks provide a money transmission service.

(b) **Providing a place for individuals, firms and government to store their wealth**. Banks compete with other financial institutions to attract the funds of individuals and firms. The banks then hold the money in two main types of account:

    (i) Current accounts
    (ii) Deposit accounts

(c) **Lending money** in the form of loans or overdrafts.

(d) **Acting as financial intermediaries** by accepting deposits and lending, and in doing so transforming the risk characteristics and maturity characteristics of the lending.

(e) **Providing customers with a means of obtaining foreign currency, or selling foreign currency**, whenever they require it. Banks play a central role in the foreign exchange markets.

The banks also provide a wide range of other **commercial and financial services** to customers which generate them earnings and facilitate trade for the banks' corporate customers.

1.3 Liquidity, profitability and security: aims of the banks

FAST FORWARD

The three goals of commercial banks are **profitability**, **liquidity** and **security**

A commercial bank has three different and potentially conflicting aims which it must try to keep in balance. These are:

(a) **Profitability.** A bank must make a profit for its shareholders. The biggest profits come from lending at higher interest rates. These are obtained with long-term lending, and lending to higher risk customers.

(b) **Liquidity**. A bank must have sufficient liquid assets. It needs enough notes and coin to meet demands from depositors for cash withdrawals. It also needs to be able to settle debts with other banks.

For example, if on a particular day, customers of the Barclays Bank make payments by cheque to customers of HSBC Bank totalling $200 millions, and customers of HSBC make payments by cheque to customers of Barclays totalling $170 millions, Barclays will be expected to pay HSBC $30 million to settle the net value of transactions. This is done by transferring funds between the bank accounts of Barclays and HSBC, which they keep with the Central Bank (as 'operational deposits'). A bank might also need to have some 'near liquid' assets which it can turn into liquid assets quickly, should it find itself with a need for more liquidity. Near-liquid assets earn relatively little interest. A bank will try to keep the quantity of such assets it holds to a safe minimum.

(c) **Security**. People deposit their money with banks because they are regarded as stable and secure institutions. A bank might lend to some high-risk customers, and suffer some bad debts, but on the whole, a bank will be expected to lend wisely and securely, with a strong likelihood that the loans will be repaid in full and with interest.

1.4 Credit creation

FAST FORWARD

The **bank multiplier** or **credit multiplier** is the name given to banks' ability to create credit, and hence money, by maintaining their cash reserves at less than 100% of the value of their deposits.

When someone deposits money in a bank, the banks are able as a result to 'create' credit of a much greater magnitude than the amount of money originally deposited, and thereby they can make profit for themselves.

Suppose, for example, that in a country with a single bank, customer deposits total $100,000. The bank, we will assume, re-lends all these deposits to other customers. The customers will use the money they have borrowed to buy goods and services and they will pay various firms and individuals for these purchases. If the firms and individuals receiving payment then put the money into their own accounts with the bank, the bank's deposits will have doubled.

It is because most additions to bank lending end up as money in someone's bank account, in turn adding to total customer deposits with the banks, that banks have this **ability to create credit**. They can do this because they know that not all of the cash that has been deposited with them will be withdrawn at the same time.

This is commonly referred to as **fractional reserve banking** because it involves the bank keeping only a fraction of customers' deposits as reserves.

The distribution of assets for all UK commercial banks aggregated together is summarised in the table below.

UK commercial banks' assets, October 2010

	%
Cash	0.2
Balances with Bank of England	0.4
Market loans	12.0
Bills of exchange	1.2
Investments	15.5
Advances	55.7
Miscellaneous	15.0
	100.0

The triple aspects of bank lending – profitability, liquidity, and security – are evident in a commercial bank's **asset structure**.

(a) About 0.5% to 1% or so of a retail bank's assets might be till money (notes and coin) and deposits with the central bank (the Bank of England in the UK). Most of these assets are held to meet the need for immediate liquidity, and they earn no interest.

(b) Some assets are 'near-liquid' which means that they can quickly be converted into liquid deposits.

The most important near-liquid assets are loans to the money markets and other money market securities. But near-liquid assets also include bills of exchange and gilt-edged security investments.

Near-liquid assets – market loans, bills of exchange and gilt-edged security investments – might represent around 15% to 20% of a retail bank's assets.

(c) The biggest returns are earned by banks on their longer term **illiquid assets** – ie their overdrafts and bank loans to customers. Advances to customers are the biggest proportion of a retail bank's assets (usually about 50%) and the rate of interest on the loans varies according to the perceived risk of the customer as well as current interest rates.

(d) Banks' assets include the normal type of fixed assets found in any large organisation – eg property and equipment. However, the value of these operational assets is small in relation to the size of loans, even for the big clearing banks.

1.5 Illustration of credit creation

Illustrating the process with some figures may be helpful. We shall assume for simplicity that there is only one bank in the banking system, and that all money lent by the bank is re-deposited by various customers.

Let us assume a customer deposits $1,000 in cash in the bank.

Although this $1,000 is an asset for the customer, for the bank, this deposit is a **liability**. However, the deposit provides funds for the bank to acquire **assets**. We shall begin by assuming that the bank holds these assets entirely in the form of cash.

If the bank keeps the full $1,000 and does nothing with it, then it would simply operate as a 'safe' in which the client's money is deposited. However, if the bank believes that the client is unlikely to claim the full $1,000 for some time, there will be some incentive to use the money rather than to keep it idle. One possibility would be to lend it to another customer. The bank would be taking a risk that it will not have the cash when its first customer wants to have it back, but at the same time it would expect to make a profit by charging interest on the sum of money it had lent to the second customer.

On one hand, the deposit of the $1,000 creates the opportunity for the bank to make a profit in the form of the interest that it can charge on the money it lends (with this incentive being accentuated if the bank is paying interest on the deposits it accepts). On the other hand, however, there is a risk that when the money is out on loan the client may claim it back. The bank will then be unable to meet its obligation to repay the cash to the client unless it can recall the loan instantly, which is unlikely.

As long as the bank feels that the likelihood its depositors will demand a substantial proportion of their deposits in cash is small, then it faces an acceptable risk in lending some of the money. In other words, the bank strikes a balance between the desire to play safe by holding the cash and the desire to make profits by lending.

Let us assume that the bank has decided (on the basis of past experience and observation) to keep 20 cents in cash for every $1 deposited, and then lend out the other 80 cents. In other words, the bank in this example is operating a 20% cash ratio. At step (1) below, the bank has $1,000 in cash.

On the basis of the 20% cash ratio, the bank manager decides to keep $200 cash, and make a loan of $800 to a business (step 2).

This business in turn pays the $800 to another company, which banks at the same bank.

The second company then decides to pay the $800 into the bank (step 3).

So the bank is now holding $1,000 in cash, but has accepted total deposits of $1,800.

On the basis of the 20% cash ratio, the bank only needs to be holding $360 (20% × $1,800) as cash.

Accordingly (step 4), the bank lends $640 to another customer seeking a loan.

	Bank's liabilities (= customer deposits)	*Bank's assets (= cash or loans to customers)*
(1)	$1,000 deposit	$1,000 cash
(2)	$1,000 deposit	$200 cash
		$800 loans
(3)	$1,000 deposit	$200 cash
	$800 deposit	$800 loan
		$800 cash
(4)	$1,000 deposit	$200 cash
	$800 deposit	$800 loan
		$160 cash
		$640 loan

The bank can continue with this process of depositing and lending as long as the cash ratio is maintained. However, even by the end of step (4) in our simple example, we can see that, through the process of credit creation, the bank now has deposits of $1,800 compared to the initial deposit of $1,000. So, it has 'created' an extra $800.

Ultimately, if the bank kept on lending, applying the 20% cash ratio, total deposits would rise to $5,000 (the initial $1,000 plus an extra $4,000 'created').

1.6 The credit multiplier

If the bank decided that the 20% cash ratio was too conservative and reduced it to 10%, then for every $1,000 cash deposited with it, the bank would only need to hold $100, and could loan out the other $900. It is important to understand that banks, in the process of lending, are also potentially creating money because clients either borrowing or receiving the proceeds of borrowers' expenditure can use their deposits to make money transactions.

The fact that banks do not need to keep a 100% cash reserve ratio automatically implies that they have the capacity to create money out of nothing. The size of this credit expansion depends primarily on the size of their **cash reserve ratio**.

We can summarise the quantitative side of credit creation in banks as follows:

Formula to learn

$$\text{Deposits} = \frac{\text{Initial cash deposit}}{\text{Cash ratio}} \text{ or } D = \frac{c}{r}$$

The relationship of the total deposits resulting from an initial deposit to that initial deposit is known as the **credit multiplier** (or deposit multiplier).

The smaller the cash ratio or credit multiplier, the bigger the total of the deposits that a given amount of cash will be able to support and hence the larger the money supply.

If a bank decides to keep a cash reserve ratio of 10%, and it receives additional deposits of $1,000, the total increase in bank deposits will be $1,000 ÷ 10% = $10,000.

Question

Credit multiplier

Learning outcome: D2 (b)

Suppose that all the commercial banks in an economy operated on a cash reserve ratio of 20%. How much cash would have to flow into the banks for the money supply to increase by $80 million?

Answer

Call the extra cash $C. Then:

$$\frac{C}{20\%} = 80 + C$$

$$C = 20\% \times (80 + C)$$

$$0.8C = 16$$

$$C = \$20 \text{ million}$$

If an extra $20 million is deposited, the total money supply will rise to $20 million ÷ 20% = $100 million. This includes the initial $20 million, so the increase is $80 million.

A **cash ratio** or similar **fractional reserve system** might be imposed on banks by the government. The People's bank of China (the central bank in China) uses changes in reserve requirements as a tool for helping to control inflation (by controlling the money supply in the economy). It raised the reserve requirement nine times during 2007.

1.7 Capital adequacy rules

We have seen how banks create credit through the credit multiplier. However, we also noted that the credit creation ratio is based on there being no leakages from the credit creation system.

However, in reality not all customers will repay the amounts they borrow and so banks will suffer bad debts.

Capital requirement rules state that credit institutions, like banks and building societies, must always maintain a **minimum amount of financial capital**, in order to cover the risks to which they are exposed. The aim is to ensure the financial soundness of such institutions, to maintain customer confidence in the solvency of the institutions, to ensure the stability of the financial system at large, and to protect depositors against losses.

The **Bank for International Settlements (BIS)** is the governing committee of central banks and is based in Basel, Switzerland. It hosts the quarterly meetings of the Basel Committee on Banking Supervision which lays down guidelines for banking supervision, the **Basel Accords.** The **Basel III Agreement** (or Basel 3) was developed in the wake of the worldwide collapse of banking in 2008 and the consequent bail-outs by governments and has added to the previous requirements that laid out banks' capital management, including the formalisation of a **capital adequacy ratio** and **minimum capital requirements** banks will be required to meet to cover credit, market and operational risk. Basel III now requires that banks maintain the equivalent 7% of their risk bearing assets as top quality debt. This is a big increase on the previous 2% requirement and reflects the experience of regulators when, from 2008, they discovered that most banks were holding lots of worthless assets as reserves, so-called **'toxic debt'.**

As well as creating a framework to **control liquidity** and **bad debt** exposure, the Basel III agreement also sought to improve controls over the banking process. It introduced a new **supervisory review process** which required financial institutions to have their own internal processes to assess their capital needs and appoint supervisors to evaluate their overall risk profile, to ensure that they hold adequate capital.

It also aimed to improve **market discipline** by requiring banks to publish certain details of their risks, capital and risk management.

1.8 Example: Lehman Brothers

Lehman Brothers traces its origins to 1858 when its founders opened its first branch in New York to trade in and finance cotton and coffee. In 2008 it filed for bankruptcy, the biggest financial failure in the history of the USA. It nearly collapsed the entire structure of world banking.

Like all banks, Lehman's core business was lending money and taking interest. The reason for its failure was excessive lending to the **sub-prime mortgage market**. This was house-buyers borrowing money but who lacked the good credit ratings of 'prime' borrowers. Lehmans was able to make a better rate of profit because it could charge higher interest rates to these borrowers. But it sacrificed **security and liquidity** to do so.

The **sub-prime mortgage crisis** in the USA began after 2006 when house prices began to fall and borrowers preferred to lose their houses rather than refinance their mortgages, and new lenders refused to lend, because the sum required was more than the house was now worth. Mortgage defaults rapidly increased and caused further pressure on house prices as the market was flooded with an increased supply of houses on which owners had defaulted, whilst at the same time demand fell due to a lack of mortgages.

The assets on the balance sheet of Lehman's fell below the value of its liabilities. Liquidity of mortgages is always poor because they are long-term loans and won't get paid back for many years. However there is traditionally a ready secondary market for good mortgage loans which means that lenders like Lehman's can sell parts of their mortgage books to other banks by bundling them up as bonds, a process called **securitisation**. However Lehman's couldn't sell its mortgages because other banks knew they were bad. It could not meet the demands of depositors for withdrawal of funds. The US government refused to lend it money to stabilise it and so it had to close. It had gone bankrupt.

The problem rippled across other banks. Some had bought securitised mortgages from Lehman's to hold as assets and now faced the same problems that Lehman's faced. Others had deposits in Lehman's, or held Certificates of Deposit issued by Lehman's, as assets which now was unlikely to be able to make payments.

Faced with similar problems in the weeks that followed the US authorities did provide emergency funding to several other banks.

2 Yield on financial instruments

FAST FORWARD

In practice, there is a variety of **interest rates**. To make a profit, institutions that borrow money to re-lend, or that accept deposits which they re-lend (eg banks) must pay lower interest on deposits than they charge to customers who borrow.

2.1 Interest rates and yields

Credit is a scarce commodity, priced through **interest rates**. Although there are many different interest rates in an economy, including banks' base rates, mortgage rates and yields on gilt-edged securities, they tend to move up or down together.

(a) If some interest rates go up, for example the banks' base rates, it is quite likely that other interest rates will move up too, if they have not gone up already.

(b) Similarly, if some interest rates go down, others are likely to follow them and move down too.

A **yield** is a general term to describe the return from an investment. It is calculated by expressing the return as a percentage of the **market price** of the investment. Note this means that yields for bonds are inversely related to bond prices. That is, as the price of the bond falls, the yield % will rise.

For example, a $100 bond with a $10 return gives a yield of 10%. But if the bond price falls to $80, yield will be 12.5% (10/80). The yield will remain at $10 because it is referenced to the nominal value of the bond rather than the current price of the bond.

Assessment focus point

You must remember that yields and interest rates are linked, and you should be able to calculate the impact that changes in interest rates have on changes in yields.

2.2 Nominal and real rates of interest

FAST FORWARD

The real value of income from investments is eroded by **inflation**. The rate of return left after inflation has been deducted is called the **real rate of interest**

Key term

Real rate of interest

$$\frac{1+\text{money rate}}{1+\text{inflation rate}} = 1 + \text{real rate}$$

Nominal rates of interest are rates expressed in money terms. For example, if interest paid per annum on a loan of $1,000 is $150, the rate of interest would be 15%. The nominal rate of interest might also be referred to as the **money rate of interest**, or the **actual money yield** on an investment.

Real rates of interest are the rates of return that investors get from their investment, adjusted for the rate of inflation. The real rate of interest is therefore a measure of the increase in the real wealth, expressed in terms of buying power, of the investor or lender. Real rates of interest are lower than nominal rates when there is price inflation. For example, if the nominal rate of interest is 12% per annum and the annual rate of inflation is 8% per annum, the real rate of interest is the interest earned after allowing for the return needed just to keep pace with inflation.

The relationship between the inflation rate, the real rate of interest and the money rate of interest is:

$(1+ \text{real rate of interest}) \times (1+ \text{inflation rate}) = 1+ \text{money rate of interest}$

We may rearrange this to find the real rate of interest in the example above.

$$\frac{1+\text{money rate}}{1+\text{inflation rate}} = 1 + \text{real rate}$$

$$\frac{1.12}{1.08} = 1.037$$

The real rate of interest is thus 3.7%.

The real rate of interest is commonly measured approximately, however, as the difference between the nominal rate of interest and the rate of inflation. In our example, this would be 12% – 8% = 4%.

FAST FORWARD

Provision of finance brings **risk**, which will be reflected in the interest charged. The higher the risk the higher the interest charged.

2.3 Interest rates and loans

The influences affecting interest rates in general will play a background part in determining the rate of interest for a particular loan. The main emphasis will be on specific factors concerning the nature of the borrowing and the status of the borrower.

The fundamental consideration in any lending decision is **risk**. The more **speculative** any borrowing proposal is believed to be, the higher will be the rate of interest. The lender is concerned not only with recovering the capital sum on the due maturity date, but also with earning a return on the money lent over the period of the loan. The time period of lending influences risk: the longer the time period, the greater the uncertainty about the ability of the borrower to repay the loan, or the greater the erosion in the value of money by inflation.

Borrowers and lenders will both take into account **real interest rates**. Consideration as to **future inflation levels** will therefore help determine the nominal rate of interest.

The **status of the borrower** will influence **perceived risk**. Those borrowers with a higher credit rating and moderate financial gearing will be granted more favourable borrowing terms and therefore relatively lower interest rates than those with a poor financial record. Whether a borrower can offer security for a loan and the quality of that security will be important: the better the collateral, the lower the rate of interest.

From both parties' points of view, but particularly that of the lender, the **type of any asset purchased by the loan is** important: is the security non-marketable on the one hand, or is it either marketable or redeemable on the other? In the latter case, there is possible escape from the financial commitment and risk, and means of adjustment to changed conditions. The more marketable/redeemable a security, the lower the interest rate.

The **amount** of any proposed loan will also be of some importance. Larger individual amounts will be less costly for a borrower to administer and this may be reflected in a marginally higher rate of interest on offer.

A lender will also be concerned in some instances with the **purpose** of any loan and the **competence of the borrower** in use of the funds. The reputation of a financial institution may be jeopardised by ill-considered lending which subsequently is adversely publicised. The greater the risk in this regard is considered to be, the higher will be the rate of interest.

2.4 Yields on short term money market instruments

Yield on Commercial paper

Commercial paper (short term debts issued by a company) can be issued at a discount from the face value, or it can be issued in interest bearing form. The investor is getting the same rate of return regardless of whether the commercial paper is purchased on a discounted or interest bearing basis.

On a discounted basis, the investor pays less than the face value or principal amount of the commercial paper and receives the full face at maturity. The quoted discount rate of interest is the discount amount expressed as a percentage of the maturing face amount.

On a interest bearing basis, the investor pays for the full face value of the commercial paper and receives the face value plus accrued interest at the time of maturity. The quoted discount or interest rate is converted to a yield to calculate the interest at maturity. This conversion is simply a restatement of the discount rate as a percentage of the initial proceeds rather than the maturing amount.

Yield on Treasury bills

Treasury bills (T-bills) are purchased by investors at less than face value and are redeemed at maturity at face value. The difference between the purchase price and the face value of the bill is the investor's return.

The following formula is used to determine the discount yield for T-bills that have three- or six-month maturities:

$$y = \frac{F - P}{F} \times \frac{360}{M}$$

F = = face value

P = purchase price

M = maturity of bill. For a three-month T-bill (13 weeks) use 91, and for a six-month T-bill (26 weeks) use 182

360 = the number of days used by banks to determine short-term interest rates

2.4.1 Example

What is the discount yield for a 182-day T-bill, auctioned at an average price of $9,719.30 per $10,000 face value?

Solution

$$y = \frac{F - P}{F} \times \frac{360}{M} = \frac{10{,}000 - 9{,}719.3}{10{,}000} \times \frac{360}{182} = 0.0555$$

The discount yield is 5.55%

When comparing the return on investment in T-bills to other short-term investment options, the investment yield method can be used. This yield is alternatively called the **bond equivalent yield**, the coupon equivalent rate, the effective yield and the interest yield.

The yield on a Treasury bill varies according to the method of computation. The discount method relates the investor's return to the face value, while the investment method relates the return to the purchase price of the bill. The discount method tends to understate yields relative to those calculated using the investment method.

The following formula is used to calculate the investment yield for T-bills that have three- or six-month maturities:

$$\text{Investment yield} = y = \frac{F-P}{P} \times \frac{365}{M}$$

Note that the investment yield method is based on a calendar year: 365 days, or 366 in leap years.

2.4.2 Example

What is the investment yield of a 182-day T-bill, auctioned at an average price of $9,719.30 per $10,000 face value?

Solution

$$y = \frac{F-P}{P} \times \frac{365}{M} = \frac{10{,}000 - 9{,}719.3}{9{,}719.3} \times \frac{365}{182} = 0.0579$$

Investment yield = 5.79%

2.5 Yields on bonds

Yields on bonds

Yield calculations on bonds aim to show the return on a gilt or bond as a percentage of either its nominal value or its current price. There are three types of yield calculation that are commonly used, the **nominal or flat yield**, the **current or running yield** and the **yield to maturity or redemption yield**:

Nominal or flat Yield

This is derived by dividing the annual coupon payment by the par value or nominal value of the bond.

$$\text{Nominal yield} = \frac{C}{F}$$

where C is the coupon and F is the nominal or par value.

2.5.1 Example

If the nominal value of a bond is $100 and the bond pays 4% what is the nominal yield on the bond?

Solution

$$\text{Nominal yield} = \frac{4}{100} = 0.04 \text{ or } 4\%$$

Current or Running Yield

This is calculated by dividing the annual coupon income on the bond by its current market price.

$$\text{Running yield} = \frac{C}{P}$$

Where P is the market price.

2.5.2 Example

If the market price of the $100 bond dropped to $96, what is the current yield on the bond?

Solution

$$\text{Running yield} = \frac{4}{96} = 0.0417 \text{ or } 4.17\%$$

Redemption Yield

The yield to maturity or redemption yield, is the rate of return investors earn if they buy the bond at a specific price (P) and hold it until maturity. Mathematically the yield to maturity (r) is the value that makes the present value of all the coupon payments equal to the purchase price.

2.6 Variations in the general level of interest rates over time

Interest rates reflect a number of things, including **inflation**, **risk**, **demand for finance** and **government monetary policy**.

Interest rates on any one type of financial asset will vary over time. In other words, the general level of interest rates might go up or down. The general level of interest rates is affected by several factors.

(a) **The need for a real return**. It is generally accepted that investors will want to earn a 'real' rate of return on their investment, that is, a return which exceeds the rate of inflation. The suitable real rate of return will depend on factors such as investment risk.

(b) **Uncertainty about future rates of inflation**. When investors are uncertain about what future nominal and real interest rates will be, they are likely to require higher interest yields to persuade them to take the risk of investing, especially in the longer term.

(c) **Changes in the level of government borrowing**. When the demand for credit increases, interest rates will go up. A high level of borrowing by the government, is likely to result in upward pressure on interest rates.

(d) **Higher demand for borrowing from individuals**. If individuals want to borrow more, for example because they feel confident about their level of future earnings, then interest rates will also tend to rise (as the demand for credit rises).

(e) **Monetary policy**. Governments (or the central banks acting on their behalf) control the level of interest rates in order to control inflation.

(f) **Interest rates abroad**. An appropriate real rate of interest in one country will be influenced by external factors, such as interest rates in other countries and expectations about the exchange rate.

2.7 The term structure of interest rates

FAST FORWARD

The rate of interest required by investors when they buy bonds varies according to **how long-dated** the assets are. Generally the **longer the loan, the higher the interest**. This gives rise to a **yield curve.**

The various interest rates can be grouped into three broad classes, according to the length of the loan period.

- Short-term interest rates
- Medium-term interest rates
- Long-term interest rates

Longer term financial assets should in general offer a higher yield than short-term lending. There are several reasons for this.

(a) The investor must be compensated for tying up his money in the asset for a longer period of time. If the government were to make two issues of 9% Treasury Stock on the same date, one with a term of five years and one with a term of 20 years (and if there were no expectations of changes in interest rates in the future) then the **liquidity preference** of investors would make them prefer the five year stock.

The concept of **liquidity preference** is that, if all other things are equal, investors will prefer to hold money (liquidity) rather than bonds or other investments.

As an extension of this, it follows that investors will initially prefer short term (more liquid) investments over longer term ones.

(b) The only way to overcome the liquidity preference of investors is to compensate them for the loss of liquidity; in other words, to offer a higher rate of interest on longer dated stock.

(c) There is a greater **risk** in lending longer term than shorter term for two reasons.

(i) **Inflation**. The longer the term of the asset, the greater is the possibility that the rate of inflation will increase, so that the fixed rate of interest paid on the asset will be overtaken by interest yields on new lending now that inflation is higher.

(ii) **Uncertain economic prospects**. The future state of the economy cannot be predicted with certainty. If an organisation wishes to borrow money now for, say, 15 years, there is no certainty about what might happen to that organisation during that time. It might thrive and prosper or it might run into economic difficulties for one reason or another.

Investors will require a higher return to compensate them for the increased risk.

(d) Note, however, that two other factors also affect the cost of borrowing.

(i) The risk associated with the perceived ability of the borrower to fulfil the terms of the loan
(ii) Whether or not the loan is secured by a mortgage on an asset

2.8 Yield curve

A yield curve shows the relationship between interest rates on similar assets with different terms to maturity. A normal yield curve will be upward-sloping, as shown in Figure 1, because of the higher interest rates which are likely to apply to longer terms of lending. Equally, as a stock nears maturity its market price will get closer to its nominal price, and therefore its yield will fall.

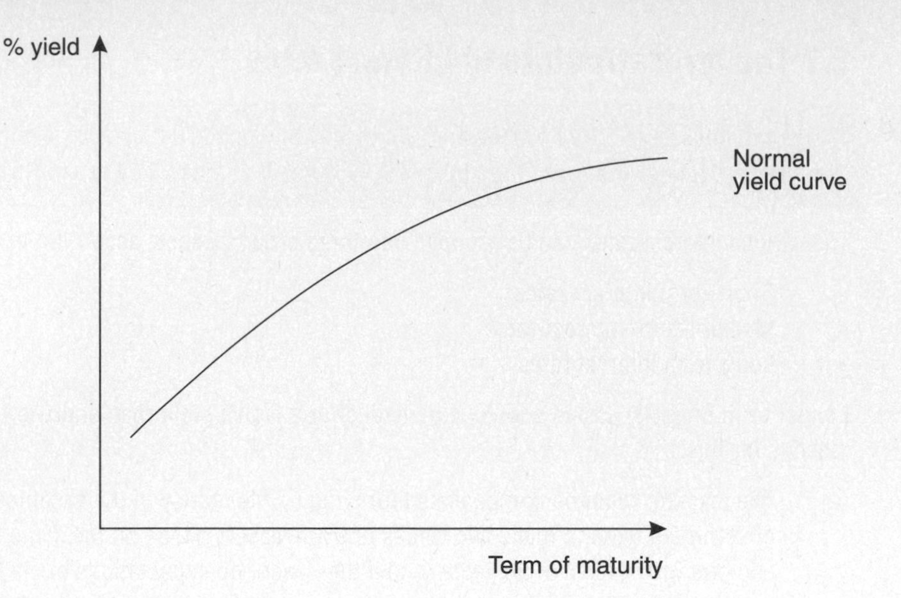

Figure 1 Yield curve

Notice that our yield curve in Figure 1 measures the percentage yield on an asset, and remember that yields rise when the market prices of the stocks falls.

One possible reason for the market prices of stocks falling is that markets for shares are bullish and so investors are looking to buy shares (either for capital growth or to earn dividends) instead of holding stocks.

2.9 Dividend yield

Dividend yield shows the return achieved from dividends as a percentage of the market price of the share.

$$\text{Dividend yield} = \frac{\text{Dividend per ordinary share}}{\text{Market price of the share}}$$

2.9.1 Example

Consider the following information on a share:

Current dividend per share	\$0.2
Market price of share	\$5.0

What is the dividend yield?

Solution

$$\text{Dividend yield} = \frac{\text{Dividend}}{\text{Market price}} = \frac{0.2}{5} = 0.04 = 4\%$$

Long term rates of return

As ordinary equities have no maturity and the dividend payments are not constant, it is difficult to calculate a return similar to the yield to maturity. However, approximate measures can be derived if we make assumptions about the dividends.

Two such assumptions are normally made. First that the dividend paid is constant forever at level D. In this case if the price is P, the return on equities is given by the dividend yield since with no growth in dividend payments there will be no growth in the value of the firm.

The second assumption made is that dividends grow at constant rate 'g'. In this case the rate of return is given by

$$k_E = \frac{D}{P}(1+g)+g$$

Where K_E = rate of return on equity
D = dividend paid
P = share price
g = dividend growth rate

2.9.2 Example

To illustrate, assume the following values for the expected growth, current dividends and current market price:

g = 0.05
D = \$0.06
P = \$2

Calculate the rate of return on equity.

Solution

$$k_E = \frac{0.06}{2}(1+0.05)+0.05 = 0.0815 \text{ or } 8.15\%$$

2.9.3 Comparing yields

Being able to calculate a yield on equity is important for the rational investor. If all the markets are operating efficiently, then, *ceteris paribus,* the yield on equities (shares) will equal the yield on bonds (stocks). If they do not, the investor will reallocate their resources towards the **higher yielding instrument**. For example, if dividend yield is 4%, but the yield on bonds is 5%, rational investors will look to hold bonds rather than shares.

This also shows that interest rates can affect the price of shares. If interest rates rise, the yield on bonds will also be rising, and so holding bonds will become relatively more attractive than holding shares.

Therefore, in an efficient market, investors will seek to transfer their funds from shares to bonds. They will sell shares and buy bonds. Selling shares will reduce the price of shares, because it means there is an inward shift in the demand curve for shares (shift from D_0 to D_1, on Figure 2).

In turn, the fall in the price of shares will raise the dividend yield, so that investors are attracted back to holding shares.

This flux will continue until an equilibrium is reached whereby the yield on bonds is equal to the yield on shares.

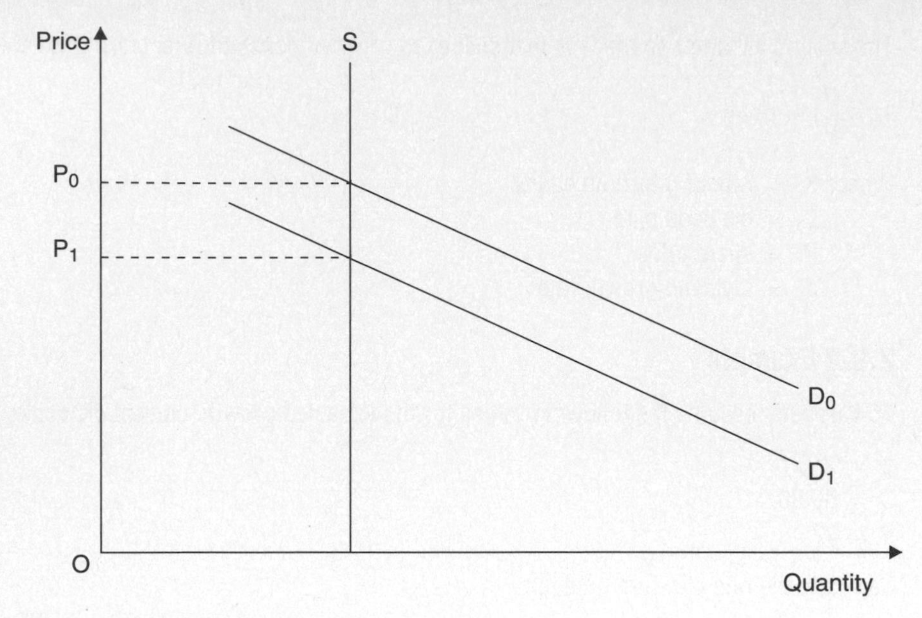

Figure 2: Reduction in demand for shares

2.10 Risk and return on financial assets

FAST FORWARD

The rate of interest required by investors also **rises as the risk of the investment rises**.

When investors invest in financial assets they receive in return an income as a compensation for giving up funds and therefore potential consumption. This income takes the form of a dividend or interest or a capital gain. Looking at the various instruments we have examined so far, we can make the following comments regarding the uncertainty surrounding the income and the capital gain element of compensation.

(a) A 91 day **Treasury bill** has no uncertainty regarding its income if it is held to maturity, since the compensation in the form of the discount yield is known at the beginning of the transaction.

(b) A **government bond** has no uncertainty regarding its income, since this is known at the time the bond is issued. It also faces no risk with regard to capital gains if it held to maturity. However, as we have noted earlier, if the bond is sold before maturity, it is possible however for the price of the bond to fall and a loss to incur.

(c) **Ordinary shares**, on the other hand, have uncertain dividend payments and uncertain selling prices, that makes the holding period return uncertain.

(d) Another aspect of risk that should be taken into account is **credit risk**. A corporate bond for example may pay fixed coupons but it may have a high risk of bankruptcy in which case even the coupon payment is rendered uncertain.

Taking these characteristics into account it is accepted that the ranking of securities in terms of risk is as follows.

Since individuals are exposed to varying degrees of risk when invest in financial assets, it follows that investors will demand a higher compensation for the higher risk. The relationship between risk and return is thus positive and the determination of the precise relationship between risk and return is the object of financial theory. The accepted relationship between risk and return is shown in the diagram below.

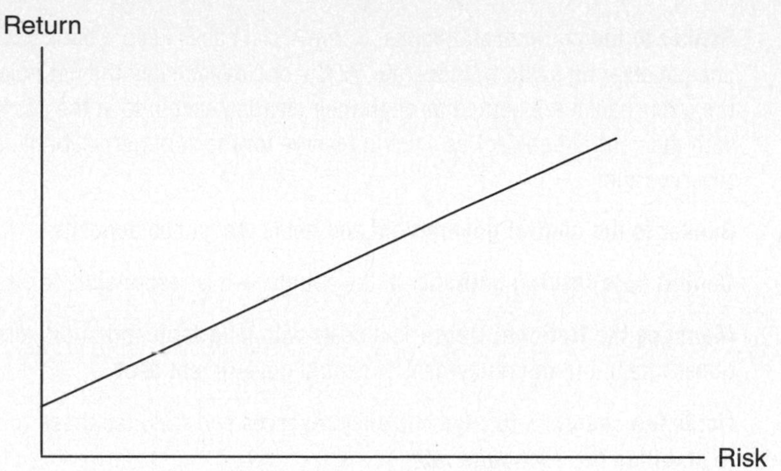

The return on any asset could be seen as made up of two components:

(a) the return from an **asset** which is **free of risk** such as government bond (a **risk free asset**) and

(b) an additional return, referred to as the **risk premium** which represents the compensation for bearing the risk.

2.11 The impact of the central bank on financial market yields

As discussed earlier, central banks may set short term interest rates. At the same time interest rates affect the yields on other financial assets. For example, an investor in equities will require a yield that would be at least equal to the prevailing short-term interest rates plus a risk premium appropriate to the equities held. If interest rates go up following an intervention by the Central Bank the required return by equity holders will go up and share prices will tend to fall.

Central banks can therefore play an important role in affecting yields and prices of financial assets.

3 Role of central banks

FAST FORWARD

The **central bank** has various functions. These include acting as a **banker to the central government** and to the **commercial banks** and has responsibility for controlling **inflation** and **interest rates**.

A central bank is a bank which acts on behalf of the government. The central bank for the UK is the Bank of England. The Bank of England ('the Bank') is a nationalised corporation run by a Court of Directors, consisting of the Governor, Deputy Governor, and some Executive Directors and part-time Directors.

3.1 Functions of a central bank

(a) **Monetary stability**. The Bank's most important function is maintaining monetary stability in the economy. This includes **setting interest rates** at the level it considers appropriate in order to meet the government's **inflation target**.

(b) The Bank also has a key role in maintaining the **stability of the financial system**. Some central banks **regulate the banking** sector.

(c) **Lender of last resort** when the banking system is short of money, the Bank will provide the money the banks need – at a suitable rate of interest.

(c) **Banker to the commercial banks**. Commercial banks keep a bank account with the Bank This enables the cheque clearing system to operate. At the end of each day the net balances on each bank's accounts with all the other banks are settled through their clearing accounts at the central bank. The funds which banks hold with the central bank act as a liquid reserve for the commercial bank, and are controlled by the fractional reserve ratio.

(d) **Banker to the central government** and holds the 'public deposits'.

(e) **Central note-issuing authority** in the country – it is responsible for issuing bank notes

(f) **Manages the National Debt** – ie it deals with long-term and short-term borrowing by the central government and the repayment of central government debt.

(g) **Holds the country's foreign currency reserves** and may use these to trade on the foreign exchange markets to **stabilise the exchange rate**

(h) **Advisor** to the government on **monetary policy**.

4 Influence of central bank over financial markets

4.1 Financial markets

FAST FORWARD

Firms may obtain long-term or medium-term capital as **share capital** or as **loan capital**. Debentures, loan stock, bonds and commercial paper are all types of loan capital.

In this section we discuss short-term instruments which can be traded in the money markets, and long-term instruments such as bonds and shares.

4.1.1 Money market instruments

In most economies, the money markets are the most important financial markets.

Money markets are operated by the banks and other financial institutions. Although the money markets largely involve wholesale borrowing and lending by banks, some large companies and the government are also involved in money market operations. **The money markets are essentially shorter term debt markets**, with loans being made for a specified period at a specified rate of interest.

Specialist banks (called Discount Houses in the UK) act as market makers for the short term treasury and commercial bills.

When the government issues treasury bills to make good a shortfall between government expenditure and reserves, any excess supply of bills in the market will be bought by the discount houses.

The price which the discount house pays for the bill reflects the market rate of interest.

A similar discounting process occurs for commercial bills, whereby a financial intermediary will discount a bill on issue, knowing that it will receive its full value at a later date. Again, the difference between the two indicates the market interest rate.

The money markets operate both as a **primary market**, in which new financial claims are issued, and as a **secondary market**, where previously issued financial claims are traded.

Amounts dealt in are relatively large, generally being above £50,000 in the UK and often in millions of pounds. Loans are transacted on extremely 'fine' terms – ie with small margins between lending and borrowing rates – reflecting the **economies of scale** involved. The emphasis is on liquidity: the efficiency of the money markets can make the financial claims dealt in virtually the equivalent of cash.

There are various markets, including the following.

(a) On **the primary market** (as already described), companies, governments or public sector institutions obtain funding through the sale of a new stock or bond issue.

(b) **The interbank market** is the market in which banks lend short-term funds to one another. An internationally recognised interest rate in this market is the London Inter-Bank Offered Rate (LIBOR), which is used by individual banks to establish their own base interest rates and interest rates for wholesale lending to large borrowers.

(c) **The Certificate of Deposit market** is a market for trading in **certificates of deposit**, a form of deposit which can be sold by the investor before maturity. A certificate of deposit (CD) is a certificate (a paper asset) issued by a bank that shows a specific amount of money has been deposited at the issuing institution. The CD bears a specific maturity date, interest rate, and denomination, and so banks can issue them to depositors who are willing to leave their money on deposit for a specified period of time. CDs are issued by banks to access funds (cash) for their finance and lending activities.

A distinction is sometimes made between the **primary market** and all the other money markets which are referred to collectively as the **parallel money markets** or 'unofficial' markets.

4.1.2 The stock market

Stock markets are a particular type of financial market which enable the trading of company stock (shares) and derivatives. Major stock markets include the New York Stock Exchange, Euronext, and the London Stock Exchange.

We will use the London Stock Exchange as an example here.

A stock exchange is an organised capital market which plays an important role in the functioning of the economy.

(a) It makes it easier for large firms and the government to raise long-term capital, by providing a market place for borrowers and investors to come together.

(b) It publicises the prices of quoted (or 'listed') securities. Investors can therefore keep an eye on the value of their stocks and shares, and make buying and selling decisions accordingly.

(c) It enforces certain rules of conduct for its listed firms and for operators in the market, so that investors have the assurance that companies whose shares are traded on the Exchange and traders who operate there are reputable. Confidence in the Stock Exchange will make investors more willing to put their money into stocks and shares.

The price of shares on a stock market fluctuate up and down.

(a) The price of shares in a **particular company** might remain unchanged for quite a long time; alternatively, a company's share price might fluctuate continually throughout each day.

(b) The **general level** of share prices, as measured by share price indices such as the All-Share Index and the FTSE 100 Index, may go up or down each minute of the day.

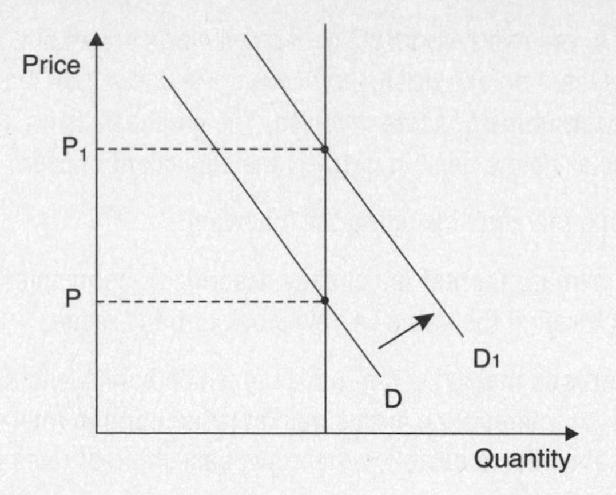

Figure 3. Impact of changes in demand on share prices

In essence, share prices on a stock market reflect the equilibrium between supply and demand in the same way that any other prices do.

For example, if a company announces very good results, demand for its shares may increase (an outward shift in its demand curve) causing share prices to rise (as in Figure 1).

Equally, a company may wish to issue new shares to generate extra capital. This new share issue represents an outward shift in the supply curve, and so, *ceteris paribus,* will lead to a fall in share price (as illustrated in Figure 4).

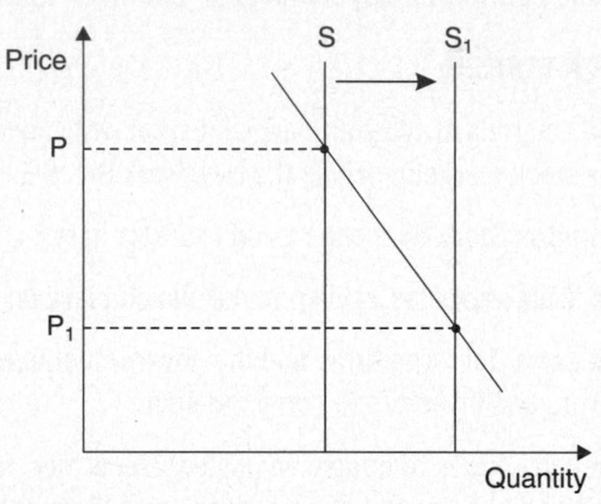

Figure 4. Impact of a new share issue on share prices

The indices of share prices on the Stock Exchange act as indicators of the state of **investor confidence** in the country's economy. For example, if investors believe that interest rates are too low to curb inflation, they may sell shares and move their funds to other countries, causing a decline in share prices. Although in theory a stock market should be an example of a perfectly competitive market, with large numbers of buyers and sellers reacting to perfect knowledge, in practice this is not the case. Factors which are not related to the market itself – such as concerns about political instability or general confidence in the economy – will affect share prices. Therefore the share price of a company may not truly reflect the value or performance of that company.

Question — Share prices

From your reading of the business pages of the newspapers (which should be a central feature in anyone's study of economics) what factors have you noticed as having an influence on share prices?

Answer

Share prices respond to:

(a) Factors related to the circumstances of individual companies – eg news of a company's annual profits, or a proposed takeover bid

(b) Factors related to the circumstances of a particular industry – eg new government legislation or regulations for an industry, such as new laws on pollution controls or customer protection measures

(c) Factors related to the circumstances of the national economy – eg optimism about economic growth, changes in interest rates, the latest official figures for the balance of trade, or price inflation

Assessment focus point

You should be aware of the types of factors set out in the Question above, but detailed knowledge of theories of share price behaviour is not expected.

4.1.3 Changes in the capital markets

Recent years have seen very big changes in the capital markets of the world.

(a) **Globalisation of capital markets**

The capital markets of each country have become internationally integrated. Securities issued in one country can now be traded in capital markets around the world. For example, shares in many UK companies are traded in the USA. The shares are bought by US banks, which then issue ADRs (American depository receipts) which are a form in which foreign shares can be traded in US markets without a local listing.

(b) **Securitisation of debt**

Securitisation of debt means creating tradable securities which are backed by less liquid assets such as mortgages and other long term loans.

(c) **Risk management (and risk assessment)**

Various techniques have been developed for companies to manage their financial risk such as swaps and options. These 'derivative' financial instruments may allow transactions to take place off-balance sheet and the existence of such transactions may make it more difficult for banks and other would-be lenders to assess the financial risk of a company that is asking to borrow money.

(d) **Increased competition**

There is much fiercer competition than there used to be between financial institutions for business. Banks have changed, with some shift towards more fee-based activities (such as selling advice and selling insurance products for commission) and away from the traditional transaction-based activities (holding deposits, making loans).

4.2 The central bank as lender of last resort

FAST FORWARD

As the **provider of liquidity** to the financial markets the central bank becomes able to **influence interest** rates by its **buying and selling of financial assets**.

The short-term money market provides a link between the banking system and central bank whereby it lends money to the banking system, when banks which need cash cannot get it from anywhere else.

(a) The Bank will supply cash to the banking system on days when the banks have a cash shortage. It does this by buying eligible bills and other short-term financial investments from approved financial institutions in exchange for cash.

(b) The Bank will remove excess cash from the banking system on days when the banks have a cash surplus. It does this by selling bills to institutions, so that the short-term money markets obtain interest-bearing bills in place of the cash that they do not want.

The process whereby this is done currently is known as **open market operations** by the Bank. This simply describes the buying and selling of eligible bills and other short-term assets between the Bank and the short-term money market.

4.3 Open market operations and short-term interest rates

Key term

Open market operations: the central bank's dealings in the money and capital markets. The Bank uses open market operations to control interest rates.

Open market operations provide central banks with a method of control over **short-term interest rates**. They are thus an important feature of the government's monetary policy, which the Bank implements on its behalf.

When bills are bought and sold, they are traded at a discount to their face value, and there is an implied interest rate in the rate of discount obtained. Discounts on bills traded in open market operations have an immediate influence on other money market interest rates, such as the London Inter-Bank Offered Rate (LIBOR), and these in turn influence the 'benchmark' base rates of the major banks.

Because the eligible bills and other assets which the Bank acquires in its money market operations are short-term assets, a proportion mature each day. The market is then obliged to redeem these claims and must seek further refinancing from the bank. This continual turnover of assets gives the Bank the opportunity to determine the level of interest rates day by day.

4.4 Government stock and interest rates

When we look at macroeconomic policy later in this text, we will look at how governments attempt to manage both economic growth and inflation. When we do so, we will see how interest rates are a vital part of economic policy.

However, for now, and in conjunction with looking at the open market operations of central banks, we should consider briefly what interest rates are.

In essence, interest rates reflect the **price of money**, or credit. And money is priced, like everything else, through the **supply and demand** for it.

We will look at what affects the demand for money later in this text, but the key aspect to consider in connection with open market operations is how to **control the supply of money** and therefore determine the level of interest rates.

Through its open market operations, a central bank will either buy government stock from commercial banks or sell government stock to them.

If the central bank **buys government stock**, the commercial banks will get extra money in return for the stocks they have sold to the central bank. Therefore, the supply of money will increase, and the banks' ability to create credit through the credit multiplier will also increase. In effect, this increase in the supply of money should make money cheaper (reduce interest rates).

Conversely, if the central bank wants to reduce the supply of money through its open market operations (and thereby raise interest rates), it will look to **sell government stocks**. In buying the stocks, the commercial banks' money base will be reduced, as will the level of credit they can subsequently create through the credit multiplier.

5 The global banking crisis

FAST FORWARD

The **global banking crisis** of 2007-2010 led to a sharp **contraction in the availability of credit** and also led to a **shakeout in the banking sector** and increased concerns over the **structural debts** of some **governments**.

5.1 The 2007 -2010 financial crisis

This crisis began with the collapse of the US sub-prime mortgage market in 2007 and rippled across the banking and financial sectors. At the time this text was written (May 2011) the financial crisis continues to throw up new challenges in a World where confidence in banks and financial institutions has fallen low, whilst at the same time banks and financial institutions are suspicious of advancing credit.

5.2 The main consequences

These have been

(a) **Collapse of property sector**. Declining or stagnant prices of commercial and residential property in many developed countries, bringing the financial collapse of many construction and property development businesses

(b) **Credit squeeze**. Tightened lending by banks reducing private sector investment and private consumption. This has been a huge fall in injections with consequent downward multiplier effects through rising unemployment and business failures. A particular casualty was automobile manufacturers.

(c) **Government intervention**. Large scale and co-ordinated intervention by governments to limit the crisis. The governments of developed economies individually and collectively took steps to reduce interest rates and also to provide funding to the banks to recapitalise them following the sharp fall in the values of their assets.

(d) **More regulation of banks and financial institutions**. A response in most countries has been to blame the banks and financial sector and to seek to regulate them more closely. Some were nationalised.

(e) **Austerity budgets.** General nervousness about banks exposure to toxic assets has led to increased scrutiny of the amount of government bills and bonds held by the banking sector.

(f) **Concern over structural deficits** are fiscal deficits that are not run as a consequence of seeking to modify the recession and depression stage of the business cycle, but rather are perpetual. There is no possibility that the government will have the funds to pay back the borrowing in the future. Many governments were accused of running structural deficits and banks became nervous of lending to them. This forced the governments to take strong steps to eliminate the structural deficits, or at least convince the banks that they meant to, in order to keep the interest rates on their debts low and manageable. Such reductions of government spending and raising of taxation exerts a further downward multiplier effect.

5.3 The causes of the 2007 -2010 financial crisis

Economists offer a range of explanations for the crisis.

(a) **The US property boom of 1997 – 2006**. Prices of US houses rose 124%, a trend echoed in some other countries. The cause initially was sub-prime mortgages which allowed persons with poor credit ratings to start bidding for homes. The price of house rose from 2.9 times average earnings in 1997 to 4.6 times in 2006. This was unsustainable because buyers could not afford the interest on their mortgages. The rising house prices had turned the market into one where buyers, and construction firms, speculated on house price rises by buying in at a low price using cheap credit and selling again soon after to make a capital gain. This was particularly attractive as such gains attracted no tax provided they didn't exceed generous thresholds. Once the growth stopped the house prices fell sharply as people tried to pay back their borrowings.

(b) **The sub-prime mortgage crisis.** The effect of the collapse of the housing boom was to leave banks holding mortgages as assets which the borrowers had no way to pay back or to maintain interest payments on. Sometimes these banks holding these were the original lenders, sometimes they had been bought by other banks and financial institutions as bonds (or securitised debt) from the original lenders. Either way the banks were holding worthless assets (called 'toxic debt' by the media) which left them having advanced too much credit without the assets to back them up. Banks and financial institutions began to fail and this forced rescue plans by governments to get additional capital into them before they pulled the entire banking system down with them.

(c) **Low market interest rates.** Central banks followed a cheap money policy during the period before 2007. These low interest rates were mainly to help stabilise equity markets that had been falling and harming personal wealth and investments. This was the result of a fall in investor confidence following poor returns from investments in the internet shares boom of the late 1990's and also concerns over the involvement of several countries in military action following the September 11th attack on USA. These low rates encouraged borrowing by consumers, house buyers and property developers but left the economies fragile once the credit was no longer available.

(d) **Poor regulation of the financial sector.** Criticism has been made of the role of central banks and other regulatory bodies in not putting a stop to high risk lending before it dragged the banks down. This has included a failure to understand the new institutions and assets of the **shadow banking sector** such as hedge funds and investment funds which gambled on the movements of asset prices and introduced instability into the markets. There were also examples of **predatory lending** in which borrowers were encouraged to borrow funds they could not repay using credit agreements, credit cards and very high mortgages. This loans were further assets that turned bad on bank balance sheets.

(e) **Excessively complex financial assets.** The period saw the development of many new financial assets which were created using very complex mathematical models to establish the risks and returns on them. One such were credit default swaps which, the users believed, insulated them from the risks of defaults by the borrows behind the mortgages they held. The investor, regulators and even the creators did not understand these fully with the effect that investors and financial institutions were exposed to risks that they had not anticipated and hence lost money as a result.

(f) **Greed and poor governance.** Financial markets traditionally rely on the integrity and fair-dealing of the institutions and people involved in them. Regulation has been limited to allow them to be flexible and to develop. The payment of huge bonuses to management and traders encouraged them to expose their clients and the institutions they worked for to inappropriate risks.

5.4 The European sovereign debt crisis

Sovereign debt is another term for debt issued by the government of a country. From late 2009 the debts issued by the governments of several European countries, including Ireland, Greece, Portugal and Spain, came under scrutiny by the world's financial markets. This was because these governments seemed to be borrowing spiralling amounts of funds which their economies would be unable to repay. Because these countries are all members of the Euro currency the crisis also become known as the **Eurozone Crisis**.

Government debt is typically 'rolled over' ie when some debt falls due for repayment the government repay with one hand with money raised on the other by new borrowing. But concern over their ability to repay had the effect was that these countries had to pay higher and higher amounts of interest each time they issued debt. Several began to borrow even more in order to be able to afford the higher interest.

A big concern was, and is, that this debt is held by commercial banks as assets. If a county became unable to repay debts out of new borrowing they would have to **default** on the debt. This would have led some commercial banks to collapse.

To avoid this various international banking institutions, including the International Monetary Fund (IMF) and the European Central Bank (ECB) loaned large amounts to the affected countries to help them repay the debts that were falling due whilst at the same time demanding these countries implemented **austerity programmes** to cut their borrowing by reducing government expenditures and raising taxation.

Chapter roundup

- Commercial banks can be separated into clearing banks, retail banks, and investment banks.
- The three goals of commercial banks are **profitability**, **liquidity** and **security**
- The **bank multiplier** or **credit multiplier** is the name given to banks' ability to create credit, and hence money, by maintaining their cash reserves at less than 100% of the value of their deposits.
- In practice, there is a variety of **interest rates**. To make a profit, institutions that borrow money to re-lend, or that accept deposits which they re-lend (eg banks) must pay lower interest on deposits than they charge to customers who borrow.
- The real value of income from investments is eroded by **inflation**. The rate of return left after inflation has been deducted is called the **real rate of interest**
- Provision of finance brings **risk**, which will be reflected in the interest charged. The higher the risk the higher the interest charged.
- Interest rates reflect a number of things, including **inflation**, **risk**, **demand for finance** and **government monetary policy**. A normal yield curve slopes upward.
- The rate of interest required by investors when they buy bonds varies according to **how long-dated** the assets are. Generally the **longer the loan, the higher the interest**. This gives rise to a **yield curve.**
- The rate of interest required by investors also **rises as the risk of the investment rises**.
- The **central bank** has various functions. These include acting as a **banker to the central government** and to the **commercial banks** and has responsibility for controlling **inflation** and **interest rates**.
- **Firms** may obtain long-term or medium-term capital as **share capital** or as **loan capital**. Debentures, loan stock, bonds and commercial paper are all types of loan capital.
- As the **provider of liquidity** to the financial markets the central bank becomes able to **influence interest** rates by its **buying and selling of financial assets**.
- The **global banking crisis** of 2007-2010 led to a sharp **contraction in the availability of credit** and also led to a **shakeout in the banking sector** and increased concerns over the **structural debts** of some **governments**.

Quick quiz

1 A 'money market' is best defined as:

A A market where organisations raise any form of finance
B A market where organisations raise long-term finance
C A market where organisations raise short-term finance
D A market where Treasury Bills are traded

2 A money market financial intermediary is best defined as:

A An institution which matches surplus funds holders to deficit funds units.
B An institution which operates on the Stock Exchange, matching buyers and sellers of stocks and shares.
C An institution which allows firms to obtain equipment from suppliers by providing leasing or hire purchase finance.
D An institution which acts as a buffer between the Bank of England and the rest of the UK banking system.

3 Define the credit multiplier

4 What three aims must a commercial bank keep in balance?

5 List the likely functions of a central bank.

6 If the banking system has liquid reserves of $225bn and seeks to maintain a reserve ratio of 13%, what will broad money supply be?

A $17bn
B $1,731bn
C $2,925bn
D $292,599bn

7 The ability of the banks to create credit is constrained by all the following except:

A Leakages of cash out of the banking system
B A reduced reserve ratio
C Low demand for loans
D Prudent lending operations

8 What is the purpose of capital adequacy rules?

9 A $100 bond which pays 4% currently has a market price of $90. What is the current yield on the bond?

A 3.6%
B 4%
C 4.44%
D 5%

10 Which of the following would be likely to lead to a rise in share prices on a stock market?

(i) An expected rise in company profits
(ii) A fall in share prices in other international stock markets
(iii) A fall in interest rates

A (i) and (ii)
B (i) and (iii)
C (ii) and (iii)
D (i), (ii) and (iii)

Answers to quick quiz

1 C Money markets deal with short-term finance. Capital markets deal with long-term finance.

2 A An institution on the Stock Exchange is a capital market player. C is a financial intermediary but is not the best definition. D is a financial intermediary but is not the best definition.

3 The credit multiplier (or bank multiplier) is the name given to banks' ability to create credit, and hence money, by maintaining their cash reserves at less than 100% of the value of their deposits.

4 Liquidity, profitability and security.

5 Setting interest rates

Banker to the government

Central issuer of banknotes

Manager of the national debt

Manager of the nation's foreign currency reserves

Banker to the clearing banks

Lender to the clearing banks (lender of last resort)

Supervision of the banking system

6 B \$225bn × credit multiplier = total deposits (broad money) therefore \$225bn × (1/0.13) = \$1,731bn

7 B A falling reserve ratio will increase the credit multiplier.

8 Capital adequacy rules are designed to ensure that banks have enough capital to cover their risk assets after allowing for the risk of potential bad debts.

9 C Current yield = $\frac{4}{90}$ = 4.44%

10 B A rise in company profits will encourage people to buy shares, so demand for shares will rise and their prices will also rise: meaning (i) is correct.

A fall in share prices in one market tends to lead to falls in share prices in other markets around the world because stock markets are linked. So (ii) is not correct.

Interest rates and share prices move in opposite directions. If interest rates are falling, people will look to buy shares instead of bonds, so this increased demand for shares will mean share prices rise. So (iii) is correct.

Now try the questions below from the Exam Question Bank

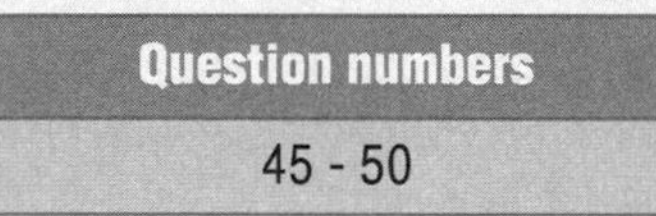

Question numbers
45 - 50

Financial systems 3 –foreign exchange markets

11

Introduction

In this chapter we look at how exchange rates are determined and how they impact on business. An awareness of the factors that cause movements in the foreign exchange rates will help businesses predict what the effects are likely to be.

First we see how the foreign exchange markets operate.

Next we go through the terminology and basic calculations and consider the main influences on exchange rates.

Finally we see that governments intervene to varying degrees to limit the fluctuations of exchange rate, and we consider various exchange rate systems.

Topic list	Learning outcomes	Syllabus references	Ability required
1 Foreign exchange markets	D2	D2(e)	Comprehension
2 Factors influencing exchange rates	D2	D2(e)	Comprehension
3 Government policies on exchange rates	D2	D2(e)	Comprehension

1 Foreign exchange markets

FAST FORWARD

Foreign exchange markets feature **large commercial banks** buying and selling currencies using **screen-based price information** but often conducting the actual **transaction over telephones**.

1.1 Nature of the foreign exchange markets

Being able to buy and sell things in different currencies is essential to trade. Once nations developed their own currencies rather than using gold and silver it became necessary to be able to exchange one currency for another. Therefore foreign exchange markets have a long history dating back to the beginnings of trade.

The globalisation of capital markets, and the growth of multinational companies has reinforced the importance of foreign exchange markets, which facilitate the sale and purchase of foreign exchange.

Foreign exchange markets serve to finance international trade, but also allow companies to manage their foreign exchange risk and deal in foreign exchange so that they can benefit from changes in exchange rates.

The assets traded in the foreign exchange markets are deposits of the currency itself and bonds denominated in foreign currencies. Funds available on the international capital markets can, like funds available on other markets, be grouped by timescale.

Timescale	Category of funds	Used for
Short	Eurocurrency	Funding working capital requirements
Medium	Eurocredit	Working capital and investment purposes
Long (> 5 years)	Eurobonds	Investment purposes and funding acquisitions

Note: Eurocurrency does not simply refer to deposits made in Euros. Eurocurrency refers to **any** currency deposited by companies or governments into banks outside their own country. For example, a deposit denominated in US dollars residing in a UK bank is a Eurocurrency deposit. (The same rules apply for Eurocredits and Eurobonds).

The main participants in the foreign exchange market (sometimes called the forex market or currency market) are:

(a) Large **commercial banks** dealing on behalf of clients or sometimes speculating on their own behalf

(b) **Central banks** needing to obtain currency for governments or trying to influence the exchange rate between currencies

(c) **Investment institutions** seeking to manage their clients; funds to gain a return and avoid the risks of having them all invested in a single currency

(d) **Businesses** which need to exchange currencies in order to buy and sell between countries

(e) **Currency speculators** who buy currencies in the expectation they will make a profit later by selling at a higher price.

1.2 Spot and forward markets

In 2010 the average daily turnover of the World's forex markets was US$3.28 trillion of which a third was trading to immediately exchange on currency for another (the 'spot' market) and two-thirds was buying for delivery of the currency in the future (the 'forward' market).

Key terms

Spot market: trades in foreign exchange for immediate delivery

Forward market: trades in foreign exchange for delivery in the future, typically 1, 3 or 6 months

Trading 'forward' for delivery in several months time is an important method of **hedging risk**. A firm from a country using the Euro may have sold a consignment of machine tools to a country that uses the dollar. Assuming trade credit terms are 90 days the firm will be receiving an amount of dollars in 90 days time. It will want to convert these to Euro to pay its costs and so on. If the exchange rate of the dollar for the Euro falls during the next 90 says this firm will get back less Euros for the dollars than it had hoped for. But if it buys a forward contract today that commits it to sell a certain amount of dollars for a set amount of Euro in 90 days time it will avoid that risk.

Trading 'spot' is for immediate delivery and is used either to pay debts in foreign currency or to make good on a forward contract.

1.3 Motives for foreign exchange dealing

FAST FORWARD

The main **motives for forex dealing** are **transactions**, to support trade, for **overseas investment**, to **hedge forex risks**, and for the purposes of **speculation**.

The foreign exchange markets originated from the **needs of trade**. But today foreign exchange instruments are **speculative assets** that are traded in the hope of gain like equities and other financial instruments.

The main motives are:

(a) **Transactions needs:** a firm, individual or government hold its bank deposits in $ but needs € to pay a supplier in a different country will exchange its balances via its bank or, for large organisations, issue a € denominated instrument to obtain the funds it needs.

(b) **Finance trade:** a firm in Europe importing a cargo from USA will borrow $ for 3 months to pay the suppliers and rely on selling the goods in € to repay the loan.

(c) **Investment projects:** a construction firm from UK building a sports stadium in France using materials and suppliers from Europe and USA will need to borrow € and £ for several years before being paid in € when the stadium is complete. It will issue corporate bonds in € and $.

(d) **Risk management:** the examples in (b) and (c) show that firms are exposed to risks in trade. For example in (b) if the € falls in value against the $ there is no guarantee that the proceeds of selling the cargo will repay the $ loan taken. For this reason the firm may hedge its position by buying a forward contract today to be able to buy a set value of $ in 3 months time in for a set value of €.

(e) **Speculation**: the value of one currency against another changes though time. If the $ is expected to appreciate (that means rise) against the € a speculator may today exchange their € assets (bank balances, bonds and so on) for assets denominated in $. If the $ rises they can sell them for € and make a profit on the transaction. Sometimes a speculator may buy in the morning and sell in the afternoon to make these profits.

2 Factors influencing exchange rates

FAST FORWARD

An exchange rates is the **price of one currency in terms of another**. Exchanges rates are determined by the **relative demand and supply** for the currency on the foreign exchange market.

2.1 The foreign exchange market diagram

Figure 1 shows the application of demand and supply analysis to the determination of exchange rates.

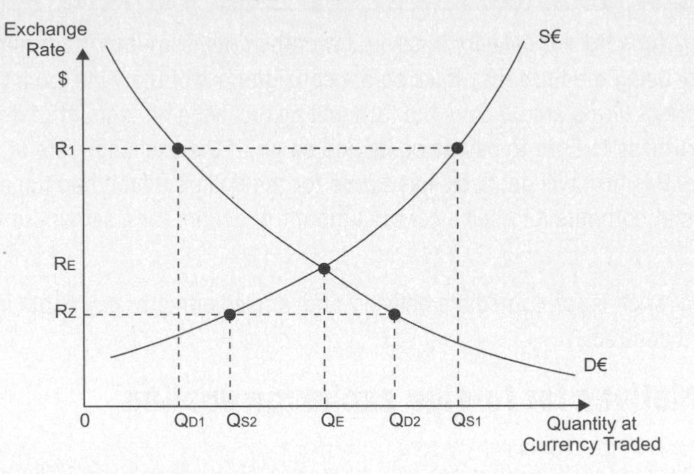

Figure 1 Determination of the exchange rate

Figure 1 shows the market for Euros. It shows the price of the Euro in terms of dollars..

(a) A high exchange rate against other currencies , such as R1, means that a given amount of $ can buy only a small amount of €. So demand for exports from Euro countries will be lower. This means demand for Euros will be lower.

(b) A low exchange rate, say R2, means the same amount of $ can buy a larger amount of €. Therefore demand for exports from Euro countries will be higher and, as a result, demand for Euros will be higher.

Understanding this diagram helps us understand two important aspects of the forex market:

(a) How foreign exchange dealing establishes a rate

(b) The factors determining the demand and supply for a currency.

2.1.1 Establishment of the exchange rate

Figure 1 represents the **spot market** for the Euro. The buyers and sellers in this market are currency traders, ie the foreign exchange dealers of commercial banks and the currency speculators.

An important point in understanding Figure 1 is to appreciate that the **foreign exchange** (forex) **dealers are the market makers** and that demand for € represents the telephone calls to forex dealers from firms, banks and governments who wish to buy €. The supply of € is the calls to forex dealers from firms, banks and governments who wish to sell €.

Forex dealers make profits in two ways:

(a) On the profit (or **turn**) between the lower rate they pay when they buy currency, and the slightly higher rate they charge when they sell it on. This is the same way that a foreign exchange bureau at an airport makes a profit, although a forex dealer will deal in narrower margins and vastly greater volumes that the forex bureau

(b) On the **appreciation** in the currency whilst they hold it. A speculator will buy currency and then wait for the exchange rate to rise before selling it at a profit.

Consider exchange rate R1 in Figure 1. This shows that the demand for € will be Q_{D1} but supply will be Q_{S1}. This means that the forex dealers will be buying Q_{S1} of currency but only selling Q_{D1}. They will drop their quoted exchange rates to eliminate this **surplus of currency** building up in their accounts (or **book** as they would term it). This **depreciation** in the exchange rate will continue until equilibrium is reached at R_E.

The forex dealers reduce the rate for two reasons:

(a) **To return** to profitable trading: if rates are too high they will be buying in currency that they cannot then sell. This ties up their capital without making any profit

(b) **To limit risk of capital loss**: the forex dealer realises that the rate is too high and will soon fall. Given they hold stocks of the currency bought at R1 they will make a loss on this as the rate falls. Therefore they drop the rate to encourage demand and so off-load their surplus stocks of currency.

Consider exchange rate R2 in Figure 1. This shows that the demand for € will be Q_{D2} but supply will be Q_{S2}. This means that the forex dealers will be buying only Q_{S2} of € but have demands from clients of Q_{D2}. They will raise their quoted exchange rates to eliminate this **shortage of currency** and this **appreciation** in the exchange rate will continue until equilibrium is reached at RE.

The forex dealers raise the rates they quote for two reasons:

(c) **To increase profits from trading**: if rates are too low they will not have enough currency to sell and so will be tuning away profit. Putting the rate up attracts sellers and gives them the currency they need to sell.

(d) **To make a capital gain**: by putting the rate up of the currency they bought at R2 they will make a capital gain by selling at a higher rate.

Of the two mechanisms described above the **stronger influence on rates is the speculative motive** to make capital gains and avoid losses. The forex market, together with bond and bill markets, are the **most price-sensitive markets** in existence. The adjustments described above take place within minutes and **adjustments are continuous** across global forex markets **24 hours a day**.

2.1.2 Factors determining the demand and supply for a currency

Figure 1 shows a downward sloping demand curve for the currency, the Euro, and an upward sloping supply curve for the Euro. These need to be understood.

The **demand for currency extends as the exchange rate falls** for three reasons:

(a) **Trade effects:** as the exchange rate depreciates the world prices of products denominated in that currency also fall. For example in Figure 1 assume that R1 = \$2 to €1. This would mean something costing €20,000 would cost \$40,000 (ie €20,00 x \$2). If the exchange rate for the Euro fell to \$1.5 to €1 then the €20,000 item would now cost only \$30,000 (€20,000 x \$1.5) If this €20,000 item were a car, a piece of machinery, or a holiday then demand for it from abroad would extend. This would mean that foreign buyers would need € to pay for it and so the demand for € on the foreign exchange market extends above Q_{D1}. The opposite effect would happen if exchange rates rose

(b) **Portfolio effects:** this refers to the demand for investment assets. A fall in the exchange rates makes foreign investment assets such as bonds and equities cheaper to buy too. This makes the **investment assets more attractive to investors** who will obtain a yield from them and also potential capital gains if the exchange rate rises again and they can sell them and buy back into their original currency. To buy the assets the investors need to buy the currency

(c) **Speculative effects:** as the rate depreciates some forex speculators will begin to buy the currency because they think it is likely to appreciate again in the future and allow them to enjoy a capital gain

The **supply of the currency** is the persons holding the currency wishing to sell it to obtain other sorts of foreign exchange or assets. Supply **contracts as the exchange rate depreciates** for the following reasons:

(a) **Trade effects**: as the exchange rate depreciates so does its purchasing power and so imported products become more expensive. Assume a rate of R1 = $2:€1 and a US product costing $10,000. This would cost a holder of Euros €5,000 (ie €10,000 x €1/$2) and might be attractive compared to European products. But if the rate fell to $1.5:€1 then the price of the US product would rise to €6,667 ($10,000 x €1/$1.5). Therefore a holder of € will not be inclined to buy the US product and so will not wish to supply € in exchange for $. Supply of € will contract.

(b) **Portfolio effects**: the weaker currency makes foreign assets more expensive and the yield lower. Holder of € will be less likely to want to exchange their € for currency to buy assets denominated in other currencies

(c) **Speculative effects**: as the rate depreciates holders of € will assume the rate will rise again and so will be reluctant to sell holdings at a lower rate.

2.2 Other influences on exchange rates

FAST FORWARD

In the short run the foreign exchange rate adjusts to equilibrium by the actions of foreign exchange traders. **Longer term shifts** in exchange rates are caused by changes in the **balance of trade**, the impact of changes in **relative interests rates**, the rate of **inflation** and **expectations** of future movement in exchange rates.

2.2.1 Impact of a fall in demand for a currency

Figure 2 shows a fall in demand for a currency causing exchange rates to fall.

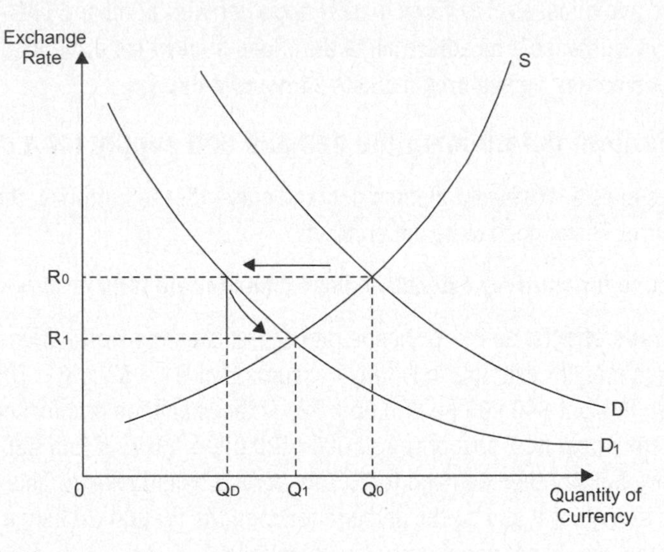

Figure 2 Impact of a fall in demand for a currency

In Figure 2 the exchange rate is initially at R_0 and the quantity demanded and supplied of the currency is Q_0. A fall in demand from Q_0 to Q_D creates a surplus of currency and the exchange rate falls to R_1.

The potential causes of this change in demand are described below.

2.2.2 Exchange rates and trade balances

Currency is demanded partly for trade purposes. Trade depends on the **competitiveness** of a country's products, their **prices** and also the **levels of economic activity** in the world.

The fall in demand shown in Figure 1 could have resulted from a decline in the value of foreign demand for the products of the country.

(a) **Loss of competitiveness:** the products have become more expensive, or less appealing, than rival products from another country. This will reduce the demand for the currency to buy them with

(b) **Fall in price of a key export:** suppose a country's currency is demanded in order to buy a key export, for example a metal or mineral such as oil or copper, or a cash crop such as tobacco. If the price (or availability) of that export falls then the demand for the currency may fall too. This is the reason that the currencies of some developing nations can be volatile due to world commodity price instability and the variability of harvests from year to year

(c) **World recession affecting exports:** if the major trading partners of the county are suffering economic recession this will reduce their demand for imports and so will reduce the demand for currency

A situation of **trade deficits** where the value of a countries imports exceeds the value of its exports will lead to a depreciation of its exchange rate. This is because the value of currency being demanded, from foreign buyers wishing to pay for its exports, will be less than the value of currency being supplied, by its residents in exchange for currency to buy imports. This causes a **surplus of domestic currency on the forex markets** that will cause the exchange rate to depreciate over time.

2.2.3 Exchange rates and interest rates

A second demand for currency is for **investment purposes**. Investment money chases higher rates of yield on assets around the world.

If the interest rates in a country fall the demand for the currency will also fall, as in Figure 2, because investors will find the yields less attractive.

2.2.4 Exchange rates and inflation rates

Key term

Inflation: the tendency for the general level of prices in an economy to rise through time. This leads to a fall in the purchasing power of its currency.

Inflation occurs when the prices in a country rise and its goods and services become more expensive. The important factor affecting exchange rates is the **relative inflation rate** of the country against its trading partners.

(a) If the country has a **higher inflation rate than its trading partners** it means that its **products are becoming more expensive** relative to the goods produced by its trading partners

(b) This will lead the demand for its exports to fall, and therefore the demand for its currency to fall

(c) The **supply of its currency will also increase** because domestic **residents will wish to buy imports** because they are relatively cheaper. Therefore they will seek to supply domestic currency to obtain the foreign currency they need to pay for the imports

(d) This will cause a **surplus of currency** on the forex markets and drive its price, the exchange rate, down.

(e) The depreciation of the currency will **continue until the relative competitiveness** of the domestic goods **is the same** as the foreign goods

This mechanism gives rise to the **purchasing power parity** theory of exchange rate determination. This predicts that a country's exchange rate against another country's currency will decline at the rate of difference in their respective inflation rates.

2.2.5 Expectations and exchange rates

Because of the huge sums of money involved the forex market is very sensitive to any data that might suggest an exchange rate is likely to rise or to fall.

The banks and corporations engaged in forex dealing are fully aware of how the factors that have been described above can affect exchange rates. Therefore they watch for signs that any of them are about to change.

Any factors that could lead to the expectation that exchange rates might fall will cause a **flight from the currency**, ie a fall in demand for it and a rush to sell it, that will act as a **self-fulfilling prophesy** because the rates will then fall as a consequence of the expectation even if it later proves to have been unfounded.

Factors that lead to a rise in an exchange rate include:

(a) Anticipation of a rise in interest rates

(b) Expectation that the relative inflation rate may fall

(c) Anticipation of better foreign trade figures

(d) Factors that improve the outlook for export earnings such as rise in price of key crop

(e) Information that suggests the country's firms may make higher profits in future and so its shares may be more attractive to foreign investors

(f) Statements from government or its central bank that they may be intending to use their influence over the exchange rate to raise it

3 Government policies on exchange rates

FAST FORWARD

Government policies on exchange rates might be to set **fixed exchange rates** or to allow **floating exchange rates**. Alternatively, governments may look for a policy somewhere between the two.

In practice, 'in-between' schemes have included:

- **Fixed rates**, but with provision for devaluations or revaluations of currencies from time to time ('adjustable pegs') and also some fluctuations ('margins') around the fixed exchange value permitted
- **Managed floating** within a desired range of values

Currency blocs and **exchange rate systems** enhance currency stability, but limit the ability of governments to pursue independent economic policies.

If several currencies adopt a **single currency**, then **transactions** between firms in different countries within the currency zone will become **cheaper** (no commission costs on currency dealings), and **financial markets** across the zone will become **more flexible.**

3.1 Free floating exchange rates

Sometimes governments will not intervene in the foreign exchange markets. Free floating or flexible exchange rates occur when **exchange rates are left to the interaction of market forces** and there is no official financing at all. In other words, the exchange rate will reflect the interaction of supply and demand for a currency.

3.1.1 Advantages of floating exchange rates

(a) Governments do not have to spend or even hold foreign currency reserves

(b) Balance of payments deficits or surpluses are automatically corrected. A deficit will result in the exchange rate falling; this will improve competitiveness, raise exports and restore equilibrium.

(c) Governments need not adopt economic policies that may be undesirable for other reasons to maintain exchange rates.

(d) Encourage efficient allocation of resources since exchange rates will reflect economic conditions.

3.1.2 Disadvantages of floating exchange rates

(a) If exchange rates **appreciate too much** under a floating rate system, then **firms' international competitiveness** may be reduced, and output and employment may fall across the economy.

(b) Uncertainty surrounding fluctuations in exchange rate could deter trade.

(c) If **exchange rates fall too much**, **import prices,** and hence **inflation**, will rise.

(d) **Currency risk** will be **maximised** under a system of floating exchange rates.

(e) The freedom afforded governments by (c) in the advantages above may mean governments do not pursue domestic policies which they should.

3.1.3 Managed floating

In practice, governments prefer generally to operate **managed floating** (or **dirty floating**) exchange rates for their currency, and a policy of allowing a currency to float entirely freely is rare. Under a system of managed floating exchange rates, governments will intervene in the market to buy or sell currency in order to achieve an exchange rate target. For example, they may wish to reduce the exchange rate to make exports more competitive, and they could, for example, achieve a reduction in the exchange rate by selling their own currency on the exchange markets.

3.2 Government intervention in foreign exchange markets

A government can intervene in the foreign exchange markets in several ways.

(a) It can **sell its own currency** in exchange for foreign currencies, when it wants to keep the exchange rate of its domestic currency low. The foreign currencies it buys can be added to the official reserves.

(b) It can **buy its own currency** and pay for it with the foreign currencies in its official reserves. It will do this when it wants to keep the exchange rate high when market forces are pushing it down

(c) The government can also intervene indirectly, by **changing domestic interest rates,** and so either attracting or discouraging investors in financial investments which are denominated in the domestic currency

(d) It can **impose exchange controls** by making it a criminal offence for its citizens and banks to hold foreign currency and instead itself becomes the **monopoly provider of foreign currency** in the country which it will only buy and sell as a set **official rate.** This tends to lead to a thriving illegal sector offering better rates for foreign currency to tourists and firms wishing to buy domestic currency at below the official rate.

By managing the exchange rate for its currency, a government does not stop all fluctuations in the exchange rate, but it tries to keep the fluctuations within certain limits.

(a) **Unofficial limits**: a government might intervene in the foreign exchange markets and sell foreign currency from its official reserves to buy the domestic currency, and so support its exchange rate, even though there is no officially declared exchange rate that it is trying to support.

(b) **Official limits**: the country may be part of a system that allows its currency to fluctuate against the other currencies within the system only within specified limits.

3.2.1 Reasons for a policy of controlling the exchange rate

(a) To **rectify a balance of trade deficit**, by trying to bring about a fall in the exchange rate.

(b) To **prevent a balance of trade surplus** from getting too large, by trying to bring about a limited rise in the exchange rate.

(c) To **emulate economic conditions** in other countries, for example lower inflation.

(d) To **stabilise the exchange rate of its currency**. Exporters and importers will then face less risk of exchange rate movements wiping out their profits. A stable currency increases confidence in the currency and promotes international trade.

3.3 Fixed exchange rates

A policy of rigidly fixed exchange rates means that the government must use its **official reserves** to create an exact match between supply and demand for its currency in the foreign exchange markets, in order to keep the exchange rate unchanged. Using the official reserves will therefore cancel out a surplus or deficit on the current account and non-official capital transactions in their balance of payments. A balance of payments surplus would call for an addition to the official reserves, and a balance of payments deficit calls for drawings on official reserves.

For simplicity and convenience, the exchange rate is fixed against a standard. The standard might be one of the following.

- Gold
- A major currency
- A basket of major trading currencies

3.3.1 Advantages of fixed exchange rates

(a) A fixed exchange rate system removes exchange rate uncertainty and so encourages international trade.
(b) A fixed rate system also imposes economic disciplines on countries in deficit (or surplus).

3.3.2 Disadvantages of fixed rates

(a) There is inevitably **some loss of flexibility** in economic policy making once a country fixes its exchange rates. A government might be **forced to reduce demand** in the domestic economy (for example by raising taxes and so cutting the demand for imports) in order to maintain a currency's exchange rate and avoid a devaluation.

(b) Countries regard **devaluation** as an indicator of failure of economic policy and often resist devaluation until long after it should have taken place.

3.4 Currency blocs

Currency blocs are where groups of countries **fix their exchange rates** against a major trading currency. The resulting stability is designed to help international trade, since the major currency used will be the currency of a country (countries) with whom members of the bloc carry out a lot of trade.

The currency may be a major world currency or it may be an artificial currency set up as part of a more formal exchange rate system.

3.5 Exchange rate systems

Exchange rate systems are systems where there is **stability** between the currencies of member currencies, even though there are fluctuations with the currencies of countries outside the systems. An example is the European Monetary System established in 1979. Part of this was the Exchange Rate Mechanism under which:

(a) Each country had a **central rate** in the system.

(b) Currencies were only allowed to **fluctuate within certain levels** (bands)

(c) Within the bands, fluctuations of a certain limit should **trigger action** by governments to prevent fluctuations beyond the bands allowed.

3.5.1 Advantages of exchange rate systems

(a) **Reduction of inflation**

Exchange rate stability within an exchange rate system may help dampen inflation by preventing a government from allowing the currency to drift downwards in value to compensate for **price inflation.**

(b) **Expectations**

There are likely to be effects on people's expectations. In particular, the **perceived risk** of **exchange rate movements** between member currencies should be **low.** As well as allowing firms to plan and forecast with greater certainty, exchange rate stability ought to make a currency **less risky to hold**.

3.5.2 Problems with exchange rate systems

The are a number of the potential problems of an exchange rate system.

(a) **Wrong initial rates.** If a country pegs its currency at **too high a rate** it becomes less competitive as exports became too expensive for consumers in foreign countries whilst domestic consumers seek imports. This creates a surplus of currency that puts pressure on the rate to fall whilst also encouraging **import penetration** and **loss of export sales** resulting in unemployment, a deep recession and a significant deficit on the balance of payments.

(b) **Interest rate levels. Interest rate policy** must be consistent with keeping the currency stable. For example using a high interest rate to keep the exchange rate high will mean that the costs of credit, home-buying and industrial investment will become prohibitively high

(c) **Vulnerability**. If the pegged rate is believed to be too high the forex markets will consider it inevitable that is will have to be lowered and will start selling the currency, with the effect that the **speculation proves self-fulfilling** and forces the government to give up supporting the exchange rate an allow it to fall.

3.6 Single currency

A single currency is where a number of countries agree to adopt a single currency, for example, the Euro. Twelve members of the European Union initially adopted a single currency, the Euro, in 2002, but by the end of 2008 this number had risen to 17.

3.6.1 Advantages of a single currency

(a) The removal of exchange rate risk makes **cross-border trade and investment easier** and less risky.

(b) The removal of conversion fees paid by business and individuals to banks when converting different currencies makes **transactions** within the currency zone **cheaper.**

(c) **Financial markets** are **opened up** across the region and are more flexible and liquid than when there are many different currencies.

(d) **Price parity** or price transparency across borders is thought to **lower prices** across the area, because it allows consumers to compare prices across borders.

(e) **Funding** is **easier to obtain**, as there is greater cross-border borrowing.

(f) **Economic stability** within the zone is thought to benefit not just the member countries of the zone but also the **world economy** as a whole.

3.6.2 Disadvantages of a single currency

(a) '**One size fits all**' currency may **not be applicable** to countries with very different industrial structures and at very different levels of economic maturity.

(b) There is a **loss of national self-determination** in monetary matters.

(c) **Agreement and coordination** between the different countries using the currency may be **difficult to achieve**

(d) Serious difficulties if a member country runs into financial difficulties because others have to support it or risk a sharp deterioration in the value of the common currency. In 2010/11 the banking crisis led to concern over the security of banks and government debts in several European countries that forced the EU members to borrow to provide stabilisation funding to those countries or otherwise run the risk of the Euro collapsing.

Question — **Floating exchange rates**

Which of the following is not a disadvantage of a government allowing a country's exchange rate to float freely?

A Floating may result in currency appreciation and a fall in competitiveness.
B Floating may result in currency depreciation and a rise in inflation.
C Floating will result in firms facing increased foreign exchange risk.
D Floating will mean that government economic policy becomes more restricted.

Answer

D Floating removes the restrictions on economic policy that are necessary to maintain exchange rates at fixed levels.

3.6.3 European Central Bank

The European Central Bank (ECB) is responsible for **monetary policy** in the eurozone (the countries using the Euro), and its primary objective is to maintain price stability therein by managing interest rates.

The bank also seeks to **support the economic policies** of the European Union, which include maintaining a high level of employment, and achieving non-inflationary economic growth.

In addition, the ECB is responsible for conducting **foreign exchange operations**, and holding / managing the official foreign reserves of the eurozone countries.

Further tasks include **issuing banknotes** for the eurozone, (which ECB has the exclusive right to do) and promoting the smooth operation of payment systems.

Chapter roundup

- Foreign exchange markets feature **large commercial banks** buying and selling currencies using **screen-based price information** but often conducting the actual **transaction over telephones**.
- The main **motives for forex dealing** are **transactions**, to support trade, for **overseas investment**, to **hedge forex risks**, and for the purposes of **speculation**.
- An exchange rates is the **price of one currency in terms of another**. Exchanges rates are determined by the **relative demand and supply** for the currency on the foreign exchange market.
- In the short run the foreign exchange rate adjusts to equilibrium by the actions of foreign exchange traders. **Longer term shifts** in exchange rates are caused by changes in the **balance of trade**, the impact of changes in **relative interests rates**, the rate of **inflation** and **expectations** of future movement in exchange rates.
- Government policies on exchange rates might be to set **fixed exchange rates** or to allow **floating exchange rates**. Alternatively, governments may look for a policy somewhere between the two.

  In practice, 'in-between' schemes have included:
- **Fixed rates**, but with provision for devaluations or revaluations of currencies from time to time ('adjustable pegs') and also some fluctuations ('margins') around the fixed exchange value permitted
- **Managed floating** within a desired range of values

  Currency blocs and **exchange rate systems** enhance currency stability, but limit the ability of governments to pursue independent economic policies.
- If several currencies adopt a **single currency**, then **transactions** between firms in different countries within the currency zone will become **cheaper** (no commission costs on currency dealings), and **financial markets** across the zone will become **more flexible.**

Quick quiz

1 Which of the following statements about the forex market is *false*

A It only trades in currencies that can be delivered immediately
B The market participants are large banks, businesses and financial institutions
C The prices it sets vary minute by minute
D Central banks seek to influence the exchange rates set by the market

2 True or false? The main volume of forex dealing is for the finance of trade?

3 A German firm is due to receive £25,000 from a UK customer. The €/£ exchange rate is 1.0650 – 1.0700. How much in € will the German firm receive?

A € 23,364
B € 23,474
C € 26,625
D € 26,750

4 What is the main advantage of a system of free floating exchange rates?

A Currency risk will be minimised
B Imposes policy discipline on governments
C Balance of payments deficits or surpluses are automatically corrected
D Consumers can compare prices across borders more easily

5 If a country has a freely floating exchange rate, which one of the following would lead to a rise (appreciation) in the rate of exchange for its currency?

A A decrease in the level of exports
B A decrease in the country's interest rates
C A decrease in the country's inflation rate
D A decrease in the level of capital inflows into the country

6 Which of tho following would normally rocult from a fall (dopreciation) in a country'c oxchango rato?

A A fall in the country's rate of inflation
B A rise in the volume of exports
C A worsening in its balance of payments
D A rise in the volume of imports

7 Which of the following would normally lead to an increase in a country's exchange rate?

A A rise in the country's rate of inflation
B An increase in a the country's balance of payments deficit
C A rise in the country's interest rate
D A decline in the forecast profits of the country's firms

8 What does Purchasing Power Parity theory predict?

Answers to quick quiz

1 A The forex market deals spot and forward contracts

2 False The main volume of dealing is speculative

3 C 25,000 × 1.0650 = €26,625. Note that we are given the €/£ exchange rate. If you chose A you divided rather than multiplied, and used the rate that was more favourable to the firm rather than the rate that was more favourable to the bank. If you chose B you divided rather than multiplied. If you chose D you used the rate that was more favourable to the firm.

4 C Free floating exchange rates mean that market forces restore equilibrium in the market. A balance of payments deficit will mean that supply > demand for a country's currency, and so its exchange rate will fall. This will improve competitiveness of the country's exports so exports will increase and restore equilibrium in the balance of payments. (Answers A and D are benefits of a single cross-border currency such as the euro).

5 A decrease in a country's inflation will make its exports cheaper, and therefore more attractive. The increase in demand for exports will lead to an increase in demand for the country's currency (for customers to pay for the exports) and this will lead to its exchange rate rising.

Conversely, a decrease in the level of exports (A) will lead to a fall in demand for a country's currency, so this will lead to its exchange rates falling.

Likewise if interest rates fall (B) it will be less attractive to invest money in a country's banks, so again there will be less demand for the country's money, from foreign investors looking to invest in it.

A decrease in the level of capital inflows will also mean demand for the currency falls, and so, again, the exchange rate will fall.

6 B The fall in the exchange rate will make a country's exports cheaper, therefore the volume of **exports will increase**. Conversely, the currency depreciation will make imports more expensive, so demand for **imports will fall**. The net of these two will lead to an improvement in the country's balance of payments. The rising price of imports will increase domestic inflation.

7 C A rise in domestic interest rates will attract portfolio investment and this increases demand for its currency

8 Purchasing Power Parity theory predicts that the exchange rate on currency for another will depreciate at the rate by which its country's inflation rate exceeds that of the other country

Now try the questions below from the Exam Question Bank

Question numbers
51 - 55

Part C

The macroeconomic context of organisations

The macroeconomic context 1 – the trade cycle

Introduction

The macroeconomic environment concerns the behaviour of the national and World economies in which organisations must operate.

The level of economic activity of a country's economy is its **national income**. We begin by understanding that factors determining **aggregate demand** and **aggregate supply** and which influence national income in general.

The **circular flow of income** provides a detailed analysis of the influences on aggregate demand for the goods produced by firms. Governments try to influence this to steer the macroeconomy away from recessions.

Historically the economy of countries and the World as a whole exhibit a cycle of growth and recession through time called a **trade cycle.** This cycle has effects on the outlook for business organisations and affects government activity in the economy.

Topic list	Learning outcomes	Syllabus references	Ability required
1 Factors affecting national income	A1	A1(a)	Comprehension
2 The circular flow of income	A1	A1(a)	Comprehension
3 Stages in the trade cycle	A1	A1(b)	Comprehension
4 Impact of the trade cycle on the business environment	A1	A1(e)	Comprehension

1 Factors affecting national income

FAST FORWARD

National income is a statistical measure of the **value of goods and services** produced in an economy **during a year**. It is an important index of **economic activity and employment**.

1.1 National income

Key term

National income: the value of goods and services produced in the economy during the year.

The governments or central banks of most economies monitor the level of economic activity in the domestic economy by measuring the national income each year.

The level of national income provides a guide to the **economic standard of living** of the population, and the levels of **employment** and **utilisation of the country's economic resources.**

The annual change in national income is called the **rate of economic growth** of the country.

National income is sometimes called:

(a) **Gross Domestic Product** (GDP): this is a measure of the value of goods and services made produced within the country's boundaries. It is the closest index to output and employment.

(b) **Gross National Product** (GNP): this measures the output from assets belonging to the country's population and therefore includes earnings from investments abroad. It is an indes of wealth and standard of living.

The analysis in this chapter will focus on GDP.

1.2 Aggregate demand and aggregate supply

FAST FORWARD

Equilibrium national income is determined using aggregate supply and aggregate demand analysis.

Key terms

Aggregate demand: the total value of demand for goods and services produced in the economy during a year

Aggregate supply: the maximum potential output of the economy during a year

Aggregate demand and supply analysis uses **market diagrams** to represent the behaviour of the entire economy rather than the markets for individual products. It is a **simplified view** but it helps convey the main points of this complex topic.

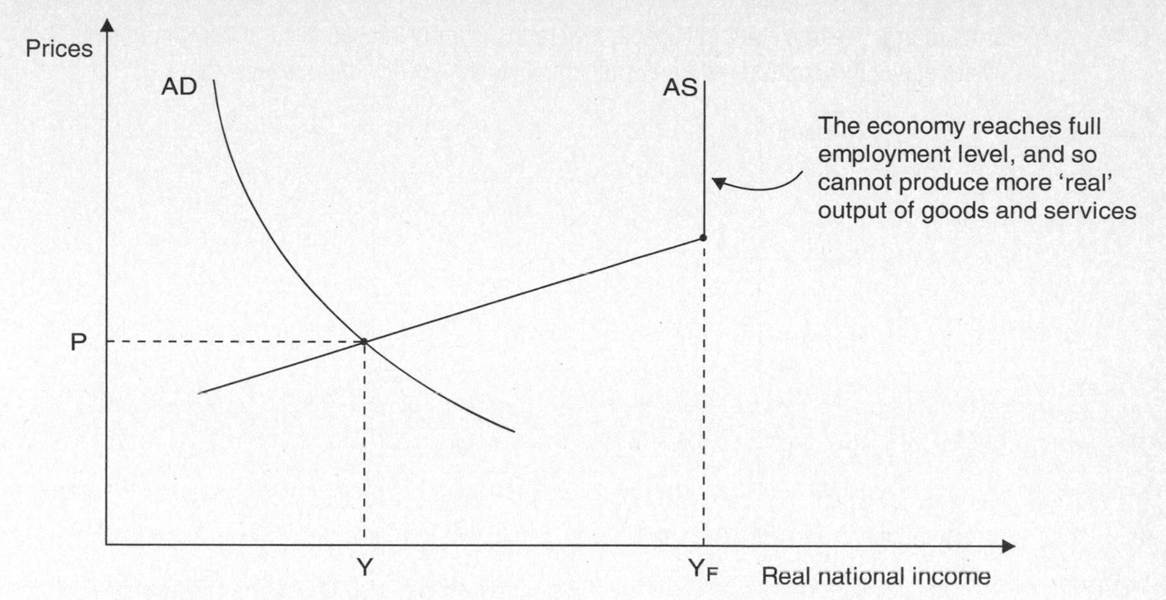

Figure 1 Equilibrium national income, using aggregate supply and aggregate demand analysis

In Figure 1 the following points should be noted:

(a) The **axes of the diagram** show national income as Y and on the vertical access the **general level of prices** in the economy

(b) **Aggregate demand** is downward sloping showing that as domestic prices rise the level of demand contracts. This is because the **higher prices** mean the **same income can buy less** output and also that the higher prices **discourage demand for exports**

(c) The **aggregate supply curve** is upward sloping showing that higher levels of output can only be achieved at the cost of higher prices. This is because **as output rises** there will arise **shortages of some productive resources**, such as labour and factory space, and their **costs will increase**.

(d) Level of output Y_F stands for **full employment**. It is a maximum potential output of the economy where all productive resources are fully used.

Figure 1 illustrates that the equilibrium level of national income will be at the intersection of the AD curve and AS curves – ie at Y. The difference between the equilibrium national income Y and the full employment national income Y_F shows how much national income could be increased with the resources at the economy's disposal. Y therefore represents the level of **satisfied** demand in the economy.

Two points follow on immediately from this initial analysis.

(a) Equilibrium national income Y might be at a level of national income below full employment national income Y_F.

(b) On the other hand, the AD curve might cut the AS curve above the point at which it becomes vertical, in which case the economy will be fully employed, but price levels will be higher than they need to be. There will be inflationary pressures in the economy.

1.3 Full-employment national income

If one aim of a country's economic policy is to achieve full employment, then the ideal equilibrium level of national income will be where AD and AS are in balance at the full employment level of national income, without any inflationary gap – in other words, where aggregate demand at current price levels is exactly sufficient to encourage firms to produce at an output capacity where the country's resources are fully employed. This is shown in Figure 2, where equilibrium output will be Y_F (full employment level) with price level P_F.

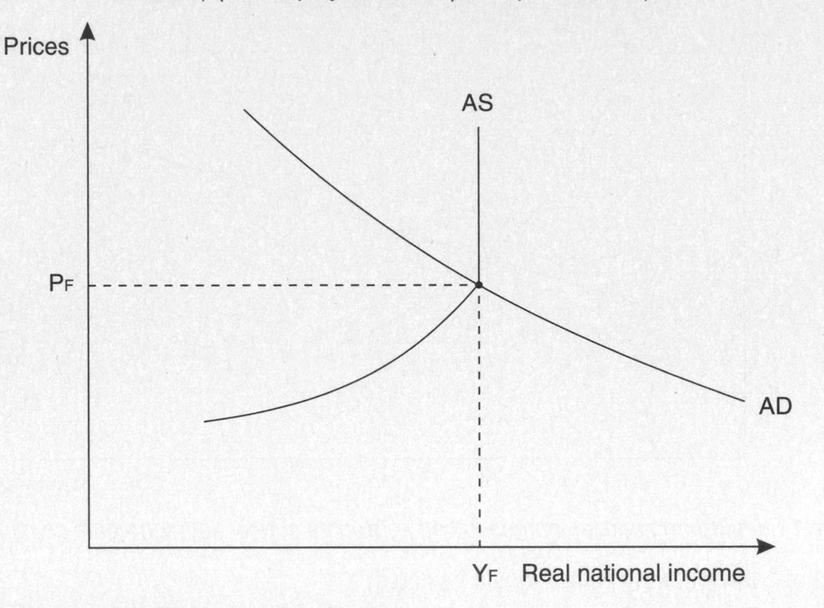

Figure 2 Full Employment Equilibrium national income

A country will usually continue to seek economic growth, but to achieve a real increase in living standards rather than simply to cause inflation, both AD and AS curves in Figure 2 will now have to shift to the right.

1.4 Inflationary gaps

Key term

Inflationary gap: a situation where the planned aggregate demand exceeds the full employment level of national income

In a situation where resources are already **fully employed**, there may be an **inflationary gap**, since increases in aggregate demand will cause price changes and not variations in real output. An inflationary gap can be described as the extent to which the aggregate demand function would have to **shift downward** to produce the full employment level of national income without price rises.

You should also note that a shift in the AD curve or the AS curve will not only change the national income, it will also change price levels (P). In Figure 3, an inflationary gap can be removed by shifting the aggregate demand curve to the left, from AD_1 to AD_2.

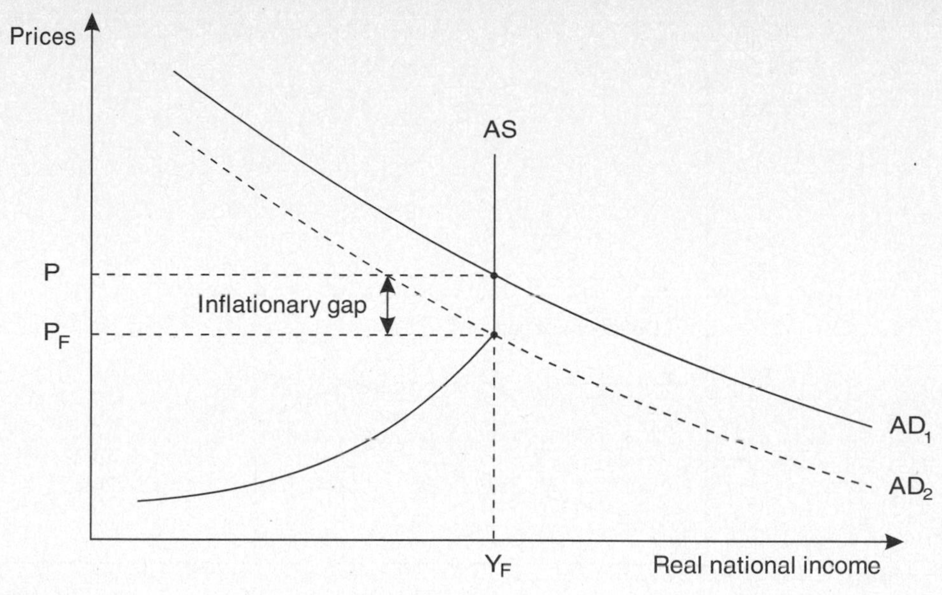

Figure 3 Inflationary gap

If you are not sure about this point, a simple numerical example might help to explain it better. Suppose that in Ruritania there is full employment and all other economic resources are fully employed. The country produces 1,000 units of output with these resources. Total expenditure (that is, aggregate demand) in the economy is 100,000 Ruritanian dollars, or 100 dollars per unit. The country does not have any external trade, and so it cannot obtain extra goods by importing them. Because of pay rises and easier credit terms for consumers, total expenditure now rises to 120,000 Ruritanian dollars. The economy is fully employed, and cannot produce more than 1,000 units. If expenditure rises by 20%, to buy the same number of units, it follows that prices must rise by 20% too. In other words, when an economy is at full employment, any increase in aggregate demand will result in price inflation.

The term **inflation** has turned into a description of rising prices in an economy. However when the term was first proposed, by the economist Keynes in 1936, it merely referred to excess demand.

1.5 Deflationary gap

Key term

Deflationary gap: where the level of planned aggregate demand is below the level needed to assure full employment.

In a situation **where there is unemployment of resources**, there is said to be a **deflationary gap** (Figure 4). Prices are fairly constant and real output changes as aggregate demand varies. A deflationary gap can be described as the extent to which the aggregate demand function will have to shift upward to produce the full employment level of national income. The economy is currently in equilibrium at Y_e (with aggregate demand AD_1) but it would need to be at Y_f (with aggregate demand AD_2) to achieve full employment.

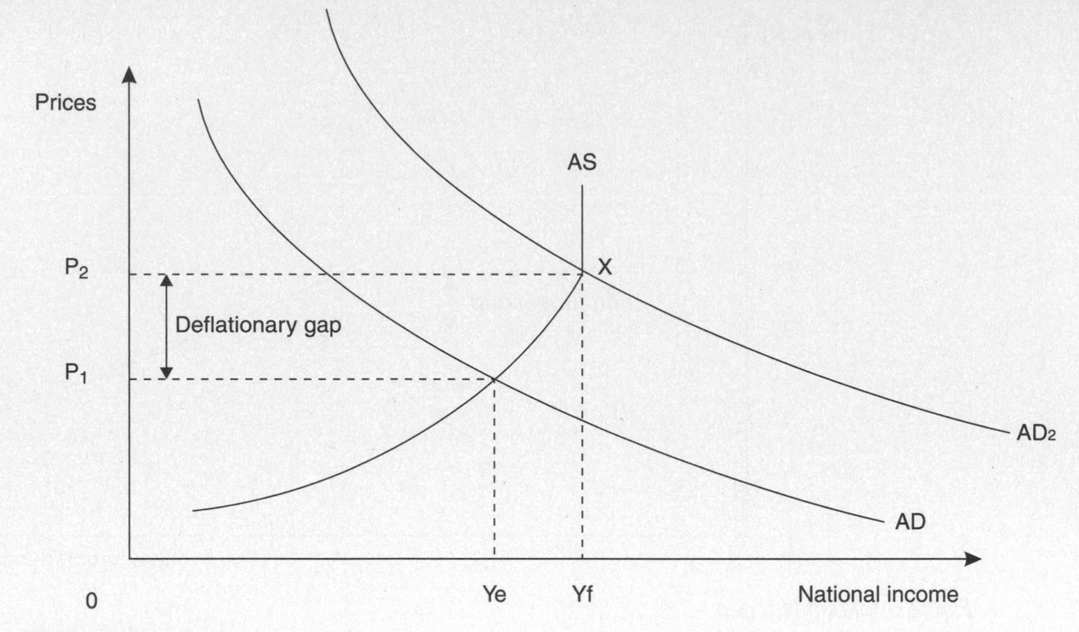

Figure 4 Deflationary gap

1.6 Shifts in Aggregate Supply

In Figures 3 and 4 we showed how changes in aggregate demand could affect the economy. However, there may also be changes in aggregate supply.

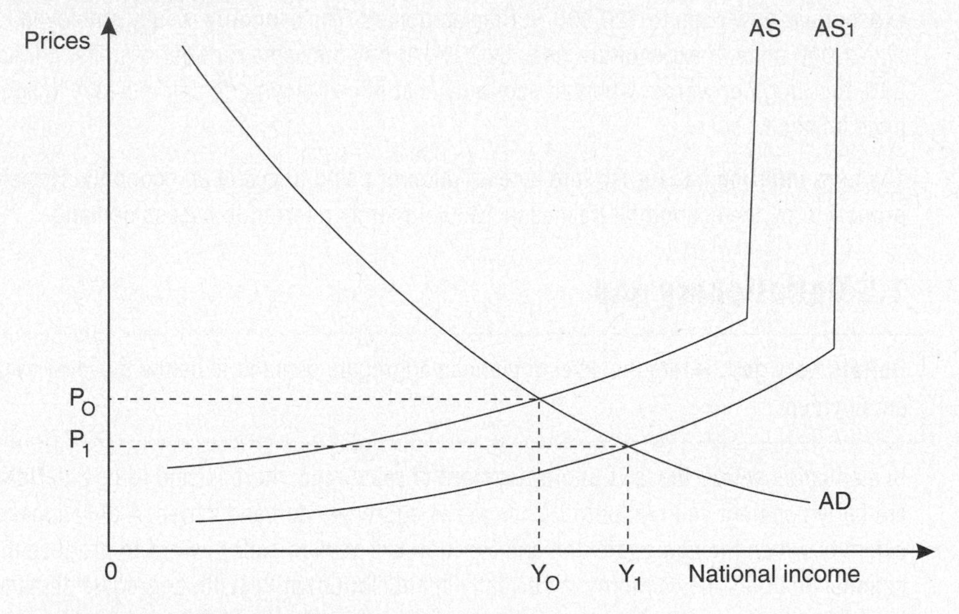

Figure 5 Increase in aggregate supply

Figure 5 shows the impact of a rise in Aggregate Supply.

(a) National income equilibrium is initially at Po Yo

(b) The rise in aggregate supply is shown by a shift of the aggregate supply curve from AS to AS1

(c) A new equilibrium level of national income is established at P1Y1

(d) This will be a position of greater employment and higher consumption than previously. This is also **non-inflationary** because the price level has fallen.

Increases in the productive characteristics of the economy, aggregate supply, take a considerably greater number of years to occur than rises in aggregate demand.

The likely **causes of rises in aggregate supply** include:

(a) Increased investment in technology and capital equipment in the economy

(b) Better training of staff to make them more productive

(c) Retraining of unemployed workers to give them skills needed to make them employable again

(d) Increased incentives for firms to employ workers and expand output in the economy

2 The circular flow of income

FAST FORWARD

The is a **circular flow of income** in an economy describes how the **incomes** earned for producing output are recycled back to provide **expenditure** to buy the outputs of the economy

2.1 Income and expenditure flows

Firms must pay households for the factors of production, and households must pay firms for goods. The income of firms is the sales revenue from the sales of goods and services.

This creates a **circular flow** of income and expenditure, as illustrated in Figure 6. This is a basic **closed economy**, without foreign trade. It assumes the economy has only two sectors (firms and households), with no government intervention and no imports or exports. In this model, we assume all household income is spent on consumption, and all the firms' goods and services are sold to the households.

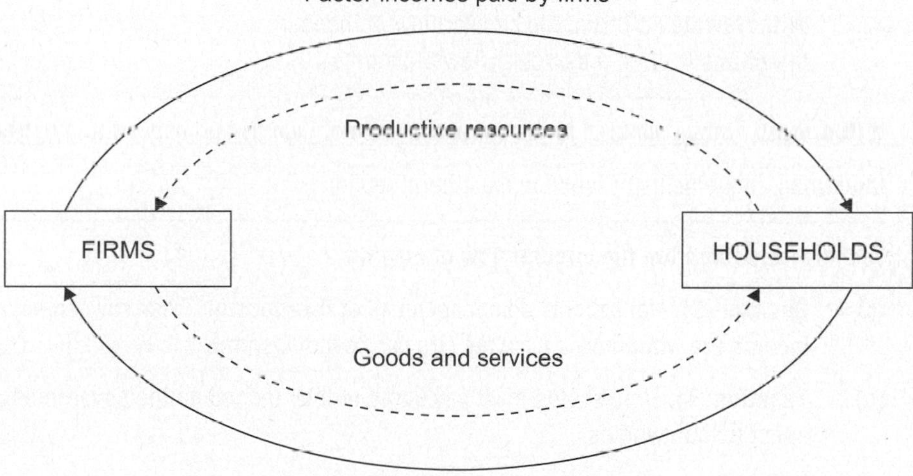

Figure 6 Circular flow of income

Households earn **income** because they have provided the factors of production which enable firms to provide goods and services. The income earned is used as **expenditure** on these goods and services that are made.

2.2 Macroeconomic equilibrium in the circular flow

FAST FORWARD

For there to be macroeconomic equilibrium **planned expenditure must equal income** ie E=Y

Key term

> **Macroeconomic equilibrium**: where the level of national income shows no tendency to change through time.

The equilibrium conditions of AD=AS can also be seen in the circular flow diagram.

Planned expenditure (E) is the value of goods and services household **intend** to purchase during the year.

Income (Y) is the **actual** earnings being generated from the production of goods and services at the economy's present level of activity. In effect Y means aggregate supply.

(a) If $E > Y$ then the level of planned expenditure exceeds the level of income this means that the **present level of output is insufficient** and therefore firms will take on additional workers and equipment to increase output. This will **raise national income**.

(b) If $E < Y$ then the level of planned expenditure is below the level of income this means that the **present level of output is excessive** and therefore firms will reduce output and employment. This will **reduce national income.**

You may recognise that (a) and (b) above describe an **inflationary gap** and a **deflationary gap** respectively.

Therefore for macroeconomic equilibrium **planned expenditure must equal actual income**.

2.3 Withdrawals and injections into the circular flow of income

FAST FORWARD

> There are **withdrawals** from the circular flow of income (**savings, taxation, import expenditure**) and **injections** into the circular flow (**investment, government spending, export income**).

Our simplified diagram of the circular flow of income in Figure 6 needs to be amended to allow for two things.

- **Withdrawals** (W) from the circular flow of income
- **Injections** (J) into the circular flow of income

Key terms

> **Withdrawals**: movements of funds out of the cycle of income and expenditure between firms and households.
>
> **Injections**: movements of funds in the other direction

Withdrawals (W) from the circular flow of income

(a) **Savings (S).** Households do not spend all of their income. They save some, and these savings out of income are withdrawals from the circular flow of income.

(b) **Taxation (T).** Households must pay some of their income to the government, as taxation. Taxes cannot be spent by households.

(c) **Imports (M)**. When we consider national income, we are interested in the economic wealth that a particular country is earning.

   (i) Spending on imports is expenditure, but on goods made by firms in other countries.
   (ii) The payments for imports go to firms in other countries, for output created in other countries.
   (iii) Spending on imports therefore withdraws funds out of a country's circular flow of income.

Be aware that **saving** is different from **investment**; saving simply means withdrawing money from circulation. Think of it as cash kept in a money box rather than being put into a bank to earn interest.

Injections (J) into the circular flow of income

(a) **Investment (I).** Investment in capital goods is a form of spending on output, which is additional to expenditure by households. Just as savings are a withdrawal of funds, investment is an injection of funds into the circular flow of income, adding to the total economic wealth that is being created by the country.

(b) **Government spending (G).** Government spending is also an injection into the circular flow of income. In most mixed economies, total spending by the government on goods and services represents a large proportion of total national expenditure. The funds to spend come from either taxation income or government borrowing.

(c) **Exports (X).** Firms produce goods and services for export. Exports earn income from abroad, and therefore provide an injection into a country's circular flow of income.

Figure 7 shows the circular flow of income, taking account of withdrawals and injections. This is an **open economy**, since it participates in foreign trade.

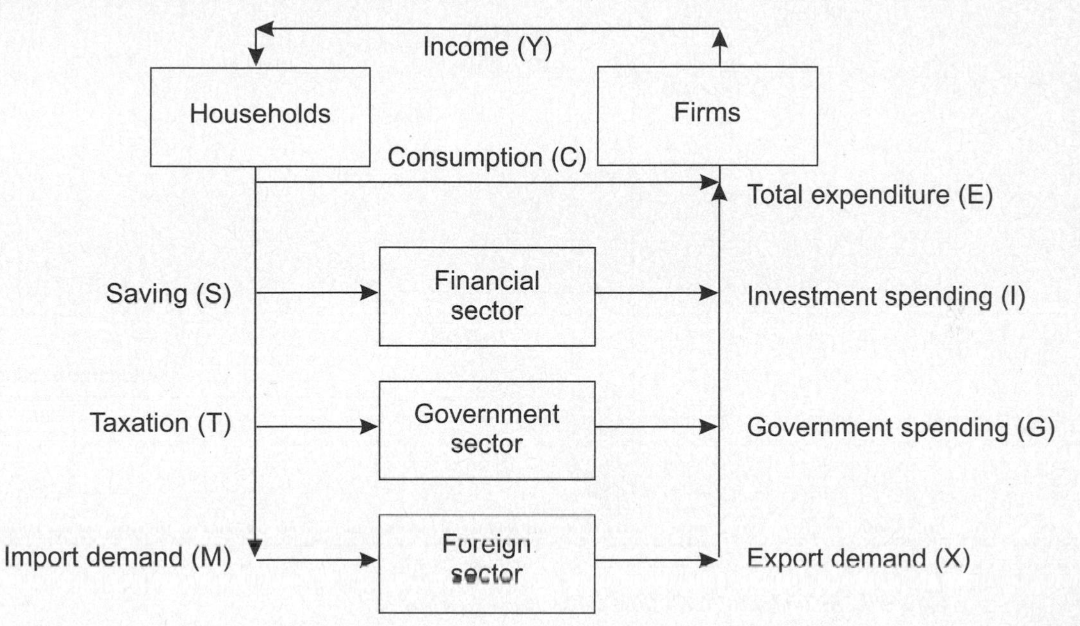

Figure 7 Circular flow of income showing withdrawals and injections

The economy is said to be in **equilibrium** when injections (J) equal withdrawals (W). So written out in full, equilibrium is reached in an economy when:

I	+	G	+	X	=	S	+	T	+	M
Investment	+	Government spending	+	Exports	=	Savings	+	Taxation	+	Imports

However, if injections are greater than withdrawals (**J>W**) the level of national income will rise. This is because it would mean that planned expenditure > income (**E>Y**) and create an **inflationary gap**.

Equally, if withdrawals are greater than injections (**W>J**) then the level of national income will fall because planned expenditure would be less than income (**Y>E**) and create a **deflationary gap**.

2.4 Consumption and savings

FAST FORWARD

Consumption expenditure depends on income. As income rises consumption will rise at a rate determined by the **marginal propensity to consume (MPC).** The increase in consumption will be less **than the rise in income due to the withdrawals** of savings, taxation and import demand.

2.4.1 Importance of consumption expenditure

Many firms require a high level of consumer demand to provide a market for their goods. It is important to understand the factors affecting consumption.

Consumption expenditure also affects the level of national income because it is a major part of aggregate demand.

2.4.2 Marginal propensities to consume and withdraw

Figure 8 shows the **consumption function** of an economy, the way **planned consumption varies as income rises.**

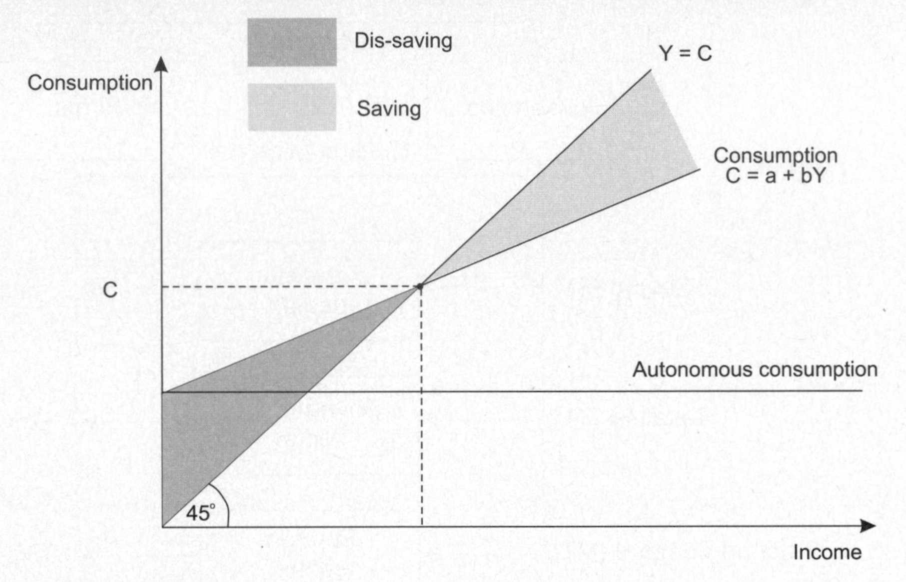

Figure 8 The consumption function

The points to notice are:

(a) There is a level of consumption spending in an economy that is **independent of income** called **autonomous consumption.** This is because in a developed economy some households will spend more than they earn during a year due to pensions, welfare benefits and the use of credit. This is called **dissaving.**

(b) The remaining consumption expenditure is **income induced** because it rises as income rises. In Figure 8 the 45° line shows what would happen if all extra income were spent on consumption, ie if C=Y. The actual consumption function is flatter than 45° which shows that **only proportion of extra income is used as consumption expenditure**.

Key term

Marginal propensity to consume (MPC): the percentage of any additional income that is spend on consumption. For the economy as a whole this will have a value of less than 1.

MPC is calculated as: $\text{MPC} = \dfrac{\text{Change in consumption}}{\text{Change in income}}$

Question

A household's disposable income has increased from $200 to $250 per week, and consumption has increased from $180 to $£220.

What is the household's marginal propensity to consume?

Answer

0.8 $\frac{\text{Change in consumption}}{\text{Change in income}} = \frac{40}{50}$

The MPC will always be less than 1 in an economy due to the inevitable impact of withdrawals.

(a) Many households will be saving. This is described by the **marginal propensity to save (MPS)**

(b) Taxation will be levied by the government at a rate termed the **marginal propensity to tax (MPT)**

(C) Some expenditure will be on imported goods and services at a rate determined by the **marginal propensity to import (MPM)**

Key term

Marginal Propensity to Withdraw: the proportion of income earned in an economy that is not directly passed on as expenditure in the circular flow of income

= MPS + MPT + MPM

= 1 – MPC (because MPC + MPW equals 1)

The MPW is the proportion of national income that is withdrawn from the circular flow of income.

2.4.3 Influences on consumption

The level of consumption expenditure will **increase** due to the following:

(a) **Rise in incomes**: this will cause consumption to rise by the value of the MPC

(b) **Redistribution of income to the less well-off**: richer households save a greater portion of their income than poorer households who need to spend most of their incomes on the basic necessities of life. Taking money from the rich and giving to the poor, by the taxation and benefits system, will increase consumption

(c) **Fall in interest rates**: this will discourage savings (a fall in a withdrawal) and also encourage consumption spending on credit (a rise in autonomous consumption)

(d) **Fall in taxation**: this leaves more income for households to spend(a fall in a withdrawal)

(e) **Fall in foreign exchange rate**: this will reduce the attractiveness of imports and encourage greater consumption of domestic product (a fall in a withdrawal)

(f) **Length of time since income rose:** the MPC increases with time as households adjust to the improved level of income and incorporate it in their spending plans

2.5 The multiplier

The **multiplier** describes the **process of circulation of income** in the national economy, whereby an **initial rise in expenditure leads to a much larger increase in national income.**

Formula to learn

Multiplier:

Or $\frac{1}{1\text{-MPC}}$ or $\frac{1}{\text{MPW}}$

Consider a situation of an economy that get an injection of extra expenditure, perhaps from the government spending on a large road-building project (a rise in injections). The firms or households receiving the injection use at least part of the money to increase their own consumption. This provides money for other firms and households to repeat the process and so on.

Key term

Multiplier: the ratio of the **total** increase in national income to an **initial injection**

Total increase in National Income/Initial increase in National Income

$$\text{Multiplier} = \frac{\text{Total increase in national income}}{\text{Initial increase in national income}}$$

The multiplier can be defined as a measure of the effect on total national income of a unit change in a component of aggregate demand: I, G or X.

Multiplier values can therefore be measured specifically for each of these separately.

$$\text{Investment multiplier} = \frac{\text{Eventual change in national income}}{\text{Initial change in investment spending}}$$

$$\text{Government spending multiplier} = \frac{\text{Eventual change in national income}}{\text{Initial change in government spending}}$$

$$\text{Export multiplier} = \frac{\text{Eventual change in national income}}{\text{Initial change in exports}}$$

2.6 Numerical illustration of the multiplier

A numerical illustration of the multiplier might help to explain it more clearly. In this example, we shall again ignore taxes, government spending, exports and imports, and assume a simple closed economy in which all income is either spent on consumption (C) or saved (S). Let us suppose that in this closed economy, marginal propensity to consume (MPC) is 0.9. This means that out of any addition to household income, 90% is consumed and 10% saved.

(a) If income goes up by $200m, $180m would be spent on consumption, and $20m saved.

(b) Because of the circular flow, the $180m spent on consumption in turn increases the income of other people, who spend 90% of it ($162m) and save $18m.

(c) This $162 in turn becomes additional income to others. We can see that a snowball effect on consumption (and income and output) occurs, as follows.

			Increase in expenditure $m	*Increase in savings* $m
Stage	1	Income rises	200.00	–
	2	90% is consumed	180.00	20.00
	3	A further 90% is consumed	162.00	18.00
	4	90% of $162 is consumed	145.80	16.20
	5	90% is consumed	131.22	14.58
		Etc	.....	.....
		Total increase in income	2,000.00	200.00

However, although we have identified that a 'snowball effect' has been created, it will not continue indefinitely, because at each stage a proportion of the extra income is lost through **withdrawals** (savings).

In this example, the initial increase in income of $200m will result in a final increase in national income of $2,000m. The multiplier is 10.

2.7 The multiplier in an open economy

The example in section 2.6 used a simplified economy in which income is either saved or spent on domestic production, and in which there is no government intervention. The real world is more complex, though, and we must now consider the effect of taxation and imports. Like savings, these are **withdrawals from the circular flow** and they therefore affect the multiplier. Thus, in an open economy, the value of the multiplier depends on three things.

(a) The marginal propensity to **save**

(b) The marginal propensity to **import**, because imports reduce national income, and if households spend much of their extra income on imports, the snowball increase in total national income will be restricted because imports are a withdrawal out of the circular flow of income.

(c) The level of **taxes**, because taxes reduce people's ability to consume and so are likely to affect the marginal propensity to consume and the marginal propensity to save.

Whereas the multiplier in a closed economy is the reciprocal of the marginal propensity to save, the multiplier in an open economy, taking into account government spending and taxation, and imports and exports, will be less. This is because government taxation and spending on imports reduces the multiplier effect on a country's economy.

For an open economy:

$$\text{Multiplier} = \frac{1}{s+m+t}$$

Where s is the marginal propensity to save

m is the marginal propensity to import

t is the marginal propensity to tax – ie the amount of any increase in income that will be paid in taxes.

The multiplier as defined in this way may still be represented as below.

$\text{Multiplier} = \frac{1}{1\text{-MPC}}$, but this is now the same as $\frac{1}{\text{MPW}}$ (reflecting the impact of withdrawals as a whole).

For example, if in a country the marginal propensity to save is 10%, the marginal propensity to import is 45% and the marginal propensity to tax is 25%, the size of the multiplier would be:

$$\frac{1}{0.1+0.45+0.25} = \frac{1}{0.80} = 1.25$$

2.8 Determinants of injections

2.8.1 Influences on investment (I)

Investment represents one of the major injections in the circular flow of income. As we will see later when looking at the multiplier effect, variations in the level of investment can affect the level of national income and the level of aggregate demand in the economy.

The total volume of desired investment in the economy depends on factors similar to those influencing 'micro-level' investment decisions by firms.

- The rate of interest on capital
- The marginal efficiency of capital (MEC) invested, that is how profitable the investment is likely to be
- Expectations about the future and business confidence, including expectations about future cash flows and profit flows arising from the investment

(a) **Higher interest rates** should make firms **less willing to invest**, because it will make some investments unable to repay the interest costs of doing them.

(b) **Lower interest rates** should have the opposite effect and encourage greater investment.

When considering an investment, a firm will be concerned with the net rate of return it will receive from its investment.

In this way, the firm will consider not only the values of future sales and costs, but also the timings of them and interest rate levels.

Interest rates are crucial to the investment decision, because if the funds used for the investment had not been invested they could have earned interest elsewhere.

Consequently, the future income stream which an investment is expected to generate has to be **discounted** to allow for the interest income foregone, and to convert it to its **net present value**.

Net present value (NPV) is the value obtained by discounting all cash outflows and inflows of a capital investment project by a chosen target rate of return or cost of capital.

The present value (PV) of a project can be shown as:

$$PV = \frac{Q}{1+r} + \frac{Q}{(1+r)^2} + \ldots + \frac{Q}{(1+r)^n}$$

Where Q is the anticipated annual inflow, r is the interest rate, and n is the time period when the inflow will occur.

From this we can see that the PV will vary inversely to interest rates, meaning that if interest rates increase, the PV of the investment will fall, *ceteris paribus*.

2.8.2 Marginal efficiency of capital

Using the NPV method, present values are calculated by discounting at a target rate of return, and the difference between the PV of costs and the PV of benefits is the NPV.

In contrast, the marginal efficiency of capital approach calculates the exact rate of return which a project is expected to achieve, in other words, the rate at which the NPV is zero.

This rate of return is termed the marginal efficiency of capital (MEC). If the MEC (or internal rate of return (IRR)) exceeds the current rate of interest, then an investment will be profitable.

A change in interest rates is likely to induce a movement along the MEC curve and prompt a change in levels of investment.

However, we could also witness shifts in the MEC curve, notably from changes in **business confidence**. If businesses are optimistic about the future they are more likely to invest. This would lead to an outward shift in the MEC curve (MEC to MEC_1 in Figure 9). The MEC curve could also be shifted by **technological innovation** (making capital more productive) or **government policy** (for example, a reduction in taxes could encourage investment). A final factor which could lead to a shift in the MEC curve is the **substitution** of other factors of production. For example, if wage costs rise, a business may look to substitute capital for labour, in effect shifting the MEC curve to the right.

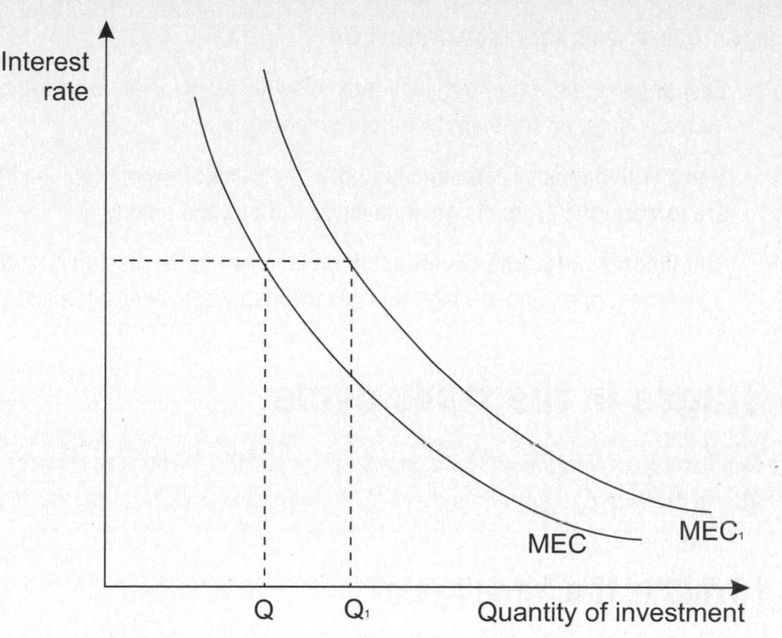

Figure 9 The marginal efficiency of capital

2.8.3 Influences on government expenditure (G)

Government expenditure includes all spending by the national and regional government agencies and departments in the country.

Government expenditure includes:

(a) **Government consumption spending**: these are the daily and monthly expenses of staff, buildings and so on

(b) **Social overhead capital formation**: this includes projects such as roads, airports, defence equipment, power generation and public buildings

(c) **Discretionary expenditure**: this is spending on one-off projects and includes wars, public events or special projects to reduce unemployment and provide training

Government expenditure is financed from taxation revenues and from borrowing from financial markets.

Governments frequently use government expenditure to influence the level of activity and employment in the economy in the following ways:

(a) **Fiscal deficits (G>T)**: the government acts as a **net injection** into the economy by spending more that it receives in taxation revenues. It borrows the balance. This is intended to **increase aggregate demand** via a multiplier effect.

(b) **Fiscal surpluses (T>G)**: the government acts as a **net withdrawal** from the economy by spending less than it receives from taxation. It uses this to repay past borrowing. This **reduces aggregate demand** via a **downward multiplier effect**.

2.8.4 Export demand (X)

Export demand is foreign spending on products produced domestically. It includes purchase of goods and services provided to the buyer's home country. It also includes spending by visitors to the domestic economy.

The main determinants of export demand are:

(a) **Exchange rates:** if the exchange rate is low this will make domestic goods more competitive and will increase demand for them from foreign countries.

(b) **Competitiveness of domestic industry:** the sales of exports will be improved if domestic production costs are low and the products are innovative and of good quality

(c) **The income of foreign countries:** if the incomes in the foreign country are high and household and investment spending are high this will inevitably spill over into increased demand for exports

3 Stages in the trade cycle

FAST FORWARD

Trade cycles (sometimes called **business cycles**) describe the tendency for economies to swing between **years of growth and high employment**, and **years of stagnation and high unemployment** on a regular basis.

3.1 What is the trade cycle?

Trade cycles or **business cycles** are the continual sequence of rapid growth in national income, followed by a slow-down in growth and then a fall in national income (recession). After this recession comes growth again, and when this has reached a peak, the cycle turns into recession once more.

3.2 Phases of the business cycle

At point A in Figure 10, the economy is entering a **recession**. In the recession phase, consumer demand falls and many investment projects already undertaken begin to look unprofitable. Orders will be cut, inventory levels will be reduced and business failures will occur as firms find themselves unable to sell their goods. Production and employment will fall. The general price level will begin to fall. Business and consumer confidence are diminished and investment remains low, while the economic outlook appears to be poor. Eventually, in the absence of any stimulus to aggregate demand, a period of full **depression** sets in and the economy will reach point B.

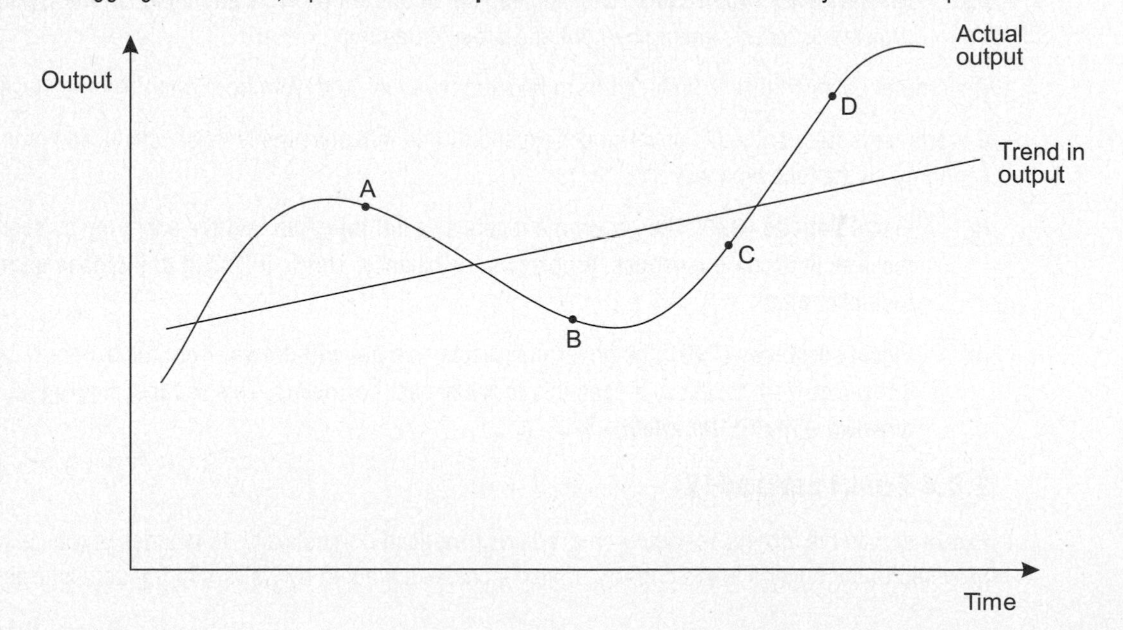

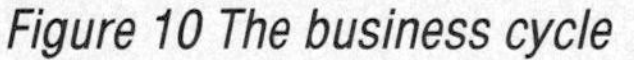
Figure 10 The business cycle

3.3 Analysis of the phases

3.3.1 Recession phase

In Figure 10 the points between A and B shows a recession.

Recessions are characterised by

(a) Negative economic growth for 2 or more successive quarters (ie for 6 months or more)

(b) Rising levels of unemployment of labour, and associated capital infrastructure

(c) Low levels of business and consumer confidence

Recession can begin relatively quickly. This is because of the speed with which the effects of declining demand will be anticipated by businesses which then run down inventories and cut back on investment in new buildings and machinery. This creates a wave of unemployment and falling incomes spreading across the economy as a **downward multiplier effect.**

In economies where governments follow **macroeconomic stabilisation policies** the governments will try to limit the decline by **limiting the fall in aggregate demand**.

These are called **demand management policies** and to boost aggregate demand the most likely policies are:

(a) **Increases to government expenditure**: the government **borrow** funds from the financial sector and spend this on infrastructure projects and other job creation schemes to **create an offsetting upward multiplier effect**

(b) **Reductions in taxation:** by reducing taxation the levels of income of households and firms are increased and this **encourages more expenditure**

(c) **Reduce interest rates:** using the influence of the central bank to reduce interest rates has the effect of **stimulating investment and consumption** on credit (and well as reducing saving). Together these help boost aggregate demand.

Point B in Figure 10 may be called the **depression phase**. This is where the economy has become stuck at low levels of national income. It is the same as a **deflationary gap**.

3.3.2 Recovery phase

At point C in Figure 10 the economy has reached the recovery phase of the cycle.

The symptoms of a recovery phase are:

(a) Modest rates of economic growth (ie rate of increase of national income, usually measured quarterly)
(b) Increase in job vacancies, job creation and reduction in levels of unemployment
(c) Improvement in profitability of business
(d) Improved consumer and business confidence, leading to greater expenditure

Once begun, the phase of recovery is likely to quicken as confidence returns. Output, employment and income will all begin to rise. Rising production, sales and profit levels will lead to optimistic business expectations, and new investment will be more readily undertaken.

The rising level of demand can be met through increased production by bringing existing capacity into use and by hiring unemployed labour. The average price level will remain constant or begin to rise slowly.

3.3.3 Boom phase

This is shown as point D in Figure 10.

The symptoms of the boom phase are:

(a) Low levels of unemployment as economy reaches full employment level of national income

(b) Excess demand for labour and capital resources leads to rising pay and other costs which feeds in to create higher prices

(c) Excess aggregate demand pulls in imports and diverts export production to serve the domestic market and leads to balance of payments deficits (X<M)

As recovery proceeds, the output level climbs above its trend path, reaching point D, in the boom phase of the cycle. During the boom, capacity and labour will become fully utilised. This may cause bottlenecks in some industries which are unable to meet increases in demand, for example because they have no spare capacity or they lack certain categories of skilled labour, or they face shortages of key material inputs. Further rises in demand will, therefore, tend to be met by increases in prices (inflation) rather than by increases in production. In general, business will be profitable, with few firms facing losses. Expectations of the future may be very optimistic and the level of investment expenditure high.

In economies where governments follow **macroeconomic stabilisation policies** the governments will try to limit the adverse effects of the boom by **limiting the rise in aggregate demand**.

The most likely policies are:

(a) **Reductions to government expenditure**: this government may use funds to repay past borrowings instead

(b) **Increases in taxation:** this reduces the growth in expenditure as incomes rise by increasing the marginal propensity to withdraw and so reduces the multiplier effect

(c) **Raise interest rates:** this will reduce investment, consumption on credit, and also increase savings.

Assessment focus point

It is important that you can not only recognise the characteristics of each phase of the business cycle, but also the appropriate policy for a government to employ at each stage.

3.4 Causes of the business cycle

There have been many theories of why business cycles occur. A famous 19th Century economist, Jevons, suggested they arose from sunspot activity affecting harvests. This is clearly not correct for an industrial economy. The most likely explanations are:

(a) **Instability of private** investment: sometimes called the **accelerator theory** this ventures that the initial recovery of an economy stimulates a disproportionate boost in investment in long-term projects that propels the economy into an unsustainable boom. Once the level of real national income ceases to rise there is a corresponding savage cut back in investment that plunges the economy into recession and depression

(b) **Business psychology**: this suggests that businesses exhibit a **herd** instinct that makes them all run in one direction and then suddenly change direction and run in the other. During a boom businesses look for the signs of recession and small events can trigger a sudden loss of business confidence and the onset of a **depression psychology.** During a recession the low expectations are reinforced by the poor state of the economy and hence little investment occurs. Once the recovery begins the psychology turns and investment takes place, sometimes long after it is warranted and turns into an unsustainable boom

(c) **Inappropriate government policy:** this may be called **fiscal** lag or **government failure** and are used by some economist who argue that the business cycle is made much worse by government activity. During the later stages of a recovery, when governments should begin to cut spending and raise taxes, they are **politically unwilling** to be seen to raise taxes and cancel social projects. This causes a boom. In a recession they maintain the high taxes too long and take too long to draw up spending plans and so the recession is deepened. They also argue that government borrowing to boost spending raises interest rates and reduces the investment funds available and this **crowds out** private investment which would have resolved the recession if left to itself.

4 Impact of the trade cycle on the business environment

FAST FORWARD

The impacts of the trade cycle on business include the **direct effects** of the changes in aggregate demand and employment, and the **secondary effects** of the resulting intervention by governments to correct it.

4.1 Direct effects of the trade cycle

The trade cycle is characterised by changes in the level of aggregate demand. These changes affect the demand for the output of a firm and so need to be responded to.

4.1.1 The recovery and boom phases

This is a time of high and rising demand in the economy. During this phase the impacts on business are:

(a) **Need to expand capacity** to cope with the higher demand. this should be planned in advance to avoid paying higher prices later. For example training its own staff will be cheaper than relying on hiring skilled staff from the labour market

(b) **Resource shortages**: The costs of materials and components will rise. Staff will need to be well-rewarded to avoid them leaving for higher paid jobs with rivals. This can drive inflation (see (e) below)

(c) **Import penetration and market entry:** the high profits and prospects will attract rivals, some from outside the country, to compete

(d) **Acquisition activity:** in a growth market banks and investors become more willing to lend, and firms need to gain capacity and additional product ranges. This can lead to **merger mania**, a wave of business amalgations.

(e) **Inflation:** rising costs will cause rising prices which in turn lead to further rising costs in a spiral of inflation. Firms will have to budget for rising prices and costs and be prepared to accommodate unanticipated cost increases

(f) **Exchange rate depreciation:** rising prices and increasing trade deficits will tend to push exchange rates down. This will increase the costs of imported components.

4.1.2 Recession and depression phases

This is where demand is falling and business and consumer confidence are low. The business impacts of this will include:

(a) **Need to rationalise output and production:** firms will suffer reduced sales. They will need to reduce production volumes, including dismissing staff or not replacing leavers, during these phases

(b) **Downward pressure on prices and profits:** with less demand firms will seek to shift unsold stock and maintain sales by price reductions. This will lead to a reduction in profits

(c) **Investor pressure:** investors will still seek constant and rising profits despite the recession. This will force firms to find ways to reduce costs, or indicate that they have a plan to reduce costs. This will normally involve **selling off** incidental lines of business, **rationalisation** of operations, and **off-shoring**

(d) **Failure of partner firms:** in a recession key customers and suppliers can become financially troubled and disappear or be acquired

4.2 Secondary effects of trade cycle

Government may attempt to regulate the trade cycle by demand management policies. This leads to secondary effects on business

4.2.1 The recovery and boom phases

During this phase the government may follow **deflationary demand management policies.**

(a) **Increases in interest rates:** many **central banks** are under instructions to ensure the **inflation rate** (the general rate of increase of prices) does not exceed a certain target. They will use the interest rate to achieve this. Interest rates are a blunt instrument that can **harm particular sectors** that depend on bank finance, such as small businesses, the housing market, and some consumer credit. This will also tend to **increase exchange rates** due to increasing demand for currency to buy domestic financial assets

(b) **Increases in taxation**: the government may seek to increase taxes. Most obviously these may be on personal incomes and company profits but less obviously may be specific taxes placed on the production or consumption of particular products, or **windfall taxes** on industries which seem to have been making excessive profits

(c) **Reductions in government spending**: this can lead to the withdrawal of particular types of funding for training, youth work, social housing and the public sector generally. This leads industries that depend on public contracts to struggle

(d) **Direct controls**: the government may seek to attack the symptoms of the boom by introducing **import restrictions** and **price freezes**. These distort the market and create uncertainty for the business.

4.2.2 Recession and depression phases

Here the government will seek to use expansionary demand management policies:

(a) Central banks will be encouraged to **extend lending** and **reduce interest rates**. This may lead to a relaxation on regulations on **consumer credit** and **lower costs of loans** to businesses.

(b) Government will launch **major spending contracts**, particularly in the construction sector, for which firms can **tender**.

(c) **Selective tax reductions** will be targeted to increases investment and employment in addition to **general tax reductions** to boost aggregate demand generally.

Chapter roundup

- **National income** is a statistical measure of the **value of goods and services** produced in an economy **during a year**. It is an important index of **economic activity and employment**.
- **Equilibrium national income** is determined using aggregate supply and aggregate demand analysis
- The is a **circular flow of income** in an economy describes how the **incomes** earned for producing output are recycled back to provide **expenditure** to buy the outputs of the economy
- For there to be macroeconomic equilibrium **planned expenditure must equal income** ie **E=Y**
- There are **withdrawals** from the circular flow of income (**savings, taxation, import expenditure**) and **injections** into the circular flow (**investment, government spending, export income**).
- **Consumption expenditure** depends on income. As income rises consumption will rise at a rate determined by the **marginal propensity to consume (MPC).** The increase in consumption will be less **than the rise in income due to the withdrawals** of savings, taxation and import demand.
- **Trade cycles** (sometimes called **business cycles**) describe the tendency for economies to swing between **years of growth and high employment**, and **years of stagnation and high unemployment** on a regular basis.
- The impacts of the trade cycle on business include the **direct effects** of the changes in aggregate demand and employment, and the **secondary effects** of the resulting intervention by governments to correct it.

Quick quiz

1 If total national expenditure is 'E', what is the equation used to show how 'E' is calculated?

2 What are the marginal propensity to consume and the marginal propensity to save?

3 How might a government try to influence the volume of investment by firms?

4 Injections into the economy are:

A Consumption and Investment
B Investment and Government Expenditure
C Investment, Government Expenditure and Export Demand
D Consumption, Investment, Government Expenditure and Export Demand

5 If a consumption function has the formula C = 750 + 0.4Y where is Y the change in national income, and injections are 500, then equilibrium national income will be at:

A 833
B 1,250
C 2,083
D 3,125

6 If the MPC is greater for the poor than the rich then a redistribution of national income in favour of the rich will:

A Raise savings out of a given income
B Increase the multiplier
C Decrease the MPS
D Stimulate import demand

7 A deflationary gap occurs when:

A Aggregate demand is insufficient to buy up all the goods and services the company is capable of producing.
B Aggregate demand is more than sufficient to buy up all the goods and services produced by an economy.
C A government attempts to spend its way out of recession.
D A government is cutting its level of expenditure.

8 What is the multiplier effect?

9 In an aggregate demand and supply diagram, what would be the consequences if the aggregate supply curve shifted inwards?

A Prices would rise and national income would rise
B Prices would fall and national income would rise
C Prices would fall and national income would fall
D Prices would rise and national income would fall

10 In an economy, the marginal propensity to consume is 0.85. What is the multiplier in that economy?

Answers to quick quiz

1 $E = C + I + G + (X - M)$

2 When a household receives an increase in income, some will be spent and some will be saved. The proportion which is spent is the marginal propensity to consume, while the proportion which is saved is the marginal propensity to save.

3 Lower interest rates, investment grants and tax incentives may encourage investment. Governments can also stimulate demand by tax cuts or lower interest rates and improve business confidence by business friendly and growth enhancing policies like deregulation and controlling inflation. Policies to encourage technological development may also lead to increased investment.

4 C Injections are any additional expenditures which do not arise from the circular flow of income itself. Consumption is part of the circular flow so it not an injection.

5 C Equilibrium occurs when E = Y. E = C + J = 750 + 0.4Y + 500. Therefore 0.6Y = 1,250, therefore Y= 2,083.

6 A The rich will save more, not spend. The MPC is greater for the poor than the rich.

7 A

8 The multiplier explains how the increase in total national income will be much greater than an initial injection into an economy, due to the injection being recycled through the economy.

9 D If the aggregate supply curve shifts to the left, national income will fall. Because the aggregate demand curve is downward sloping, shifting the supply curve to the left will mean the intersection between supply and demand is at a higher price: prices will rise.

This combination of rising prices and falling national income is characteristic of stagflation.

10 6.67 The multiplier is $\frac{1}{1-MPC}$

$$\frac{1}{1-0.85} = \frac{1}{0.15}$$

Now try the questions below from the Exam Question Bank

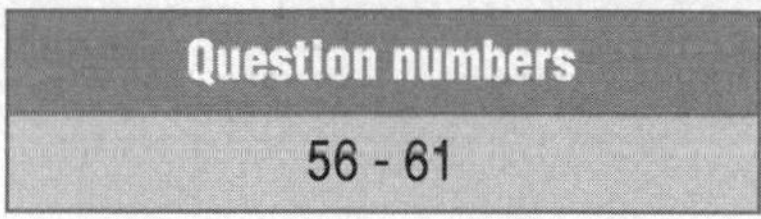

Question numbers
56 - 61

BPP
LEARNING MEDIA

The macroeconomic context 2 – the role of government

Introduction

This chapter follows on from Chapter 12 by dealing in more detail with the **policy goals** of government and the **policy instruments** used to modify the trade cycle. Despite the long topic list the sections are relatively short and many of the concepts will be familiar to you from Chapter 12.

The first main topic is a reminder of the **principles of public finance** and the role of the government budget and borrowing.

Two key problems that government seek to deal with are **unemployment** and **inflation** and these are covered in the two sections that follow.

This leads on to a detailed discussion of the main fiscal, monetary, and supply side policy instruments available to governments

Topic list	Learning outcomes	Syllabus references	Ability required
1 Government macroeconomic policy goals	A1	A1(d)	Comprehension
2 The elements of public finance	A1	A1(d)	Comprehension
3 Unemployment	A1	A1(d)	Comprehension
4 Inflation	A1	A1(d)	Comprehension
5 Fiscal policy	A1	A1(d)	Comprehension
6 Monetary policy	A1	A1(d)	Comprehension
7 Supply side policies	A1	A1(d)	Comprehension

1 Economic policy objectives

FAST FORWARD

The main macroeconomic policy goals of governments is to sustain economic growth, limit price inflation, achieve low unemployment, and to achieve balance of payments equilibrium

All modern governments are expected to manage their national economies to some extent. People generally suppose that government action can support or hinder the growth of prosperity in their country and look to their government for serviceable macroeconomic policies. There are four main objective of economic policy, though debate continues about their relative priority.

(a) **To achieve economic growth**, and growth in national income per head of the population. Growth implies an increase in national income in real terms. Increases caused by price inflation are not real increases at all.

(b) **To control price inflation** (to achieve stable prices). This has become a central objective of UK economic policy in recent years.

(c) **To achieve full employment**. Full employment does not mean that everyone who wants a job has one all the time, but it does mean that unemployment levels are low, and involuntary unemployment is short-term.

(d) **To achieve a balance between exports and imports** (on the country's balance of payments accounts) over a period of years. The wealth of a country relative to others, a country's creditworthiness as a borrower, and the goodwill between countries in international relations might all depend on the achievement of an external balance over time.

2 The elements of government finance

FAST FORWARD

Government finance consists of the outgoings of **expenditure** and its receipts from **taxation and other sources**. The main reason for government budgets is to **enable the state to carry out its work**. A side-effect of this is the ability of government to **influence aggregate demand** through use of **budget deficits and surpluses**.

2.1 The size of the government budget

The size of the government budget depends on the extent to which political culture of the country requires or allows state involvement, as well as particular factors such as the stage of the trade cycle or the existence of a wartime economy.

The table below shows the size of the state budget in some selected countries

Country	Tax burden (% of GDP)	Government expenditure (% of GDP)
Denmark	49.0	51.2
France	44.6	52.8
Germany	40.6	43.7
Hong Kong	13.0	18.6
India	18.6	27.2
Switzerland	29.4	32.0
United Kingdom	38.9	47.3
United States	26.9	38.9

(Estimated 2011: Source Wall Street Journal)

This means that government spending is **more than half of total aggregate demand in some developed countries** like Denmark and France (and Sweden). The highest in the World is Zimbabwe with 97.8, mainly the government spending overseas aid into a collapsed economy, and Iceland with 57.8% but this was to overcome the huge recession caused by the collapse of the country's banking system.

2.2 The makeup of government expenditure

The three main categories of government expenditure are:

(a) **Government final consumption expenditure**: this is acquisition of goods and services to be used by the population. This includes payment to state employees providing these goods and services

(b) **Government gross fixed capital formation**: the building of roads and infrastructure

(c) **Transfer payments**: welfare benefits and grants to individuals and organisations

Taking the UK as an example, the planned total spending for the year to April 2013 is 683.6bn made up as follows:

Pensions	£138.1bn
Health care*	£126.2bn
Education*	£97.2bn
Defence	£46.4bn
Welfare	£117.0bn
Protection	£32.0bn
Transport	£18.5bn
General government	£17.9bn
Interest payments	£45.1bn
Balance	£(3.5bn)

Source: UK Office of Budget Responsibility

Notes

*the UK provides free healthcare to its population and free education up to the age of 16+

2.3 Committed and discretionary government spending

Although governments will seek to use their spending to manipulate the level of aggregate demand in practice it is **easier to boost government expenditure than it is to cut it**.

(a) Much government spending is **committed under complex laws** covering health provision, welfare payments, rights to education and so on. These cannot be reduced without complex legislation and political turmoil

(b) Many government **projects are long-term** such as building new roads, providing for the regeneration of an ailing city, or providing funds to train workers in new skills. They cannot be cut quickly without leaving the job half-done

In practice many democratic governments find they have discretion on about 4% of their spending after which they need to undertake radical **structural reforms** to the large budget items.

2.4 Cyclical and structural deficits

Key terms

Cyclical deficit: the fiscal deficit being run by a government due to the phase of the trade cycle

Structural deficit: the element of fiscal deficit that is not due to the trade cycle but rather is a consequence of the size of the role the government has assumed in the economy

2.4.1 Causes of cyclical deficits

Governments tend to increase government spending during recessions due to two factors:

(a) **Automatic stabilisers:** as recession progresses and unemployment rises the government automatically increases welfare spending as the number of people eligible for payments increases. Higher unemployment also results in lower taxation revenues from wages, profits and on spending

(b) **Discretionary spending:** these are deliberate increases in spending to limit unemployment and recession. For example a youth training scheme will provide incomes to trainees, employers and training providers

Cyclical deficits come and go with the trade cycle. The borrowing needed to pay for the deficit can be repaid when the economy returns to growth, unemployment declines leading to lower welfare payments and higher taxation revenues.

Financial institutions are usually **willing to lend to finance cyclical deficits** because they see it as **responsible government** behaviour and they believe the government will be **able to afford the interest** and to **pay the borrowing back eventually**.

2.4.2 Structural deficits

Structural deficits arise from a number of sources together:

(a) **Increases in the role of government**: this is largely political in nature and involves issues such as the public's desire for **state ownership of industry**, the commitment to the **welfare state** and free education, health, housing and so on

(b) **Past failures in control over expenditure**: part of the deficit will be the interest on past borrowings by government. Governments that borrow heavily to fund development and growth rely on the spending to generate higher national income in the future from which the taxes will repay the interest and borrowings. If this original money was squandered then the state has higher interest to pay but no additional tax revenues

(c) **Emergency borrowing:** a major war, natural disaster, or state rescue of a collapsed firm or industry can create fiscal deficits independently of the trade cycle. For example in 2008 the US Congress voted to borrow $700bn to provide a fund to rescue its auto industry and banking sectors. In the same year the UK government set aside £500bn to rescue its financial services sector.

Government borrowing depends on willing lenders and since the banking crisis of 2007-2010 international financial institutions have become **unwilling to lend to governments with high structural deficits**. This is because investors believe that the deficit each year, when added to the existing debts of the country, will lead to **a total debt that the country will not be able to pay the interest on** and therefore will eventually **default on its national debt**.

This has led to escalating interest rates for the government bonds of countries with high structural deficits as investors demand a **risk premium** to invest in them. The interest on this contributes further to the deficit and so a **vicious downward spiral** begins.

Policies to deal with the financial crisis of countries with structural deficits include:

(a) **Emergency loans** from other national governments and international institutions at low interest rates to finance the present deficit

(b) **Austerity measures** adopted, often as a condition of receiving the emergency loans, to cut public spending and increase taxation. This includes seeking efficiency savings in the state sector and can extend to removal of pension benefits, dismissal of public sector workers, and curtailing the role of the government

(c) **Sale of state assets:** governments may be required to sell nationalised industries, mines, land rights and public buildings to private investors to raise the funds needed to repay some it past borrowings.

The danger of austerity measures to reduce structural deficits is that it represents a **huge reduction in aggregate demand** and this can cause a **deep and prolonged recession** that causes misery and also worsens the deficit by reducing tax revenues.

2.5 Functions of taxation

Taxation has several functions.

(a) **To raise revenues for the government** and to finance the provision of public and merit goods such as defence, health and education.

(b) **To manage aggregate demand**. Aggregate demand could be boosted by lowering taxes, or it could be reduced by increasing taxes.

(c) **To provide a stabilising effect on national income**. Taxation reduces the effect of the multiplier, and so can be used to dampen upswings in a trade cycle – ie higher taxation when the economy shows signs of a boom will slow down the growth of money GNP and so take some inflationary pressures out of the economy.

The size of the multiplier, remember, is $\left(\frac{1}{s+m+t}\right)$ where t is the marginal rate of taxation.

(d) **To cause certain products to be priced to take into account their social costs**. For example, smoking entails certain social costs, including the cost of hospital care for those suffering from smoking-related diseases, and the government sees fit to make the price of tobacco reflect these social costs.

In a similar way, taxes could be used to discourage activities which are regarded as undesirable.

(e) **To redistribute income and wealth**. Higher rates of tax on higher incomes will serve to redistribute income. UK inheritance tax goes some way towards redistributing wealth.

(f) **To protect industries from foreign competition.** If the government levies a duty on all imported goods much of the duty will be passed on to the consumer in the form of higher prices, making imported goods more expensive. This has the effect of transferring a certain amount of demand from imported goods to domestically produced goods.

2.6 Qualities of a good tax

Adam Smith (in his seminal work *Wealth of Nations*) ascribed **four features to a good tax system.**

(a) **Equity**. People should pay according to their ability.

(b) **Certainty**. The tax should be well-defined and easily understood by all concerned.

(c) **Convenience**. The payment of tax should ideally be related to how and when people receive and spend their income (eg PAYE is deducted when wages are paid, and sales tax is charged when goods are bought).

(d) **Economy**. The cost of collection should be small relative to the yield.

Further features of a good tax can be identified.

- **Flexibility**. It should be adjustable so that rates may be altered up or down. For example, in the UK, the rate of sales tax (VAT) was reduced from 17.5% to 15% in 2008 to try to boost aggregate demand in the economy then increased to 20% in 2011 to help reduce the country's structural deficit.
- **Efficiency**. A tax needs to achieve its objective efficiently, and avoidance should be difficult. However, the tax should not undermine other aims or taxes.
- It should attain its purpose **without distorting economic behaviour**.

2.6.1 Types of taxation

Taxation can be classified into three categories on the basis of what is being taxed.

(a) **Income** – income tax, corporation tax, national insurance
(b) **Expenditure** – sales tax (VAT), duties and levies.
(c) **Capital** – inheritance tax, capital gains tax

Taxes can also be categorised according to the percentage of income which is paid as tax by different groups in society.

(a) A **regressive tax** takes a higher **proportion** of a poor person's salary than of a rich person's. Television licences (the annual licence fee people have to pay in the UK to watch television) are an example of regressive taxes since they are the same for all people. Sales taxes (such as VAT) are also regressive because poorer households spend more of their income than do richer ones (ie they have a higher MPC), and therefore a greater proportion of their income suffers the tax

(b) A **proportional tax** takes the **same proportion** of income in tax from all levels of income. So an income tax with a basic rate of tax at 22% is a proportional tax

(c) A **progressive tax** takes a **higher proportion** of income in tax as income rises. Income tax as a whole in the UK is progressive, since the first part of an individual's income is tax-free due to personal allowances and the rate of tax increases in steps up as taxable income rises.

FAST FORWARD

Direct taxes have the quality of being **progressive** or **proportional**. Income tax is usually progressive, with higher rates of tax charged on higher bands of taxable income. **Indirect taxes** can be **regressive**, when the taxes are placed on essential commodities or commodities consumed by poorer people in greater quantities.

2.7 Advantages and disadvantages of progressive taxation

Arguments in favour of progressive direct taxes

(a) **They are levied according to the ability of individuals to pay**. Individuals with a higher income are more able to afford to give up more of their income in tax than low income earners, who need a greater proportion of their earnings for the basic necessities of life. If taxes are to be raised according to the ability of people to pay (which is one of the features of a good tax suggested by Adam Smith) then there must be some progressiveness in them.

(b) **Progressive taxes enable a government to redistribute wealth from the rich to the poor in society**. Such a redistribution of wealth will alter the consumption patterns in society since the poorer members of society will spend their earnings and social security benefits on different types of goods than if the income had remained in the hands of the richer people. Poorer people are also likely to have a higher marginal propensity to consume than richer people, so leaving more income in the hands of the poorer people is likely to increase aggregate demand in the economy as a whole.

(c) **Indirect taxes tend to be regressive and progressive taxes are needed as a counter-balance** to make the tax system as a whole more fair.

Arguments against progressive taxes

(a) **In an affluent society, there is less need for progressive taxes than in a poorer society**. Fewer people will live in poverty in such a society if taxes are not progressive than in a poorer society.

(b) **Higher taxes on extra corporate profits might deter entrepreneurs** from developing new companies because the potential increase in after-tax profits would not be worth the risks involved in undertaking new investments.

(c) **Individuals and firms that suffer from high taxes might try to avoid or evade paying tax** by transferring their wealth to other countries, or by setting up companies in tax havens where corporate tax rates are low. However, tax avoidance and evasion are practised whether tax rates are high or low. High taxes will simply raise the relative gains which can be made from avoidance or evasion.

(d) When progressive taxes are harsh, and either tax high income earners at very high marginal rates or tax the wealthy at high rates on their wealth, **they could act as a deterrent to initiative**. Skilled workers might leave the country and look for employment in countries where they can earn more money.

Question

Taxation types

Below are details of three taxation systems, one of which is regressive, one proportional and one progressive. Which is which?

	Income before tax	*Income after tax*
	$	$
System 1	10,000	8,000
	40,000	30,000
System 2	10,000	7,000
	40,000	28,000
System 3	10,000	9,000
	40,000	38,000

Answer

	Tax paid on low income	*Tax paid on high income*	*Nature of tax*
	%	%	
System 1	20	25	Progressive
System 2	30	30	Proportional
System 3	10	5	Regressive

2.8 Direct and indirect taxes

FAST FORWARD

A government must decide how it intends to raise tax revenues, from **direct or indirect taxes**, and in what proportions tax revenues will be raised from each source.

A **direct tax** is paid direct by a person to the Revenue authority. Examples of direct taxes in the UK are income tax, corporation tax, capital gains tax and inheritance tax. A direct tax can be levied on income and profits, or on wealth. Direct taxes tend to be progressive or proportional taxes. They are also usually unavoidable, which means that they must be paid by everyone.

An **indirect tax** is collected by the Revenue authority from an intermediary (a supplier) who then attempts to pass on the tax to consumers in the price of goods they sell, for example, as with VAT in the UK. Indirect taxes are of two types:

- A **specific tax** is charged as a *fixed sum* per unit sold.
- An **ad valorem tax** is charged as a *fixed percentage* of the price of the good.

2.9 Disincentive effects of taxation

A direct tax on **profits might act as a disincentive to risk-taking and enterprise**. The tax will reduce the net return from a new investment and any disincentive effects will be greater when the tax is progressive. In addition, a tax on profits will reduce the ability to invest. A considerable part of the finance for new investment comes from retained profits, so any tax on corporate profits will reduce the ability of firms to save and therefore limit the sources of funds for investment.

High taxation acts as a disincentive to work for legitimate employees because if **marginal tax rates** (ie the proportion of additional income taken as tax) are high, this is likely to lead to:

(a) Individuals **forgoing opportunities to increase income** through additional effort on the basis that the increase in net income does not adequately reward the effort or risk

(b) A **brain-drain** of high earning individuals and firms to other countries where tax rates are lower

(c) **Tax avoidance**: firms and individuals will pay tax experts to find loopholes in the law that enable them to save tax

(d) **Tax evasion**: growth of the parallel 'black' economy where incomes are not declared to avoid paying the tax.

2.10 The Laffer curve and tax yields

Key term

Laffer curve: a curve depicting the relationship between tax revenue and the average tax rate, designed to illustrate the thesis that there is an optimal tax rate at which tax revenues are maximised.

The **Laffer curve** (named after Professor Arthur Laffer) illustrates the effect of tax rates upon government revenue and national income.

In the hypothetical economy depicted in Figure 1 a tax rate of 0% results in the government receiving no tax revenue irrespective of the level of national income. If the rate is 100% then nobody will work because they keep none of their earnings and so once again total tax revenue is zero. In our example, at 25% tax rates the government will achieve a total tax take of $30bn; the same as the revenue they enjoy tax at rates of 75%. By deduction, the level of national income when taxes are 25% must be $120bn compared with only $40bn if taxes are 75%. High taxation appears to operate as a disincentive and reduce national income.

The government will be keen to identify the tax rate 'T_r' which maximises revenue, and it will not want to set taxes higher than that, because if it does the taxes become a disincentive to work.

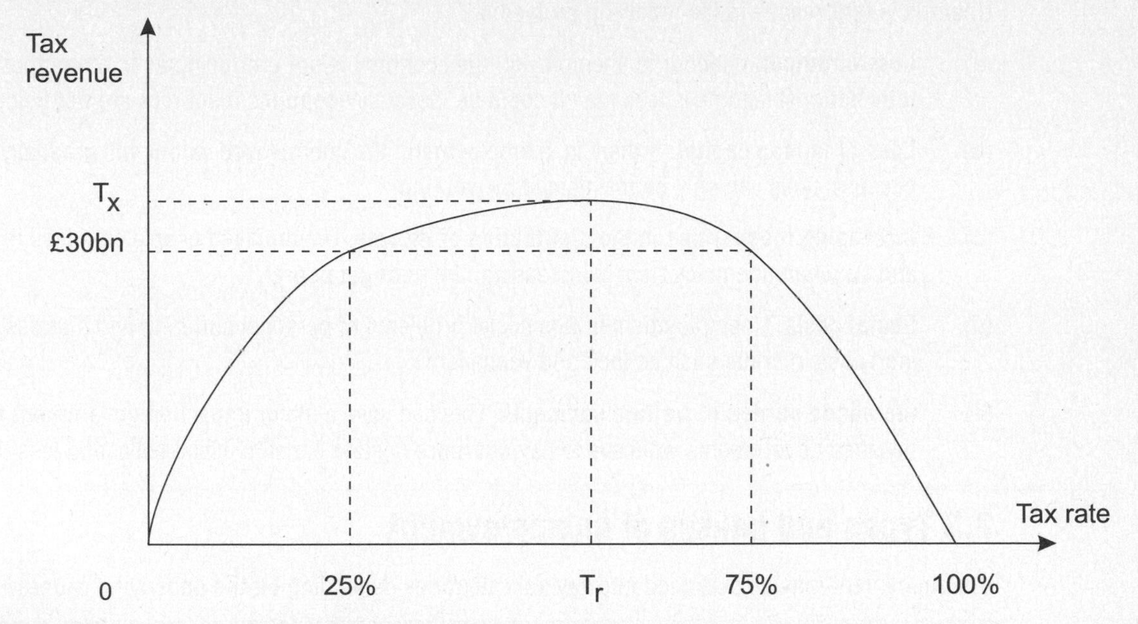

Figure 1 Laffer curve for a hypothetical economy

Three consequences flow from this Laffer curve analysis.

(a) **High rates of taxation act as a disincentive to work** and accordingly reduce output and employment, because people will substitute leisure for work. This is known as the **disincentive effect**.

(b) Governments cannot always expect to increase tax revenue by increasing tax rates. There appears to be a crucial tax rate beyond which the fall in national income resulting from the erosion of incentives and effort outweighs the increased tax rate. In Figure 1 the maximum tax revenue is T_x, at average tax rate T_r. If tax rates are above T_r, the government can increase tax revenues by cutting tax rates.

(c) There will always be two tax rates available which can yield the same total tax revenue: one associated with a high level of national income and another associated with a lower level. In consequence, governments committed to high government expenditure need not necessarily be associated with high rates of tax. Taxes could be set at the lower of the two rates and earn just the same amount of revenue as if they had been set at the higher amount.

3 Unemployment

FAST FORWARD

Unemployment is where not all workers willing to take a job at the present level of wages can find work. Most government seek to reduce the level of unemployment.

3.1 The rate of unemployment

The **rate of unemployment** in an economy can be calculated as:

$$\frac{\text{Number of unemployed}}{\text{Total workforce}} \times 100\%$$

The number of unemployed at any time is measured by government statistics. If the flow of workers through unemployment is constant then the size of the unemployed labour force will also be constant.

3.2 Consequences of unemployment

Unemployment results in the following problems.

(a) **Loss of output**. If labour is unemployed, the economy is not producing as much output as it could. Thus, total national income is less than it could be, because economic resources are not being fully used.

(b) **Loss of human capital**. If there is unemployment, the unemployed labour will gradually lose its skills, because skills can only be maintained by working.

(c) **Increasing inequalities in the distribution of income**. Unemployed people earn less than employed people, and so when unemployment is increasing, the poor get poorer.

(d) **Social costs**. Unemployment brings social problems of personal suffering and distress, and possibly also increases in crime such as theft and vandalism.

(e) **Increased burden of welfare payments**. This can have a major impact on government **fiscal policy**, because governments will have to pay out more in state benefits whilst collecting less through tax revenue.

3.3 Types and causes of unemployment

Unemployment may be classified into several categories depending on the underlying causes.

Category	Comments
Frictional unemployment	It is inevitable that some unemployment is caused not because there are not enough jobs to go round, but because of the *friction* in the labour market (difficulty in matching quickly workers with jobs), caused perhaps by a lack of knowledge about job opportunities. These are imperfections in the labour market. In general, it takes time to match prospective employees with employers, and individuals will be unemployed during the search period for a new job. Frictional unemployment is temporary, lasting for the period of transition from one job to the next.
Seasonal	This occurs in certain industries, for example building, tourism and farming, where the demand for labour fluctuates in seasonal patterns throughout the year and where staff are often employed on temporary contracts.
Structural	This occurs where long-term changes occur in the conditions of an industry. It is likely to result from either a long-term fall in demand for the good or service, or from changes in production methods which mean that labour-intensive production is replaced by capital-intensive production (technology). A feature of structural unemployment is high regional unemployment in the location of the industry affected.
Technological	This is a form of structural unemployment, which occurs when new technologies are introduced. (a) Old skills are no longer required. (b) There is likely to be a labour saving aspect, with machines doing the job that people used to do. With automation, employment levels in an industry can fall sharply, even when the industry's total output is increasing.

Category	Comments
Cyclical or demand-deficient	Past experience has shown that domestic and foreign trade go through cycles of boom, decline, recession, recovery, then boom again, and so on. (a) During recovery and boom years, the demand for output and jobs is high, and unemployment is low. (b) During decline and recession years, the demand for output and jobs falls, and unemployment rises to a high level. Here unemployment is a result of insufficient aggregate demand in the economy. Cyclical unemployment can be long-term, and a government might try to reduce it by doing what it can to minimise a recession or to encourage faster economic growth.
Real wage unemployment	This type of unemployment is caused when the supply of labour exceeds the demand for labour, but real wages do not fall for the labour market to clear. This type of unemployment is normally caused by strong trade unions which resist a fall in their wages. Another cause of this type of unemployment is the minimum wage rate, when it is set above the market clearing level. Some people argue that real wage unemployment is a type of voluntary unemployment.
Voluntary	This occurs when people are unwilling to work at existing wage rates.

Assessment focus point

You need to be familiar with all the different types and causes of unemployment for your assessment.

3.4 Government employment policies

Job creation and reducing unemployment should often mean the same thing, but it is possible to create more jobs without reducing unemployment.

(a) This can happen when there is a greater number of people entering the jobs market than there are new jobs being created. For example, if 500,000 new jobs are created during the course of one year, but 750,000 extra school leavers are looking for jobs, there will be an increase in unemployment of 250,000.

(b) It is also possible to reduce the official unemployment figures without creating jobs. For example, individuals who enrol for a government-financed training scheme are taken off the unemployment register, even though they do not have full-time jobs.

A government can try several options to create jobs or reduce unemployment.

(a) **Spending more money directly on jobs** (for example hiring more civil servants)

(b) **Encouraging growth** in the private sector of the economy. When aggregate demand is growing, firms will probably want to increase output to meet demand, and so will hire more labour.

(c) **Encouraging training in job skills**. There might be a high level of unemployment amongst unskilled workers, and at the same time a shortage of skilled workers. A government can help to finance training schemes, in order to provide a 'pool' of workers who have the skills that firms need and will pay for.

(d) **Offering grant assistance to employers** in key regional areas

(e) **Encouraging labour mobility** by offering individuals financial assistance with relocation expenses, and improving the flow of information on vacancies

Other policies may be directed at **reducing real wages to market clearing levels**.

(a) Abolishing '**closed shop**' agreements, which restrict certain jobs to trade union members

(b) Reviewing **minimum wage regulations**, to assess whether the level set for the minimum wage is preventing employers taking on new staff.

Question

Types of unemployment

Match the terms (1), (2) and (3) below with definitions A, B and C.

(1) Structural unemployment
(2) Cyclical unemployment
(3) Frictional unemployment

A Unemployment arising from a temporary difficulty in matching unemployed workers with available jobs
B Unemployment occurring in the downswing of an economy in between two booms
C Unemployment arising from a long-term decline in a particular industry

Answer

The pairings are (1) C, (2) B and (3) A.

4 Inflation and its consequences

FAST FORWARD

High rates of **inflation** are harmful to an economy. Inflation redistributes income and wealth. Uncertainty about the value of money makes business planning more difficult. Constantly changing prices impose extra costs.

4.1 Inflation

Key term

Inflation is the name given to an increase in price levels generally. It is also manifest in the decline in the purchasing power of money.

An economic policy objective which now has a central place in the policy approaches of the governments of many developed countries is that of stable prices.

4.1.1 Consequences of inflation

(a) **Redistribution of income and wealth** Inflation leads to a redistribution of income and wealth in ways which may be undesirable. Redistribution of wealth might take place from suppliers to customers. This is because amounts payable or receivable lose 'real' value with inflation. For example, if you owed $1,000, and prices then doubled, you would still owe $1,000, but the **real value** of your debt would have been halved. In general, in times of inflation those with economic power tend to gain at the expense of the weak, particularly those on fixed incomes. Their nominal income will stay the same but the amount of goods and services they can buy with that income (its purchasing power) will fall.

(b) **Balance of payments effects** If a country has a higher rate of inflation than its major trading partners, its exports will become relatively expensive and imports into it will be relatively cheap. As a result, the balance of trade will suffer, affecting employment in exporting industries and in industries producing import-substitutes. Eventually, the exchange rate will be affected (the **purchasing power parity** effect)

(c) **Uncertainty of the value of money and prices** If the rate of inflation is imperfectly anticipated, no one has certain knowledge of the true rate of inflation. As a result, no one has certain knowledge of the value of money or of the real meaning of prices. A further problem is that once the rate of inflation has begun to increase, a serious danger of **expectational inflation** will occur. This means that, regardless of whether the factors that have caused inflation are still persistent or not, there will be a perception of what inflation is likely to be, and so, to protect future income, wages and prices will be raised by the expected amount of future inflation. This can lead to the vicious circle known as the **wage-price spiral**, in which inflation becomes a relatively permanent feature, because of people's expectations that it will occur.

(d) **Wage bargaining** Wage demands (particularly from trades' unions) will be increased in times of high inflation. If they are successful then a wage/price spiral will take hold, which will reinforce the problem.

(e) **Consumer behaviour** People may stockpile goods fearing price increases later. This could create shortages for other people who haven't already stockpiled themselves.

4.2 Causes of inflation

There are **three main causes of inflation**: demand pull factors, cost push factors, and excessive growth in the money supply

4.2.1 Demand pull inflation

FAST FORWARD

Demand pull inflation arises from an excess of aggregate demand over the productive capacity of the economy.

Key term

Demand pull inflation: inflation resulting from a persistent excess of aggregate demand over aggregate supply, due to constraints on supply in the economy, for example if full employment levels have been reached.

Demand pull inflation occurs when the economy is buoyant and there is a high aggregate demand, in excess of the economy's ability to supply.

(a) Because aggregate demand exceeds supply, prices rise.

(b) Since supply needs to be raised to meet the higher demand, there will be an increase in demand for factors of production, and so factor rewards (wages, interest rates, and so on) will also rise.

(c) Since aggregate demand exceeds the output capability of the economy, it should follow that demand pull inflation can only exist when unemployment is low.

There are two main causes of demand pull inflation.

(a) **Fiscal deficits**. Government policies affect aggregate demand in an economy. For example, an increase in government spending or a reduction in taxes and interest rates will raise demand in the economy.

(b) **Imported excess demand.** If a trading partner has a booms of excess demand in their domestic economy this will lead them to increase their demand or imports. This will spill into our domestic economy as an **increase in the injection for export demand** and will set off a **multiplier effect** of rising demand.

4.2.2 Cost push inflation

FAST FORWARD

Cost push inflation arises from increases in the costs of production.

Cost push inflation occurs where the costs of factors of production rise regardless of whether or not they are in short supply, and where the rise in costs is not matched by an increase in productivity.

Key term

> **Cost push inflation**: inflation resulting from an increase in the costs of production of goods and services, e.g. through escalating prices of imported raw materials or from wage increases.

The main sources of cost push inflation are

(a) **Real wage increases**: this is where workers obtain wage increases in excess of inflation without corresponding increases in output. This has the effect of pushing up production costs which feeds through into increase prices.

(b) **Commodity price increases**: occurs when the cost of essential products, often imports, rise due to rises in the world prices of them. To have a general impact requires that these are essential goods that are price inelastic in demand such as oil, gas, and foodstuffs.

(c) **Exchange rate depreciation:** this can drive up the price of imports generally.

4.2.3 Money supply growth

This is a special form of demand pull inflation put forward by economists who are termed **monetarists**. They argue that **increases in the supply of money in excess of increases in output** lead holders of the money in bank accounts to seek security and a return by exchanging money for goods and services. This causes excess demand for goods and services.

Monetarism as a theory states that the money value of national income is determined by the quantity of money in circulation (the quantity theory of money).

Key term

> **Quantity theory of money**: theory which argues that changes in the level of prices are caused predominantly by changes in the supply of money.

The **quantity theory of money** is expressed as: MV = PT (the **Fisher equation**)

Where M = money stock: the total value of bank desposits

V = velocity of circulation: how quickly bank deposits are used for spending to finance transactions

P = the average price of each transaction

T = the number of transactions in a year

In other words the money value of national income in a year (Prices x Transactions) is equal to the amount of money spent on it in a year (Money stock x Velocity of circulation).

The Fisher equation basically says that $10 worth of money buys $10 worth of goods. This is not a very startling finding.

Monetarists take this forward by making two key assertions:

(a) **Velocity of circulation** is constant in the short run because money is held merely to finance the transactions of firms and households.

(b) **Number of transactions** are constant in the short run. This is the same as saying the economy is at full employment and cannot produce more.

In essence they argue that if the money stock increases that it will flood bank accounts with funds that are in excess of the amount needed by households and firms to finance normal transactions. Therefore holders will seek security by exchanging the surplus money for other assets such as houses, jewellery and so on. Because these are in fixed supply the extra demand will bid their price up and this will begin an inflationary spiral.

The key point about monetarist theory is that they argue the increases money stock occurs due to **excessive borrowing by governments** to support fiscal deficits. This borrowing floods the financial markets with new bonds which are held by banks as reserve assets and credit is loaned on the basis of them.

Therefore the monetarist theory of inflation is the same as a demand pull theory of inflation. The difference is the **transmission mechanism** by which fiscal deficits cause excess demand. Demand pull says that it is excess demand for labour and resources that bids up costs and prices (after reducing unemployment) whereas monetarists say it is investors with excess cash chasing non-financial investment assets that causes the prices of these to rise directly without any beneficial impact on unemployment.

Question — **Money supply and inflation**

According to the Fisher equation, if an economy's money supply increases, what will happen to the level of prices in that economy?

Answer

The increase in the money supply will lead to an increase in price levels in the future.

FAST FORWARD

There appears to be a connection between the **rate of inflation** and **unemployment**. The **Phillips curve** has been used to show the relationship between wage inflation and unemployment.

4.3 Unemployment and inflation

Managing unemployment and inflation are two of the key aspects that governments try to manage, and the two are often thought to be linked. It has been found that boosting demand to increase the level of employment can cause a higher rate of inflation. However, growth in unemployment can also be associated with a rising rate of inflation.

4.3.1 The meaning of full employment

The term full employment does not mean a situation in which everyone has a job. There will always be at least a certain **natural rate of unemployment**, which is the minimum level of unemployment that an economy can expect to achieve.

An aim of government policy might be to reduce unemployment to this minimum natural rate, and so get as close as possible to the goal of full employment. On the basis that unemployment cannot be kept below its natural rate without causing inflation, the natural rate of unemployment is sometimes called the **non-accelerating inflation rate of unemployment (NAIRU)**.

4.3.2 The Phillips curve

In 1958, *A W Phillips* found a statistical relationship between unemployment and the rate of money wage inflation which implied that, in general, **the rate of inflation falls unemployment rose and vice versa**. A curve, known as a **Phillips curve**, can be drawn linking inflation and unemployment (Figure 2).

Key term

Phillips curve: a graphical illustration of the inverse relationship which historically existed between the rate of wage inflation and the rate of unemployment.

Note the following two points about the Phillips curve.

(a) The curve crosses the horizontal axis at a positive value for the unemployment rate. This is the rate of natural unemployment (or NAIRU) above and means that zero inflation will be associated with some unemployment; it is not possible to achieve zero inflation and zero unemployment at the same time.

(b) The shape of the curve means that the lower the level of unemployment, the higher the **rate of inflation**.

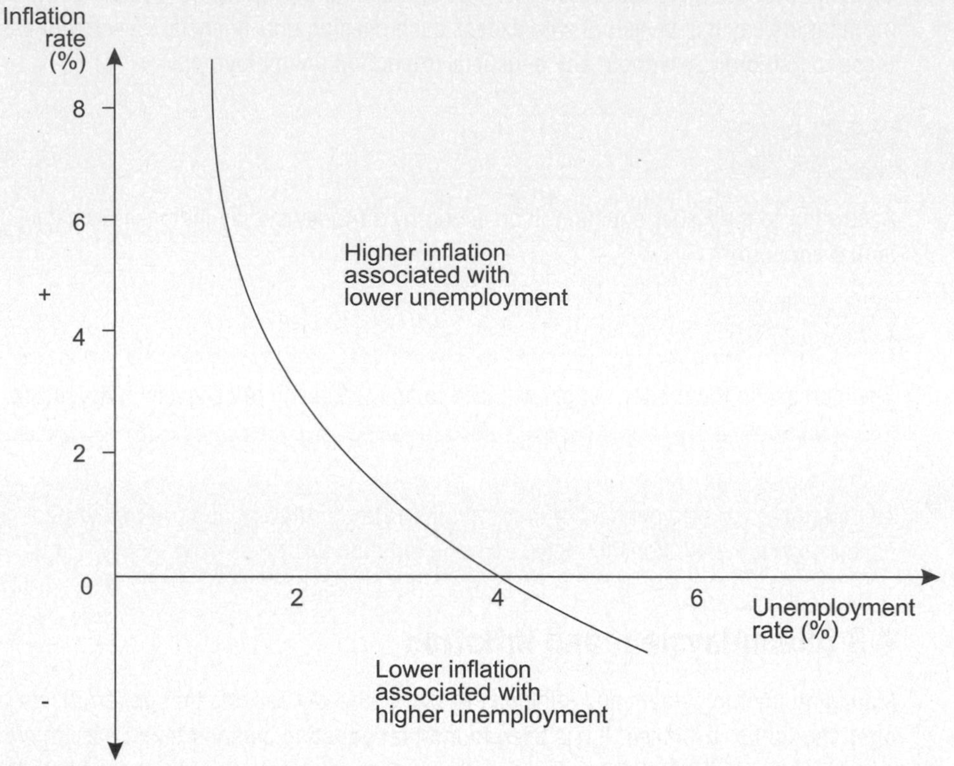

Figure 2 Phillips curve

The existence of a relationship between inflation and unemployment of the type indicated by the Phillips curve suggests that the government should be able to use **demand management policies** to take the economy to acceptable levels of inflation and unemployment.

The Phillips curve indicated that a government had to make a **choice between inflation or unemployment**. Price stability and full employment could not both be achieved together.

However, the Phillips curve relationship between inflation and unemployment broke down at the end of the 1960s when many countries began to experience **rising inflation at the same time as rising unemployment** (stagflation).

4.3.3 Stagflation and the expectations augmented Phillips curve

But by the 1980s the relationship between inflation and unemployment had re-appeared, although at a higher absolute level of unemployment. The Phillips curve could be re-plotted, but it had shifted to the right.

The monetarist economist, Milton Friedman put forward a theory that adjusted the Phillips curve to reflect the fact that **expectations** distort the inflationary process.

Friedman's model is known as the **expectations augmented Phillips curve**, and indicates that, although in the short run there may be trade-offs between inflation and unemployment, in the long run an economy is faced with a **vertical Phillips curve**, and there are inflationary expectations which reflect the rates of inflation that workers expect in the future.

Figure 3 illustrates why. The economy is initially in equilibrium with unemployment of U, and with very low inflation (PE_0).

The government tries to boost aggregate demand in the economy, and this reduces unemployment to U_1. However, it also creates excess demand in the labour market which prompts wage inflation.

This wage inflation in turn becomes price inflation, so workers are no better off in real terms than they were before the wage rise. In this case, the labour supply and hence unemployment returns to its previous level: U. Therefore the economy has found a new equilibrium with higher inflation (PE_1) and the original unemployment (U), because the price expectations in the market mean that the equilibrium rate of unemployment can now only be achieved at this higher rate of (wage) inflation. In effect, the short-run Phillips curve has shifted outwards from PC to PC_1.

These shifts in the **short-run** Phillips curves illustrate that a cycle of wage inflation has been created, but note that **long term** unemployment rate remains the same (at U on Figure 3). This means that governments can no longer base policies on the simple trade off between inflation and unemployment as proposed in the original Phillips curve.

Moreover, instead of trying to eradicate unemployment, governments need to accept that there is a natural rate of unemployment in the economy, and that this will also be the level at which inflation rates will be stable.

This natural rate of unemployment is called the **non-accelerating inflation rate of unemployment** (NAIRU), the level at which the rate of inflation is stable. (The NAIRU is also sometimes referred to as the natural rate hypothesis).

NAIRU is a logical extension of the expectations-augmented Phillips curve, and is represented by U in Figure 3.

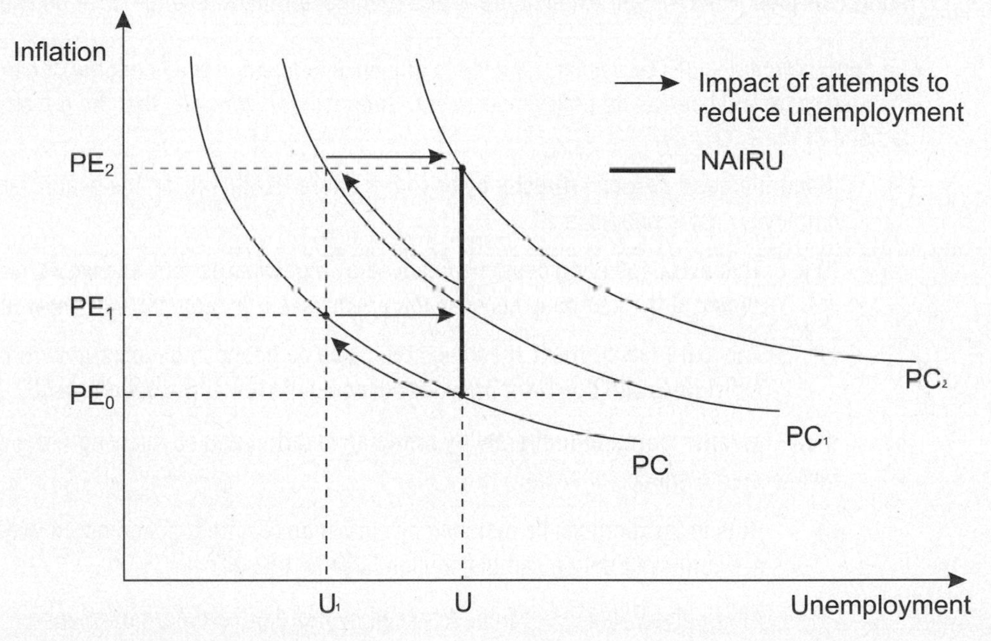

Figure 3 Expectations augmented Phillips curve

5 Fiscal policy

FAST FORWARD

The government has several types of **macroeconomic policy instrument** at its disposal. These are **fiscal policy**, **monetary policy**, and **supply side policies**.
Fiscal policy provides a method of managing **aggregate demand** in the economy via taxation and government spending.

Key terms

Fiscal policy relates to government policy on taxation, public borrowing and public spending.

Monetary policy is concerned with government policy on the money supply, the monetary system, interest rates, exchange rates and the availability of credit.

Fiscal and monetary policy attempt to attain the macroeconomic policy objectives by influencing **aggregate demand** in an economy.

Supply Side policies, on the other hand, attempt to the attain the macroeconomic policy objectives by shifting the aggregate supply curve in an economy.

5.1 Budget surplus and budget deficit

Key terms

Budget deficit: Government expenditure exceeds government revenue from taxation income.

Budget surplus: Government expenditure is less than government revenue from taxation income.

If a government decides to use fiscal policy to influence demand in the economy, it can choose either expenditure changes or tax changes as its policy instrument. Suppose, for example, that the government wants to stimulate demand in the economy.

(a) **It can increase demand directly by spending more itself** – eg on the health service or education, and by employing more people itself.

  (i) This extra spending could be financed by higher taxes, but this would reduce spending by the private sector of the economy because the private sector's after-tax income would be lower.

  (ii) The extra government spending could also be financed by extra government borrowing. Just as individuals can borrow money for spending, so too can a government.

(b) **It can increase demand indirectly by reducing taxation** and so allowing firms and individuals more after-tax income to spend (or save).

  (i) Cuts in taxation can be matched by cuts in government spending, in which case total demand in the economy will not be stimulated significantly, if at all.

  (ii) Alternatively, tax cuts can be financed by more government borrowing.

5.2 Fiscal policy and aggregate demand

Fiscal policy is concerned with **government spending** (an injection into the circular flow of income) and **taxation** (a withdrawal from the circular flow).

(a) If government spending is increased, there will be an increase in the amount of **injections**, expenditure in the economy will rise and so national income will rise (either in real terms, or in terms of price levels only; that is, the increase in national income might be real or inflationary).

(b) If government taxation is increased, there will be an increase in **withdrawals** from the economy, and expenditure and national income will fall. A government might deliberately raise taxation to take inflationary pressures out of the economy.

A government's **'fiscal stance'** may be **neutral, expansionary** or **contractionary,** according to its effect on national income.

(a) **Spending more money** and financing this expenditure by borrowing would indicate an expansionary fiscal stance.

(b) **Collecting more in taxes** without increasing spending would indicate a contractionary fiscal stance.

(c) Collecting more in taxes in order to **increase spending**, thus diverting income from one part of the economy to another would indicate a broadly neutral fiscal stance.

5.3 Fiscal policy and unemployment

Fiscal policy can be used to reduce unemployment and provide jobs.

(a) More government spending on capital projects would create jobs in the construction industries.

(b) Government-funded training schemes are a means of spending by government to improve training, so as to make people more qualified for jobs in private industry.

(c) A government might tax companies on the basis of the numbers and pay levels of people they employ (as with employers' national insurance contributions). Lower employment taxes would possibly make employers more willing to take on extra numbers of employees.

If government raises taxes and government spending by the same amount, so that the budget remains in balance, there will be an **increase in aggregate monetary demand**. This is because tax payers would have saved some of the money they pay in increased tax while the government spends all of its revenue within the economy. This effect is called the **balanced budget multiplier**.

Government spending, however, might create inflationary pressures. Fiscal policy must therefore be used with care, even to create new jobs.

5.4 Other effects

Since government spending or tax reductions might be inflationary, and higher domestic prices make imports relatively cheaper and exports less competitive in foreign markets, fiscal policy has possible implications for the **balance of payments** (which we will discuss in the chapters on international trade later in this Study Text).

The impact of changes in fiscal policy is not always certain, and fiscal policy to pursue one aim (eg lower inflation) might, for a while at least, create barriers to the pursuit of other aims (eg employment).

5.5 Crowding out

Deficit budgets have been criticised on the grounds that they '**crowd out**' private sector activity; that is, the government spending merely replaces private spending with no net increase in aggregate demand. In particular, it is suggested that increased government borrowing to finance government expenditure inevitably leads to higher interest rates, which, in turn, lead to a reduction in private borrowing for both consumption and investment. The Keynesian response to this criticism is to say that crowding out will not occur when there are **idle resources** within the economy, such as a large number of unemployed people.

6 Monetary policy

FAST FORWARD

Monetary policy focuses on the relationship between interest rates and the supply of money in an economy, and how the two of them together can influence aggregate demand.

6.1 Objectives of monetary policy

Assessment focus point

Questions on monetary policy will often focus on its impact on the business sector. It is important that you understand how changes in interest rates could affect business decisions.

Monetary policy can be used as a means towards achieving ultimate economic objectives for inflation, the balance of trade, full employment and real economic growth. To achieve these **ultimate objectives**, the authorities will set **intermediate objectives** for monetary policy.

Increasingly monetary policy is under the control of independent central banks. They focus on maintaining the rate of inflation at a sustainable low level. The intermediate objectives of monetary policy have related to the level of interest rates, growth in the money supply, the exchange rate for the currency and the expansion of credit.

6.2 The money stock as a target of monetary policy

To monetarist economists, the **money stock** is an obvious intermediate target of economic policy. This is because they claim that an increase in the money stock will raise prices and incomes and this in turn will raise the demand for money to spend.

The approach is sometimes called **money base control** and it involves the following elements:

Establishment of **measures of money stock**. Sometimes called measures of **bank liquidity** these range from **narrow measures** of money base such as notes and coins and the banks own operational balances at the central bank, to **broad measures** which include all bank deposits belonging to customers plus a range of financial assets such as bills and bonds.

(a) Setting of **targets for the growth in the money stock**. The goal is for money stock to grow only at the same rate as the output of the economy. Hitting these targets is intended to give the financial markets confidence that the central bank has the supply of money under control

(b) **Restriction of growth of money base** by limiting government borrowing and other influences on the ability of banks to create credit.

6.3 The effects of changing interest rates

6.3.1 Uses of the interest rate

Interest rates can be used in three ways by monetary policy

(a) As a **target**: here the interest rate is being used to **influence aggregate demand directly** through its effects on investment, consumption and savings

(b) As an **indicator** to help **achieve money stock targets.** Higher rates of interest discourage borrowing and so limit the ability of banks to create credit and boost the money stock

(c) As an **indicator** to help **achieve exchange rate targets**. Higher rates of interest will tend to increase the exchange rate for the currency by attracting portfolio investment.

6.3.2 The impacts of a rise in interest rates

Impact	Comment
Spending falls	Higher interest rates increase the cost of credit and thereby deter spending. The higher interest rates are, the more attractive it is to hold money rather than to spend it.
Investment falls	The increased rate will increase the opportunity cost of investment and reduce the net present value of the investment. This will discourage firms from investing. The increased interest rates will make borrowing more expensive.
Foreign funds are attracted into the country	Interest rates are the reward for capital, so a rise in interest rates will encourage overseas investors because of the increased rate of return relative to other countries.
Exchange rate rises	The inflow of foreign funds (above) increases the demand for currency and therefore increases the exchange rate. A rise in exchange rates will make exports more expensive, and imports cheaper. The impact this will have on the balance of payments current account will depend on the relative price elasticities of imports and exports.
Inflation rate falls	This is the overall goal of an interest rate rise. The reduction in spending and investment will reduce aggregate demand in the economy. Higher exchange rates will force producers to make prices more competitive by cutting costs.
Bond prices fall	There is an inverse relationship between bond prices and the rate of interest.

An increase in interest rates will have a **deflationary** impact on the economy.

6.3.3 Benefits of using interest rate policy

The main benefits of using interest rates are:

(a) **Quick adjustment:** Interest rates can be changed within hours by interventions and signals from the central bank. Fiscal policy takes many months due to the need to pass legislation to raise taxes

(b) **Discipline over government borrowing:** the government's borrowing will be held in check by the interest rate target. For example a low interest rate policy would be undermined by a sudden decision to expand government bond issues and drive their price down.

6.3.4 Drawbacks of interest rate policy

(a) **Unpredictable in effect:** raising an interest rate affects aggregate demand by reducing investment and increasing savings. However it is not easy to judge how much of an increase will be needed to bring the required effect

(b) **Indiscriminate effects:** higher interest rates penalise borrowers and reward savers. Therefore they work against small businesses and young families. Families with savings might actually increase spending because their income has risen.

6.4 The exchange rate as a target of monetary policy

Why the exchange rate is a target

(a) If the exchange rate falls, exports become cheaper to overseas buyers and so more competitive in export markets. Imports will become more expensive and so less competitive against goods produced by manufacturers at home. A fall in the exchange rate might therefore be good for a domestic economy, by giving a **stimulus to exports** and **reducing demand for imports**.

(b) An increase in the exchange rate will have the opposite effect, with dearer exports and cheaper imports. If the exchange rate rises and imports become cheaper, though there should be a reduction in the rate of domestic inflation. A fall in the exchange rate, on the other hand, tends to increase the cost of imports and adds to the rate of domestic inflation.

When a country's economy is heavily dependent on overseas trade, as the UK economy is, it might be appropriate for government policy to establish a target exchange value for the domestic currency. However, the exchange rate is dependent on both the domestic rate of inflation and the level of interest rates. Targets for the exchange rate cannot be achieved unless the rate of inflation at home is first brought under control.

6.5 Instruments of monetary policy

There are a number of techniques or instruments which are available to the authorities to achieve their targets for monetary policies.

- Changing the level and/or structure of **interest rates** through **open market operations**
- **Reserve requirements**
- **Direct controls**, which might be either quantitative or qualitative
- **Intervention to influence the exchange rate**

6.6 Control over the level and structure of interest rates

When a government uses interest rates as an instrument of policy, it can try to influence either the general level of interest rates or the term structure of interest rates. It could do this by influencing either short-term interest rates or long-term interest rates. Central banks set short-term interest rates through open market operations – by buying or selling government securities in order to control their price, and consequently to control their interest rates.

6.7 Reserve requirements on banks as a means of controlling the money supply

As another technique for controlling money supply growth, the government might impose **reserve requirements** on banks. A reserve requirement might be a compulsory minimum cash reserve ratio (ie ratio of cash to total assets) or a minimum liquid asset ratio.

You will recall that any initial increase in bank deposits or building society deposits will result in a much greater eventual increase in deposits, because of the credit multiplier.

Ignoring leakages, the formula for the credit multiplier is:

$$D = \frac{C}{r}$$

Where C is the initial increase in deposits
r is the liquid assets ratio or reserve assets ratio
D is the eventual total increase in deposits

If the authorities wished to control the rate of increase in bank lending and building society lending, they could impose minimum reserve requirements – ie a minimum value for r. **The bigger the value or r, the lower size of the credit multiplier would be**.

There are drawbacks to reserve requirements as a monetary policy instrument.

(a) Unless the same requirements apply to all financial institutions in the country, some institutions will simply take business from others..

(b) Similarly, restrictions on domestic financial institutions which do not apply to foreign banks would put the domestic financial institutions at a competitive disadvantage in international markets. This is one reason why international co-operation on the capital adequacy of banks (the Basel agreement) is an important step towards better regulation of financial markets.

6.8 Direct controls as a technique of monetary control

Another way of controlling the growth of the money supply is to impose direct controls on bank lending. Direct controls may be either quantitative or qualitative.

(a) **Quantitative controls** might be imposed on either bank lending (assets), for example a 'lending ceiling' limiting annual lending growth, or bank deposits (liabilities). The purpose of quantitative controls might be seen as a means of keeping bank lending in check without having to resort to higher interest rates.

(b) **Qualitative controls** might be used to alter the type of lending by banks. For example, the government (via the Bank) can ask the banks to limit their lending to the personal sector, and lend more to industry, or to lend less to a particular type of firm (such as, for example, property companies) and more to manufacturing businesses.

6.9 Quantitative controls

Controls might be temporary, in which case, in time, interest rates would still tend to rise if the money supply growth is to be kept under control. However, the advantage of a temporary scheme of direct quantitative controls is that it gives the authorities time to implement longer term policy. Quantitative controls are therefore a way of bridging the time-lag before these other policies take effect.

Quantitative controls might be more permanent. If they are, they will probably be unsuccessful because there will be financial institutions that manage to escape the control regulations, and so thrive at the expense of controlled institutions.

Direct controls on banks, for example, might succeed in reducing bank deposits but they will not succeed in controlling the level of demand and expenditure in the economy if lending is re-directed into other non-controlled financial instruments of non-controlled financial institutions. For example, large companies might use their own bank deposits to set up a scheme of lending themselves.

Direct controls are therefore rarely effective in dealing with the source rather than the symptom of the problem. Direct controls tend to divert financial flows into other, often less efficient, channels, rather than to stop the financial flows altogether, ie 'leakages' are inevitable.

6.10 Qualitative controls

Qualitative controls might be **mandatory** or they might be applied through **moral suasion**. Mandatory directives of a qualitative nature are unlikely in practice, because they are difficult to enforce without the co-operation of banks and other financial institutions. Moral suasion, on the other hand, might be used frequently. This is a process whereby the Central Bank appeals to the banks to do one or more things.

- To restrain lending
- To give priority to certain types of lending such as finance for exports or for investment
- Refuse other types of lending such as loans to private individuals

Moral suasion might therefore be a temporary form of control.

6.11 Monetary policy and fiscal policy

Monetary policy can be made to act as a subsidiary support to fiscal policy and demand management. Since budgets are once-a-year events, a government must use non-fiscal measures in between budgets to make adjustments to its control of the economy.

(a) A policy of **low interest rates** or the absence of any form of credit control might stimulate bank lending, which in turn would increase expenditure (demand) in the economy.

(b) **High interest rates might** act as a deterrent to borrowing and so reduce spending in the economy.

(c) Strict **credit controls** (for example restrictions on bank lending) might be introduced to reduce lending and so reduce demand in the economy.

6.12 Monetary policy, inflation control and economic growth

Monetarists argue that monetary control will put the brake on inflation, but how does this help the economy? We have already suggested that inflation seems to hinder economic growth, and so we could argue like this.

(a) High inflation increases **economic uncertainty**. Bringing inflation under control will restore business confidence and help international trade by stabilising the exchange rate.

(b) A resurgence of business confidence through lower interest rates (due to less uncertainty and lower inflation) will **stimulate investment** and **real output**.

(c) A **controlled growth in the money supply** will provide higher incomes for individuals to purchase the higher output.

7 Supply side policies

FAST FORWARD

Supply side policies provide a method of managing **aggregate supply** in the economy.

7.1 The supply side approach

Demand management relies upon the proposition that the level of aggregate demand determines the level of national income and prices, since demand creates supply. Demand can be controlled either through fiscal or monetary policy.

The **supply side approach**, on the other hand, focuses policy upon the **conditions of aggregate supply**, taking the view that the availability, quality and cost of resources are the long term determinants of national income and prices. Supply side approaches put resources to work, and anticipate that the economy will automatically generate the additional incomes necessary to purchase the higher outputs.

Key term

> **Supply side economics** can be defined as an approach to economic policymaking which advocates measures to improve the supply of goods and services (eg through deregulation) rather than measures to affect aggregate demand.

Supply side economics is characterised by the following propositions.

(a) The predominant long-term influences upon output, prices, and employment are the conditions of aggregate supply.

(b) Left to itself, the **free market** will automatically generate the highest level of national income and employment available to the economy.

(c) **Inflexibility in the labour market** through the existence of trade unions and other restrictive practices retain wages at uncompetitively high levels. This creates unemployment and restricts aggregate supply.

(d) The rates of **direct taxation** have a major influence upon aggregate supply through their effects upon the **incentive** to work.

(e) There is only a **limited role for government** in the economic system. Demand management can only influence output and employment 'artificially' in the short run, whilst in the long run creating inflation and hampering growth. Similarly state owned industries are likely to be uncompetitive and accordingly restrict aggregate supply.

7.2 Supply side economic policies

The main supply side policies are:

(a) **Reduction in government expenditure** and greater involvement of the private sector in the provision of services.

(b) **Reduction in taxes** in order to increase incentives.

(c) **Increasing flexibility** in the labour market by curbing the power of trade unions.

(d) **Increasing competition** through deregulation and privatisation of utilities.

(e) **Abolition of exchange controls** and allowing the free movement of capital.

7.3 The role of aggregate supply

The **central role of aggregate supply** is demonstrated in Figures 4(a) and (b).

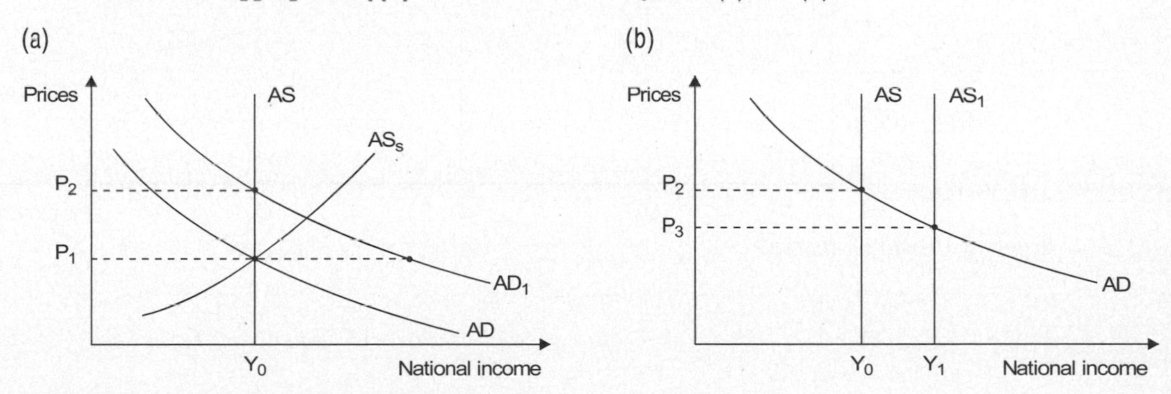

Figure 4 The importance of aggregate supply

Figure 4(a) shows the effect of a rise in aggregate demand, perhaps as the result of expansionary demand management policies. The aggregate demand schedule shifts from AD to AD_1, but in the long run national income remains at Y_0. AS_S is the short run supply schedule, so in the short run there will be a degree of expansion in national income. However, in the long run, aggregate supply is inelastic, represented by AS. The effect of the rise in aggregate demand will be to increase prices from P_1 to P_2. While supply side theorists accept that in the short run, national income may rise along the short-run aggregate supply curve AS_S, they contend that ultimately national income will fall to its long-run level of Y_0 because supply cannot be maintained above its long run level. Consequently aggregate demand by itself is powerless to increase long-run output or employment.

Figure 4(b) illustrates a rise in aggregate supply from AS to AS_1. The income generated from the higher employment causes aggregate demand to extend and consequently national income rises from Y_0 to Y_1. This demonstrates the supply side view that **only changes in the conditions of aggregate supply can lead to a sustained increase in output and employment**. The vertical aggregate supply curve suggests that changes in aggregate demand do not affect output but rather only influence prices.

The economy will self-regulate through the action of the price mechanism in each market. Flexible prices in goods and factor markets will ensure that at the microeconomic level each market tends towards a market-clearing equilibrium. At the macroeconomic level, the maximum attainable level of national income is at the level of full employment. Advocates of supply side economics argue that **flexible wages** will ensure the economy reaches this point.

7.4 Flexible wages

The importance of flexible wages is shown in Figure 5. When the wage rate is at W_0 the demand for labour is Q_d whilst the total supply of labour stands at Q_s. This creates involuntary unemployment of $(Q_s - Q_d)$ at the prevailing wage rate. By accepting lower wages workers can 'price themselves back into jobs' and consequently unemployment falls. If wages were perfectly flexible downwards then the market would restore full employment at wage rate W_1. This would leave unemployment at its natural rate.

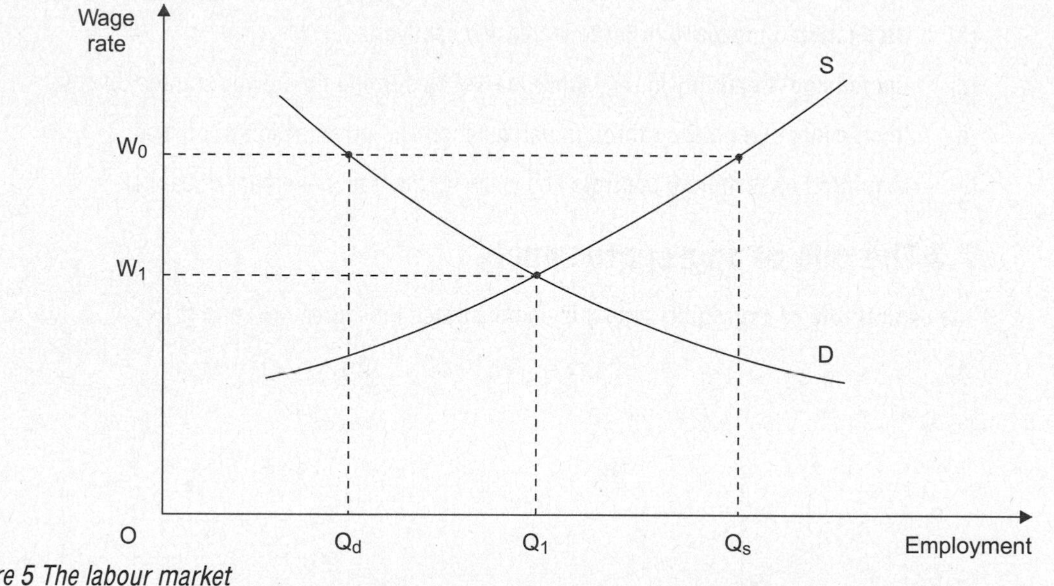

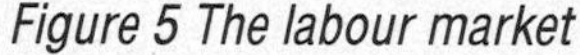
Figure 5 The labour market

Chapter roundup

- The main macroeconomic policy goals of governments is to sustain economic growth, limit price inflation, achieve low unemployment, and to achieve balance of payments equilibrium
- **Government finance** consists of the outgoings of **expenditure** and its receipts from **taxation and other sources**. The main reason for government budgets is to **enable the state to carry out its work**. A side-effect of this is the ability of government to **influence aggregate demand** through use of **budget deficits and surpluses**.
- **Direct taxes** have the quality of being **progressive** or **proportional**. Income tax is usually progressive, with higher rates of tax charged on higher bands of taxable income. **Indirect taxes** can be **regressive**, when the taxes are placed on essential commodities or commodities consumed by poorer people in greater quantities.
- A government must decide how it intends to raise tax revenues, from **direct or indirect taxes**, and in what proportions tax revenues will be raised from each source.
- Unemployment is where not all workers willing to take a job at the present level of wages can find work. Most government seek to reduce the level of unemployment.
- High rates of **inflation** are harmful to an economy. Inflation redistributes income and wealth. Uncertainty about the value of money makes business planning more difficult. Constantly changing prices impose extra costs.

  Demand pull inflation arises from an excess of aggregate demand over the productive capacity of the economy.

  Cost push inflation arises from increases in the costs of production.
- There appears to be a connection between the **rate of inflation** and **unemployment**. The **Phillips curve** has been used to show the relationship between wage inflation and unemployment.

  The government has several types of **macroeconomic policy instrument** at its disposal. These are **fiscal policy**, **monetary policy**, and **supply side policies**.
- **Fiscal policy** provides a method of managing **aggregate demand** in the economy via taxation and government spending
- **Fiscal policy** provides a method of managing **aggregate demand** in the economy via taxation and government spending.
- **Monetary policy** focuses on the relationship between interest rates and the supply of money in an economy, and how the two of them together can influence aggregate demand.
- **Supply side policies** provide a method of managing **aggregate supply** in the economy.

Quick quiz

1. What is the difference between fiscal policy and monetary policy?
2. Outline how the government may use fiscal policy to influence aggregate demand.
3. What is:

   (a) A regressive tax?
   (b) A proportional tax?
   (c) A progressive tax?

4. Distinguish between direct taxation and indirect taxation.
5. The government of a certain country decides to introduce a poll tax, which will involve a flat rate levy of $200 on every adult member of the population. This new tax could be described as:

   A Regressive
   B Proportional
   C Progressive
   D Ad valorem

6. High rates of personal income tax are thought to have a disincentive effect. This refers to the likelihood that the high rates of tax will:

   A Encourage illegal tax evasion by individuals
   B Lead to a reduction in the supply of labour
   C Lead to a reduction in savings by individuals
   D Discourage consumer spending and company investments

7. Which of the following will *not* be the immediate purpose of a tax measure by the government?

   A To discourage an activity regarded as socially undesirable.
   B To influence interest rates.
   C To influence the level of aggregate demand
   D To raise revenue to spend on public or merit goods

8. What will be the consequence for bond prices of an increase in interest rates?
9. What effect does an increase in interest rates have on the exchange rate?
10. What is the crowding-out effect?
11. How do supply side policies affect inflation and unemployment?

    Answer in terms of the effect on the aggregate supply curve.

Answers to quick quiz

1 A government's fiscal policy is concerned with taxation, borrowing and spending; and their effects upon the economy. Monetary policy is concerned with money, the money supply, interest rates, inflation and the exchange rate.

2 A government can increase demand by spending more itself or by reducing taxation so that firms and households have more after-tax income to spend.

3 A regressive tax takes a higher proportion of a poor person's income than a rich person's. A progressive tax takes a higher proportion of a rich person's income and a lower proportion of a poor person's. A proportional tax takes the same proportion of all incomes.

4 Direct taxes are levied on income while indirect taxes are levied on expenditure. Indirect taxes are regressive. Direct taxes can be progressive.

5 A A flat-rate poll tax, with no concession for the lower-paid, would take a higher proportion of the income of lower-income earners than of higher income earners. This is a regressive tax system.

6 B The disincentive effect refers specifically to the disincentive of individuals to work.

7 B The main purpose of taxation will be to raise revenue for the government. Other aims might be to redistribute wealth or affect demand in the economy. Changes in rate of tax do not have a direct influence on interest rates, which can be influenced by a government's *monetary* policies.

8 Bond prices will fall until the fixed income they provide equates to the rate of interest.

9 A rise in interest rates attracts foreign investment, thus increasing the demand for the currency. The currency typically strengthens as a result.

10 The crowding-out effect is the monetarist argument that public (government) expenditure merely displaces private sector spending in an economy rather than adding to it and boosting output.

11 By shifting the supply curve to the right, a new equilibrium between aggregate supply and aggregate demand will be reached with levels of lower inflation and higher output (lower unemployment).

Now try the questions below from the Exam Question Bank

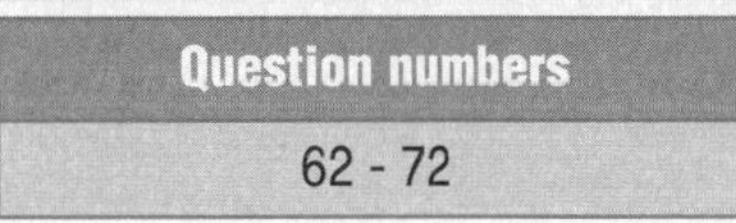

Question numbers
62 - 72

The international context

14

Introduction

In this final chapter, we examine the makeup of the balance of payments and the factors . This is followed by an explanation of the financial consequences of deficits on the balance of payments and the policies available to deal with them.

The includes a review of some of the global financial institutions that have been established to assist countries with balance of payments and financial difficulties.

In this final chapter the contemporary topic of globalisation is discussed.

The origins of the worldwide patterns of consumption and production are described and the role of multinational enterprises and global financial institutions is described.

The various types of institutional arrangements to encourage globalisation are reviewed.

The chapter concludes with an evaluation of the benefits from globalisation.

Topic list	Learning outcomes	Syllabus references	Ability required
1 The make-up of the balance of payments	C2	C2 (a)	Comprehension
2 Causes of imbalances in the balance of payments	C2	C2 (a)	Comprehension
3 Policies to eliminate current account deficits	C2	C2 (b)	Comprehension
4 The terms of trade	C2	C2 (a)	Comprehension
5 The role of global financial institutions	C3	C3(b)	Comprehension
6 The nature and causes of globalisation	C3	C3 (a)	Comprehension
7 Trade agreements and trading blocks	C3	C3 (b)	Comprehension
8 Impacts of globalisation	C3	C3 (a)	Comprehension

1 The make-up of the balance of payments

FAST FORWARD

The **balance of payments accounts** consist of a current account with visibles and invisibles sections and transactions in capital (external assets and liabilities including official financing). The sum of the balances on these accounts must be zero, although in practice there is a balancing figure for measurement errors.

1.1 The nature of the balance of payments

Assessment focus point

Students often confuse the balance of payments with the government budget. Make sure that the distinction is clear in *your* mind. A government cannot correct a balance of payments current account deficit through its own budget. The two are quite separate.

Most countries publish balance of payments accounts. These use standard rules and conventions laid down by the International Monetary Fund (IMF) in its **Balance of Payments and International Investment Position Manual** .

These rules are summarised as:

(a) Receipts in the balance of payments (external balance) come from **exports** of goods and services and inflows of capital. These have a **positive sign** as income earned by the country

(b) Payments in the balance of payments come from **imports** of goods and services and outflows of capital. These have a **negative sign** as expenditure by the country

The balance of payments accounts have three parts:

1.1.1 Current account

The **current account** can be subdivided as follows:

Visibles	Invisibles
• Trade in goods	• Trade in services • Income (interest, profit, dividends) • Transfers

Before 1996, the term **visibles** was used for trade in goods and the term **invisibles** was used for the rest: services, transfers and repatriated interest, profits and dividends. These terms have now been dropped in order to give more emphasis to the balances for trade in goods and services.

Trade in goods relates to exports and imports of tangible goods, such as oil, machinery, transport equipment, electrical goods, clothing etc.

Trade in services relates to exports and imports of services, and includes such things as international transport, travel, financial services and business services.

Income is divided into two parts.

(a) Income from employment of the country's residents by overseas firms
(b) Income from capital investment overseas (such as dividends and interest earned)

Transfers are also divided into two parts:

(a) Public sector payments to, and receipts from, overseas bodies such as the EU or World Bank. Typically these are interest payments

(b) Non-government sector payments to and receipts from bodies such as the EU or IMF

1.1.2 Capital account

The **capital account** balance is made up of public sector flows of **capital** into and out of the country, such as government loans to other countries.

1.1.3 Financial account

The balance on the **financial account** is made up of flows of capital to and from the non-government sector, such as direct investment in overseas facilities; portfolio investment (in shares, bonds and so on); and speculative flows of currency ('hot money'). Movements on government foreign currency reserves are also included under this heading.

If a multinational company invests in the country this would be shown as an inflow on that country's balance of payments under the investment section of the financial account.

Similarly, if speculators buy up its currency in response to interest rate or exchange rate movements, these 'hot money' movements will still be shown as inflows in the financial account even though they are short-term capital movements.

1.2 Net errors and omissions

A balancing item appears in the balance of payments accounts because of errors and omissions in collecting statistics for the accounts (for example, sampling errors for items such as foreign investment and tourist expenditure and omissions from the data gathered about exports or imports). A positive balancing item indicates unrecorded net exports: a negative one, net imports.

The sum of the balance of payments accounts must always be zero (ignoring statistical errors in collecting the figures). This is for the same reason that a statement of financial position must always balance: for every debit there must be a credit.

So if the current account is in **deficit** it must be matched by a **surplus** on the capital or financial accounts.

If a country is suffering a current account deficit, it will need to attract additional capital and financial inflows into it. It can do this either by attracting **foreign direct investment** from multinational companies, or attracting foreign funds. It will achieve the latter through having a more attractive level of interest rates than other countries. This could lead to conflict between a domestic need for low interest rates and the need for higher interest rates to attract foreign funds.

1.3 Example: the UK balance of payments accounts

The UK balance of payments account is summarised below, showing how the deficit on the current account is matched by the surplus on capital and financial accounts.

UK balance of payments accounts (2008)

	£m	£m	£m
Current account	*Exports*	*Imports*	*Net*
Trade in goods	251,102	343,979	(92,877)
Trade in services	170,399	115,920	54,479
Income	263,703	236,763	26,940
Transfers	15,422	29,032	(13,610)
Current balance	700,626	725,694	(25,068)
Capital account	5,590	2,197	3,393
Financial account	(637,083)	(655,204)	18,121
	69,133	72,687	(3,554)
Net errors and omissions	3,554	–	3,554
	72,687	72,687	0

[*Source:* United Kingdom Balance of Payments: The Pink Book (2009)]

1.4 What is meant by a balance of payments?

Given that the balance of payments in principle sums to zero, you may wonder what is meant by a surplus or deficit on the balance of payments.

When journalists or economists speak of the balance of payments they are usually referring to the deficit or surplus on the current account, or possibly to the surplus or deficit on trade in goods only (this is also known as the **balance of trade**).

A surplus on the current account is generally regarded as desirable, because the **current account affects national income**. If a country has a current account deficit this represents a net withdrawal from the circular flow of income, and so a deficit on a country's current account will be **deflationary**.

Question — Balance of payments

'If the balance of payments always balances why do we hear about deficits and surpluses?'

Answer

The sum of the three balance of payments accounts must always be zero, because every transaction in international trade has a double aspect. Just as accounting transactions are recorded by matching debit and credit entries, so too are international trade and financing transactions recorded by means of matching plus and minus transactions.

If an exporter sells goods to a foreign buyer:

(a) The value of the export is a plus in the current account of the balance of payments

(b) The payment for the export results in a reduction in the deposits held by foreigners in the country's banks (a minus in the assets and liabilities section)

When we use the phrases 'deficit' or 'surplus on the balance of payments' what we actually mean is a deficit or surplus on the current account. If there is a surplus (+) on the current account we would expect this to be matched by a similar negative amount on the assets and liabilities section. This will take the form of:

(a) Additional claims on non-residents (for example, overseas loans)
(b) Decreased liabilities to non-residents (paying off loans abroad)

This will involve not only banks and other firms but it may also involve the government too, since it is responsible for the 'reserves'.

If there is a deficit (-) on the current account the result will be a similar positive amount on the assets and liabilities section. This will consist of inward investment and/or increased overseas indebtedness, representing how the deficit has been 'financed'. This means that banks and other firms will owe more money abroad and the government may also be borrowing from abroad.

Assessment focus point

Do not equate a trade surplus or deficit with a 'profit' or 'loss' for the country. A country is not like a company and the trade balance has nothing to do with profits and losses as such.

1.5 Foreign currency and international trade

With international trade, there is often a need for foreign currency for at least one of the parties to the transaction.

(a) If a UK exporter sells goods to a US buyer, and charges the buyer £20,000, the US buyer must somehow obtain the sterling in order to pay the UK supplier. The US buyer will do this by using some of his US dollars to buy the £20,000 sterling, probably from a bank in the USA.

(b) If a UK importer buys goods from Germany, he might be invoiced in euros, say €100,000. He must obtain this foreign currency to pay his debt, and he will do so by purchasing the euros from a UK bank in exchange for sterling.

(c) If a UK investor wishes to invest in US capital bonds, he would have to pay for them in US dollars, and so he would have to sell sterling to obtain the dollars.

Thus **capital outflows**, such as investing overseas, not just payments for imports, cause a demand to sell the domestic currency and buy foreign currencies. On the other hand, exports and capital inflows to a country cause a demand to buy the domestic currency in exchange for foreign currencies.

Exporters might want to sell foreign currency earnings to a bank in exchange for domestic currency, and importers may want to buy foreign currency from a bank in order to pay a foreign supplier.

1.6 Exchange rates and the UK balance of payments

As in any other market, the market for foreign exchange is a market in which buyers and suppliers come into contact, and 'prices' (exchange rates) are set by supply and demand. Exchange rates change continually. Significant movements in the exchange rate for a country's currency can have important implications for the country's balance of payments.

1.7 Equilibrium in the balance of payments

A balance of payments is in equilibrium if, over a period of years, the exchange rate remains stable and autonomous credits and debits are equal in value (the annual trade in goods and services is in overall balance). However, equilibrium will not exist if these things require the government to introduce measures which create unemployment or higher prices, sacrifice economic growth or impose trade barriers (eg import tariffs and import quotas).

2 Causes of imbalances in the balance of payments

2.1 Surplus or deficit in the current account

FAST FORWARD

When newspapers and the press talk about a surplus or deficit on the balance of payments, they usually mean a **surplus or deficit on the current account**.

A problem arises for a country's balance of payments when the country has a deficit on its current account year after year, although there can also be problems for a country which enjoys a continual current account **surplus**.

The problems of a **deficit** on the current account are probably the more obvious though. When a country is continually in deficit, it is importing more goods and services that it is exporting.

2.2 Reasons for deficits

The table below summarises the main reasons why a country might be suffering a current account deficit.

Increased import penetration	Poor export performance
Lower production costs mean overseas competitors can produce goods more cheaply than domestic producers.	Exports are not competitively priced and so overseas demand will fall.
Over-valuation of domestic currency makes imports relatively cheaper than domestic products.	Over-valuation of domestic currency makes exports relatively more expensive.
High income elasticity of demand for imports increases demand for imports as national income grows.	Low income elasticity of demand in foreign markets, so demand for exports only grows slowly despite foreign national incomes growing. Equally a country might have low exports because its own domestic market is growing, hence its producers will concentrate on domestic sales rather than looking to export.
Non-price features of imported goods (eg performance, service care) better than domestic goods.	Non-price features of exported goods (eg performance, service care) worse than those of home-produced goods in target markets.

2.3 Consequences of balance of payments deficits

FAST FORWARD

A key consequence of perpetual balance of payments deficits is the **rise in external debt** as the central bank borrows currency to provide to bank to make up the shortfall between earnings from selling exports and the greater expenditure on imports. Eventually the government will **run out of places to borrow** from.

A current account deficit will have been paid for in foreign currency. This is because it is the excess of expenditure abroad over earnings from abroad. It leads to three possible consequences.

(a) A country may borrow more and more from abroad, to build up external **liabilities** which match the deficit on its current account, for example encouraging foreign investors to lend more by purchasing the government's bonds.

(b) A country may sell more and more of its **assets**. This has been happening in the USA in the early 2000s, for example, where a large deficit on the US current account has resulted in large purchases of shares in US companies and property by foreign investors.

(c) **Reserves** of foreign currency held by the central bank may be run down.

Note, however, that none of these three can continue indefinitely, for example because reserves and assets will eventually run out and if liabilities increase too far foreigners will become unwilling to lend fearing their loans will be irrecoverable.

A current account deficit will also mean the demand to buy the country's currency in the foreign exchange markets will be weaker than the supply of the country's currency for sale. As a consequence, there will be pressure on the exchange rate to **depreciate in value**.

2.4 Consequences of a balance of payments surplus

If a country has a **surplus** on current account year after year, it might invest the surplus abroad or add it to official reserves. The balance of payments position would be strong.

There is the problem, however, that if one country which is a major trading nation (such as China) has a continuous surplus on its balance of payments current account, other countries must be in continual deficit. These other countries can run down their official reserves, perhaps to nothing, and borrow as much as they can to meet the payments overseas, but eventually, they will run out of money entirely and be unable even to pay their debts.

Political pressure might therefore build up within the importing countries to impose tariffs or **import quotas** or calls on the country with the surplus to raise its exchange rate and/or buy more imports.

3 Policies to eliminate current account deficits

FAST FORWARD

The main **policies for dealing with a current account** deficit are to **depreciate/devalue the currency**, or to introduce **protectionist measures**, or to reduce demand for imports and encourage exports by **deflating the economy**.

The government of a country with a balance of payments deficit will usually be expected to take measures to reduce or eliminate the deficit. A deficit on current account may be rectified by one or more of the following measures.

3.1 Depreciation/devaluation of the currency

Generally a balance of payments deficit will **automatically cause a currency to depreciate** in value due to the excess supply of domestic currency it creates on the forex market. However sometimes governments maintain the currency at a high level to avoid rising costs of imports. The government could decide to set its exchange rate target lower

[Note: A devaluation occurs when the value of a currency is lowered in a fixed exchange rate system. A depreciation occurs when an exchange rate is reduced under a floating exchange rate system.]

As a result of a fall in the value of the currency, exports would become relatively cheaper to foreign buyers, and so the demand for exports would rise.

The extent of the increase in export revenue would depend on several factors.

(a) The price elasticity of demand for the goods in export markets.

(b) The extent to which industry is able to respond to the export opportunities by either producing more goods, or switching from domestic to export markets.

(c) It may also depend on the price elasticity of supply. With greater demand for their goods, producers should be able to achieve some increase in prices (according to the law of supply and demand), and the willingness of suppliers to produce more would then depend on the price elasticity of supply.

The effects of a fall in the exchange rate (for example, due to a government policy of devaluation) are likely to vary in the short term and the long term. The immediate effects will depend on the elasticity of demand for imports. Demand is likely to be fairly inelastic in the short term and so total expenditure on imports will rise. Exports will be cheaper in overseas markets (in foreign currency) but in the short term exporters might be unable to increase their output to meet the higher demand.

Until domestic industry adjusts to the change and increases its output of exported goods and home produced substitutes for imported goods, there will be a deterioration in the current account of the balance of payments.

After a time lag, production of exports and import substitutes can be expected to rise, so that the volume of exports will rise, thereby increasing the value of exports (despite the domestic currency's lower exchange rate) and the volume of imports will fall further. This will improve the current account balance.

The improvement in the balance of payments will have some limit, and the current balance should eventually level off. The effect of the falling exchange rate on the current balance through time has been portrayed in the form of the so-called **J curve** (Figure 1).

3.2 The J Curve effect

Key term

J curve effect: the effect on the balance of payments of a falling exchange rate. Inelasticity of both supply and demand means that the current account will deteriorate at first but then improve.

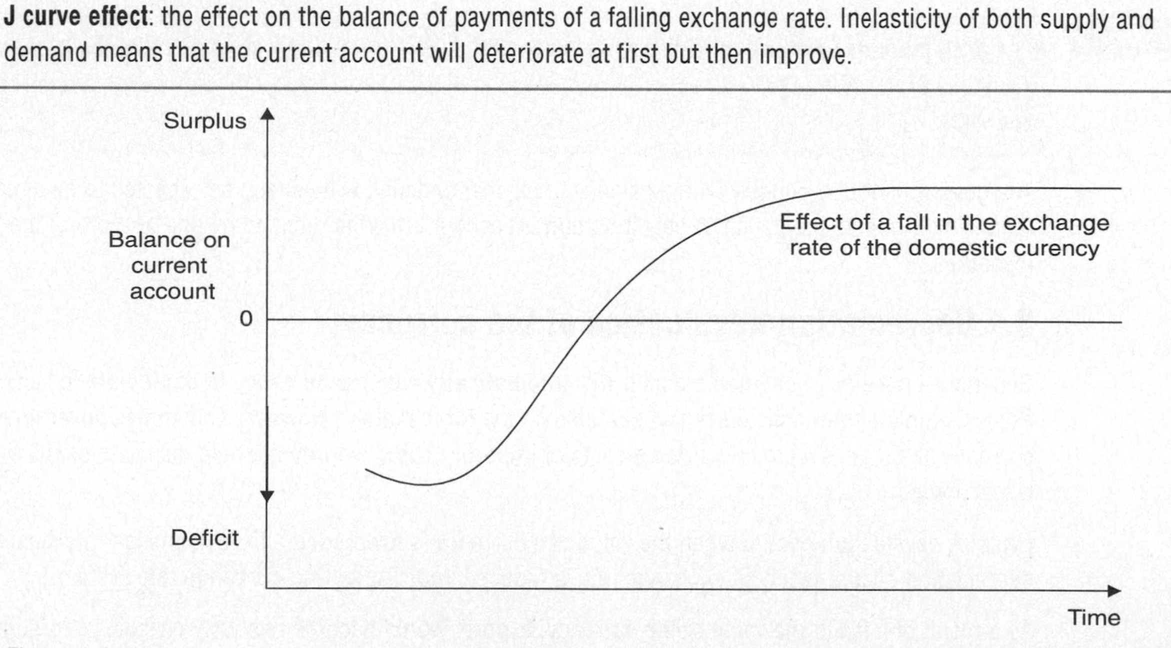

Figure 1 J curve

The upside in the J curve is based on the **Marshall-Lerner conditions** being met. These state that provided the sum of the price elasticity of demand coefficients for **exports and imports is greater than one**, then a fall in the exchange rate will reduce a balance of payments deficit. If demand for both imports and exports is inelastic (which it will be in the short run) then a currency depreciation will lead to a worsening of the balance of payments position. This is why the J curve falls initially.

3.3 Protectionist measures

Another way of attempting to rectify a balance of payments deficit is to take direct protectionist measures as if trying to **reduce the volume of imports**. These measures might include the following:

(a) Import **tariffs**

(b) Import **quotas**

(c) A **total ban** or embargo on imports from a certain country

(d) Placing **administrative burdens** on importers (for example increasing the documentation required or safety standards that imported goods must comply with)

(e) Exchange control regulations which make it difficult for importers to obtain foreign currency to buy goods from abroad

(f) Providing export subsidies to encourage exports, and other measures of financial support to exporters

Import restrictions and export subsidies give rise to counter-measures by other countries. They are therefore potentially dangerous measures for a country whose economy relies heavily on external trade.

Exchange control regulations might be essential, however, for a country with a balance of payments deficit, low official reserves and one which has great difficulty in borrowing capital from abroad.

3.4 Domestic deflation

Deflation can be used to adjust a balance of trade deficit. When the total volume of expenditure and demand for goods in a country's economy is too high, the government can take steps to reduce it, by reducing its own expenditure, raising interest rates to deter borrowing, and cutting private consumption by raising taxes. This fall in demand should lead to a fall in prices or at least to a reduction in the rate of domestic inflation. Unfortunately, it might also lead, in the short term at least, to a reduction in industrial output and a loss of jobs in the country's economy. Certainly, the country must accept a lowering of its standard of living if severe deflationary measures are taken. The effect of deflation is not only to dampen domestic inflation rates, but to force domestic manufacturers, who will be faced with lower domestic demand for their goods, to switch more effort into selling to export markets.

Deflationary measures include cutting government spending, increasing taxation and raising interest rates. They have three purposes.

(a) To reduce the demand for goods and services at home, and so to reduce imports

(b) To encourage industry to switch to export markets, because of the fall in domestic demand

(c) To tackle domestic inflation, which might be undermining the beneficial effect for exports of a depreciating domestic currency by raising the prices of exported goods in terms of the domestic currency

Sometimes, a government's domestic economic policies are not deflationary, despite a balance of payments deficit, and on the contrary, the government's economic policies might encourage increasing demand, which will both boost demand for imports, and cause more inflation and a falling exchange rate. Economic policies which boost demand in the economy in spite of a balance of payments deficit will worsen, rather than improve, the deficit.

4 The terms of trade

FAST FORWARD

The balance of trade depends not only on the volumes of goods traded, but on the **relative prices** of exports and imports (ie on the **terms of trade**).

4.1 What are the terms of trade?

The **balance of trade** for any country depends on two things.

- The volume of goods exported and imported
- The relative prices of exports and imports

Key term

Terms of trade: a measure of the relative prices of a country's exports to its imports.

In effect, the **terms of trade** are an 'export:import' price ratio, which measures the relative prices of a country's exports and imports. The terms of trade for a country continually change as export prices and import prices change.

The terms of trade determine the volume of exports necessary to pay for a given volume of imports or, meaning the same thing, the volume of imports that can be purchased with the proceeds of a given volume of exports.

Other things being equal, if the price of exports falls relative to that of imports (a fall in the terms of trade) the trade balance will deteriorate, or *vice versa*.

Note that trade balance depends not just on the physical volume of exports and imports, but on the prices at which they are traded.

Assessment focus point

Note that the 'terms of trade' and the 'balance of trade' are two distinct measures. Make sure you know what each is, and do not confuse the two.

Question — **Trade effects**

A country's electronics industry, which is its major export industry, switches from the production of mass low cost, low profit margin microchips to the production of more high powered, high cost, high profit margin custom-built microchips. Which one of the following effects would you expect to occur?

A An improvement in the balance of trade
B A deterioration in the balance of trade
C An improvement in the terms of trade
D A worsening in the terms of trade

Answer

The answer is C. This is one example of how a country's terms of trade might improve. By switching from low priced to high priced products in a major export industry, unit export prices will go up and the terms of trade will improve. The change in the *balance* of trade depends on changes in the *volume* of exports and imports *as well as changes in export and import prices.* The question doesn't give any indication about the expected volume of exports, so we cannot tell what the likely effect of this change in the balance of trade will be.

4.2 Measuring the terms of trade

The terms of trade are measured as:

$$\frac{\text{Unit value of exports}}{\text{Unit value of imports}}$$

In practice, economists are usually concerned not with a measurable value for the terms of trade but with a measure of *changes* in the terms of trade, (eg from one year to the next).

Using indices for the average prices of imports and exports, the movement in the terms of trade between 2008 and 2009 would be computed as:

$$\frac{\text{Price of exports 2009/price of exports 2008}}{\text{Price of imports 2009/price of imports 2008}}$$

4.3 Changes in the terms of trade

Change in a country's terms of trade occur for two reasons.

(a) A change in the composition of exports or imports. In the UK, two main things have improved the UK's terms: lower oil imports, and manufacturers trading up to higher-price products for export.

(b) Lower or higher prices of imports/exports.

A government has limited powers to influence its country's terms of trade, since it cannot directly influence the composition nor the prices of imports and exports – although it *can* affect the terms of trade through a revaluation or devaluation of the currency which would alter relative import/export prices.

(a) If a country's terms of trade **worsen**, the unit value of its imports will rise by a bigger percentage than the unit value of its exports. The terms of trade will worsen when the exchange rate of the currency depreciates in value against other currencies.

(b) If a country's terms of trade **improve**, the unit value of its exports will rise by a bigger percentage than the unit value of its imports. The terms of trade will improve when the exchange rate of the country's currency appreciates in value against other currencies.

It would seem logical to assume that an improving terms of trade is good for a country and a worsening terms of trade is bad for it. But this is not necessarily the case.

4.4 Terms of trade and the balance of payments

The effect of a change in the terms of trade should be considered in the context of the country's balance of payments. If the terms of trade worsen for a country, the country will be unable to afford the same volume of imports, or else its balance of payment position will deteriorate. By contrast, a country with improving terms of trade will be able to afford more imports or will improve its balance of payments.

Changes in the terms of trade affect a country's balance of payments via the price elasticity of demand for the goods traded. If a country's terms of trade improve, so that the price of its exported goods rises relative to the price of its imported goods, there will be a relative fall in the volume of goods exported and a rise in the volume of imports. The size of this fall in exports and increase in imports will depend on the price elasticities of demand for exported goods in foreign markets and imported goods in the country's domestic markets.

Note, however, that the terms of trade only measure trade in goods and not trade in services. So while the terms of trade can give an indication of a country's competitive position and balance of payments, it is not a definitive indicator.

Question

Terms of trade and balance of trade

From your knowledge of the theory of elasticity of demand, analyse what will happen to the current balance of trade when the terms of trade improve, on the assumptions that:

(a) Demand for exported goods and demand for imported goods are both *inelastic*
(b) Both demands are *elastic*

Answer

(a) If the demand for exported goods is inelastic the total value of exports will rise if their price goes up.
(b) If the demand for imported goods is inelastic the total value of imports will fall if their price falls.

Provided that price elasticity of demand for both exports and imports is inelastic, an improvement in the terms of trade will result in an improvement in the current balance of trade.

On the other hand if the price elasticity of demand for both exports and imports is elastic, an improvement in the terms of trade will lead to a worsening current balance of trade, because:

(a) A rise in export prices would reduce total export revenue
(b) A fall in import prices would increase total payments for imports

An improvement in the terms of trade might therefore result in a better or a worse balance of payments position. The same applies to worsening terms of trade.

5 Role of global financial institutions

FAST FORWARD

Global financial institutions like the **World Bank**, the **IMF** and the **G20** act to help countries that are **suffering financial problems due to deficits** and lack of borrowing power in the interests of promoting trade.

5.1 The goals of international financial institutions

A number of Institutions are central to the stability of the world economy including the World Bank Group (WB), the International Monetary Fund (IMF), and the Group of Twenty (G-20)

Together these seek to provide:

(a) Short-term stabilisation measures for particular countries or the world economy as a whole;

(b) Medium and long term financial help to countries seeking to restructure and invest in their economies

(c) Co-ordination of policies of member countries on financial regulation and economic policies to avert crises and simulate world economic growth.

5.2 The World Bank Group

The World Bank was formed in 1945 initially to help affected countries recover and rebuild after the damage of the Second World War.

It comprises five agencies although generally the term 'World Bank' is used to refer to just the IBRD and IDA together.

1. **International Bank for Reconstruction and Development (IBRD)**: mission is to fight poverty in middle-income countries. It borrows funds from commercial banks by issuing bonds. Its credit rating is very high and so it can get these funds at much lower rates of interest than could the central bank of a developing country. It loans these funds to governments and public enterprises in developing countries at a low rate of interest to help them invest in development projects. Generally the IBRD lends using tight criteria that ensure the investment can be repaid. The IBRD requires a 'sovereign charge' – ie that the government of the country undertakes to repay the loan.

2. **International Development Association (IDA):** a sister agency to IBRD using the same staff and premises. Its focus is on helping the 80 poorest countries by issuing no-interest loans and grants (called 'credits') to local governments and public enterprises. These loans are long term (35 to 40 years). These help restructuring and also tackling environmental and health issues. Its funds come from donor countries, ie richer developed countries. A sovereign charge is taken for these too.

3. **International Finance Corporation (IFC):** in effect a consultancy and introducer to assist *private sector* investment projects. It has funds of its own to provide initial investment but also relies on encouraging private capital to invest. Where funds are raised by IFC they issue bonds and pass them on with a slight margin for administration to the private borrower. Any guarantees to repay are taken from the borrow and not a sovereign charge.

4. **Multilateral Investment Guarantee Agency (MIGA):** this insures investors against political risk of investing in developing countries. It also provides reports and a forum for sharing information on the risks of investing in particular countries.

5. **International Centre for Settlement of Investment Disputes (ICSID):** this resolves disputes on investments between member countries.

5.3 The International Monetary Fund

The IMF was formed in 1946. Its members are 187 countries belonging to the United Nations.

The IMF supports its membership by providing

(a) policy advice to governments and central banks based on analysis of economic trends and cross-country experiences

(b) research, statistics, forecasts, and analysis based on tracking of global, regional, and individual economies and markets

(c) loans to help countries overcome economic difficulties

(d) concessional loans to help fight poverty in developing countries

(e) technical assistance and training to help countries improve the management of their economies.

Unlike the World Bank, which focuses on eliminating poverty in poor and middle income countries, the IMF provides its services equally to developed countries.

The IMF focuses on helping countries which have balance of payments problems and need more foreign exchange to pay their way.

The IMF members deposit sums of their local currencies with the IMF and in return enjoy Special Drawing Rights (SDRs) that enable them to call on these funds to pay foreign debts.

A nation may become unable to raise foreign currency by issuing bonds to foreign banks. This is because the investment community is having doubts about the ability of that country to repay its debt and fears default. They will either refuse to lend or will charge very high rates of interest to lend. These high rates of interest deepen the

problem because the country will require foreign currency to pay them and so they make the balance of payments deficit, and the need to borrow, deeper.

The IMF will lend at a much lower rate. However it will normally do so subject to the borrowing government agreeing to implement a Structural Adjustment Programme designed by the IMF to bring public finance into better order.

Typical cases where the IMF become involved are:

(a) **Temporary cyclical problems** where the boom stage of a trade cycle has led a country to run temporary balance of payment deficits. Normally drawing down on SDRs is sufficient to deal with this problem

(b) **Structural deficits** where the government of the country has been borrowing heavily to fund the growth of the economy but the growth is delayed or not likely to come about. The government has huge external interest payments and a bad credit rating such that it cannot borrow to pay the interest. . This became very important during the European sovereign debt crisis (or Eurozone crisis) that began in 2009.

(c) **Sectoral problems** such as a threatened collapse of the banking and financial system that requires huge sums to recapitalise the balance sheets of the banks

The IMF is also involved in laying down standards for data dissemination, such as the calculation of Balance of Payments data.

5.4 The Group of 20

The **Group of Twenty Finance Ministers and Central Bank Governors (G-20)** is a group of finance ministers and central bank governors from 20 economies: 19 countries plus the European Union, the latter is represented by the President of the European Council and by the European Central Bank. Together these countries are home to two-thirds of the World's population and account for 85% of the World's GDP.

The G20 holds annual summits, or meetings, to discuss global financial issues. These have included

(a) Dealing with financial crises such as the banking crisis of 2007-2010

(b) Harmonisation of taxation policies across countries to reduce tax avoidance

(c) Agreeing policies to detect and reduce illegal transfers of money from the proceeds of crime, terrorism and so on

The G20 has become very influential since it was formed in 2008 and has essentially replaced other groupings of rich countries such as the G7 and G8.

6 The nature and causes of globalisation

FAST FORWARD

Globalisation refers to a **widespread extension of trade** between countries and a high degree of **interdependence of production** between countries

6.1 Globalisation

Globalisation may be defined as the interdependence and integration of different national economies. It reflects the tendency of markets to become global rather than national and for it to be difficult to view any national economy as a stand-alone entity.

6.2 Factors driving globalisation

(a) Improved communications, for example the speed of access to the internet

(b) Reduction of transport costs

(c) Political realignments, for example the collapse of the Soviet block

(d) Growth of global industries and institutions

(e) Break down of some trade barriers by free trade organisations and treaties

6.3 The size and significance of multinational enterprises

A **multinational company** is one that has production or service facilities in more than one country. Multinational enterprises range from medium-sized companies having only a few facilities (or subsidiaries or 'affiliates') abroad to giant companies having an annual turnover larger than the gross national product (GNP) of some smaller countries of the world. Indeed the largest – the US multinationals Ford, General Motors and Exxon have each been reported to have a turnover larger than the GNPs of all but 14 countries of the world.

The size and significance of multinationals is increasing. Many companies in middle-income countries such as Singapore are now becoming multinationals, and the annual growth in output of existing multinationals is in the range 10-15%.

6.4 Globalisation of production

FAST FORWARD

Globalisation has been assisted by the **globalisation of production** by multinational enterprises (MNEs) and the **globalisation of capital markets**.

Transnational companies are tending more and more to take a global view of production facilitated by technological advances which make it easier to do business internationally. Production facilities may be located in particular countries for a variety of reasons.

- To give access to markets protected by tariffs
- To reduce transport costs
- To exploit national or regional differences in demand for goods, and thereby expand sales
- To take advantage of low labour costs, and thereby reduce production costs
- To secure supply through backward vertical integration

Centralisation of manufacturing can bring important **economies of scale**. These must be balanced against transport costs and barriers to trade. And the companies must have a suitably developed organisational structure to control their operations overall.

6.5 Globalisation of capital markets

Globalisation describes the process by which the capital markets of each country have become internationally integrated. The process of integration is facilitated by improved telecommunications and the deregulation of markets in many countries. Securities issued in one country can now be traded in capital markets around the world. This trend can only increase as stock exchanges are linked electronically as has happened with markets like NASDAQ.

For companies planning international investment activities (also known as foreign direct investment (FDI)), easy access to large amounts of funds denominated in foreign currencies can be very useful. Such funds are available in the eurocurrency markets. The eurocurrency markets can also help to bypass official constraints on international business activities.

6.6 Forms of foreign investment

Foreign direct investment (FDI) provides an alternative to growth restricted to a firm's domestic market. A firm might develop horizontally in different countries, replicating its existing operations on a global basis (**horizontal integration**). **Vertical integration** might have an international dimension through FDI to acquire raw material or component sources overseas (backwards integration) or to establish final production and distribution in other countries (forward integration). Diversification might alternatively provide the impetus to developing international interests.

6.7 Impact of MNCs and FDI on national economies

For	Against
Improve economic welfare by introducing new capital.	Inward investment may not create new investment, but displace existing domestic investment.
Introduce new technologies (**technology transfer**).	Technology transfer may only be at a low level.
MNCs will provide **direct employment**, and may also create additional indirect employment through supplier firms. Possible multiplier effect resulting from new investment.	May not be new employment; may displace existing employment if MNCs displace existing firms.
Local producers establish direct linkages with MNCs and supply to them. Improve productivity of local producers.	
Balance of payments gains from inflows of FDI.	Profits from the investment are repatriated to the host country of the MNC.
Governments can get **tax revenue** from MNC profits.	MNCs likely to minimise tax liability through **transfer pricing**. Government offer grants and subsidies to attract MNC investment so may end up worse off.

7 Trade agreements and trading blocks

FAST FORWARD

Trade agreements include **free trade areas**, **common markets** and **economic unions**.

7.1 Types of trade agreement

7.1.1 Free trade areas

A **free trade area** exists when there is no restriction on the movement of goods and services between countries although individual member countries can impose their own restrictions on non-member countries.

A free trade area may be extended into a **customs union** when there is a free trade area between all member countries of the union, and in addition, there are **common external tariffs** applying to imports from non-member countries into any part of the union. In other words, the union promotes free trade among its members but acts as a protectionist bloc against the rest of the world

7.1.2 Common markets

A **common market** encompasses the idea of a customs union but has a number of additional features. In addition to free trade among member countries there are also free markets in each of the **factors of production**. A British citizen has the freedom to work in any other country of the European Union, for example. A common market will also aim to achieve stronger links between member countries, for example by harmonising government economic policies and by establishing a closer political confederation.

7.1.3 Economic union

An **economic and monetary union** harmonises national economic policies, such as financial regulations, and by introducing its own central bank and currency.

7.2 The World Trade Organisation

The World Trade Organisation (WTO) was formed in 1995 as a successor to the General Agreement on Tariffs and Trade (GATT). In 2009 WTO had 153 countries as members. The main objective of WTO is to encourage free trade by policies such as the reciprocal dropping of tariffs between trading countries and the elimination of other forms of protectionism. It is also a forum for governments to negotiate trade agreements and to settle trade disputes.

7.3 The European Union

The European Union (EU) (formerly the European Community) is one of several international economic associations. It was formed in 1957 by the Treaty of Rome and now consists of 27 nations (2009), and there are three more candidate countries waiting to join.

The European Union has a **common market** combining different aspects, including **a free trade area** and a **customs union**.

The **European Central Bank (ECB)** is the central bank for Europe's single currency (the Euro). Its main task is to maintain price stability in the euro area.

However, this means the ECB has to balance the two potentially conflicting objectives in Article 2 of the Treaty on European Union: a high level of employment, and sustainable and non-inflationary growth.

In addition, as prescribed by Article 105.2 of the Treaty, the ECB's tasks are to:

- Define and implement **monetary policy** for the eurozone area
- Conduct **foreign exchange operations**
- Manage the official **foreign reserves** of the eurozone countries
- Promote the smooth operation of **payment systems** within the eurozone countries

7.4 COMESA

The Common Market for Eastern and Southern Africa (COMESA) comprises 19 member states with a combined GDP of US$360bn and a combined population of over 400mn. Its members include Burundi, Comoros, Djibouti, the Democratic Republic of Congo (DRC), Egypt, Eritrea, Ethiopia, Kenya, Libya, Madagascar, Malawi, Mauritius, Rwanda, Seychelles, Sudan, Swaziland, Uganda, Zambia and Zimbabwe. It was formed in 1992.

The aim of COMESA is to create an economic community between its members. It seeks to so this in the same way as the European Union developed.

7.5 The North American Free Trade Agreement (NAFTA)

Canada, the USA and Mexico formed the North American Free Trade Agreement (NAFTA) in 1993. This free trade area covering a population of approximately 445 million (2008) is similar in size to the European Economic Area.

7.6 Opinions on trading blocs

Not surprisingly, opinion on regional trading blocs is divided. Proponents of it argue it encourages trade creation by removing restrictions to trade. Opponents argue it leads to trade diversion and uneconomic behaviour, as member countries buy within that bloc when goods and services may be cheaper elsewhere. Critics also argue trading blocs will foster a fortress mentality and encourage protectionism worldwide, contravening the logic of free trade.

8 Impacts of globalisation

FAST FORWARD

Globalisation was once assumed to bring **higher standards of living and growth** to economies but increasingly concerns have been expressed about its potential for allowing the **exploitation of developing countries.**

Globalisation used to be the unquestioned model for economic growth and stability but there are now many critics of the phenomena.

8.1 Arguments in favour of globalisation

(a) Emergence of new growth markets, for example in the less developed countries
(b) Enhanced competitiveness as more producers and customers make up the global marketplace
(c) Growth of previously poor economies, such as China
(d) Cross-national business alliance and mergers
(e) International support for poorer nations and assistance provided in development of their economies
(f) World economic equalisation

8.2 Criticisms of globalisation

(a) The main institutions of globalisation follow the collective will of the G8 countries (USA, Japan, Germany, Canada, Italy, France, the UK and Russia) and are more concerned therefore in aiding the economic wealth of these countries.

(b) IMF, WB and G20 along with powerful multinational organisations dictate economic policy in countries but do not include real representation of these countries within their organisations. This lack of accountability has been called 'global governance without global government' (*Joseph Stiglitz*, Globalisation and its Discontents).

(c) World poverty is still an issue and many fear that the policies adopted by WB, IMF and others, for example in restricting subsidy in Africa and opening up their markets for Western imports that are produced under subsidy, actually makes some nations poorer.

(d) There is no enduring political and economic stability in the world and the collapse of one part of the economy, for example in South America, could have disastrous knock on effects for the rest of the world.

(e) Not all countries are included in global activity. Instead there is an increasing tendency for groups of counties, usually located in the same region to become involved in each others economies, for example the countries in the Eurozone.

Chapter roundup

- The **balance of payments accounts** consist of a current account with visibles and invisibles sections and transactions in capital (external assets and liabilities including official financing). The sum of the balances on these accounts must be zero, although in practice there is a balancing figure for measurement errors.
- When newspapers and the press talk about a surplus or deficit on the balance of payments, they usually mean a **surplus or deficit on the current account**.
- A key consequence of perpetual balance of payments deficits is the **rise in external debt** as the central bank borrows currency to provide to bank to make up the shortfall between earnings from selling exports and the greater expenditure on imports. Eventually the government will **run out of places to borrow** from.

  The main **policies for dealing with a current account** deficit are to **depreciate/devalue the currency,** or to introduce **protectionist measures**, or to reduce demand for imports and encourage exports by **deflating the economy**.
- The balance of trade depends not only on the volumes of goods traded, but on the **relative prices** of exports and imports (ie on the **terms of trade**).
- Global financial institutions like the **World Bank**, the **IMF** and the **G20** act to help countries that are **suffering financial problems due to deficits** and lack of borrowing power in the interests of promoting trade.

  Globalisation refers to a **widespread extension of trade** between countries and a high degree of **interdependence of production** between countries
- Globalisation has been assisted by the **globalisation of production** by multinational enterprises (MNEs) and the **globalisation of capital markets**,
- Trade agreements include **free trade areas**, **common markets** and **economic unions**.
- Globalisation was once assumed to bring **higher standards of living and growth** to economies but increasingly concerns have been expressed about its potential for allowing the **exploitation of developing countries.**

Quick quiz

1 What does the J curve describe?

2 How do deflationary measures help to eliminate a balance of payments deficit?

3 What is the balance of trade?

A The balance of payments on current account
B Net visible trade
C Net visible and invisible trade
D The theory of gains from trade

4 Which of the following statements concerning international trade are true?

(1) The J curve effect will work in reverse if there is a depreciation when the current account is in deficit.
(2) Protectionism could reduce exports.
(3) Devaluation of the domestic currency could reverse a current account deficit.

A (1) and (3) only
B (1), (2) and (3)
C (1) and (2) only
D (2) and (3) only

5 From a given base year, a country's export prices rise by 8% and import prices rise by 20%. During this period, the terms of trade will have:

A Risen from 100 to 111.1
B Risen from 100 to 112
C Fallen from 100 to 90
D Fallen from 100 to 88

6 A devaluation will only benefit the UK balance of payments if:

A The sum of the price elasticities of demand for imports and exports is less than 1
B The sum of the price elasticities of demand for imports and exports is greater than 1
C The sum of the price elasticities of demand for imports and exports is less than 0
D The sum of the price elasticities of demand for imports and exports is greater than 0

7 Assume that two small countries, X and Y, produce two commodities P and Q, and that there are no transport costs. One unit of resource in Country X produces 4 units of P or 8 units of Q. One unit of resource in Country Y produces 1 unit of P or 3 units of Q. Which one of the following statements is true?

A Country X has an absolute advantage over Country Y in producing P and Q, and so will not trade.
B Country X has a comparative advantage over Country Y in producing Q.
C Country Y has a comparative advantage over Country X in producing Q.
D Country X has a comparative advantage over Country Y in producing both P and Q.

8 The balance of payments current account will include which of the following items?

(i) Expenditure in a country by overseas visitors
(ii) The inflow of capital investment by multinational companies
(iii) Exports of manufactured goods

A (iii) only
B (i) and (iii)
C (ii) and (iii)
D (i), (ii) and (iii)

Answers to quick quiz

1 The J curve shows the effect on the balance of payments of a falling exchange rate. A falling exchange rate will eventually reduce demand for imports and increase demand for exports. However, in the short term, both domestic and export demand are likely to be inelastic and the ability of domestic industry to meet any increase in export demand will be limited. The volume of goods and services traded is therefore unlikely to change in the short term, but imports will cost more in foreign currency and exports will sell for less. It is therefore likely that there will be a deterioration in the balance of payments in the short term.

2 Domestic deflation cuts demand, including demand for imports. Industry is therefore encouraged to switch to export markets.

3 B Learn this definition. The balance of trade is the surplus or deficit on trade in goods only.

4 D The J curve would work in reverse if there were a surplus and the currency appreciated, so (i) is not true. Protectionism could reduce exports if other countries react hostilely to a country introducing import restrictions. Devaluation of the domestic currency should make exports cheaper, and so should help reduce a current account deficit.

5 C $108/120 \times 100 = 90$.

6 B In order to benefit, internal demand must react to a rise in the price of imports and external demand must react to a fall in the price of UK exported goods.

7 C Country X has an *absolute* advantage over Country Y in making both P and Q, because 1 unit of resource in Country X will make more of either P or Q than one unit of resource in Country Y. However, international trade should still take place because of *comparative* advantage in producing P and Q. The opportunity costs of producing a unit of P is 2 units of Q in Country X and 3 units of Q in Country Y. Similarly, the opportunity cost of producing a unit of Q is 1/2 a unit of P in Country X and 1/3 of a unit of P in Country Y. Country X has a comparative advantage in producing P and Country Y has a comparative advantage in the production of Q. International trade should be beneficial for both countries, with country X exporting P and Country Y exporting Q.

8 B Exports of manufactured goods are part of the balance of trade element of the current account. Expenditure by tourists is part of the trade in services in the 'invisibles' part of the current account. Foreign investment by multi-national companies is part of the financial account.

Now try the questions below from the Exam Question Bank

Question numbers
73 - 78

Appendix – Mathematical tables

Present value table

Present value of $1 ie (1+r)-n where r = interest rate, n = number of periods until payment or receipt.

Periods	Interest rates (r)									
(n)	1%	2%	3%	4%	5%	6%	7%	8%	9%	10%
1	0.990	0.980	0.971	0.962	0.952	0.943	0.935	0.926	0.917	0.909
2	0.980	0.961	0.943	0.925	0.907	0.890	0.873	0.857	0.842	0.826
3	0.971	0.942	0.915	0.889	0.864	0.840	0.816	0.794	0.772	0.751
4	0.961	0.924	0.888	0.855	0.823	0.792	0.763	0.735	0.708	0.683
5	0.951	0.906	0.863	0.822	0.784	0.747	0.713	0.681	0.650	0.621
6	0.942	0.888	0.837	0.790	0.746	0.705	0.666	0.630	0.596	0.564
7	0.933	0.871	0.813	0.760	0.711	0.665	0.623	0.583	0.547	0.513
8	0.923	0.853	0.789	0.731	0.677	0.627	0.582	0.540	0.502	0.467
9	0.914	0.837	0.766	0.703	0.645	0.592	0.544	0.500	0.460	0.424
10	0.905	0.820	0.744	0.676	0.614	0.558	0.508	0.463	0.422	0.386
11	0.896	0.804	0.722	0.650	0.585	0.527	0.475	0.429	0.388	0.350
12	0.887	0.788	0.701	0.625	0.557	0.497	0.444	0.397	0.356	0.319
13	0.879	0.773	0.681	0.601	0.530	0.469	0.415	0.368	0.326	0.290
14	0.870	0.758	0.661	0.577	0.505	0.442	0.388	0.340	0.299	0.263
15	0.861	0.743	0.642	0.555	0.481	0.417	0.362	0.315	0.275	0.239
16	0.853	0.728	0.623	0.534	0.458	0.394	0.339	0.292	0.252	0.218
17	0.844	0.714	0.605	0.513	0.436	0.371	0.317	0.270	0.231	0.198
18	0.836	0.700	0.587	0.494	0.416	0.350	0.296	0.250	0.212	0.180
19	0.828	0.686	0.570	0.475	0.396	0.331	0.277	0.232	0.194	0.164
20	0.820	0.673	0.554	0.456	0.377	0.312	0.258	0.215	0.178	0.149

Periods	Interest rates (r)									
(n)	11%	12%	13%	14%	15%	16%	17%	18%	19%	20%
1	0.901	0.893	0.885	0.877	0.870	0.862	0.855	0.847	0.840	0.833
2	0.812	0.797	0.783	0.769	0.756	0.743	0.731	0.718	0.706	0.694
3	0.731	0.712	0.693	0.675	0.658	0.641	0.624	0.609	0.593	0.579
4	0.659	0.636	0.613	0.592	0.572	0.552	0.534	0.516	0.499	0.482
5	0.593	0.567	0.543	0.519	0.497	0.476	0.456	0.437	0.419	0.402
6	0.535	0.507	0.480	0.456	0.432	0.410	0.390	0.370	0.352	0.335
7	0.482	0.452	0.425	0.400	0.376	0.354	0.333	0.314	0.296	0.279
8	0.434	0.404	0.376	0.351	0.327	0.305	0.285	0.266	0.249	0.233
9	0.391	0.361	0.333	0.308	0.284	0.263	0.243	0.225	0.209	0.194
10	0.352	0.322	0.295	0.270	0.247	0.227	0.208	0.191	0.176	0.162
11	0.317	0.287	0.261	0.237	0.215	0.195	0.178	0.162	0.148	0.135
12	0.286	0.257	0.231	0.208	0.187	0.168	0.152	0.137	0.124	0.112
13	0.258	0.229	0.204	0.182	0.163	0.145	0.130	0.116	0.104	0.093
14	0.232	0.205	0.181	0.160	0.141	0.125	0.111	0.099	0.088	0.078
15	0.209	0.183	0.160	0.140	0.123	0.108	0.095	0.084	0.074	0.065
16	0.188	0.163	0.141	0.123	0.107	0.093	0.081	0.071	0.062	0.054
17	0.170	0.146	0.125	0.108	0.093	0.080	0.069	0.060	0.052	0.045
18	0.153	0.130	0.111	0.095	0.081	0.069	0.059	0.051	0.044	0.038
19	0.138	0.116	0.098	0.083	0.070	0.060	0.051	0.043	0.037	0.031
20	0.124	0.104	0.087	0.073	0.061	0.051	0.043	0.037	0.031	0.026

Cumulative present value table

This table shows the present value of $1 per annum, receivable or payable at the end of each year for n years $\frac{1-(1+r)^{-n}}{r}$.

Periods (n)	Interest rates (r) 1%	2%	3%	4%	5%	6%	7%	8%	9%	10%
1	0.990	0.980	0.971	0.962	0.952	0.943	0.935	0.926	0.917	0.909
2	1.970	1.942	1.913	1.886	1.859	1.833	1.808	1.783	1.759	1.736
3	2.941	2.884	2.829	2.775	2.723	2.673	2.624	2.577	2.531	2.487
4	3.902	3.808	3.717	3.630	3.546	3.465	3.387	3.312	3.240	3.170
5	4.853	4.713	4.580	4.452	4.329	4.212	4.100	3.993	3.890	3.791
6	5.795	5.601	5.417	5.242	5.076	4.917	4.767	4.623	4.486	4.355
7	6.728	6.472	6.230	6.002	5.786	5.582	5.389	5.206	5.033	4.868
8	7.652	7.325	7.020	6.733	6.463	6.210	5.971	5.747	5.535	5.335
9	8.566	8.162	7.786	7.435	7.108	6.802	6.515	6.247	5.995	5.759
10	9.471	8.983	8.530	8.111	7.722	7.360	7.024	6.710	6.418	6.145
11	10.368	9.787	9.253	8.760	8.306	7.887	7.499	7.139	6.805	6.495
12	11.255	10.575	9.954	9.385	8.863	8.384	7.943	7.536	7.161	6.814
13	12.134	11.348	10.635	9.986	9.394	8.853	8.358	7.904	7.487	7.103
14	13.004	12.106	11.296	10.563	9.899	9.295	8.745	8.244	7.786	7.367
15	13.865	12.849	11.938	11.118	10.380	9.712	9.108	8.559	8.061	7.606
16	14.718	13.578	12.561	11.652	10.838	10.106	9.447	8.851	8.313	7.824
17	15.562	14.292	13.166	12.166	11.274	10.477	9.763	9.122	8.544	8.022
18	16.398	14.992	13.754	12.659	11.690	10.828	10.059	9.372	8.756	8.201
19	17.226	15.679	14.324	13.134	12.085	11.158	10.336	9.604	8.950	8.365
20	18.046	16.351	14.878	13.590	12.462	11.470	10.594	9.818	9.129	8.514

Periods (n)	Interest rates (r) 11%	12%	13%	14%	15%	16%	17%	18%	19%	20%
1	0.901	0.893	0.885	0.877	0.870	0.862	0.855	0.847	0.840	0.833
2	1.713	1.690	1.668	1.647	1.626	1.605	1.585	1.566	1.547	1.528
3	2.444	2.402	2.361	2.322	2.283	2.246	2.210	2.174	2.140	2.106
4	3.102	3.037	2.974	2.914	2.855	2.798	2.743	2.690	2.639	2.589
5	3.696	3.605	3.517	3.433	3.352	3.274	3.199	3.127	3.058	2.991
6	4.231	4.111	3.998	3.889	3.784	3.685	3.589	3.498	3.410	3.326
7	4.712	4.564	4.423	4.288	4.160	4.039	3.922	3.812	3.706	3.605
8	5.146	4.968	4.799	4.639	4.487	4.344	4.207	4.078	3.954	3.837
9	5.537	5.328	5.132	4.946	4.772	4.607	4.451	4.303	4.163	4.031
10	5.889	5.650	5.426	5.216	5.019	4.833	4.659	4.494	4.339	4.192
11	6.207	5.938	5.687	5.453	5.234	5.029	4.836	4.656	4.486	4.327
12	6.492	6.194	5.918	5.660	5.421	5.197	4.988	4.793	4.611	4.439
13	6.750	6.424	6.122	5.842	5.583	5.342	5.118	4.910	4.715	4.533
14	6.982	6.628	6.302	6.002	5.724	5.468	5.229	5.008	4.802	4.611
15	7.191	6.811	6.462	6.142	5.847	5.575	5.324	5.092	4.876	4.675
16	7.379	6.974	6.604	6.265	5.954	5.668	5.405	5.162	4.938	4.730
17	7.549	7.120	6.729	6.373	6.047	5.749	5.475	5.222	4.990	4.775
18	7.702	7.250	6.840	6.467	6.128	5.818	5.534	5.273	5.033	4.812
19	7.839	7.366	6.938	6.550	6.198	5.877	5.584	5.316	5.070	4.843
20	7.963	7.469	7.025	6.623	6.259	5.929	5.628	5.353	5.101	4.870

Question bank

1 The 'divorce of ownership from control' in a modern economy describes:

A The growth of government regulation

B Management of companies by salaried personnel who do not have significant shareholding in their company

C Enhancement of employee rights over conditions of work

D Expansion of share ownership through privatisation

2 Which of the following sectors would include a sole trader

A Not for profit sector
B Incorporated sector
C Private sector
D Voluntary sector

3 What do the letters PPP stand for?

A Private-sector Profit Pursuing
B Private Profit Partnership
C Public Profit Partnership
D Public Private Partnership

4 In stakeholder theory, how is a shareholder classified?

A Internal stakeholder
B Connected stakeholder
C External stakeholder
D Voluntary stakeholder

5 Which of the following is *not* a source of shareholder power in a quoted company

A Voting rights at General Meetings
B Ability to sell shares and make firm vulnerable to takeover
C Ability of groups of institutional investors to act as a dominant coalition
D Right to attendance at Board meetings

6 The following are summary financial data for a company for the year ending 31.12.20X9

	$m
Profit before interest and tax	120
Interest payments	15
Tax payments	27

Capital employed at 31.12.20X9 was $990m
Capital employed at 31.12.20X8 was $930m

What was the company's return on capital employed (ROCE)?

A 7.9%
B 8.1%
C 12.1%
D 12.5%

7 What relationship is described by the shareholders' risk-return curve?

A That shareholders are only willing to take on higher risk if they anticipate a higher return from the success of the business

B That most shareholders prefer a risk free rate

C That profits are always higher if a shareholder is prepared to take a bigger risk

D That risk and return are related

8 Which of the following does EPS measure?

A The dividend the ordinary shareholder has received in the past year

B The amount of capital gain (or loss) on each share in the past year

C The amount of post tax profit attributable to each ordinary share from the most recent year's business activity

D The likely profits per share that will arise from the coming year's activity

9 Why is a rate of discount applied to future earnings to arrive at a value for the firm's shares?

A Because some of the claims made about future profits must be disregarded
B Because investors place a time value on money
C To allow for the interest on the funds the investor borrowed to buy the shares
D To provide for the shareholder the chance to make a capital gain

10 If all other factors remain unchanged, which one of the following would lead to a fall in share prices?

A A reduction in the rate of tax which companies have to pay
B Forecasts predicting a rise in company profits
C A rise in interest rates
D A reduction in the number of shares issued

11 If the cost of milk rises, and milk is a major ingredient in yoghurt, then the:

A Demand curve for yoghurt shifts to the left
B Supply for yoghurt curve shifts to the left
C Supply curve for yoghurt shifts to the right
D Demand and supply curves for yoghurt both shift to the right

12 Which of the following is *not* one of the roles performed by prices in a market economy?

A A signal to consumers
B A signal to producers
C A way of allocating resources between competing uses
D A way of ensuring a fair distribution of incomes

13 Indicate whether the following will cause a shift in the demand curve for a normal good, a shift in its supply curve, or neither:

	Shift in demand	*Shift in supply*	*Neither*
(i) An increase in household incomes			
(ii) A rise in wage costs			
(iii) A fall in the price of raw materials			
(iv) A fall in the price of the good			

14 Which of the following best describes price elasticity of demand?`

A Some goods go up in price more than others when demand rises

B A $1 price fall lead to a bigger change in the quantity demanded of price elastic goods than of price inelastic goods

C The proportionate increase in quantity demand for a given proportionate change in price is bigger in some markets than in others

D People always buy more of a good when its price falls

15 Which of the following statements about a demand curve of unit price elasticity along its length is *false*?

A Changes in price will not affect the firm's total revenue
B If price is increased then quantity demanded will fall in the same proportion
C All rectangle drawn beneath it will have the same area
D Quantity demanded doesn't change when price changes

16 Which of the following will tend to make the price elasticity of supply lower?

A The ability to store the good and sell it when demand rises
B The good is made by skilled labour which is in short supply
C The elapse of more time since the price changed
D The change in demand is expected to be permanent

17 Which of the following statements about a market with a downward sloping straight line demand curve is *false*?

A It will have an angle of 45^0 from the vertical
B At the mid point it will have unit price elasticity of demand
C Price elasticity of demand falls as total quantity rises
D Firms are unlikely to produce output to the right of the midpoint of the curve

18 There are three special cases of elasticity of supply.

Put correct labels in the boxes on this diagram.

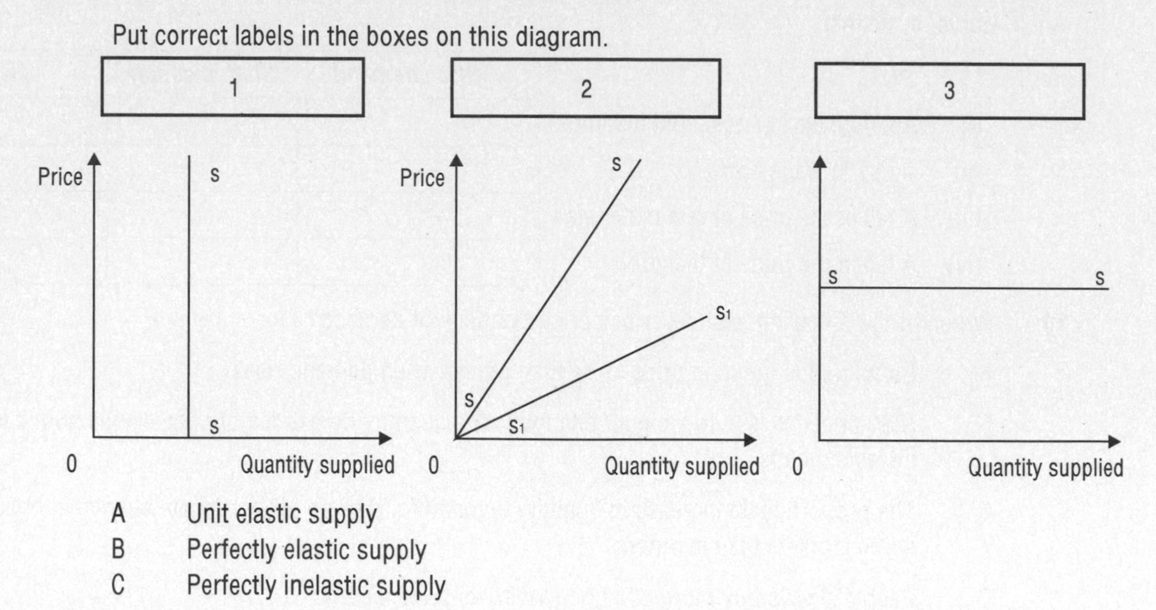

A Unit elastic supply
B Perfectly elastic supply
C Perfectly inelastic supply

19 In the diagram below, point 5 represents equilibrium. If the government starts to pay a cash subsidy to producers of the commodity, what will the new equilibrium be?

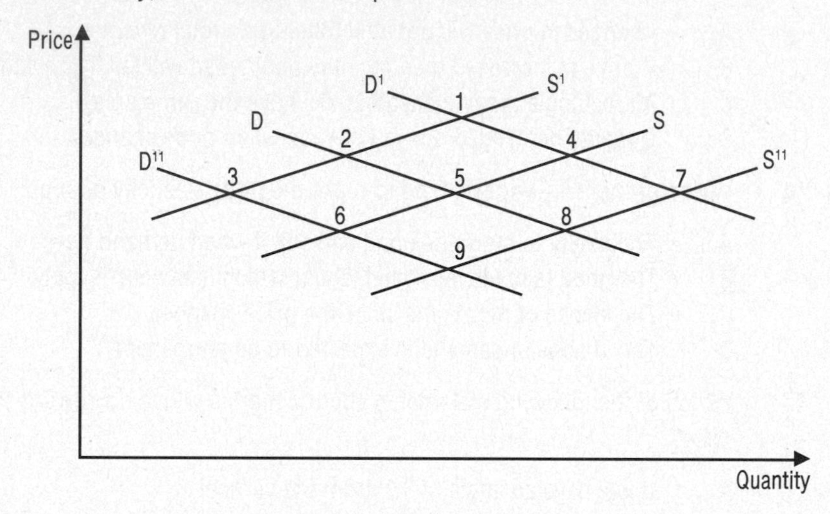

A Point 2
B Point 4
C Point 6
D Point 8

20 The table below shows a market demand schedule and a market supply schedule for beans.

Price per tonne $	*Quantity demanded per month* ('000 tonnes)	*Quantity supplied per month* ('000 tonnes)
280	4,000	9,200
260	5,000	8,800
240	6,400	8,200
220	7,400	7,400
200	8,200	6,600

180	9,000	5,800
160	9,800	4,800

What would be the consequences of the introduction by the government of a maximum price for beans of $200 per tonne? Assume that supply quantities can be readily adjusted to any new market conditions.

1 There would be a need for rationing of beans
2 There would be a 'bean mountain'
3 There would be a shortage of 1,600,000 tonnes per month
4 There would be a surplus of 1,600,000 tonnes per month
5 The price for beans would be unchanged

A Consequences 1 and 3 only
B Consequences 2 and 4 only
C Consequence 5 only
D Consequence 4 only

21 Which of the following statements about the purpose of a guaranteed minimum price is *false*?

A It will help to assure farm incomes
B It will encourage production of the good
C It will make it cheaper for consumers
D It will ensure farmers survive in times of good harvests

22 Which one of the following would be a symptom of a maximum price set below free market price?

A Stockpiles of unsold product
B Suppliers extending quantity supplied
C Waiting lists for the product
D Demand contracting in favour of substitutes

23 The table below shows a firm's total cost (TC), average cost (AC) and marginal cost (MC) for certain levels of output. Which is which?

Units of output	*1* $	*2* $	*3* $
1	1.10	1.10	1.10
2	0.80	0.50	1.60
3	0.58	0.15	1.75
4	0.50	0.25	2.00
5	0.50	0.50	2.50
6	0.52	0.62	3.12

A 1 = AC, 2 = TC, 3 = MC
B 1 = AC, 2 = MC, 3 = TC
C 1 = MC, 2 = AC, 3 = TC
D 1 = TC, 2 = AC, 3 = MC

24 Which of the following descriptions of fixed cost is *false*?

A The total costs at zero output
B Costs that do not increase as output rises within the relevant range
C Costs of production that are fixed by long term contract and so do not rise through time
D The difference between total costs and total variable costs at any given level of output

25 What is the significance of the total variable cost curve being drawn as a straight line

A It ensures the total cost curve is parallel to it
B It assumes that efficiency of production does not change as output changes
C It shows that making more of the product always costs more
D It means that marginal cost will have the same value as unit cost

26 Which of the implications of curvilinear cost curves below is *false*?

A It shows one unique level of output at which unit cost is lowest

B It shows that variable costs per unit are not constant if the firm makes large changes in output

C It shows that there are no fixed costs

D It shows that increasing output leads to initially improving efficiency then, at some point, declining efficiency

27 Which of the following statements best distinguishes an external economy of scale from an internal economy of scale?

A They enable unit costs to fall as the firm adopts a larger scale of production

B At the minimum efficient scale they are fully utilised

C They are only available in the long run

D They result from a growth in the size of the industry and not from the growth in the size of an individual firm

28 Which one of the following statements about the total revenue curve is *false*?

A It curves because of the operation of the law of demand
B It assumes the amount the firm sells does not influence price
C The highest point of the curve is where price elasticity of demand equal 1
D It intersects the origin on the diagram

29 What point on the total cost and total revenue diagram shows the point of maximum profit?

A The point where the total cost and total revenue curves have the same slope
B The point where the two curves intersect
C The highest point on the total revenue curve
D The point where the total revenue and total cost curves cease converging

30 Which one of the following *would not* contribute to lower prices in markets served by e-commerce?

A The greater availability of substitutes due to ease of entry to the market
B The reduction in search costs available by using the internet
C The low or zero variable cost per unit for downloads
D The high fixed costs of setting up an e-commence business

31 Which one of the following statements explains the trend by ACT businesses to develop proprietary product platforms?

A They are expensive to produce
B They reduce the price elasticity of demand for games and songs that run on them
C They benefit from economies of scale
D They increase the availability of substitute products to use with them

32 Which one of the following will tend to increase the number of firms in an industry?

A Significant barriers to entry
B Economies of scale
C High transport costs
D High advertising costs

33 Which of the following are public goods in economic terms?

(i) Health service
(ii) Public transport
(iii) Street lighting

A (i) and (ii)
B (i) and (iii)
C (ii) and (iii)
D (iii) only

34 Recent government legislation in County T has meant that car manufacturers there now have to install anti-pollution devices in all their cars.

Which of the following outcomes is a result of this action?

A An increase in private costs and a reduction in negative externalities
B An increase in private costs and an increase in negative externalities
C An increase in social costs and a reduction in negative externalities
D An increase in social costs and an increase in negative externalities

35 Which of the following statements about externalities is true?

(i) Externalities are the differences between the private and social costs or benefits of a transaction
(ii) Externalities are the benefits provided by merit goods
(iii) Monopolistic market transactions are characterised by the absence of positive externalities

A (I) and (III) only
B (ii) only
C (i), (ii) and (iii)
D (i) only

36 A selective indirect tax will have predictable effects.

In this diagram, an indirect tax has been imposed and supply has shifted from S_0 to S_1.

Put the correct labels in the boxes on the diagram.

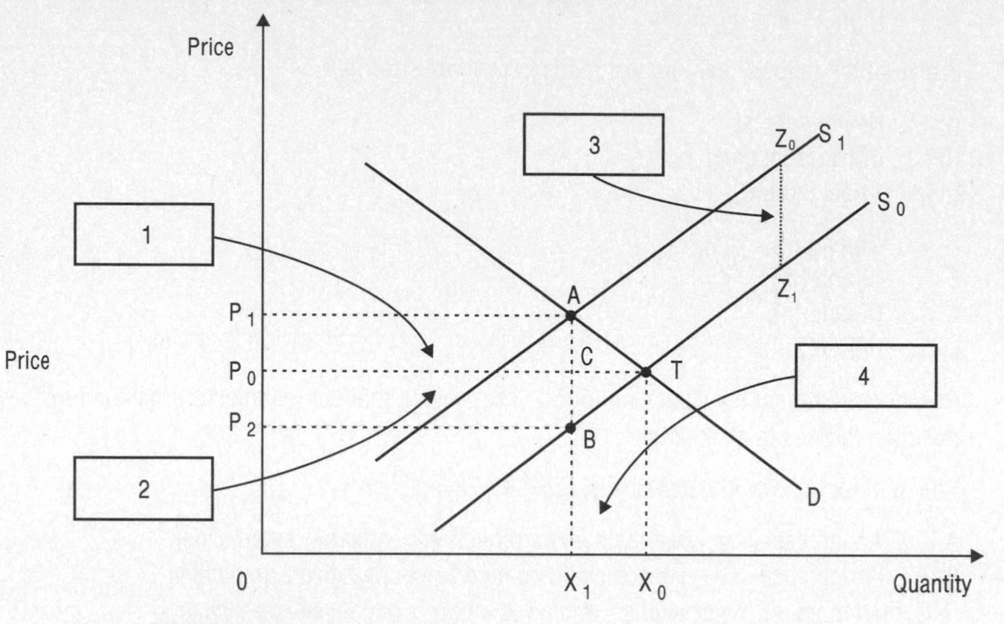

A Fall in output
B Tax borne by supplier
C Tax borne by customer
D Supernormal profit
E Tax imposed per unit

37 A horizontal merger combines two firms:

A At different stages in the production chain
B In the same country
C Working in different industries
D Producing the same goods or services

38 Which one of the following statements is *incorrect*?

A If the effect of privatisation is to increase competition, the effect might be to reduce or eliminate allocative inefficiency

B Privatisation means selling off nationalised industries by the government to the private sector

C The effect of denationalisation could be to make firms more cost-conscious, because they will be under the scrutiny of stock market investors

D The government may appoint consumer watchdogs to regulate privatised industries

39 Highfly Co is looking to raise finance to fund the construction of a new airport terminal, which is a major long-term investment project it expects to take approximately 10 years to complete.

Which one of the following is the most suitable source of finance for Highfly Co to use?

A Renegotiating its bank overdraft
B Issuing new shares
C Taking out a new, five year, bank loan
D Issuing a bill of exchange

40 What is maturity transformation?

A The rolling-over of government debt at its maturity date into new long-term bonds

B The packaging up of small investor deposits into large loans

C The conversion of short-term capital into long-term capital

D The banking practice of allowing depositors to withdraw funds at short notice while making long-term loans

41 What is meant by a lack of synchronisation between payments and receipts?

A That people don't have enough income to live on
B That banks make errors on the cash they pay out sometimes
C That the time when money is spent may be different from the time in which it is received
D That there will always be deficit and surplus units

42 Which of the following *is not* an asset issued by governments to help them borrow?

A Treasury bills
B Banknotes and coins
C Treasury bonds
D Equities

43 What is mezzanine finance?

A Borrowing that combines the features of debt and equity
B Finance that is borrowed short-term whilst longer term loans are arranged
C Finance on which the interest rate is set at the mid-market rate
D Another name for medium term finance

44 Which of the following *is not* an example of debt finance?

A Debentures
B Bank overdrafts
C Mortgages
D Retained earnings

45 A money market is most closely described as:

A The market for short-term capital, enabling businesses and government to maintain liquidity
B The market for trading unquoted company shares
C The market for mortgages, enabling individuals to buy their own homes
D A government agency for raising finance

46 The slope of a normal yield curve is:

A Upwards because of government monetary policy
B Upwards because of uncertainty about the future
C Downwards because of price inflation
D Downwards because of reducing demand

47 Foxy Bank is the only bank in Foxland and it maintains a cash reserve ratio of 20%.

The bank has recently received a new cash deposit of $5 million. What will be the subsequent, additional increase in bank deposits in Foxland as a result of this?

A $25 million
B $20 million
C $5 million
D $1 million

48 Which one of the following is NOT a function of a central bank?

A Act as lender of the last resort to the banking system
B Issue notes and coin in an economy
C Ensure banks have sufficient capital to meet problems arising from business losses
D Advise companies on money management and share issues

49 Which of the following is the most liquid asset of a commercial bank?

A Customers' deposits
B Government Bonds
C Cash
D Operational balances with the central bank

50 Fixed interest securities that pay $1.50 every six months are trading at a price of $40 each, though their face value is $50 each. What is the current rate of annual interest available on investments of this type?

A 6%
B 3¾%
C 7½%
D 3%

51 Which of the following statements about exchange rates is correct?

(i) If Country A has 8% inflation and Country B has 12% inflation, Country A's currency will tend to weaken against that of Country B.

(ii) A country that has a persistent large deficit on its balance of trade cannot have a stable exchange rate in the short-term.

(iii) Foreign currency reserves are necessary when the exchange rate is fixed.

A (i) and (iii)
B (ii) only
C (ii) and (iii)
D (iii) only

52 Which one of the following would be the most likely to occur if the Euravian dollar depreciates significantly against the currencies of its major trading partners?

A There will be an increase in demand for goods imported into Euravia
B There will be an increase in imported inflation in Euravia
C There will be a decrease in the cost of travelling overseas from Euravia
D There will be a decrease in the demand for exports from Euravia

53 Which one of the following statements about the foreign exchange market is *false*?

A The main market participants are banks, investments funds, commercial firms and speculators
B It conducts trades for immediate delivery
C It conducts trades for future delivery
D It is regulated by the central bank of the country

54 Brazainia is suffering a falling exchange rate. Which of the following *would not* be a consequence of this

A Increased demand for the exports of Brazainia
B Increase in the supply of the currency of Brazania on the foreign exchange markets
C Reduction in demand for imports
D Speculation against the currency of Brazainia

55 The government of Brazainia is divided on whether to adopt a fixed exchange rate policy. Which of the following arguments is likely to be advanced by the opponents of a fixed exchange rate approach?

A It will encourage greater trade
B It will discourage speculation against the country's currency
C It will take away the governments ability to manage its domestic economic policy
D It will give help stop inflation due to rising import costs

56 This diagram applies supply and demand to the macroeconomy.

Label the diagram.

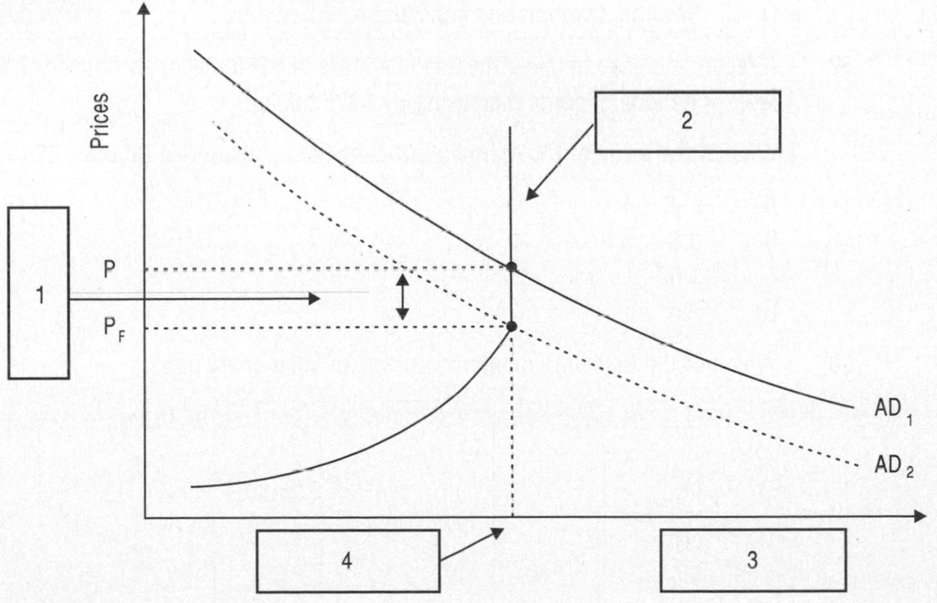

A Full employment level of output
B National income
C Inflationary gap
D Aggregate supply

57 There is a circular flow of value around the macroeconomy

Label the diagram.

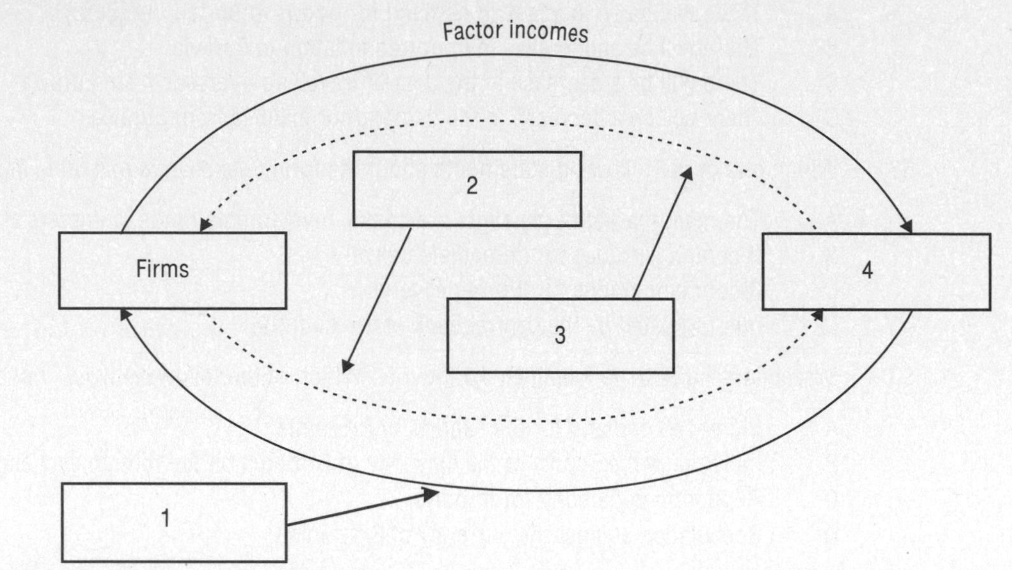

A Households
B Expenditure on goods and services
C Factors of production
D Goods and services produced and sold

58 Withdrawals from the circular flow of income in an economy are:

A Savings, investments and exports
B Investment, taxation and imports
C Investment, government spending and exports minus imports
D Savings, taxation and imports

59 A recent increase in investment expenditure of $150 million in Country Z has resulted in the equilibrium level of national income increasing by $375 million.

What is the value of the marginal propensity to consume in Country Z?

A 0.4
B 0.6
C 1.67
D 2.5

60 Which of the following diagrams shows an inflationary gap?

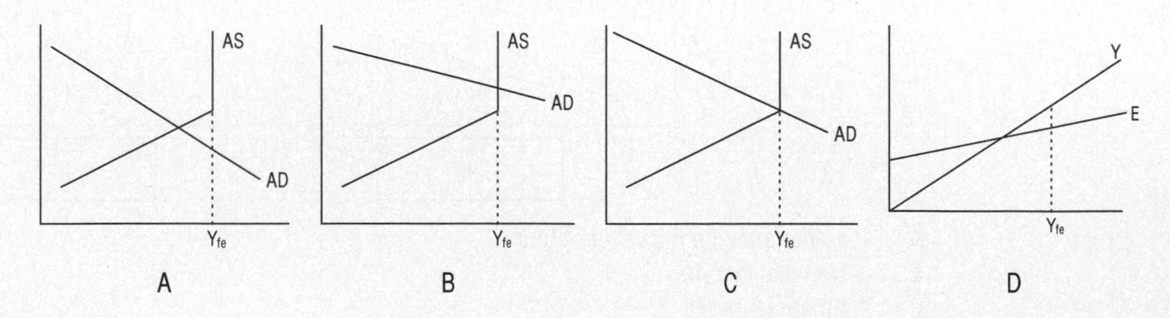

61 The government of Autoland is considering different ways of increasing the rate of economic growth in its country.

Which one of the following would NOT be a suitable policy for it to introduce?

A Reducing rates of direct tax
B Reducing interest rates
C Reducing the level of government spending
D Increasing investment in training to help reduce unemployment

62 The level of unemployment in Jobland is currently at its natural rate.

However, recent government policies have prompted an increase in aggregate demand in Jobland.

What will be the initial impact of this increase in aggregate demand in Jobland?

A An increase in prices and a decrease in the level of unemployment
B An increase in prices, but no change in the level of unemployment
C No change in prices but a decrease in the level of unemployment
D A decrease in prices and a decrease in unemployment

63 Which of the following would lead to cost push inflation:

(i) An increase in indirect taxation
(ii) An increase in consumer expenditure resulting in aggregate demand exceeding aggregate supply
(iii) An increase in wages and salaries

A (i) and (ii)
B (i) and (iii)
C (ii) and (iii)
D (iii) only

64 Which of the following is an example of structural unemployment?

A A computer programmer leaves his job and moves abroad
B A construction worker is always unemployed during the winter months
C A worker loses her job during a recession
D A car worker is replaced by a robot

65 Recent increases in tax rates in Messiland have led to a number of skilled workers leaving the country to work in neighbouring countries.

Assuming other factors remain unchanged, what is the most likely consequence of the resulting decrease in the supply of skilled labour in Messiland?

A The quantity of skilled labour employed will fall, but wage levels will remain unchanged

B A decrease in the quantity of skilled labour employed, but an increase in the equilibrium wage level in Messiland

C An increase in structural unemployment in Messiland, and a fall in wage rates

D A decrease in the quantity of skilled labour employed and a decrease in the equilibrium wage level in Messiland

66 The relationship between money supply and prices can be expressed in the quantity theory of money. What is the correct formula?

A MV = PT
B M/V = P/T
C MP = VT
D MT = VP

67 A government wishes to continue to combine an expansionary fiscal stance with anti-inflationary monetary policy. What combination of policy instruments should it choose?

A Taxation up, borrowing down, interest rates up
B Spending down, taxation down, interest rates down
C Interest rates stable, taxation greater than spending
D Spending greater than taxation, interest rates up

68 The government of Country X has adopted a restrictive monetary policy to try to control the rate of economic growth in its country.

Which one of the following is NOT likely to occur as a result of this policy?

A Demand for goods in Country X, especially consumer durables, is likely to decline
B Business investment in new capital projects is likely to decline
C The exchange rate for Country X's currency on the foreign exchange markets is likely to depreciate
D The level of savings in Country X is likely to increase

69 If a government is trying to achieve economic growth in its country by pursuing a supply side policy, which one of the following will its policy be designed to achieve:

A An increase in the money supply in the economy

B A reduction in the supply of labour in order to reduce unemployment levels

C Introducing measures (such as education and training) to improve the supply of goods and services in the economy

D A reduction in the level of government borrowing in the economy

70 The most likely effect of a cut in the basic rate of income tax (direct tax) is:

A A rise in the value of the pound
B A fall in the value of the pound
C A fall in the government's borrowing
D A fall in the amount of VAT receipts

71 The economy of Fastland is currently experiencing high levels of demand pull inflation, and the government is keen to reduce this.

What would be the most appropriate macroeconomic policy to try to achieve this goal?

A Increased government expenditure, increased taxation and increased interest rates
B Decreased government expenditure, increased taxation and decreased interest rates
C Decreased government expenditure, increased taxation and increased interest rates
D Increased government expenditure, decreased taxation and decreased interest rates

72 Here is some summary economic data for a country

	$m		$m
Savings	325	Investment	300
Taxation	375	Government expenditure	450
Imports	240	Exports	215

Which one of the following statements about the economy is true?

A Economic activity is increasing, and the country has a budget surplus
B Economic activity is increasing, but the country has a budget deficit
C Economic activity is decreasing, and the country has a budget deficit
D Economic activity is decreasing, but the country has a budget surplus

73 Which one of the following statements is *not* true?

A The balance of payments accounts always balance to zero

B Current account deficits have to be financed by surpluses on the capital or financial accounts

C The J curve shows that the short term effect of a depreciation in currency is the reduction in a current account deficit

D A rise in the exchange rate is likely to reduce domestic inflation

74 The trade accounts for Exland for 20X9 show the following figures:

	$m
Trade in goods (net position of exports minus imports)	–325
Trade in services (net position of exports minus imports)	260
Income from capital investments overseas	125
Capital flows	100
Transfers to overseas bodies	–80
Investment flows on the financial account	–75
Net errors and omissions	–5

What is the balance on Exland's balance of payments' current account for 20X9?

A $80m
B $60m
C Zero
D $-20m

75 Which one of the following options would a government attempting to reduce the deficit on its country's balance of payments current account deficit be most likely to employ?

A An expansionary fiscal policy
B A depreciation of its currency
C An reduction in interest rates
D Provide incentives for foreign companies to invest in its country

76 Which of the following describe functions of the World Trade Organisation (WTO)?

(i) Settling trade disputes between member countries
(ii) Monitoring developments in world trade and reviewing barriers to international trade
(iii) Providing financial assistance to developing countries to help them develop international trade

A (i) and (ii)
B (i) and (iii)
C (ii) and (iii)
D All of them

77 Which of the following organisations *is not* a member of the World Bank Group

A International Monetary Fund
B International Bank for Reconstruction and Development
C International Finance Corporation
D International Development Agency

78 Which of the following states the key difference between a customs union and a free trade area?

A Trade is encouraged between member state
B There is freedom of movement of labour
C There is a common external tariff
D It is a less integrated form of trading block

Answer bank

1 B Smaller companies are often 'owner-managed', but larger public companies generally use hired managers to serve shareholders. This can also be expressed as the principal-agent problem.

2 C Sole traders seek profit as unincorporated entities and are not voluntary

3 D Public Private Partnership

4 B Connected stakeholder

5 D Shareholders have a right to attend General Meetings but no rights to attend Board meetings unless also appointed as Directors

6 D Note because you are given capital employed for both 20X9 and 20X8 you must use an average of the two figures when calculating the ROCE.

$$\text{ROCE} = \frac{\text{Profit before interest and tax}}{\text{Average capital employed}} = \frac{120}{960} = 12.5\%$$

7 A The remaining options are technically wrong statements except D which doesn't explain the relationship

8 C The remaining options are technically wrong statements

9 B

10 C A reduction in corporation tax, and expectations of increased profits, will both increase the *demand* for shares. A reduction in the number of shares issued reduces the *supply* of shares. As the price of shares is determined by demand and supply (for shares) these options will cause the price of shares to rise.

However, a rise in interest rates will lead to other investments becoming relatively more attractive instead of shares, so demand (and therefore price) for shares will fall.

11 B Demand conditions, and therefore the demand curve, are unchanged. However, less will be supplied at any given price and so the supply curve will move to the left.

12 D A government may intervene, for example through progressive taxation, to make the distribution of income fairer.

13

	Shift in demand	*Shift in supply*	*Neither*
(i) An increase in household incomes	X		
(ii) A rise in wage costs		X	
(iii) A fall in the price of raw materials		X	
(iv) A fall in the price of the good			X

An increase in household incomes will lead to an increase in the quantity demanded at all prices, and so will lead to an outward shift in the demand curve.

A rise in wage costs will lead to an inward shift (contraction) of the supply curve, while a fall in the price of raw materials will lead to an outward shift (expansion) of the supply curve.

A fall in the price of the good will lead to a movement along both the demand and supply curves, but will not lead to a shift in either of them.

14	C	The proportionate increase in quantity demand for a given proportionate change in price is bigger in some markets than in others
15	D	The remaining responses are technically correct statements
16	B	If demand rises the firm will not be able to expand output without cost increases due to labour shortages
17	A	
18	1 C	Quantity available to purchase remains the same no matter what price is offered.
	2 A	Any straight line passing through the origin shows unit elasticity.
	3 B	Any desired quantity is available at the prevailing price, none at a lower price.
19	D	The effect of a cash subsidy is to shift the supply curve to the right. Producers are willing to supply bigger quantities at the same market price, because they will get a cash subsidy from the government in addition to the market price. The new supply curve goes through points 7, 8 and 9, and so the new equilibrium, given no shift in the demand curve, is at point 8.
20	A	Before the maximum price regulations were introduced, the equilibrium price was $220, with 7,400,000 tonnes demanded and supplied each month. With a maximum price of $200, demand will be 8,200,000 tonnes per month and supply only 6,600,000 tonnes per month. With demand exceeding supply, there will be a bean shortage and a need for rationing - since prices cannot be raised to eliminate the excess demand.
21	C	to have an effect a guaranteed minimum price must be higher than market price
22	C	If you have been incorrect on the last two questions ensure you are careful to distinguish between minimum and maximum prices
23	B	3 must be TC as it is the largest of any level of output greater than one unit. 2 is MC since it shows the increase in TC for each extra unit of production. Therefore 1 must be AC. Also 1 is equal to 3 divided by the units of output.
24	C	Costs of production that do not rise through time
25	B	Straight line curves assume constant variable cost per unit which ignores the impact of changing efficiency of production
26	C	The total cost curve still has a positive intercept showing the level of fixed costs
27	D	The other options are true statements but they don't deal with the difference between internal and external economies of scale
28	B	The slope of the total revenue curve declines because price falls as the firm sells more
29	A	This defines MC = MR
30	D	These would tend to increase prices
31	B	A consumer with a proprietary platform has no option but to buy software for that platform
32	C	Barriers to entry will restrict the number of firms which can join the industry. High advertising costs are a barrier to entry and so will tend to restrict numbers.

33	D	Public goods are indivisible and non-diminishable, meaning that the benefits from them cannot be restricted solely to those people who have paid for them, and consequently that they would not be provided by a private company. It would be possible to restrict the provision of health services or transport systems to those people who have paid for them, but everybody benefits from street lighting.
34	A	The cost of installing the devices is a private cost to the manufacturer. However, the reduction in pollution which results benefits society as a whole, and therefore is a reduction in negative externalities.
35	D	This is a point of definition. It is true to say that merit goods have merit because of the extensive positive externalities their provision creates, but this is not a definition of externalities. Monopolies are just as likely to generate externalities, both positive and negative, as any other market form. Economies of scale will mean that the industry is likely to contain a few large firms rather than lots of smaller ones. However, if transport costs are high we would expect to see lots of small, local firms because being local will allow them to minimise the transport costs involved in distributing goods or services to their customers.
36	1 C	Customer now pays P_1 instead of P_0
	2 B	Supplier receives P_2 net of tax instead of P_0
	3 E	The supply curve shifts vertically by the amount of the tax
	4 A	Demand is lower at the higher price
37	D	A horizontal merger involves two firms producing similar goods at the same stage of production. A is vertical integration; C would be conglomerate diversification; B may be any kind of merger: there is no enough information to tell.
38	B	Privatisation *could* mean selling off nationalised industries, but it can also refer to deregulation of industries to allow private firms to compete with state-run business (eg private bus companies) and contracting out work previously done by government employees to private firms (eg refuse collection). Statement C is correct, and refers to the influence of stock market competition on newly-privatised monopolies. Statement D is correct: an example in the UK is the regulatory body Oftel
39	B	The project is a long-term project and so it must be financed with a long-term financial instrument.
40	D	Maturity transformation is undertaken by banks. They can borrow short and lend long because they are confident that new depositors will continue to provide funds as time goes by
41	C	
42	D	Equities are issued only by companies
43	A	So-called because they are halfway between debt and equity (a mezzanine floor is a small floor between main floors in a building)
44	D	Retained earnings are equity
45	A	The money market meets short term capital requirements of companies and government.
46	B	The interest charged on a long term loan is likely, *ceteris paribus*, to be higher than that charged on a short term loan because of the greater risk involved in committing money for the longer term.

47	B	As the bank maintains a 20% cash ratio, the credit multiplier is $\frac{1}{20\%}$ = 5 times. This means the total increase in bank deposits is \$5 million x 5 = \$25 million. However, this \$25 million includes the initial deposit of \$5 million, so the additional increase is only \$25 million - \$5 million = \$20 million.
48	D	Advising companies on money management, and advising / underwriting new share issues are functions of a merchant bank not of a central bank.
49	C	Cash is the most liquid asset of all. (Note: customers' deposits (option A) are a liability for the bank).
50	C	A \$40 investment produces an annual return of \$3. This is equivalent to 7½%. Note: rate is calculated using trading price not face value.
51	D	If Country A has 8% inflation and Country B has 12% inflation, Country A's currency will tend to strengthen against Country B's. A large deficit on the balance of trade can persist for many years if there are adequate inward capital flows. A fixed exchange rate makes foreign currency reserves essential.
52	B	The depreciation in Euravia's currency means that imports into Euravia will become more expensive, leading to imported inflation. However, as a result of imported goods becoming more expensive demand for imports is likely to decrease rather than to increase. In effect, the cost of travelling overseas is like an import, and so it also becomes more expensive. By contrast, exports from Euravia are likely to become cheaper, so we would expect demand for exports from Euravia to increase.
53	D	The forex market is international and therefore cannot be regulated by one country although individual banks trading in the market could be subject to the regulations of the country in which they are operating
54	B	If import demand is falling the supply of the Brazaninan currency will fall also
55	C	Interest rates and fiscal policy may need to be employed to avoid inflation and balance or payments deficits in order to stop the exchange rate falling

56	1	C	With the economy at full employment, there is no spare capacity so an increase in aggregate demand produces inflation.
	2	D	Aggregate supply cannot increase once full employment is reached.
	3	B	National income and national output are the same thing.
	4	A	Full employment places an upper limit on output.
57	1	B	Expenditure is financed by factor incomes
	2	D	Goods and services are produced by firms and consumed by households
	3	C	Productive resources are land, labour, capital and enterprise
	4	A	Households supply factors of production to firms

58 D This is a point of definition.

59 A The multiplier in Country Z is 2.5 (375/150 = 2.5)

The multiplier is $\frac{1}{1-\text{MPC}}$

If $\frac{1}{1-\text{MPC}}$ = 2.5, then '1 – MPC' = 0.4, so MPC = 0.6

60 B A and D show a deflationary gap. C shows an economy at ideal equilibrium.

61 C Government spending is a component of aggregate demand in the economy (C + I + G + X). Reducing government expenditure will therefore reduce the level of aggregate demand, which will lead to a reduction in the rate of economic growth rather than the desired increase.

62 A Although the economy was already at its natural rate of unemployment, the increase in demand will initially lead to a reduction in unemployment.

It is only later that the short run Phillips curve will shift outwards returning the level of unemployment to its natural rate, as illustrated below.

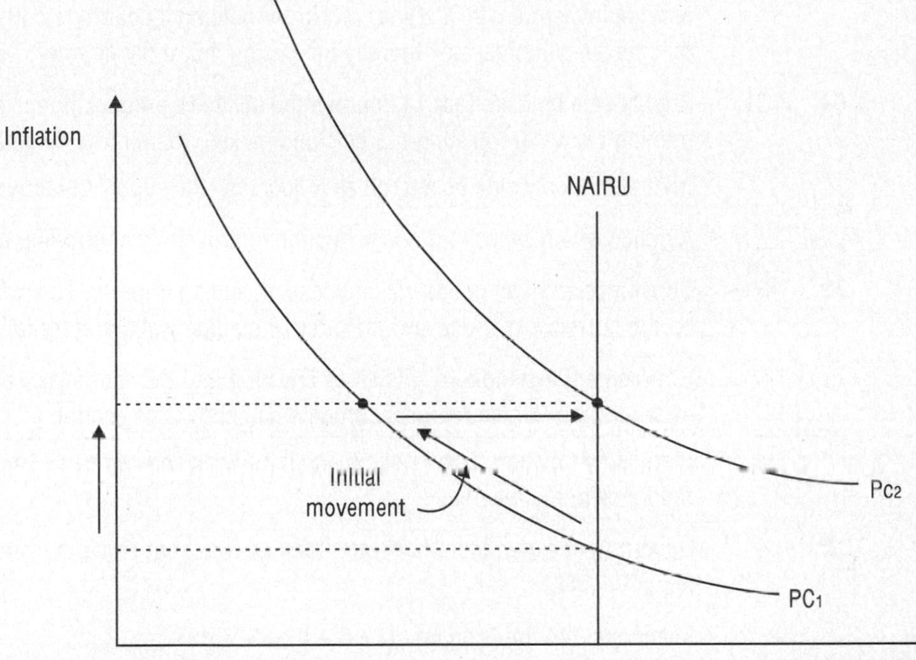

63 B Option (ii) will result in demand pull inflation, but options (i) and (iii) will both result in cost push inflation.

A rise in indirect taxation (eg sales tax) will lead to the cost of goods and services increasing, which could, in turn, increase workers' demands for higher wages.

64 D Structural unemployment is where long-term changes such as automation occur.

65 B As workers leave Messiland to work in other countries, the labour supply curve in Messiland shifts to the left.

Given the assumption that demand for labour remains unchanged, this shift in the supply curve means that the equilibrium between the supply and demand for labour will now be at a higher price (higher wage level) but lower quantity than before.

66	A	The quantity theory of money identity states that MV = PT.
67	D	B would reduce the size of the state sector, which would be contractionary; the reduction in interest rates might lead to sufficient private sector demand for the economy to expand overall, or it may not. The effect of such a policy combination on inflation is impossible to say. A would control inflation by making a public sector debt repayment possible, as well as via interest rate control. However, this is not an expansionary fiscal stance. C is a contractionary fiscal stance and a neutral policy on inflation.
68	C	A restrictive monetary policy will mean that interest rates in Country X are being raised. This is likely to lead to a fall in aggregate demand, and in particular, a fall in demand for larger, more expensive goods, such as consumer durables, which are likely to be bought on credit. By contrast, a rise in interest rates will make saving more attractive, and so the level of savings is likely to increase. Higher interest rates will lead to a reduction in investment in new capital projects, because the rise in interest rates will lead to a reduction in the NPV of these projects. Higher interest rates will lead to an increase in a country's exchange rate. Rising interest rates provide investors with a higher return for holding a country's currency, and so will mean demand for that currency increases – thereby increasing its exchange rate.
69	C	Supply side policies seek to improve the ability to produce goods and services, either by improving training or by deregulating markets and making them more flexible. In effect, supply side policies seek to increase the supply of labour rather than decreasing it. A policy which seeks to manage economic growth by controlling money supply is a monetary policy.
70	B	Consumption of all goods will increase, including imports. This will increase the supply of sterling on the currency markets and the price of sterling will therefore fall.
71	C	Government expenditure acts as an injection into the economy, so decreasing government expenditure will help reduce aggregate demand in the economy. Increasing taxation (fiscal policy) and increasing interest rates (monetary policy) will also help reduce aggregate demand.
72	B	Government expenditure is greater than government receipts from taxation, so the country has a budget deficit. Injections into the economy (I + G + X) = $965m Withdrawals from the economy (S + T + M) = $940m Because injections are greater than withdrawals, economic activity will be increasing.
73	C	In the short run the depreciation will increase the deficit. It only reduces it in the long run. A is true by definition, because of B; D is true because a risk in the exchange rate will reduce the price of imports.

74 D The balance on the current account is made up of:

	$m
Trade in goods (net position of exports minus imports)	–325
Trade in services (net position of exports minus imports)	260
Income from capital investments overseas	125
Transfers to overseas bodies	–80
Total	–20

Capital flows are recorded in the capital account, and investment flows in the financial account.

75 B Reducing the country's exchange rate will make its exports cheaper in other countries (increasing demand for its exports) and will make imports into it more expensive (reducing demand for exports).

An expansionary fiscal policy and a reduction in interest rates will both increase aggregate demand in the country, and in doing so are likely to increase the demand for imports.

If a foreign company invests in the country, this will be recorded in the financial account, not the current account.

76 A The WTO's main functions are to promote free trade, resolve trade disputes and provide a framework of rules for international trade to operate within. However, it has no financing or banking functions.

77 A International Monetary Fund

78 C There is a common external tariff

Index and key terms

Note: **Key Terms** and their references are given in **bold**.

BPP
LEARNING MEDIA

Review Form – Paper C04 Fundamentals of Business Economics

Please help us to ensure that the CIMA learning materials we produce remain as accurate and user-friendly as possible. We cannot promise to answer every submission we receive, but we do promise that it will be read and taken into account when we up-date this Study Text.

Name: ______________________ **Address:** ______________________

____

____

How have you used this Interactive Text?
(Tick one box only)

- ☐ Home study (book only)
- ☐ On a course: college ______________
- ☐ With 'correspondence' package
- ☐ Other ______________

Why did you decide to purchase this Interactive Text? *(Tick one box only)*

- ☐ Have used BPP Texts in the past
- ☐ Recommendation by friend/colleague
- ☐ Recommendation by a lecturer at college
- ☐ Saw information on BPP website
- ☐ Saw advertising
- ☐ Other ______________

During the past six months do you recall seeing/receiving any of the following?
(Tick as many boxes as are relevant)

- ☐ Our advertisement in *Financial Management*
- ☐ Our advertisement in *PQ*
- ☐ Our brochure with a letter through the post
- ☐ Our website www.bpp.com

Which (if any) aspects of our advertising do you find useful?
(Tick as many boxes as are relevant)

- ☐ Prices and publication dates of new editions
- ☐ Information on Text content
- ☐ Facility to order books off-the-page
- ☐ None of the above

Which BPP products have you used?

Text	☑	*Home Study Package*	☐
Kit	☐	*Interactive Passcard*	☐
Passcard	☐	*i Pass*	☐

Your ratings, comments and suggestions would be appreciated on the following areas.

	Very useful	*Useful*	*Not useful*
Introductory section (Key study steps, personal study)	☐	☐	☐
Chapter introductions	☐	☐	☐
Key terms	☐	☐	☐
Quality of explanations	☐	☐	☐
Case studies and other examples	☐	☐	☐
Assessment focus points	☐	☐	☐
Questions and answers in each chapter	☐	☐	☐
Fast forwards and chapter roundups	☐	☐	☐
Quick quizzes	☐	☐	☐
Question Bank	☐	☐	☐
Answer Bank	☐	☐	☐
Index	☐	☐	☐
Icons	☐	☐	☐

Overall opinion of this Study Text *Excellent* ☐ *Good* ☐ *Adequate* ☐ *Poor* ☐

Do you intend to continue using BPP products? *Yes* ☐ *No* ☐

On the reverse of this page are noted particular areas of the text about which we would welcome your feedback.

The BPP author of this edition can be e-mailed at: adriansims@bpp.com

Please return this form to: Adrian Sims, CIMA Publishing Director, BPP Professional Education, FREEPOST, London, W12 8BR

Review Form (continued)

TELL US WHAT YOU THINK

Please note any further comments and suggestions/errors below